HEROINES OF DIXIE

To
The memory of my Grandmother
Mary Turner Garrison
Wife of
Lieutenant William David Garrison
16th South Carolina Regiment, C.S.A.

HEROINES OF DIXIE

Confederate Women Tell
Their Story of the War

BY KATHARINE M. JONES

SMITHMARK

This edition published in 1995 by SMITHMARK Publishers,
a division of U.S. Media Holdings, Inc., 16 East 32nd Street,
New York, NY 10016.

SMITHMARK books are available for bulk purchase for sales
promotion and premium use. For details write or call the
manager of special sales, SMITHMARK Publishers Inc.,
16 East 32nd Street, New York, NY 10016; (212) 532-6600.

This edition published by special arrangement with Scribner,
an imprint of Simon & Schuster Inc. and W.S. Konecky
Associates, Inc.

ISBN: 0-8317-6676-X

Printed in the United States of America

10 9 8 7 6 5 4 3 2

INTRODUCTION

In some of the more recent studies of the subject it has been strongly suggested that the prime reason for the defeat of the Confederacy was a decline in, or loss of, the will to fight. There is a certain merit in the point though the more remarkable fact, considering the course of the conflict, is that the will to fight remained so strong so long.

For that, the women of the Confederacy were in large measure responsible. Not every woman could be classed as a "heroine of Dixie," as the title of the present work puts it, but it was commonly observed at the time by foe and friend alike, and has been repeatedly noted since, that it was among the women of the South that the spirit of resistance flamed highest.

The harder part of war is the woman's part. True of all wars, this was particularly true of the war of the Sixties in the South. For a few women, some of whom left memoirs which have become famous, there were the excitement and sustaining sense of accomplishment to be derived from contact with stirring events and association with notable personalities. For the great majority, however, there was more of strain and anxiety, of fear and loneliness, and of hardship and privation than there was of glamour and excitement. To all these were added, in large sections of the South, the aggravation and frustration of invasion and occupation by Federal troops—or, even worse, the depredations of the lawless freebooters of either side, or neither, in those areas which were strongly held by neither army.

The story of the life of women in these years is scattered through diaries and letters written without thought of publication, as well as through the comparatively small number of published memoirs. Of the latter, even, not many are well known and readily available. Searching out the facts about the lives of Confederate women, therefore, calls for diligence and patience, while presentation of the facts found requires judgment in selection and skill in organization. Miss Jones has brought to her work the qualities requisite for producing what is, in effect, a composite autobiography of Confederate women.

In doing so, she lets the actors tell the story in their own words, with a minimum of connective tissue to keep events in focus. There is no attempt to round up views from all sources on each phase of the story but the quotations given are each of sufficient length to preserve their flavor and effect.

The treatment is basically chronological, carrying the story forward from the first secession conventions to the last meeting of the Confederate Cabinet at Washington, Georgia, after which Miss Eliza Frances Andrews noted that "this, I suppose, is the end of the Confederacy."

The familiar passages from well-known diarists dealing with the Richmond scene are here but here also are bits of everyday life such as that on a remote farm in Texas where saving the meat at hog-killing time was a problem and where a hundred bales of cotton would "neither pay debts or buy groceries"—with touches of all the range of living in between.

To the author who has so patiently assembled and skillfully presented the story of the women of the Confederacy, the thanks of those interested in that story today are eminently due.

ROBERT S. HENRY

Alexandria, Virginia

EDITOR'S FOREWORD

The military records and reports do not tell the story of the women of the Confederacy. They told it themselves—a few in magazine articles, pamphlets and books; many in letters and diaries. Only a part of it has been published; much survives in manuscripts cherished in family, historical society, public library and university collections. All manner of women told it—the rich and the poor, the educated and the ignorant.

A handful of these Confederate women saw active service as spies, hospital nurses, government clerks. The great majority were left back home, whether home was the big house or a cabin. They had vital work to do there. But almost from the outbreak of the struggle homes were broken up and women became exiles.

So their story is increasingly a story of refugees, of invaded and occupied cities, of burned and devastated dwellings, of hunger and want, of bitterness and human frailty. But it is also a story of love, of courage, of personal loyalty transcending heartbreak.

When the curtain rose, they expected the play to be over soon by a peaceful yielding of the North or a defeat of the Northern army. There were then some gleams of glamour about war—especially a war that might be over before it was well begun. With proud hearts these women watched the parade of their brave lads marching off to certain and easy victory, with the flags the women had made waving over them. Romances flowered quickly in those days. There was a gay, unquenchable humor in the ranks; anxiety and privation would leave little room for it behind the lines. There was the excitement of combat for the soldiers; there was a little waltzing on happy, rare occasions but much more waiting, watching, work for the women.

Though their Southern patriotism was intense, for the women devotion to the family came first—always—and none of them would knowingly and willingly have chosen a course of war that reversed this order of devotion. At the very start—just after the Act of Secession was passed—a woman of South Carolina said, "What do I care for patriotism? My husband is my country. What is my country to me if he be killed?" As they faced the grim reality of a long and bitter struggle, this became more and more the secret or avowed question of their deeply troubled hearts.

From Virginia to Texas I have searched out and read every piece of their writing I could lay hands on. I have selected what I humbly hope may bring their varied story into focus and continuity—their autobiography of the war years.

ACKNOWLEDGMENTS

This anthology has been compiled with a constant sense of gratitude to all the people who have had a part in its making—the ladies of the Confederacy, whose diaries and letters I have shared, and the families of the ladies, the advisers, librarians and archivists who have helped me in my task. I owe a great debt to them for their contributions, their many kindnesses and valuable assistance.

I am grateful to Mr. Robert Selph Henry for completing the book with his introduction, for reading the galley proofs and for the usefulness of his book *The Story of the Confederacy.* I am indebted also to Dr. Bell I. Wiley of Emory University, who carefully read the proofs and offered suggestions. Of course, responsibility for any error is mine.

I wish to thank also those persons who have helped me find or given me permission to use the material reprinted in this book:

Mrs. Mary Verner Schlaefer, Mrs. T. B. Stackhouse, Mrs. Charles Blackburn, Mrs. Fitz Hugh McMaster, all of Columbia, South Carolina. Mr. Albert Neely Sanders of Furman University. Dr. James Rabun of Emory University. Dr. Robert H. Woody of Duke University. Dr. Harriet Holman of Erskine College. Mr. Zack Spratt of Washington, D. C. Dr. Mary Elizabeth Massey of Winthrop College. The library staff of Winthrop College. Mr. Frank Wardlaw, Director of the University of Texas Press. Dr. Llerena Friend, Librarian of the Barker Texas History Center, University of Texas Library. Miss Ruth Blair and Miss Bessie Duke Small of the Atlanta Historical Society. Miss Mary Verhoeff and Miss Mabel C. Weaks of the Filson Club, Louisville, Kentucky. Miss Margaret Jemison and Mr. Richard B. Harwell of Emory University Library. Mr. and Mrs. E. R. Dobbins of Atlanta, Georgia. Mrs. Marie Bankhead Owen, Mrs. Hattie M. Allen, Miss Maud McLure Kelly, Mr. Peter Brannon, of the Alabama State Department of Archives and History. Mr. David C. Mearns, Chief, Manuscript Division of the Library of Congress. Miss Anna Loe Russell, Reference Librarian of the George Peabody College. Mr. Dan M. Robinson, State Librarian and Archivist. Mrs. Gertrude Morton Parsley, of the Tennessee State Library and Archives. Mr. V. L. Bedsole and Miss Marcelle F. Schertz of the Department of Archives, Louisiana State University. Miss Mattie Russell, Curator of Mss., Duke University Library. Dr. James Welsh Patton, Director, and Miss Anna Brooke Allen, Mrs. Carolyn Daniel, Mrs. Patterson Fisher and Mrs. John Watters, all of the Southern Historical Collection, University of North Carolina. Dr. William D. McCain, Director, Department of Archives and History, Jackson, Mississippi. Miss Georgia Clark, Reference Librarian, University of Arkansas. Mrs. Lilla M. Hawes, Director of the Georgia Historical Society. Miss Elizabeth Hodge, Reference Librarian, Public Library, Savannah, Georgia. The staff of the Georgia State Archives. Miss India Thomas, House Regent of the Confederate Museum, Richmond, Virginia. Dr. and Mrs. Robert Meriwether of the South Caroliniana Library, University of South Carolina. Mr. Henry R. Dwight of Pinopolis, South Carolina. Miss Georgia Faison, Reference Librarian, University of North Carolina Library. Mrs. Frank M. Ladd and Mr. Francis H. Inge of Mobile, Alabama. Mrs. Alfred S. Gaillard of Columbia, South Carolina. Mr. A. L. Alexander of Savannah, Georgia. Miss Susan Ware Eppes and Miss Alice B. Eppes of Tallahassee, Florida. Mr. Hunter McDonald and Mrs. Jesse E. Wills of Nashville, Tennessee. Mr. J. Lewis Scoggs of Berryville, Virginia. Mr. Warrington Dawson of Versailles, France. Mrs. M. D. Chase and Mr. Charles Stow of the Greenville Public Library. Miss Alice Adams of the Furman University Library. Miss Slann L. C. Simmons of the South Carolina Historical Society, Charleston, South Carolina.

Finally, I wish to express my appreciation to Mrs. Rosemary York and Mr. D. Laurance Chambers of The Bobbs-Merrill Company, whose understanding, wisdom and guidance made this book possible.

TABLE OF CONTENTS

HEROINES OF DIXIE

". . . . it may truly be said of the Southern women of *1861-1865* that the simple narrative of their life and work unfolds a record of achievement, endurance, and self-sacrificing devotion that should be revealed and recognized as a splendid inspiration to men and women everywhere."

—MATTHEW PAGE ANDREWS

I

THE UNION IS DISSOLVED

December 1860—May 1861

From the city of Charleston, South Carolina, on December 20, 1860, news was flashed to the outside world that the state of South Carolina had been proclaimed an independent Commonwealth. One hundred and sixty-nine delegates had unanimously passed an Ordinance of Secession from the Union.

"We the People of the State of South Carolina in Convention Assembled, do declare and ordain, and it is hereby declared and ordained, That the Ordinance adopted by us in Convention, on the twenty-third day of May, in the year of our Lord one thousand seven hundred and eighty-eight under the name of the 'United States of America' is hereby dissolved."

By February 1, 1861, Mississippi, Florida, Alabama, Georgia, Louisiana and Texas had passed Ordinances of Secession. Delegates from the seceded states met in Montgomery, Alabama, on February 4 to form a provisional government. On the ninth they sent a message to Mr. Jefferson Davis of Mississippi: "Sir: We are directed to inform you that you were this day unanimously elected President of the Provisional Government of the Confederate States of America, and to request you to come to Montgomery immediately."

The convention elected Alexander H. Stephens of Georgia Vice-President. The inaugural ceremonies were held on February 18. "The man and the hour have met," said Mr. William L. Yancey and the crowds cheered and a new song called "Dixie" was sung.

In early March, General Pierre Gustave Toutant Beauregard arrived in Charleston to command preparations for the defense of the harbor from an expected attack by United States vessels. Repeated demands for the surrender of Fort Sumter met with refusal by Major Robert Anderson, its commander. On April 11 the Confederate Congress ordered the capture of the fort. On the fourteenth, after a bombardment of three days, Major Anderson departed from battered Sumter and a new flag was raised.

The Virginia state convention voted on April 17 to submit the

*Ordinance of Secession to the people, and three days later Robert E.
Lee resigned his commission in the United States Army and was
given chief command of the Virginia state forces. On May 6 an
Arkansas convention voted for secession 69 to 1; on the seventh the
Tennessee legislature submitted an ordinance to referendum vote;
and on the twentieth North Carolina seceded.*

1. EMMA E. HOLMES—SOUTH CAROLINA
SECEDES FROM THE UNION

*Emma E. Holmes, young lady of Charleston, South Carolina,
was lame as a result of recent illness. This affliction prevented her
active participation in the events associated with the secession of
her state, and to relieve pent-up feelings she began a diary. Carefully and neatly penned, it became a record of life in her home city
during 1861 and 1862.*

Charleston, South Carolina

On the 17th of December 1860 delegates elected by the people of
South Carolina met in solemn convention in Columbia to withdraw
our State from the Union. Smallpox was so prevalent there, that they
as well as the Legislature adjourned to Charleston. On the 20th The
Ordinance of Secession, declaring South Carolina a free and Independent Republic was passed unanimously at quarter past one, P.M.
That evening the two Bodies met and marched in procession to
Secession Hall, where it was signed amidst an immense throng. But
few ladies were present, as it was so late before it was determined
to sign it the same evening instead of the next day, as had been at
first proposed.

The news flew upon the wings of the wind. . . .

2. SUSAN BRADFORD—FLORIDA PASSES
THE ORDINANCE OF SECESSION

*Susan Bradford, daughter of Dr. Edward Bradford of Pine Hill
plantation, Leon County, Florida, was born in 1846. Her forebears,
who were descendants of Governor William Bradford of Plymouth
Colony, had come to Florida in early territorial days and been lead-*

*ers in the making of the new state. Susan's father had vast holdings
of land. The plantation house was cared for by thirty servants, and
more than three hundred slaves occupied the quarters and tilled the
land. There was a French landscape gardener, and a New York
governess for Susan. In the summer the family journeyed to the
springs at Montvale or to resorts in the North. Susan was "just a
little girl" when she began the diary which she kept through the
years of conflict. It tells of the war as it touched her home and the
surrounding Florida country.*

Pine Hill Plantation
Leon County, Florida

January 1, 1861.—A New Year has come to us now. As we sat
around the long table today the conversation turned on the convention, so soon to meet in Tallahassee. Father said he considered this
the most momentous year in the history of the South. He is for
Secession and he does not think that war will necessarily follow.
Brother Junius is a strong Union man and he thinks we will certainly have war; he says we will have war in any event. If the South
secedes the North will fight to keep us, and if we do not secede all
property rights will be taken from us and we will be obliged to fight
to hold our own. He says he is for the fight but he wants to fight in
the Union not out of it. Father thinks it is more honorable to take
an open and decided stand and let all the world know what we are
doing. Everyone at table who expressed an opinion was firmly set
against the Republican party. Mother says she wants the negroes
freed but she wants the United States Government to make laws
which will free them gradually. All agree on one point, if the negroes
are freed our lands will be worthless.

January 2, 1861.—Uncle Richard and Uncle Tom spent the morning with Father, the three brothers are going to Tallahassee tomorrow to the opening of the Secession Convention. They are so deeply
interested,

January 3, 1861.—I would not write this morning because I
wanted to put down in my diary the first news of the convention.
Tonight Father has told me what they did; it was simply to organize
and then they adjourned. Some of the delegates had not arrived and
this will give them the opportunity to get to Tallahassee and present

their credentials. Father says the Capitol was full of men from all over the State and they look very serious.

January 4, 1861.—I can hardly keep my mind on my books I am thinking so much of the probable action of the convention. I know Father must have been glad when the school bell rang this morning, it seems impossible for me to refrain from asking him questions, which, of course, must be troublesome.

January 5, 1861.—This is Saturday and Mother lets Lula make candy on Saturday and if she, my black mammy, will let us, we help with it. Cousin Rob is spending the day here and Lula has promised to teach us how to make the candy baskets. Cousin Rob does not care about the convention, he is going to school in town but comes home Friday after school and goes back Monday morning.

January 6, 1861.—This morning we went to Mount Zion to hear Mr. Blake preach. Today he spoke so earnestly of the representatives of the people of Florida, now in convention assembled in Tallahassee. He spoke of the heavy responsibility resting on them; of the high compliment paid them by the people of Florida, in trusting them with an issue of such paramount importance. He said we, none of us knew which way was best; we must trust in God and do good.

Mr. Blake took dinner with us and Eddie[1] came with him. He is just the shyest boy. When the company were all gone Father told me to ask Lula to get me ready to go with him to town next morning. He said he was going to show me what a convention was like. I was so happy at the thought of going and my heart fell when Mother said: "Surely, Dr. Bradford, you are not going to take the child away from school?" but Father said, "Yes, I am going to take her with me in the morning, this is history in the making, she will learn more than she can get out of books, and what she hears in this way she will never forget." I am so glad. I am so excited I cannot hold my pencil steady but I must write this down.

January 7, 1861.—I am so glad it is not raining today. I am really going and, little diary, I will tell you all about the day when we get home.

8:30 P.M. We have just finished supper. Mother would not let me

[1] Mr. Blake was the Bradfords' neighbor as well as minister, and Eddie was his son.

write until we had eaten, now she says I can only have one hour because I am going again tomorrow and must have a good sleep.

The convention was assembling in the hall of representatives when we entered the Capitol, and soon everybody was in place and Dr. DuBose made a very fine prayer.

After the preliminaries were disposed of a communication from the Governor was read and the first thing I knew Aunt Mary, who was sitting next caught me by the hand and said, "Look, there is the ambassador from South Carolina." A small man very erect and slender was being introduced by Mr. Villepigue as Mr. Leonidas Spratt of South Carolina. Mr. Spratt bowed gravely and looking around upon the audience with a pair of brilliant, beautiful eyes, he began somewhat in this manner, though I probably will not get it quite right.

He said he felt some delicacy in appearing before this convention, coming as he did from a foreign power, but the heart of South Carolina was filled with love and sympathy for Florida, who now was standing where Carolina had so lately stood. Then he read aloud a communication from his state, recounting the grievances, which had led her to sever the ties which bound her to the Union. You never heard such cheers and shouts as rent the air, and it lasted so long. When quiet was restored Mr. Villepigue introduced Colonel Bulloch, of Alabama. He made a fine address but a short one. Said his own state was now deliberating as to what course she should pursue and had sent him to assure Florida of her cordial good-will. He sat down amid cheers for "Bulloch and Alabama."

Mr. Edmund Ruffin, of Virginia,[1] was introduced and said he came to tell us that Virginia was with her Southern sisters in feeling and, if the worse came to the worst, she would be with them, heart and soul. He is a splendid looking man, quite old and yet he is perfectly erect and only his snow-white hair shows his age. He reminds me very much of dear Grandpa, who is taking such a warm interest in these proceedings, though he is so far away. I believe it will break his heart if North Carolina does not secede.

When the speaking was over and a few resolutions had been passed the convention adjourned and we came home. We left a noisy crowd behind us. As far as we could hear there were cheers for South Caro-

---

[1] He is generally accredited with firing the first shot on Fort Sumter. In spite of the fact that he was sixty-seven years old, he joined the Palmetto Guards and they gave him this honor. See *Battles and Leaders of the Civil War*, I, 47.

lina; cheers for Mississippi; cheers for Alabama and for Florida.
Never before have I seen such excitement. It even throws the horse
races in the shade. What will tomorrow bring?

January 8, 1861.—We are at home again after a day filled to over-
flowing with excitement and interest. We were in such a hurry to get
to town that the convention had not assembled when we reached the
Capitol. There were groups of men talking earnestly and there were
other men running hither and thither with papers in their hands.
Father has a great many friends and I stood quietly beside him while
he and they discussed the situation. The ambassador from South
Carolina had evidently made an impression on his audience of yesterday and somebody had been busy last night, for in every direction
could be seen Palmetto cockades, fastened with a blue ribbon; there
were hundreds of them. When at last the hall of representatives was
opened and Father and I took seats, Judge Gwynn came in and
pinned a cockade on Father and one on me. Oh, I was so proud.

The members of the convention took their seats and Mr. Blake,
our dear Mr. Blake, whom we love so well, opened the day's session
with prayer. I had never seen a convention until Father brought me
here and it is strange to me. I wish I could tell all I heard today but
the language the members used is not familiar to me and some of the
things they talk about are just as new. Then, too, I am just a little
girl. A message was read on the floor of the convention, from Governor Brown of Georgia, to Governor Milton. As near as I can
remember it was this way: "Georgia will certainly secede. Has
Florida occupied the fort?"

Mr. Sanderson was very interesting. He recounted the rights
which the states retained when they delegated other rights to the
general government in the Constitution. He made it so perfectly
clear that all and every state had the right to withdraw from the
Union, if her rights and liberty were threatened. He said the Committee on Ordinances had carefully examined into the question and
they could find no reason why Florida should not exercise her right
to withdraw from a compact, which now threatened her with such
dire disaster. I am going again tomorrow. My palmetto cockade lies
on the table beside me.

January 9, 1861.—There has been a hot time in the convention
today; the nearer they get to a final decision the hotter it gets. Colo-

nel Ward made a most eloquent address to the convention. He told them that he was a Union man but it was in this way: in his opinion the South had done more to establish that Union than any other section; it was a Southern man who wrote the Declaration of Independence, it was a Southern man who led the American army, it was Southern men who framed the Constitution, a Southern man wrote our National Anthem and, in so doing, had immortalized the Star-spangled Banner and he proposed to hold on to that which we had done so much to bring about. He was willing to fight, if fight we must, but he wanted to fight in the Union and under that flag which was doubly ours. The heartiest applause greeted him as he sat down. It was plain to see that his audience was tremendously affected but the next speaker tore his fine argument to shreds. So it went on all day, some committee business would interrupt now and then but the most of the time was spent in debate for or against secession.

Our old friend, Mr. Burgess, says: "If Mrs. Harriet Beecher Stowe had died before she wrote 'Uncle Tom's Cabin,' this would never have happened." He says, "she has kindled a fire which all the waters of the earth cannot extinguish." Isn't it strange how much harm a pack of lies can do?

January 10, 1861.—It is night and I am very tired but there is much to tell. The Ordinance of Secession was voted on today. Bishop Rutledge made the opening prayer and it was very impressive. He pleaded so earnestly for God's guidance for these members, in whose hands lay the future of Florida. These men feel their responsibility I am sure, their faces are so serious and yet so alert. I heard something today about a flag which had been presented to Florida but I have not seen it yet.

After the committees were disposed of the Ordinance of Secession was voted on. The vote was 62 for and 7 against. The ordinance was declared adopted at 22 minutes after 12 o'clock. It was resolved that at one o'clock on the next day, January 11th, the Ordinance of Secession should be signed on the east portico of the Capitol. The convention then adjourned until the afternoon session.

Mississippi seceded last night and it seems we will have plenty of company. The Union men in the hall looked very sad. They have worked hard for their side, but they had only a few followers.

January 11, 1861.—We did not try to be early this morning, as the big event of the day did not take place until one o'clock. Capitol

Square was so crowded you could see nothing but heads and the Capitol itself was full of people looking from the windows, which looked out on the east portico. Somehow Father and I had seats on the portico itself, close up to the wall where we were not in the way and yet we could both see and hear.

There was a table already there with a large inkstand and several pens, nothing more. A subdued murmur came from the assembled citizens but there was none of the noise and excitement which had prevailed on other days; all seemed impressed with the solemnity of the occasion for oh, it is solemn! I did not realize how solemn until Mr. Sanderson read the Constitution and I understood just why it was necessary for Florida to secede.

As the old town clock struck one, the Convention, headed by President McGehee, walked out on the portico. In a few moments they were grouped about the table on which some one had spread the parchment on which the Ordinance of Secession was written. It was impossible for me to tell in what order it was signed, the heads were clustered so closely around the table, but presently I heard Col. Ward's familiar voice. There was a little break in the crowd and I saw him quite plainly. He dipped his pen in the ink and, holding it aloft, he said, in the saddest of tones, "When I die I want it inscribed upon my tombstone that I was the last man to give up the ship." Then he wrote slowly across the sheet before him, "George T. Ward."

The stillness could almost be felt. One by one they came forward. When at length the names were all affixed, cheer after cheer rent the air; it was deafening. Our world seemed to have gone wild.

General Call is an old man now; and he is a strong Union man. Chancing to look toward him I saw that the tears were streaming down his face. Everybody cannot be suited and we are fairly launched on these new waters; may the voyage be a prosperous one.

Nearly everybody seems to be happy and satisfied. The Supreme Court Judges, into whose hands the document just signed has been placed, have carried it to Miss Elizabeth Eppes to engross or adorn it with blue ribbon; the judges selected Miss Bettie because she is a granddaughter of Thomas Jefferson. I hope President Jefferson likes our Ordinance—I believe those who are gone know all we are doing here below.

Father says the rest of the proceedings of this convention will be confined to business matters and though he is planning to attend, he will leave me at home and let me go on with my studies. I wonder if I can collect my wits enough to learn my lessons. I will have Saturday to rest up in and Lula will make us some candy. . . .

3. AUGUSTA J. KOLLOCK—"WE ARE A FREE AND INDEPENDENT PEOPLE"

Augusta J. Kollock was the young daughter of George J. Kollock of Savannah, Georgia. When the state seceded on January 19, her three brothers and various cousins were away at school. Augusta carried on an active correspondence with the absent members of her family despite the fact that her father, who was a Yale man, repeatedly reprimanded her for careless mistakes in spelling. Her brother George was at Virginia Military Institute, a pupil of Professor Thomas Jonathan Jackson. To this brother, waiting impatiently for his father's permission to enlist, Augusta wrote from their plantation home on the third day after the secession of Georgia.

The Retreat
Chatham Co.
Republic of Georgia
Jan. 22nd [1861]

To George J. Kollock Jr.
V.M.I.
Lexington, Virginia
Dear Brother, I suppose you have seen by the papers that our good State has seceded, and that now we are a *free & independent people.* . . . The whole city has been wild with excitement ever since Sumter was taken, & has just begun to get a little quiet, but I suppose we must prepare for hot times now, that is if the Federal Government persists in the insane policy of coercion. It is the most absurd thing I ever heard of, & I rather think if they attempt it, they will find to their cost, that it is not quite so easy to subdue us as they fancied. They will be obliged to exterminate us. Of course you know that our troops have possession of Pulaski. We cannot have any parties, (though in truth no one has any heart for them) because all the beaux are down at the Fort. Detachments of the Guards, Blues, & Oglethorpe are down there all the time. Eddie Kollock either has joined or is about to join, a new company commanded by Col. Jones, the Pulaski Guards. If there is any war Uncle George is pledged to

join another new corps, under Capt. Gallie, called the Savannah Artillery. In it are all the old men in the city, I believe. Think of Uncle G! You must know he is the only Unionist in the family, except Uncle William & James W., but Coercion has turned even him out. George J. has joined the Huzzars. The latter corps has adopted what they call a "service uniform" which consists of a plain pair of dark blue pants, with a duck-tail, tight fitting sack coat of the same, buttoned up the front with large silver buttons of the corps. Both garments are made of *Georgia cassimere.* The pretty dress uniform has been laid aside for a year, on account of the expense, which you know deterred many from joining the corps, & it is surprising how many recruits they have had, they now number 75 or more active members. Father says if there is war he will join again. There are three other new companies, the "Savannah Rifles," The "Blue Caps," Bob Grant commanding, (would you not like to join that corps) & the "Rattlesnakes." These three include all the rowdies in town, I believe. The Rattlesnakes was originally a secret society, a sort of vigilance committee I think, & the most extraordinary notices used to appear in the papers, for instance "Attention, Rattlesnakes! Come out of your holes, and meet at the Canal bridge, at 9 o'clock this evening.

> By order of President Grand Rattle
> POISON FANG, Secretary"

Then the next day the notice would be to "crawl into your holes."

Fights & weddings are the order of the day. Notwithstanding the times there have been more weddings this winter than for several years. . . . My Christmas presents were not ready to send on in Mothers box, so they will have to go in the next. All are quite well here except Mother, she was complaining yesterday, but seems quite bright today. Goodnight, it is getting late. Love to you both. Yr. affectionate sister.

P.S. Fido is quite well, so is Pluto.

4. ELEANOR NOYES JACKSON—MONTGOMERY
WELCOMES JEFFERSON DAVIS

Eleanor Noyes Jackson, a native of Boston, Massachusetts, was the wife of Jefferson Franklin Jackson of Montgomery, Alabama.

After her marriage she became an ardent Southerner and supported the Confederate cause with enthusiasm. When delegates from the seceding Southern states met in Montgomery to form their new provisional government, Mrs. Jackson witnessed the inauguration on the front steps of the Capitol. She saw President Davis ride up in a carriage drawn by six horses. She heard William L. Yancey say, "The man and the hour have met." The next day she wrote to her sister, Mary Noyes, of Boston, Massachusetts.

Montgomery, Ala. Feb. 19, 1861

. . . I was one of the mass of people in front of the portico. The balconies and every front window were filled with ladies who went early.

My share of the interesting occasion was to furnish a most beautiful wreath of japonicas and hyacinths and small Spring magnolias—also a large bunch of flowers for the Vice-President.[1] I did not begin to collect the flowers until 9 o'clock in the morning, and went to the Garrett's place with a basket and brought it away full of those crimson and red variegated japonicas. The green of the wreath was arbor vitae and box. The front of the wreath was elevated and composed of a large crimson japonica, a small one and white hyacinths in the point against a back of arbor vitae. Below the japonicas were purple and white double hyacinths. On either side of the center were half-opened pink japonicas and the whole wreath was of dark and light flowers alternating. As the procession came through the capitol grounds I handed the flowers to Mr. Watts who was of the committee. After the inauguration Howell Cobb[2] handed him the wreath which he slipped on his arm, and gave Mr. Stephens his flowers. The ladies threw down small bunches of flowers which he gathered and held in his hand. . . .

A levee was held last night in Estelle and Concert Halls. The ladies trimmed Estelle Hall beautifully. Oh! the crowd, and such a one. The greatest variety of costumes you can imagine. People from town, people from country, young and old. Mrs. Watts Fitzpatrick just from Washington with black velvet dress—pointed lace bertha and sleeves trimmed with same—pearl ornaments. A lady next to her, perhaps with her head covered and shawl on. Men in fine

[1] Alexander H. Stephens.
[2] Member of U.S. Congress from Georgia 1843-1851 and 1855-1857 (Speaker 1849-1851); Governor of Georgia 1851-1853; Secretary of the Treasury 1857-1860; President of the Confederate Congress 1861-1862.

clothes and men in homespun suit. Most of our ladies dressed prettily. Mrs. Thorington came with bonnet and cloak. I wore my brown silk with blue brocaded flowers which had been entirely made over into a low-necked dress with skirt in puffs and ruffles. On my neck I wore my pretty colarett, and black lace shawl thrown around my shoulders. My head dress was of blue velvet with black and gold ornaments. My jewelry is blue you know. . . .

Every house, little and big, was illuminated from the capitol to the Exchange last night. The theater was illuminated, also Rocketts and bengal lights were thrown from opposite sides of the street constantly by the Estelle Hall. In short yesterday was a great day for Montgomery. . . .

5. VARINA HOWELL DAVIS—"I COULD NOT COMMAND MY VOICE TO SPEAK"

Varina Howell Davis was thirty-five years old and the mother of three children when she became the First Lady of the Confederacy. She was described by William Howard Russell, the English war correspondent, as "a comely, sprightly woman, verging on matronhood, of good figure and manners, well dressed, ladylike and clever." She liked to wear a rose in her dark hair and she had a preference for gorgeous white silk dresses. She was above the average height, carried her head well and dressed her hair simply. One who saw her for the first time remarked, "She is brimming with zest for life."

Varina Howell was born in Natchez, Mississippi, on May 7, 1826, the daughter of William B. Howell and Margaret Louisa Kempe of Virginia. Her grandfather, Richard Howell, served as governor of New Jersey for eight successive terms. Varina, after a series of governesses, attended Madame Greenland's school in Philadelphia.

She met thirty-six-year-old Jefferson Davis in 1844. They were married the following year and lived at "Briarfield" near Natchez. That same year her husband was elected to Congress, and thereafter Varina found herself occupying various successive roles. She was a soldier's wife when Colonel Davis served in the Mexican campaigns, a senator's wife, a Cabinet member's wife when he was Secretary of War under President Pierce and a senator's wife again from 1857 until his resignation in 1861.

Mrs. Davis did not reach Montgomery in time to see her husband inaugurated Provisional President of the Confederate States of America. "Upon my weary heart," he wrote her, "was showered smiles, plaudits, and flowers; but, beyond them, I saw troubles and thorns innumerable. . . . I thought it would have gratified you to have witnessed it, and have been a memory to our children. . . ." She joined him on March 4.

It was necessary to close up our home and abandon all we had watched over for years, before going to Montgomery; our library, which was very large and consisted of fine well-chosen English books, was the hardest to relinquish of all our possessions. After all was secured in the best manner practicable, I went to New Orleans en route to Montgomery, and remained a few days at my father's house. While there, Captain Dreux, at the head of his battalion, came to serenade me, but I could not command my voice to speak to him when he came on the balcony; his cheery words and the enthusiasm of his men depressed me dreadfully. Violets were in season, and the captain and his company brought several immense bouquets. The color seemed ominous. Perhaps Mr. Davis's depression had communicated itself to me, and I could not rally or be buoyed up by the cheerfulness of those who were to do battle for us. My journey up the Alabama River to join Mr. Davis in Montgomery was a very sad one, sharing his apprehensions, and knowing our needs to be so many, with so little hope of supplying them. . . .

When we reached the hotel where the President was temporarily lodged, the Provisional Congress had assembled, he had been inaugurated, and the day of my arrival the Confederate flag had been hoisted by the daughter of Colonel Robert Tyler, and the granddaughter of the ex-President. . . . [The flag had] a blue union containing the stars in white at equal distances; . . . one broad white and two red stripes the same width. Under it we won our victories, and the memory of its glory will never fade. It is enshrined in our hearts forever. . . .

The house chosen for us was a gentleman's residence, roomy enough for our purposes, on the corner of a street and looking toward the State Capitol. There were many charming people there, who were all intent on kind services to us; our memory of Montgomery was one of affectionate welcome, and if we should have judged from the hampers of blossoms poured out before us, it was a flowery kingdom. . . .

6. CAROLINE HOWARD GILMAN—CHARLESTON
PREPARES FOR WAR

Mrs. Gilman, daughter of a Boston shipwright, had lived in Charleston since 1819 where her husband Samuel Gilman, author of "Fair Harvard," served as pastor of the Unitarian church. Before the war she had published The Rosebud, *one of the earliest periodicals for children; she had written* The Poetry of Travelling in the United States, Recollections of a New England Housekeeper, Recollections of a Southern Matron *and many stories and poems.*

Mrs. Gilman had been a widow for a number of years when war came. The members of her family were divided in their loyalties. Two of her four daughters, her sister, and her niece Mrs. James Russell Lowell lived in Massachusetts and were ardent Northern sympathizers. With Mrs. Gilman in Charleston were the other daughters and their children, three of whom, Frank, Willie and Washington, had recently enlisted in the Confederate service.

To the daughters in Massachusetts, Mrs. Pickering Dodge of Salem and Mrs. Charles J. Bowen of Kingston, Mrs. Gilman wrote the letter that follows. She assumes, it seems, that they will share her attitude. The secessionist post office at Charleston was certainly exercising no censorship on mail going north that might give information to the enemy.

Charleston, S.C., March 31, 1861

My dear Children:—

I was able to give the Wilkies great pleasure, by taking them with my permit to Sullivan's Island on Friday. The wharf presents a very animated appearance from the number of soldiers and the different uniforms—the Zouaves I think the most picturesque. Lieut. W. met us at the Cove, after we had passed the guard. In a short time Willie and Washington joined us. Lieut. W. borrowed the State wagon, and putting some of our chairs for extra seats, the party were made very comfortable for a drive to Fort Washington, the quarters of the Washington Light Infantry. Washington drove me in a buggy. The first battery on the way, now finished and mounted, is the next lot to mine, the terrible cannon pointing Sumter-wise. We stopped to see the recruits (regulars) drill. The second battery is on Mrs. McDowell's lot; the third is Fort Moultrie, where the fearful

A GALLERY
OF
CONFEDERATE
LADIES

☆ SUSAN BRADFORD

She was the daughter of Dr. Edward Bradford of Pine Hill plantation, Leon County, Florida. When war broke out he had vast holdings of land and over 300 slaves. This was her background when, still not quite fifteen, she watched her state secede. Scarcity resulting from the blockade made her inventive, and three years later she proudly reported making herself sandals with soles of corn shucks which she braided ingeniously. This picture was taken in 1865, when she was about nineteen.

☆ ROSE O'NEAL GREENHOW

Mrs. Greenhow, a native of Maryland, was the widow of Robert Greenhow, a prominent Washingtonian. She was a dedicated and determined Southerner and, as prison records later described her, "a dangerous, skillful spy." Two code messages from her to General Beauregard, revealing General McDowell's plans, supplied the basis for the Confederate defense at First Manassas. Her arrest followed on August 23.

☆ BELLE BOYD

The most sensational and romantic of the Southern spies, Belle Boyd was the daughter of a well-known family in Martinsburg. Her beauty and charm made her a favorite of Washington society in 1860-1861. She became a spy and courier, working in the Valley with Stuart, Beauregard and especially Jackson. She tells how Jackson rewarded her with a captain's commission and an appointment as honorary aide-de-camp.

☆ CORNELIA PEAKE McDONALD

Mrs. McDonald, the daughter of Humphrey and Anne Linton Lane Peake, was born at Alexandria, Virginia, in 1822. After some travel, she married Angus McDonald, a lawyer of Winchester, Virginia, and bore him seven children. When he rode away in the spring of 1862 as a colonel with the Stonewall Brigade, he urged his wife to keep a diary. It relates the varying fortunes of war in Winchester.

☆ SARAH MORGAN

Sarah was one of the nine children of Judge Thomas Gibbes Morgan of Baton Rouge. She was twenty when he died in '61. She started her diary in '62 to relieve her feelings, she said, so as not to make an exhibition of herself by talking, as some women did. She wrote with good sense, spirit and humor even under distressing circumstances such as getting her mother and sisters out of Baton Rouge under fire from Federal gunboats.

☆ ELIZABETH McGAVOCK HARDING

Mrs. Harding was the wife of General William G. Harding and mistress of the Belle Meade plantation near Nashville, famous throughout the South for its hospitality, its fine blooded horses and its many servants. After the Federal occupation of Nashville, General Harding was arrested for refusing to take the oath of allegiance demanded. He was sent to Fort Mackinaw in northern Michigan and held until 1866. Meanwhile Mrs. Harding ran the plantation. In 1862 she was forty-four, about ten years younger than her husband.

Picture by courtesy of Mrs. Jesse E. Wills of Nashville, great-granddaughter of Mrs. Harding

☆ VARINA HOWELL DAVIS

Varina Howell was born in Natchez, Mississippi, in 1826. She married Jefferson Davis in 1845 when he was thirty-seven. When she was thirty-five and had three children, she became First Lady of the Confederacy. She was above average height and carried her head well. She liked to wear a rose in her hair and had a preference for dresses of white silk. This picture shows her with her husband at a Presidential reception.

☆ LaSALLE CORBELL PICKETT

LaSalle Corbell's courtship and marriage had a romantic storybook quality. At Old Point Comfort in 1851, when she was eight, she met a young lieutenant from Richmond, George E. Pickett. His wife had just died. With little-girl devotion LaSalle loved him from the start and confidently prepared to become a soldier's wife. Their paths crossed but seldom until 1863. Then, encamped near her home, he fell in love with her. Returning from Pennsylvania as the hero of Gettysburg, he pressed her for an immediate wedding.

Picture from Soldier of the South: General Pickett's War Letters to His Wife, ed., Arthur Crew Inman (Houghton Mifflin Company, 1928), used by permission of the publisher

☆ ISSA DESHA BRECKINRIDGE

*Daughter of Dr. John R. Desha and granddaughter
of Governor Joseph Desha of Kentucky, Issa married
Colonel W. C. P. Breckinridge of Lexington. His family
was deeply divided, about half adhering to the Union
and others, like him, bearing arms for the Confederacy.
He rode with Morgan's cavalry. Issa, denied a pass to
join her husband in the South and feeling her security
threatened in Federal-held territory, fled to Canada.*

☆ SARA RICE PRYOR

*Daughter of Samuel Blair Rice of Halifax County,
Virginia, she married Roger A. Pryor when she was
eighteen. Serving his second term in Congress, he
resigned his seat to become a Confederate officer as war
approached. After First Manassas, Sara followed his
movements to be with him whenever possible. She endured many risks and hardships, especially during the
siege of Petersburg, when Roger could seldom see her.
After the war they lived in New York, where he was a
journalist and distinguished judge, and she wrote.*

☆ ELIZA FRANCES ANDREWS

Eliza was one of the seven children of Judge Garnett Andrews of Washington, Georgia. Though her father was bitterly opposed to secession, her brother enlisted in the Confederate Army, and Eliza gave her heart to the Southern cause. It was in the old bank building on the north side of the town square of little Washington that Jefferson Davis signed his last paper as President of the Southern Confederacy, on May 3, 1865. Eliza helped entertain the notable leaders who reached Washington and was an intimate observer of the last hours of the Confederacy.

machinery of war is so artistically arranged; the fourth and fifth are near the Curlew grounds, and the Myrtles. After our drive of three miles, so different from our Summer associations, we turned at East End, and saw the battery now named Fort Washington, which our boys have been blistering their hands in building. Lieut. Wilkie ordered the guns to be fired that we might see the force of their action. The first regiment of rifles, including the Washington Light Infantry, are all in tents, at the East End, and form quite a picturesque village. We went first to the Officers' tent, where Lieut. Wilkie unrolled a new flag beautifully wrought with a Palmetto symbol and recently presented by Mrs. Beauman of Charleston. Knowing where to touch the heart of a W. L. I. man, I asked to see the old Eutaw Standard. He unrolled it reverently. It is of red damask and in tatters.

From the Officers' tent we went to Willie's. Willie was full of fun as waiter, with his tin drinking cups, and Washington was overrunning with sentiment about Carrie, who was absent, and for whom he made a charming bouquet, with an appropriate kiss sentiment hidden in the centre. After about an hour of chat and inspection we drove home, with Fort Sumter in view, the calm waters and glittering beach in all their old beauty. Fort Sumter looks like a noble stag at bay, with Morris Ft. where the largest force is stationed, and James Fort bristling with cannon in the rear, Sullivan's in front; and the floating battery ready for the first note of reinforcement, for Beauregard says all is ready. When will it be surrendered? The men, ours, have finished their work, and are growing impatient of delay. It requires all the wisdom of their superiors to keep them cool. Think of so many thousand men leaving plantations, mercantile life, shops, colleges, and every department of labor, since December, and working like journeymen. The dragoons, who have been waited on all their lives, curry their own horses.

Such is my faith in peace, that I carried down a gardener to arrange my flower beds.

MOTHER

7. EMMA E. HOLMES—FORT SUMTER SURRENDERS

While two famous visitors to Charleston, Mrs. James Chesnut and William Howard Russell of the London Times, *were writing*

their accounts of the bombardment and surrender of Fort Sumter,
the lame girl, Emma E. Holmes, whose house shook from the thunder
of the guns, sat at her desk and painstakingly set down the new
scenes and new deeds in the once-quiet city of her birth.

Charleston, South Carolina

Thursday 11th [April 1861] is a day never to be forgotten in the annals of Charleston. A despatch was received from Jeff. Davis with orders to demand the surrender of Fort Sumter immediately. At 2 P.M. two aide-de-camps went to Anderson with the summons, giving him until six to decide. The whole afternoon and night the Battery was thronged with spectators of every age and sex, anxiously watching and waiting with the momentary expectation of hearing the roar of cannon, opening on the fort, or on the fleet which was reported off the bar. Everybody was restless and all who could go, were out.

Friday April 12 1861

Carrie went up yesterday morning to Hattie's to help, in company with two or three others, to make a Confederate flag for the "Pride." When it was half finished, Mr. Hughes went home and told them Mr. Stevens had no flag to raise on his battery so they immediately got the material necessary and worked hard at night and early this morning they finished it and sent it down.

Beauregard went a second time last night at ten to urge the surrender but Anderson refused. The first time Anderson said if the fort was not battered he would have to surrender in three days for want of food. All last night the troops were under arms and at half past four this morning the heavy booming of cannon woke the city from its slumbers. The Battery was soon thronged with anxious hearts, and all day long they have continued—a dense, quiet, orderly mass —but not a sign of fear or anguish is seen. Everybody seems relieved that what has been so long dreaded has come at last, and so confident of victory that they seem not to think of the danger of their friends. Everybody seems calm and grave.

I am writing about half past four in the afternoon—just about twelve hours since the first shot was fired—and during the whole time shot and shell have been steadily pouring into Fort Sumter from Fort Stevens where our "Palmetto boys" have won the highest praise from Beauregard, from Fort Moultrie and the floating battery, placed at the cove. These are the principal batteries and just before dinner we received despatches saying *no one* has yet been hurt on either Morris or Sullivan's island and though the floating battery and Fort Stevens have both been hit several times, *no damage* has been done, while two or three breaches have been made in Fort Sumter. For more than two hours our batteries opened on Anderson, before he returned a single shot, as if husbanding his resources. At times the firing has been very rapid, then slow and irregular and at times altogether upon Fort Moultrie.

Though every shot is distinctly heard and shakes our house, I feel calm and composed. . . .

There are some few ladies who have been made perfectly miserable and nearly frantic by their fear of the safety of their loved ones, but the great body of the citizens seem to be so impressed with the justice of our Cause that they place entire confidence on the God of Battles.

Every day brings hundreds of men from the up-country and the city is besides filled with their anxious wives and sisters and mothers who have followed them.

Saturday April 13, 1861.

All yesterday evening and during the night our batteries continued to fire at regular intervals. About six in the afternoon the rain commenced and poured for some hours. The wind rose and it became quite stormy. But this morning was clear and brilliantly beautiful. Yesterday was so misty it was difficult to see what was going on at the forts. The wind was from the west today, which prevented us from hearing any firing and we were becoming anxious to know the meaning of stillness, when Uncle James sent to tell us Fort Sumter was on fire.

I could not wait for the Dr.'s permission but drove hurriedly to cousin Sallie's, whence I had a splendid view of the harbor—with the naked eye. We could distinctly see the flames amidst the smoke. All the barracks were on fire. Beyond lay the fleet of four or five vessels off the bar, their masts easily counted. They did not make the slightest effort to go to Anderson's relief. . . .

The scene at Fort Sumter must have been awful beyond description. They had soon been compelled to leave their barbette guns, from their exposed situation, many being disabled by our balls. Anderson fired his guns until he was compelled to retire to the case mates from the fury of the fire, on three sides at one time. . . .

Both on Friday and Saturday, Anderson put his flag at half-mast as a signal of distress—the barracks being on fire three times on Friday —but "his friends" took no notice of it, and was not understood by our men though all sympathized deeply with him, and shouted applause every time he fired.

In the meantime the scene to the spectators in the city was intensely exciting. The Battery and every house, house top and spire was crowded. On White Point Garden were encamped about fifty cadets, having in charge, five, six, & twelve pounders placed on the eastern promenade. It was thought the vessels might attempt to come in and bombard the city, and workmen were busy all day in mounting four twenty-fours directly in front of Cousin S.'s.

With the telescope I saw the shots as they struck the fort, and the masonry crumbling, while on Morris Island we saw the men moving about on the sand hills. All were anxious to see, and most had opera-glasses which they coolly used till they heard a report from Sumter, when they dodged behind the sand hills. . . .

During the morning a demand for cartridge bags for the Dahlgreen guns was made. The elder ladies cut and about twenty girls immediately went to work, all seated on the floor, while we set one to watch and report.

Soon the welcome cry was heard "the flag is down" but scarcely had the shout died away, when it was reported to be up again, but only visible with the glass. The staff being shot off, it was hastily fastened just above the parapets and very soon after at one o'clock the stars and stripes were struck and the white flag floated alone. We could scarcely believe it at first but the total cessation of hostilities soon proved it true.

After the staff was shot off Mr. Wigfall,[1] who was on Morris Island, not being able to see the flag when it was replaced, determined to demand the surrender in Beauregard's name. He sprang into a boat rowed by three Negroes, asked H. Gourdin Young of the P.G. to accompany him and went to the fort while shot and shell were falling all around from the batteries on Sullivan's Island. He crept into a port hole, asked to see Anderson and demanded the surrender. He was asked why the batteries continued firing as the White flag was up beside the U.S. flag. Wigfall answered that as long as the latter floated the firing would continue. It was immediately hauled down.

---

[1] Louis T. Wigfall was U. S. Senator from Texas when his state seceded. He immediately resigned and became a member of the Confederate Congress.

In the meantime a steamer had started from the City with several other aides, but they found Wigfall had anticipated them. The terms granted are worthy of South Carolina to a brave antagonist. Major Anderson and his garrison are to be allowed to march out with military honors—saluting their flag before taking it down. All facilities will be afforded for his removal together with company arms and property and all private property. He is allowed to determine the precise time of yielding up the Fort and may go by sea or land as he chooses. He requested that he might be sent on in the "Isabel" to New York.

What a change was wrought in a few moments in the appearance of the harbor. Steamers with fire engines were immediately despatched to the Fort. The garrison gathered on the wharf to breathe the fresh air and numbers of little sailing boats were seen darting like sea-gulls in every direction, conveying gentlemen to the islands to see their friends.

During the afternoon, a small boat came with a white flag from the fleet, bearing an officer who wished to make arrangements with Anderson about his removal.

As soon as the surrender was announced, the bells commenced to ring, and in the afternoon, salutes of the "magic seven" were fired from the cutter, "Lady Davis," school ship, and "Cadet's Battery" in honor of one of the most brilliant and bloodless victories in the records of the world. After thirty three hours consecutive cannonading not one man hurt on either side—no damages of any consequence done to any of our fortifications, though the officers quarters at Fort Moultrie and many of the houses on Sullivan's Island were riddled, and though the outer walls of Fort Sumter were much battered and many of the guns disabled, besides the quarters burnt, still as a military post it is uninjured. . . .

Sunday 14th. Major Anderson appointed 12 o'clock today to give up the fort. The Governor, his wife & suite, General Beauregard—suite—and many other military men besides Mrs. Isaac Hayne and Hattie Barnwell who went down with Lieut. Davis' sister, went down on board a steamer, whence they witnessed the ceremony of raising the Confederate and Palmetto flags. . . . Anderson and his men embarked on board the "Isabel" but as the tide prevented them from leaving immediately, they were obliged to be witnesses of the universal rejoicing. . . .

Sunday afternoon I went on the Battery, which was more crowded than ever. The cadets had a dress-parade at sunset and the harbor was gay with steamers with flags flying from every point. It did not seem at all like Sunday! . . .

8. MARY ANNA JACKSON—"OUR HOME GREW LONELY"

Mary Anna Morrison, daughter of the Reverend R. H. Morrison, Presbyterian minister of Charlotte, North Carolina, was married on July 16, 1857, to Professor Thomas Jonathan Jackson, of the Virginia Military Institute, Lexington, Virginia. He was thirty-three and she twenty-six. She had attended the Moravian School in Salem, North Carolina, where she was popular with both students and faculty. The groom's gift to his lovely, black-haired bride was a gold watch and a dainty set of seed pearls. After their wedding journey he brought her to Lexington, where Professor Jackson purchased a small house and a few acres of land. They planted a garden which was the source of much pleasure to them. Many friends enjoyed the hospitality of their home. In the following year, their first child, a daughter, was born to live for only a few short weeks.

On April 21, 1861, Professor Jackson, a graduate of West Point and a veteran of the Mexican campaign, was commissioned a colonel in the Virginia forces and ordered to Richmond. After his departure Mrs. Jackson went about the dreary work of settling their business affairs, packing up, and disposing of no-longer-needed furniture. Acting on the wish and advice of her husband, she went back to her girlhood home in North Carolina.

Lexington, Virginia, April 21, 1861

About the dawn of that Sabbath morning, April 21, 1861, our door-bell rang, and the order came that Major Jackson should bring the cadets to Richmond immediately. Without waiting for breakfast, he repaired at once to the Institute, to make arrangements as speedily as possible for marching, but finding that several hours of preparation would necessarily be required, he appointed the hour for starting at one o'clock P.M. He sent a message to his pastor, Dr. White, requesting him to come to the barracks and offer a prayer with the command before its departure. All the morning he was engaged at the Institute, allowing himself only a short time to return to his home about eleven o'clock, when he took a hurried breakfast, and completed a few necessary preparations for his journey. Then, in the privacy of our chamber, he took his Bible and read that beautiful chapter in Corinthians beginning with the sublime hope of the resurrection—"For we know that if our earthly house of this tabernacle be dissolved, we have a building of God, a house not made with hands, eternal in the heavens"; and then, kneeling down, he committed himself and her whom he loved, to the protecting care of his Father in heaven. Never was a prayer more fervent, tender, and touching. His voice was so choked with emotion that he could scarcely utter the words, and one of his most earnest petitions was that "if consistent with His will, God would still avert the threatening danger and grant us peace!" . . .

When Dr. White went to the Institute to hold the short religious service which Major Jackson requested, the latter told him the command would march precisely at one o'clock, and the minister, knowing his punctuality, made it a point to close the service at a quarter before one. Everything was then in readiness, and after waiting a few moments an officer approached Major Jackson and said: "Major, everything is now ready. May we not set out?" The only reply he made was to point to the dial-plate of the barracks clock, and not until the hand pointed to the hour of one was his voice to ring out the order, "Forward, march!"

After he had taken his departure for the army, our home grew more lonely and painful to me from day to day. . . .

9. MARY CUSTIS LEE—"THE PROSPECTS BEFORE US ARE SAD"

Mary Custis Lee, wife of Robert E. Lee and mother of seven children, was in her fifty-fifth year when war came. The daughter of George Washington Custis and great-granddaughter of Martha Washington, she had spent almost her entire life at Arlington, across the Potomac from Washington. It was the scene of her courtship and marriage, the birthplace of her children—a beautiful and gracious home filled with heirlooms from Mount Vernon.

As the wife of an army officer she had lived for brief intervals in many places. After her father's death she edited a series of his articles which appeared in 1860 under the title of Recollections and

Private Memoirs of Washington, by his Adopted Son, George Washington Parke Custis, with a Memoir of the Author, by his daughter.

On the day when her husband, after thirty years' distinguished service, resigned his commission in the United States Army, she wrote to their daughter Mildred at boarding school in Winchester, Virginia.

> Arlington, Virginia
> April 20, 1861

With a sad heavy heart, my dear child, I write, for the prospects before us are sad indeed & as I think both parties are wrong in this fratricidal war, there is nothing comforting even in the hope that God may prosper the right, for I see no *right* in the matter. We can only pray that in his mercy he will spare us.

10. JUDITH BROCKENBROUGH McGUIRE—"I HEARD THE DRUMS BEATING IN WASHINGTON"

Judith McGuire was the wife of the Reverend John P. McGuire, principal of the Episcopal High School near Alexandria, Virginia. Born in Richmond in 1813, the daughter of Judge William Brockenbrough of the Virginia Supreme Court, she was widely connected throughout the state. Two sons enlisted in the Confederate Army. Her daughters were in school. Mrs. McGuire kept a diary from May 1861 till the war's end "for the members of my family who are too young to remember these days."

> Alexandria, Virginia

At Home, May 4, 1861.—I am too nervous, too wretched to-day to write in my diary, but that the employment will while away a few moments of this trying time. Our friends and neighbors have left us. Every thing is broken up. The Theological Seminary is closed; the High School dismissed. Scarcely any one is left of the many families which surrounded us. The homes all look desolate; and yet this beautiful country is looking more peaceful, more lovely than ever, as if to rebuke the tumult of passion and the fanaticism of man. We are left lonely indeed; our children are all gone—the girls to Clarke, where they may be safer, and farther from the exciting scenes which may too soon surround us; and the boys, the dear, dear boys, to the camp, to be drilled and prepared to meet any emergency. Can it be that our country is to be carried on and on to the horrors of civil war? I pray, oh how fervently do I pray, that our Heavenly Father may yet avert it. I shut my eyes and hold my breath when the thought of what may come upon us obtrudes itself; and yet I cannot believe it. It will, I know the breach will be healed without the effusion of blood. The taking of Sumter without bloodshed has somewhat soothed my fears, though I am told by those who are wiser than I, that men must fall on both sides by the score, by the hundred, and even by the thousand. But it is not my habit to look on the dark side, so I try to employ myself, and hope for the best. To-day our house seems so deserted, that I feel more sad than usual, for on this morning we took leave of our whole household. Mr. McGuire and myself are now the sole occupants of the house, which usually teems with life. I go from room to room, looking at first one thing and then another, so full of sad associations. The closed piano, the locked bookcase, the nicely-arranged tables, the formally-placed chairs, ottomans and sofas in the parlor! Oh for some one to put them out of order! and then the dinner-table, which has always been so well surrounded, so social, so cheerful, looked so cheerless to-day, as we seated ourselves one at the head, the other at the foot, with one friend,—but one,—at the side. I could scarcely restrain my tears, and but for the presence of that one friend, I believe I should have cried outright. After dinner, I did not mean to do it, but I could not help going into the girls' room. . . . I heard my own foot-steps so plainly, that I was startled by the absence of all other sounds. There the furniture looked so quiet, the beds so fixed and smooth, the wardrobes and bureaux so tightly locked, and the whole so lifeless! But the writing-desks, work-boxes, and the numberless things so familiar to my eyes! Where were they? I paused, to ask myself what it all meant. Why did we think it necessary to send off all that was so dear to us from our own home? I threw open the shutters, and the answer came at once, so mournfully! I heard distinctly the drums beating in Washington. The evening was so still that I seemed to hear nothing else. As I looked at the Capitol in the distance, I could scarcely believe my senses. That Capitol of which I had always been so proud! Can it be possible that it is no longer *our* Capitol? And are our countrymen, under its very eaves, making mighty preparations to drain our hearts' blood? And must this Union, which I was taught to revere, be rent asunder? Once I thought such a suggestion sacrilege; but now that it is dismembered, I trust it may never, never be reunited. We must be a separate people—our nationality must be different, to insure lasting peace and good-will. Why cannot we part in peace?

11. MARY CUSTIS LEE—I SET MY HOUSE IN ORDER

Although the General wrote repeatedly from Richmond urging his wife to leave Arlington, and although she had been warned to leave by her young cousin, William Orton Williams, who was attached to General Scott's office in Washington, brave Mrs. Lee could not bring herself to go. She must first place in best available security what they owned of intrinsic value or historic interest. Now she had for a brief interval the help of her son Custis who had been stationed at Fort Washington, a little way down the Potomac. The family plate and the Washington letters and papers she sent to Richmond. The family portraits and Washington's camp bed and equipment were among the things she sent to Ravensworth, the country home of her aunt, Maria Fitzhugh, near Alexandria. The Order of the Cincinnati china and the State china from Mount Vernon with other cherished possessions she stored in the closets and cellar of Arlington.

Finally, a few days after she wrote this letter to her husband, she followed her three daughters to Ravensworth.

Arlington, Virginia
May 9, 1861

I suppose ere this, dear Robert, you have heard of the arrival of our valuables in Richmond. We have sent many others to Ravensworth & all our wine & stores, pictures, piano etc. I was very unwilling to do this; but Orton was *so* urgent & even intimated that the day was fixed to take possession of these heights, that I did not feel it was prudent to risk articles that could never be replaced. Aunt Maria has been very kind in offering us an asylum there & in taking care of all our things. . . . I sent the girls up last evening. . . . I thought they could return if all was quiet. Custis was not ready to go; so I determined to remain with him, being very uneasy lest he should be arrested. I begin now to think, though it is all suspicion, that Orton was made the tool of some of the authorities in Washington to alarm us, either to bring you out to defend your home or get us out of the house. They are anxious at present to keep up appearances & would gladly, I believe, have a pretext to invade. . . . All day yesterday Gov. steamers were going up to Georgetown—transports, steam tugs & all kinds of crafts. Rumor Harpers Ferry is to be taken. Custis astonishes me with his calmness; with a possibility of having his early & beautiful home destroyed, the present necessity of abandoning it, he never indulges in invectives or a word of reflection on the cruel course of the Administration. He leaves that for his Mamma & sisters.

12. VARINA HOWELL DAVIS—"THEY ARE THE FINEST SET OF MEN"

Mrs. Davis and her children—Maggie, aged six, Jeff, Jr., aged three, and baby Joe—arrived in Montgomery in March to occupy the lovely two-story dwelling which was now called the White House of the Confederacy. She brought with her some of their heirlooms from "Briarfield." Over the mantel of her husband's new room she hung a sampler on which was embroidered "Thy Will Be Done." "Queen Varina" entered into her new duties with enthusiasm. The White House was the center of much social activity. There were brilliant levees, dinners and luncheons. But social life was not the First Lady's chief concern. She accompanied her husband on a hard, dangerous trip to examine the coast defenses of the Confederacy. She found time to keep her absent friends informed of the state of the nation. One such old friend was Clement Claiborne Clay, Jr., U.S. Senator from Alabama, 1853-1861, now in ill health at his mountain home "Cosy Cot" near Huntsville, but expecting to take his seat in the Confederate Senate in the autumn. In this letter she pays her incidental respects left-handedly to some Republican Senators in Washington.

Executive Mansion [Montgomery, Alabama]
May 10th, 1861

My dear Mr. Clay,
Could I have supposed my letter could prove a tolerable substitute to you for Mr. Davis I should long since have written to you. Mr. Davis seems just now only conscious of things left undone, and to ignore the much which has been achieved, consequently his time seems all taken up with the cabinet planning (I presume) future

operations. He comes home to eat his meals but always eats under a protest against the time occupied. "Oft in the stilly night," when he has seen his cabinet fall "like leaves in wintry weather" he is forced to come home for there is no one to help him to work. Sometimes the cabinet sans scotch cap depart surreptitiously, one at a time, and Mr. Davis while making things as plain as did the preacher "the virtues of the baptismal," finds his demonstrations made to one weak weary man, who has no vim to contend, to make the long short, he over-works himself & all the rest of mankind, but is so far quite well, though not fleshily inclined. There is a good deal of talk here of his going to Richmond as commander of the forces. I hope it may be done for to him military command is a perfect system of Hygiene and unless Mr. Spinola is around somewhere I don't suppose there is much danger. There have been some here who thought with a view to our sanitary condition that the government had better be moved to Richmond, and also that it would strengthen the weak fleshed, but willing spirited Border States.

For my part the only preference I have is be nearer Mr. Davis. I shall not attempt to stay here this summer. The children cannot stand warm weather.

This is a very pretty place and were not the climate as warm as is the enthusiasm of the people, it would be pleasant—but really all my patriotism oozes out, not unlike Bob Acres courage, at the pores, and I have deliberately come to the conclusion that Roman matrons did up their chores, patriotism, and such like public duties in the winter. I wish your health would suffice for you to come to see the Congress. They are the finest looking set of men I have ever seen collected together, grave, quiet, and thoughtful looking. Men, with an air of refinement which makes in my mind's picture gallery a gratifying pendant to Hamlen,[1] Durkee,[2] Dolittle[3] & Chandler.[4]

We are Presidents in embryo here. Shorn of much of our fair pro-portions, for instance Edward would carry prestige with him by insulting good friends, instead we have a negro door servant, who is disposed to believe all the people in the world bent on civility, and is happy to be rung up if he can testify his appreciation of their politeness.

The market is forlorn but this we give our best, and a warm wel-

[1] Hannibal Hamlin, of Maine, seems intended—U. S. Senator 1848-1861, Vice-Presi-lent 1861-1865.
[2] Charles Durkee, U. S. Senator from Wisconsin, 1855-1861.
[3] James R. Doolittle, U. S. Senator from Wisconsin, 1857-1869.
[4] Zachariah Chandler, U. S. Senator from Michigan, 1857-1875.

come, and I hope are spared many of the critiques we have heard in Washington upon the indifferent fare of the entertainers, because our guests eat with l'entente cordiale, which I now find exists out of diplomatic papers, & is not a myth.

If you are able to come with your wife, and make us a visit we will have the concordances of Washington & Montgomery. I should sincerely rejoice to see you, and to show my little ones to you. Believe me time has not cooled the affectionate gratitude I feel for all your sympathy during Mr. Davis' illness, to me the darkest hour of my life, and it would be a happiness in your hour of prostration to say so to you. You are not able to bear hotel inconvenience, but if you will come to us, need only see people when you please. I think too Mrs. Clay would enjoy seeing the many friends and acquaintances she has here. Come immediately so as to see Mr. Davis before he leaves here for Virginia.

As to the children, I think you must like them, at best your God child—he is pretty as was Maggie in her babyhood, and so very gentle & loving, gets occasions of tenderness while playing, and runs up and puts his dirty little hands on either side of my face to kiss me. He talks sporadically—the words pronounced quite plainly, sometimes whole sentences, and then it is a month before another word is enunciated. Jeff is beaming, blustering, blooming, burly and blundering as ever. The repository of many hopes, promising of but little definite as yet. Little Maggie is gentle & loving, and considerate. She and I are good friends.

We all think of going out to Mrs. Fitzpatrick this evening with C. Brown & his wife, and Mr. and Mrs. Toombs to spend a night & day. We expect much pleasure. The Madam seems to be in fine spirits, as is also the Governor. Ben I have not seen—Mrs. Mallory is in town on a short visit. Mrs. Pope Walker is here, Mrs. Memminger, and Mrs. Toombs. The latter is the only person who has a house.[1] I could gossip on ad infinitum, but were my paper longer, my gossip might be stronger. Four pages are enough for a sick man one hopes to see soon.

Faithfully, your friend

VARINA DAVIS

[1] Mrs. Fitzpatrick was the handsome wife of Benjamin Fitzpatrick, former U. S. Senator. Ben was the Senator. C. Brown was "Constitution" Browne, i.e., R. M. Browne, *ad interim* Secretary of State and Assistant Secretary of State of the Confederacy, who had been editor of the Atlanta *Constitution*. The Governor of Alabama was Andrew B. Moore. In the Provisional Cabinet Robert Toombs, of Georgia, was Secretary of State; S. R. Mallory, of Florida, Secretary of the Navy; L. P. Walker, of Alabama, Secretary of War; C. G. Memminger, of South Carolina, Secretary of the Treasury.

II

THE CONFEDERACY IS INVADED

May 1861—February 1862

On May 23, 1861, the people of Virginia ratified the Ordinance of Secession, and the very next day Union troops carried out the threat of which Orton Williams had warned Mrs. Lee two weeks or so before. They crossed the Potomac from Washington and occupied Arlington and the little towns of Alexandria and Fairfax. Ben Butler —his name was to become a byword and a hissing to Southern women—started an advance from Fortress Monroe up the peninsula between the York and the James rivers toward Richmond. He did not get far, being turned back at Big Bethel.

On June 8 Tennessee ratified secession—the eleventh state to leave the Union. The roster of the Confederacy was now complete. Maryland wavered but stayed out. Kentucky strove vainly to be neutral. Some counties in western Virginia seceded into the Union. The Provisional Congress moved to Richmond.

In July Major-General Irvin McDowell with approximately 35,000 men invaded Virginia from the Washington camp. "On to Richmond!" they shouted. They would promptly quench this fiery rebellion. At Manassas, twenty-five miles southwest of the Northern capital, they encountered Generals Beauregard and Joseph E. Johnston with about 31,000. On the twenty-first after some initial success the Union army was decisively defeated at what was later called in the South the First Battle of Manassas (Bull Run). Congressmen and others, men and women, who had come out in holiday spirit to view the spectacle of certain victory, skedaddled back to Washington in panic, adding to the confusion of the routed soldiers. During the battle Thomas Jonathan Jackson, commanding the Virginia brigade, won his first recognition and a new name. "There stands Jackson like a stone wall," cried Brigadier-General Barnard E. Bee, soon to die. President Davis and the Southern commanders on the field did not feel they were strong enough to follow up the success with determined pursuit.

Elsewhere the South was not so fortunate in repelling invasion. The North was already intent on effecting a blockade of Southern

*ports. On August 29 Fort Hatteras and Hatteras Inlet on the North
Carolina coast were captured by a Union fleet and army. Port Royal,
Hilton Head, Beaufort and the surrounding sea islands off South
Carolina fell to the enemy in November.*

*Further disasters came early in the New Year of 1862. The Con-
federate fortifications and garrison under General Henry A. Wise on
Roanoke Island, scene of Sir Richard Grenville's abortive colony,
were lost to an amphibious operation. In the West things went very
badly indeed. Fort Henry on the Tennessee River was yielded to
General Ulysses S. Grant on February 6, and on the sixteenth he
took Fort Donelson on the Cumberland, and some 14,000 men, after
a four days' siege. But the intrepid and resourceful Nathan Bedford
Forrest, who was utterly opposed to the surrender, got his cavalry
regiment out of Donelson in time. With the river forts gone, Nashville had to be evacuated by General Albert Sidney Johnston.*

*The day before that happened, Washington's Birthday, the Con-
federate permanent government had been inaugurated in Richmond.*

*Now the women speak as the tide of war flows toward them and
some begin to withdraw before it.*

1. JUDITH BROCKENBROUGH McGUIRE—
VIRGINIA IS INVADED

*During four days when Mrs. McGuire neglected her diary the
sound of military activities over the river in Washington grew more
ominous. Now she resumes—*

Alexandria, Virginia

May 10 1861. Since writing last, I have been busy, very busy,
arranging and rearranging. We are now hoping that Alexandria will
not be a landing-place for the enemy, but that the forts will be attacked. In that case, they would certainly be repulsed, and we could
stay quietly at home. To view the progress of events from any point
will be sad enough, but it would be more bearable at our own home,
and surrounded by our family and friends. With the supposition that
we may remain, and that the ladies of the family at least may return
to us, I am having the grounds put in order, and they are now so
beautiful! Lilacs, crocuses, the lily of the valley, and other spring
flowers, are in luxuriant bloom, and the roses in full bud. The green-

house plants have been removed and grouped on the lawn, verbenas in bright bloom have been transplanted from the pit to the borders, and the grass seems unusually green after the late rains; the trees are in full leaf; every thing is so fresh and lovely. "All, save the spirit of man, is divine."

War seems inevitable, and while I am trying to employ the passing hour, a cloud still hangs over us all and all that surrounds us. For a long time before our society was so completely broken up, the ladies of Alexandria and all the surrounding country were busily employed sewing for our soldiers. Shirts, pants, jackets, and beds, of the heaviest material, have been made by the most delicate fingers. All ages, all conditions, meet now on one common platform. We must all work for our country. Our soldiers must be equipped. Our parlor was the rendezvous for our neighborhood, and our sewing-machine was in requisition for weeks. Scissors and needles were plied by all. The daily scene was most animated. The fires of our enthusiasm and patriotism were burning all the while to a degree which might have been consuming, but that our tongues served as safety-valves. Oh, how we worked and talked, and excited each other! One common sentiment animated us all; no doubts, no fears were felt. We all have such entire reliance in the justice of our cause and the valor of our men, and, above all, on the blessing of Heaven! These meetings have necessarily ceased with us, as so few of any age or degree remain at home; but in Alexandria they are still kept up with great interest. We who are left here are trying to give the soldiers who are quartered in town comfort, by carrying them milk, pies, cakes, etc. I went in yesterday to the barracks, with the carriage well filled with such things, and found many young friends quartered there. All are taking up arms; the first young men in the country are the most zealous. Alexandria is doing her duty nobly; so is Fairfax; and so, I hope, is the whole South. We are very weak in resources, but strong in stout hearts, zeal for the cause, and enthusiastic devotion to our beloved South; and while men are making a free-will offering of their life's blood on the altar of their country, women must not be idle. We must do what we can for the comfort of our brave men. We must sew for them, knit for them, nurse the sick, keep up the faint-hearted, give them a word of encouragement in season and out of season. There is much for us to do, and we must do it. The embattled hosts of the North will have the whole world from which to draw their supplies; but if, as it seems but too probable, our ports are blockaded, we shall indeed be dependent on our own exertions, and great must those exertions be.

The Confederate flag waves from several points in Alexandria: from the Marshall House, the Market-house, and the several barracks. The peaceful, quiet old town looks quite warlike. I feel sometimes, when walking on King's street, meeting men in uniform, passing companies of cavalry, hearing martial music, etc., that I must be in a dream. Oh that it were a dream, and that the last ten years of our country's history were blotted out! Some of our old men are a little nervous, look doubtful, and talk of the impotency of the South. Oh, I feel utter scorn for such remarks. We must not admit weakness. Our soldiers do not think of weakness; they know that their hearts are strong, and their hands well skilled in the use of the rifle. Our country boys have been brought up on horseback, and hunting has ever been their holiday sport. Then why shall they feel weak? Their hearts feel strong when they think of the justice of their cause. In that is *our* hope.

Walked down this evening to see——.[1] The road looked lonely and deserted. Busy life has departed from our midst. We found Mrs. —— packing up valuables. I have been doing the same; but after they are packed, where are they to be sent? Silver may be buried, but what is to be done with books, pictures, etc.? We have determined, if we are obliged to go from home, to leave every thing in the care of the servants. They have promised to be faithful, and I believe they will be; but my hope becomes stronger and stronger that we may remain here, or may soon return if we go away. Everything is so sad around us! We went to the Chapel on Sunday as usual, but it was grievous to see the change—the organ mute, the organist gone; the seats of the students of both institutions empty; but one or two members of each family to represent the absentees; the prayer for the President omitted. When Dr. —— came to it, there was a slight pause, and then he went on to the next prayer—all seemed so strange! Tucker Conrad, one of the few students who is still here, raised the tunes; his voice seemed unusually sweet, because so sad. He was feebly supported by all who were not in tears. There was night service, but it rained, and I was not sorry that I could not go.

---

[1] It was not uncommon for the diarists to omit names so as not to endanger their friends in case their journals should fall into enemy hands.

May 15.—Busy every moment of time packing up, that our furniture may be safely put away in case of a sudden removal. The parlor furniture has been rolled into the Laboratory, and covered, to keep it from injury; the books are packed up; the pictures put away with care; house linen locked up, and all other things made as secure as possible. We do not hope to remove many things, but to prevent their ruin. We are constantly told that a large army would do great injury if quartered near us; therefore we want to put things out of the reach of the soldiers, for I have no idea that officers would allow them to break locks, or that they would allow our furniture to be interfered with. We have a most unsettled feeling—with carpets up, curtains down, and the rooms without furniture; but a constant excitement, and expectation of we know not what, supplants all other feelings. Nothing but nature is pleasant, and that is so beautiful! The first roses of the season are just appearing, and the peonies are splendid; but the horrors of war, with which we are so seriously threatened, prevent the enjoyment of any thing.

I feel so much for the *Southerners* of Maryland; I am afraid they are doomed to persecution, but it does seem so absurd in Maryland and Kentucky to talk of armed neutrality in the present state of the country! Let States, like individuals, be independent—be something or nothing. I believe that the very best people of both States are with us, but are held back by stern necessity. Oh that they could burst the bonds that bind them, and speak and act like freemen! The Lord reigneth; to Him only can we turn, and humbly pray that He may see fit to say to the troubled waves, "Peace, be still!" We sit at our windows, and see the bosom of our own Potomac covered with the sails of vessels employed by the enemies of our peace. I often wish myself far away, that I, at least, might not *see* these things. The newspapers are filled with the boastings of the North, and yet I cannot feel alarmed. My woman's heart does not quail, even though they come, as they so loudly threaten, as an avalanche to overwhelm us. Such is my abiding faith in the justice of our cause, that I have no shadow of doubt of our success.

May 16.—To-day I am alone. Mr. McGuire has gone to Richmond to the Convention, and so have Bishop Johns and Dr. Stuart. I have promised to spend my nights with Mrs. Johns. All is quiet around us. Federal troops quartered in Baltimore. Poor Maryland!

The North has its heel upon her! I pray that we may have peaceful secession.

May 17th.—Still quiet. Mrs. Johns, Mrs. B., and myself, sat at the Malvern windows yesterday, *spying* the enemy as they sailed up and down the river. Those going up were heavily laden, carrying provisions, etc., to their troops. I think if all Virginia could see their preparations as we do, her vote would be unanimous for secession.

May 21st.—Mr. McGuire has returned. Yesterday evening we rode to the parade-ground in Alexandria; it was a beautiful but sad sight. How many of those young, brave boys may be cut off, or maimed for life. I shudder to think of what a single battle may bring forth. The Federal vessel *Pawnee* now lies before the old town, with its guns pointing towards it. It is aggravating enough to see it; but the inhabitants move on as calmly as though it were a messenger of peace. It is said that an undefended, indefensible town like Alexandria will hardly be attacked. It seems to me strange that they do not go immediately to the Rappahannock, the York, or the James, and land at once in the heart of the State. I tremble lest they should make a direct attack upon Richmond. Should they go at once to City Point, and march thence to the city, I am afraid it could hardly be defended. Our people are busy in their preparations for defense; but time is necessary—every day is precious to us. Our President and military chiefs are doing all that men can do to forward preparations. My ear is constantly pained with the sound of cannon from the Navy-Yard at Washington, and to-day the drum has been beating furiously in our once loved metropolis. Dr. S. says there was a grand dress parade—brothers gleefully preparing to draw their brothers' blood!

Day after to-morrow the vote of Virginia on secession will be taken, and I, who so dearly loved this Union, who from my cradle was taught to revere it, now must earnestly hope that the voice of Virginia may give no uncertain sound; that she may leave it with a shout. I am thankful that she did not take so important a step hastily, but that she set an example of patience and long-suffering, and made an earnest effort to maintain peace; but as all her efforts have been rejected with scorn, and she has been required to give her quota of men to fight and destroy her brethren of the South, I trust that she may now speak decidedly.

Fairfax C. H., May 25.—The day of suspense is at an end. Alexandria and its environs, including, I greatly fear, our home, are in the hands of the enemy. Yesterday morning, at an early hour, as I was in my pantry, putting up refreshments for the barracks preparatory to a ride to Alexandria, the door was suddenly thrown open by a servant, looking wild with excitement, exclaiming, "Oh, madam, do you know?" "Know what, Henry?" "Alexandria is filled with Yankees." "Are you sure, Henry?" said I, trembling in every limb. "Sure, madam! I saw them myself. Before I got up I heard soldiers rushing by the door; went out, and saw our men going to the cars."

"Did they get off?" I asked, afraid to hear the answer. "Oh, yes, the cars went off full of them, and some marched out, and then I went to King Street, and saw such crowds of Yankees coming in! They came down the turnpike, and some came down the river; and presently I heard such noise and confusion, and they said they were fighting, so I came home as fast as I could."

I lost no time in seeking Mr. ——, who hurried out to hear the truth of the story. He soon met Dr. ——, who was bearing off one of the editors in his buggy. He more than confirmed Henry's report, and gave an account of the tragedy at the Marshall House. Poor Jackson (the proprietor) had always said that the Confederate flag which floated from the top of his house should never be taken down but over his dead body. It was known that he was a devoted patriot, but his friends had amused themselves at this rash speech. He was suddenly aroused by the noise of men rushing by his room-door, ran to the window, and seeing at once what was going on, he seized his gun, his wife trying in vain to stop him; as he reached the passage he saw Colonel Ellsworth[1] coming from the third story, waving the flag. As he passed Jackson he said, "I have a trophy." Jackson immediately raised his gun, and in an insant Ellsworth fell dead. One of the party immediately killed poor Jackson. The Federals then proceeded down the street, taking possession of public houses, etc. I am mortified to write that a party of our cavalry, thirty-five in number, was captured. It can scarcely be accounted for. It is said that the Federals notified the authorities in Alexandria that they would enter the city at eight, and the captain was so credulous as to believe them.

[1] E. Elmer Ellsworth, of the 11th New York or "First Fire Zouaves."

Poor fellow, he is now a prisoner, but it will be a lesson to him and to our troops generally. Jackson leaves a wife and children. I know the country will take care of them. He is the first martyr. I shudder to think how many more there may be.

The question with us was, what was next to be done? Mr. McGuire had voted for secession, and there were Union people enough around us to communicate every thing of the sort to the Federals; the few neighbors who were left were preparing to be off, and we thought it most prudent to come off too. Pickets were already thrown out beyond Shuter's Hill, and they were threatening to arrest all secessionists.

With a heavy heart I packed trunks and boxes, as many as our little carriage would hold; had packing-boxes fixed in my room for the purpose of bringing off valuables of various sorts, when I go down on Monday; locked up every thing; gave the keys to the cook, enjoining upon the servants to take care of the cows, "Old Rock," the garden, the flowers, and last but not least, J——'s splendid Newfoundland. Poor dog, as we got into the carriage how I did long to take him! When we took leave of the servants they looked sorrowful, and we felt so. I promised them to return to-day, but Mr. —— was so sick this morning that I could not leave him, and have deferred it until day after to-morrow. Mr. —— said, as he looked out upon the green lawn just before we set off, that he thought he had never seen the place so attractive; and as we drove off the bright flowers we had planted seemed in full glory; every flower-bed seemed to glow with the "Giant of Battles" and other brilliant roses. In bitterness of heart I exclaimed " Why must we leave thee, Paradise!" and for the first time my tears streamed. As we drove by "The Seminary," the few students who remained came out to say "Good-by." One of them had just returned from Alexandria, where he had seen the bodies of Ellsworth and Jackson, and another, of which we had heard through one of our servants who went to town in the morning. When the Federal troops arrived, a man being ordered to take down the secession flag above the market-house, and run up the "stars and stripes," got nearly to the flag, missed his foothold, fell, and broke his neck. This remarkable circumstance was told me by two persons who saw the body. Is it ominous? I trust and pray that it may be.

When we got to Bailey's Cross Roads, Mr. McGuire said to me that we were obliged to leave our home, and as far as we have a *right* to any other, it makes not the slightest difference which road we take

—we might as well drive to the right hand as to the left—nothing remains to us but the barren, beaten track. It was a sorrowful thought; but we have kind relations and friends whose doors are open to us, and we hope to get home again before very long. The South did not bring on the war, and I believe that God will provide for the homeless.

About sunset we drove up to the door of this, the house of our relative, the Rev. Mr. Brown and were received with the warmest welcome. As we drove through the village we saw the carriage of Commodore Forrest[1] standing at the hotel door, and were soon followed by the C.'s of our neighborhood and many others. They told us that the Union men of the town were pointing out the houses of the Secessionists, and that some of them had already been taken by Federal officers. When I think of all this my heart quails me. Our future is so dark and shadowy, so much may, nay must, happen before we again become quiet, and get back, that I feel sad and dreary. I have no fear for the country—that must and will succeed; but our dear ones! the representatives of every State, almost every family, from the Potomac to the Gulf of Mexico—how must they suffer, and how must we at home suffer in their behalf!

This little village has two or three companies quartered in it. It seems thoroughly aroused from the quiescent state which it was wont to indulge. Drums are beating, colors flying, and ever and anon we are startled by the sound of a gun. At Fairfax Station there are a good many troops, a South Carolina regiment at Centreville, and quite an army is collecting at Manassas Station. We shall be greatly outnumbered, I know, but numbers cannot make up for the zeal and patriotism of our Southern men fighting for home and liberty.

May 29.—I cannot get over my disappointment—I am not to return home! The wagon was engaged. E. W. had promised to accompany me; all things seemed ready; but yesterday a gentleman came up from the Seminary, reporting that the public roads are picketed far beyond our house, and that he had to cross fields, etc., to avoid an arrest, as he had no pass. I know that there are private roads which we could take, of which the enemy knows nothing; and even if they saw me, they surely would not forbid ingress and egress to a quiet elderly lady like myself. But Mr. —— thinks that I ought not to risk it. The fiat has gone forth, and I am obliged to submit.

---

[1] Commodore French Forrest, whose home was "Claremont." He was later to command the Confederate navy yard at Norfolk.

I hear that the house has been searched for arms, and that J's old rifle has been filched from its corner. It was a wonderfully harmless rifle, having been innocent even of the blood of squirrels and hares for some time past. I wonder if they do suppose that we would leave good fire-arms in their reach when they are so much wanted in the Confederacy, or if it is a mere pretext for satisfying a little innocent curiosity for seeing the interior of Southern homes? Ah, how many Northerners—perhaps the very men who have come to despoil these homes, to kill our husbands, sons and brothers, to destroy our peace —have been partakers of the warm-hearted hospitality so freely offered by our people! The parlours and dining-rooms now so igno-miniously searched, how often have they been opened, and the best cheer which the houses could afford set forth for them! I do most earnestly hope that no Northern gentleman, above all, no Christian gentleman, will engage in this wicked war of invasion. It makes my blood boil when I remember that our private rooms, our chambers, our very sanctums, are thrown open to a ruthless soldiery. But let me not do them injustice. I believe that they took nothing but the rifle, and injured nothing but the sewing-machine. Perhaps they knew of the patriotic work of that same machine—how it had stitched up many a shirt and many a jacket for our brave boys, and therefore did it wrong. But this silent agent for our country's weal shall not lie in ruins. When I get it again, it shall be repaired, and shall

> "Stitch, stitch, stitch,
> Band, and gusset, and sea,"

for the comfort of our men, and it shall work all the more vigorously for the wrongs it has suffered. . . .

29th, Night.—Several of our friends from Alexandria have passed to-day. Many families who attempted to stay at home are escaping as best they may, finding that the liberty of the hoary-headed fathers of patriotic sons is at stake, and others are in peril for opinion's sake. It is too provoking to think of such men as Dr. —— and Dr. —— being obliged to hide themselves in their houses, until their wives, by address and strategy, obtain passes to get them out of town! Now they go with large and helpless families, they know not whither. Many have passed whom I did not know. What is to become of us all?

Chantilly, June 1.—We came here (the house of our friend Mrs. Stuart) this morning, after some hours of feverish excitement. About three o'clock in the night we were aroused by a volley of musketry not far from our windows. Every human being in the house sprang up at once. We soon saw by the moonlight a body of cavalry moving up the street, and as they passed below our window we distinctly heard the commander's order, "Halt." They again proceeded a few paces, turned and approached slowly, and as softly as though every horse were shod with velvet. In a few moments there was another volley, the firing rapid, and to my unpractised ear there seemed a discharge of a thousand muskets. Then came the same body of cavalry rushing by in wild disorder. Oaths loud and deep were heard from the commander. They again formed, and rode quite rapidly into the village. Another volley, and another, then such a rushing as I never witnessed. The cavalry strained by, the commander calling out "Halt, halt," with curses and imprecations. On, on they went, nor did they stop.

While the balls were flying, I stood riveted to the window, unconscious of danger. When I was forced away, I took refuge in the front yard. Mrs. B. was there before me, and we witnessed the disorderly retreat of eighty-five of the Second United States Cavalry (regulars) before a much smaller body of our raw recruits. They had been sent from Arlington, we suppose, to reconnoitre. They advanced on the village at full speed, into the cross-street by the hotel and courthouse, then wheeled to the right, down by the Episcopal church. We could only oppose them with the Warrenton Rifles, as for some reason the cavalry could not be rendered effective. Colonel Ewell,[1] who happened to be there, arranged the Rifles, and I think a few dismounted cavalry, on either side of the street, behind the fence, so as to make it a kind of breastwork, whence they returned the enemy's fire most effectively. Then came the terrible suspense; all was confusion on the street, and it was not yet quite light. One of our gentlemen soon came in with the sad report that Captain Marr of the Warrenton Rifles, a young officer of great promise, was found dead. The gallant Rifles were exulting in their success, until it was whispered that their captain was missing. Had he been captured? Too soon the uncertainty was ended, and their exultant shouts hushed. His body was found in the high grass—dead, quite dead. Two of our men

---

[1] Richard S. Ewell was to become a lieutenant-general and one of the Confederacy's great corps commanders. He was commissioned brigadier-general on June 17, 1861.

received slight flesh-wounds. The enemy carried off their dead and wounded. We captured four men and three horses. Seven of their horses were left dead on the roadside. They also dropped a number of arms, which were picked up by our men.

After having talked the matter over, we were getting quite composed, and thought we had nothing more to fear, when we observed them placing sentinels in Mr. B's porch, saying that it was a high point, and another raid was expected. The gentlemen immediately ordered the carriages, and in half an hour M. B's family and ourselves were on the way to this place. . . .

This evening we have been enjoying a walk about these lovely grounds. Nature and art have combined to make it one of the most beautiful spots I ever saw—"So clean, so green, so flowery, so bowery," as Hannah More wrote of Hampstead; and we look on it sadly, fearing that the "trail of the serpent may pass over it all." Can it be that other beautiful homes are to be deserted? The ladies of the family are here alone, the sons are where they should be, in the camp; and should the Northern army sweep over it, they cannot remain here. Colonel Gregg and others of a South Carolina regiment dined here yesterday. They are in fine spirits, and very sanguine.

June 5.—Still at Chantilly. Every thing quiet; nothing particularly exciting; yet we are so restless. Mrs. Casenove and myself rode to the camp at Fairfax Court-House a day or two ago to see many friends; but my particular object was to see my nephew, W. B. Newton, first lieutenant in the Hanover troop. He looks so cheerful, full of enthusiasm and zeal; but he feels that we have a great work before us, and that we have entered a more important revolution than our ancestors did in 1775. His bright political prospects, his successful career at the bar, his future in every respect so full of hope and promise—all, all laid aside. But it is all right, and when he returns to enjoy his unfettered country, his hardships will be all forgotten, in joy for his country's triumphs. . . .

Mrs. General Lee has been with us for several days. She is on her way to the lower country, and feels that she has left Arlington for an indefinite period. They removed their valuables, silver, etc., but the furniture is left behind. I never saw her more cheerful, and she seems to have no doubt of our success. We are looking to her husband as our leader with implicit confidence; for besides his great military abilities, he is a God-fearing man, and looks for help where alone it is to be found. Letters from Richmond are very cheering. It is one great barracks. Troops are assembling there from every part of the Confederacy, all determined to do their duty. Ladies assemble daily, by hundreds, at the various churches, for the purpose of sewing for the soldiers. They are fitting out company after company. The large stuccoed house at the corner of Clay and Twelfth streets, so long occupied by Dr. John Brockenbrough,[1] has been purchased as a residence for the President. I am glad that it has been thus appropriated. . . .

2. BETTY HERNDON MAURY—"WE LEFT WASHINGTON"

Betty was the eldest of the eight children of famous Matthew Fontaine Maury, whom Robert S. Henry characterizes as "father of the science of oceanography, discoverer of the Gulf Stream, once the great scientific light of the United States," and later on to be "one of the three naval commissioners through whose zeal and efforts the Confederacy was able to secure the ships that became her cruisers, and her only mobile Navy."

Betty was born in Fredericksburg, Virginia, in 1835. She was a child when the family moved to Washington, D. C., and her father began his distinguished career with the United States Naval Observatory. She often accompanied him on his lecture tours and in 1852 went with him to the Brussels Conference. Before they sailed home they were lavishly entertained in many foreign cities.

When she was twenty-one Betty married her cousin, Will A. Maury, a lawyer, whose father had been mayor of Washington. A daughter, Nannie Belle, was born to them in 1859.

When war came the Will Maurys withdrew to Fredericksburg and lived with John Minor, one of their numerous Virginia cousins and brother of Mary Berkeley Minor Blackford. Betty's father resigned his position in Washington and reported in Richmond. The Governor of Virginia appointed him to his council. Then, with the rank of commander in the Confederate Navy, he was put in charge of the Torpedo Bureau where he carried out dangerous experiments with electric mines. The two brothers nearest to Betty in age, John and Dick, enlisted in the army. Brother-in-law Tom was a surgeon who helped take care of the wounded. Cousin Dabney Herndon Maury

[1] Mrs. McGuire's cousin.

rose from captain of cavalry to commander of the District of the Gulf with headquarters at Mobile.

Fredericksburg, Va.
At Cousin John Minor's
June 3d, 1861

A diary, faithfully kept, in such eventful times as these, must be interesting to our children even though it be indifferently written.

I commenced one about three weeks ago at our home in Washington, but in the hurry and confusion of getting off it was forgotten. I shall commence where I left off there, hoping to get that, one of these days, though God knows when or where we shall ever see our possessions there again. Will left his business, furniture and everything to come here and be with his people on the right side.

Last Thursday and Friday we got letters from Papa by private hand (there are no mails now between the North and the South) commanding us to come out of Washington at once.

On Friday Will went down to Alexandria to see if he could get a wagon, or conveyance of any kind to carry us to Manassas Junction. While he was gone it occurred to me that I had better go to the War Department and try to get a pass for us to leave the next day. So I got a hack and drove to the Department, intending to get Major John Lee[1] to go with me to see General Mansfield[2] and ask for the pass. Major Lee was out. After waiting half an hour for him I went over to General Mansfield's office. He refused to give us a pass. Refused even to give one to Nannie Belle and myself without Will. Said no one was allowed to cross the lines now. My heart died within me, and my eyes filled with tears. I began to despair. Just then Major Lee came in. He heard I had been waiting for him and had followed me over. He took me back to the Department and said we would go and ask the Secretary of War (Mr. Cameron). So we went up to Mr. Cameron's office, but he was home sick. Then we applied to General Scott. He gave one for Nannie Belle and myself but refused to allow Will to go. But when Major Lee learned that we were going in a hack across the country and through the "rebel camp" alone, he said it would never do for us to go without Mr. Maury.

Upon second application General Scott gave a pass to Will, first inquiring whether he was any relation to Captain Maury of the Ob-

---

[1] Major John F. Lee, in charge of the Bureau of Military Justice.
[2] Major-General J. K. F. Mansfield commanded the Department of Washington.

servatory now in Richmond. The clerk who carried a note making the second application did not know, and said he was not. The old General little knew that I was his daughter.

Will was delighted when he saw the pass. Said that he could never have gotten it. I felt like all the strong minded women I knew.

Mr. Hasbrouck of Newburg, N.Y. came to see us that night. He came down hoping to get to Richmond to see Papa but was told there was danger of his being arrested so he gave it up. He could have come with perfect safety. Papa could get him back.

He speaks with the greatest regret and grief of Papa's resignation —talks as if he were dead. I told him that I was a hundred times prouder of my father now. That if he had considered his own personal welfare he would have remained with the North. The people of the North have always honored and appreciated him far more than those of the South. But he could not take sides against his own people, against his native state and against the RIGHT.

Mr. Hasbrouck wanted Will and myself to come up to Newburg and stay until the troubles were over. Saturday morning we left Washington. We gave up our house and stowed our furniture at cousin Charles's. Left a great many things undone but I reckon Mother will attend to them. There was a good deal of furniture in the house still to be moved. We missed the boat and came all the way to Alexandria in a hack. Will paid $25. for a carriage to take us to Manassas Junction. It could only take two small trunks, so I had to leave mine with the greater part of my clothes.

We were stopped by a sentinel every fifteen minutes of our ride for eight miles out of Alexandria. Nannie Belle was so delighted at the prospect of seeing her Grand Ma and Aunt Lucy that she would sing "Dixie" all the way. I was afraid it would make the soldiers suspect us. So in order to stop her I had to give her a sugar cracker whenever we came to a sentinel. She soon understood it and would call out "Mama here is another soldier. Give me a sugar tacker."

We were told that we would find a company of Federal cavalry close to the "rebel lines." So when it was nearly dark and we were near Fairfax court house, we were stopped by two dragoons. I was struck by their gentlemanly appearance. They looked very different from the pickets we had passed. Will handed them General Heintzleman's[1] pass that he had gotten in Alexandria. They said that was signed by none of their officers and would not do. Will then gave

[1] Major-General Samuel P. Heintzelman.

them General Scott's pass. They laughed and said, they belonged to the Southern troops. I exclaimed "Thank God, we are among our own people at last."

They told us we might go on to Fairfax courthouse but must get a pass there. The night before (Friday) a company of eighty horse had ridden into the village and attacked our troops, fifty in number. They were repulsed with the loss of three killed and three prisoners. They were expected again that night. We lay down in our clothes, but were not disturbed.

Rose at four oclock and started at five for Manassas. We stopped at the court-house and jail to get our pass. There among a crowd of soldiers and horses I discovered our brother Tom. He had arrived in the night with a company from Manassas. Were only stopped three or four times between Fairfax and Manassas Junction. About three miles below Manassas a South Carolina regiment is stationed. They are fortifying themselves and throwing up breastworks. We reached Manassas too late for the eight oclock train and had to stay there till Monday morning. There were no accommodations for us. The tavern was filled with soldiers. I spent the day in the carriage under the trees, with men, horses and tents all around us.

We had services during the day, the first time Nannie Belle had ever been to "church." It was an imposing and affecting sight to see so many soldiers worshiping God under the broad canopy of Heaven. I was the only woman present. I saw a great many acquaintances and friends there. We got a room at night, but did not take off our clothes. The place was too public.

Our troops are fewer and more indifferently armed than I expected to see. But with such indomitable spirits, and such mothers and wives they can never be beaten. I saw some plain country people there telling their sons and husbands good bye. I did not hear the first word of repining or grief; only encouragement to do their best and be of good service. One woman after taking leave of her husband said to two youths when telling them goodbye, "Don't mind my tears, boys, they don't mean a thing."

After they left, their mother shamed her and said: "How could you let them see you crying? It will unman them." These were plain people who talked about "Farfax" and said "farwell."

Will went to Richmond. I arrived here Monday evening in time for tea. Mama did not expect us, so there was no one at the cars to meet us.

Tuesday June 4th 1861

I went up to the sewing society with Aunt Mary and Molly.[1] The ladies are busy making tents for the soldiers and sheets and pillow cases for the hospitals.

Wednesday June 5th

Fanny (our cook) was not to be found this morning. She has gone off with all her possessions. It seems that she and Nanny[2] had some difficulty about ten days ago and Papa told her if she did not apologize to Nanny, he would send her to Farley Vale to Mr. Corbin.

Monday, June 10th 1861

My mother returned from Farley Vale on Saturday and Father came up from Richmond. He is rather blue—doesn't know how Jeff Davis and his "clique" will work. He has made it understood that now Virginia is given up to him and is one of the Confederate States, all the commissions and appointments given by her are null and void, and that if any retain their places it is a gift from him. Governor Wise is forming a legion for the protection of *Western* Virginia. It is likely to be very popular. Charley Blackford[3] is Captain in it.

Nanny and Mr. Corbin came up Sunday. The latter was dressed in a uniform Nanny had made for him. He had Papa's old navy buttons on his blue flannel shirt. Nanny says the U.S. stands for "United South." Mr. Corbin wears a sword taken from a French officer at Waterloo. Papa returned to Richmond this morning.

Fri. June 14, 1861

Went to church yesterday. Heard a sermon on patriotism. I fall far short of the mark of a true patriot. I am selfish and narrow minded. Nanny puts me to the blush continually. She is so patriotic and unselfish.

Sunday, June 16, 1861

Mr. Corbin came up this morning. He has been with his company to Mathias' Point. Says there is no battery there.

There is great jealousy between the Virginia and the Confederate forces. Papa thinks that the Confederate officers and politicians want

[1] Molly Maury, Betty's sister.
[2] Nanny Maury, another sister, wife of S. W. Corbin of Farley Vale plantation.
[3] Son of Mary Berkeley Minor Blackford.

to usurp too much power and are unjust towards many of the Virginia soldiers. I hope Tom will be able to keep his place.

Papa's post as one of the Governor's council is to be abolished tomorrow. We do not know what will become of him then.

Wed. June 19th

Papa returned to Richmond Monday morning. He has a scheme to blow up the enemy's vessels in the different rivers by submarine works of some kind.

I do not know whether he will be able to carry it out. It is a great secret now.

Will received a very cordial letter from Judge Badger a few days ago welcoming him to the South and inviting him to his house in Raleigh. Will would like very much to go and only hesitates because of the expense. But I suspect the temptation will prove too strong for him.

I have been busy for the last two days making a shirt for one of the soldiers.

Molly has a very devoted beau, who comes very often and stays very late.—But Johnny Scott will never do. He has a grandfather, two uncles and an aunt that are crazy!!!

Thur. June 20, 1861

The Convention in Richmond were surprised and delighted to see how much good the Governor's Council had done. Thought the state could not do without it. But the Council thought they were unnecessary now that everything has been handed over to the Confederate States. So it has been abolished.

Papa is going up Saturday to see cousin Frank Minor. What a warm and true friend he is. He is very anxious that Papa shall be sent as Minister to England. Thinks it would be an appointment that would please the people and he would have more influence abroad than any other man. Cousin Frank need not take to himself the credit of having first thought of it. I have been wishing for it for more than a month. It is the only office in the gift of the Government that I covet for Papa. They surely would not send him into active service. He is too valuable and great a man for that.

Dick is chafing at being kept so long in Lexington. He wants to be in active service somewhere. Says he thirsts for Yankee blood and cannot bear to be up there in Lexington behind those mountains when so many others are in the fields.

I have found an old satin cloak that I have been looking for to make a puffing round the bottom of my *three year old* brown silk to make it long enough. It is the only thick dress I have with me. All of my handsomest clothes were left in the trunk in Alexandria.

It is strange how one can become accustomed to almost any mode of life. Here we are now *almost* as happy as in our best days and we cannot look into the future of this world at all. We cannot form an idea as to where or in what condition we may be one month hence.

Fri. June 21—1861

Was interrupted yesterday to go down and see a soldier. It turned out to be my friend Nick Hill, one of *our* old law students. He came South to join the army more than a month ago and was sent back to Maryland on recruiting service. He came back yesterday morning and swam his horse across the Potomac. He brought a good many Marylanders with him and more will follow today. They went to Mr. Corbin's and he sent them up in a wagon. This is their place of rendezvous. Mr. Hill asked me to make some shirts for them. He is to bring the material today from Richmond.

Sat. June 22/61

Mr. Hill has not made his appearance yet with the shirts.

No tidings of Fanny. I think she is too smart to be caught.

Wed. June 26th 1861

Have been hard at work this week on the clothes for Mr. Hill.

Six pairs of pantaloons, six jackets and eight shirts and havelocks —and all to be done in three days. I was in despair at first—but the ladies are so kind and ready to help. Every one that I asked took a part and the work now is comparatively easy. It will be done by tomorrow.

There are upwards of one hundred and fifty soldiers in the hospitals here. The sick suffer a great deal for want of proper medical attendance and good nursing. Many of the soldiers are laid on the floor when brought there and are not touched or their cases looked into for 24 hours.

Thurs. June 27/61

I never saw anything like the spirit here. The women give up the greater part of their time either to nursing the sick or sewing for the soldiers. It is the same case throughout the South.

Some of Papa's secret schemes are to be carried out now I am sure.

This is the time that Mr. Hill's clothes were to be done, and he has not brought me a single button or come to see anything about them. These suits are presents to the gentlemen that are with him.

Monday July 1st. 1861

Well! our secret expedition has returned.

Yesterday afternoon we heard a steam whistle and knew that no boat was expected here for a week. In a few minutes all Fredericksburg was at the wharf. It was the *St. Nicholas!* a prize! a Yankee Steamer that runs between Baltimore and Washington.

About two weeks ago Captain Hollins and Col. Thomas (a man that dresses like a Japanese)[1] went over to Maryland and arranged with friends there to take the *St. Nicholas* by strategy. Col. Thomas went to Baltimore and with six or eight friends got on board the steamer as passengers. When they reached Point Lookout, Captain Hollins with a few friends came on board as passengers also, and when the boat was fairly out in the stream they walked up to the Captain and told him that he was their prisoner and that the boat was in the hands of Confederate officers. He made some show of resistance at first, but soon saw that it was of no use and surrendered. The boat was then run into Coan Creek on the Virginia shore opposite to Point Lookout, where Captain Lewis's party, including the four hundred Tennesseeans were awaiting them. They had left the *Virginia* near the mouth of the Rappahannock and marched across country to Coan Creek the night before.

The plan was for the whole party to embark and under the Federal flag go up the Potomac, take the *Pawnee* and *Freeborn* at Aquia Creek. (They would never have suspected that the *St. Nicholas* was in the hands of Confederate officers until they were boarded) and then come around the mouth of the Rappahannock, take the blockading force there and come up with flying colors. But the Secretary of War would not allow the Tennesseeans to embark. Said they might

[1] Richard Thomas was a wealthy Marylander. After he captured the *St. Nicholas* he was commissioned a colonel of Virginia Volunteers. He was himself captured and jailed in Baltimore.

do any fighting that was necessary on shore, but not on board ship.

As it was, all embarked except Captain Lewis and a few others and went out into the Bay to see what they could find. The first vessel they met was a brig laden with coffee. It made no resistance. Some of the men were dreadfully frightened and begged on their knees for their lives. The Captain and crew were ordered aboard the steamer and two officers and five men were detailed to man the brig.

They then met a schooner filled with ice and another with coal both of which were taken in the same way. Mr. Thorburn and Dick were detailed for the coal schooner. Two of the Captains had their wives with them. One of them begged most piteously that her husband's life might be spared. There were thirty-nine prisoners in all. I saw them as they came by. They thought they were to be hung.

The Mayor went down last night to relieve their minds and say that no harm would be done them.

The passengers that were on the *St. Nicholas* were put off at Coan Creek. Clarence H. of Washington—Alice's old beau—was among the number. He was returning from a fishing excursion. Expressed much surprise at seeing Dick. The two Captains' wives were at work yesterday cutting up their flags and making them into Confederate flags. The bunting of the South has given out. Col. Thomas went on board the *St. Nicholas,* dressed as a woman. The party on board did not know each other *very well*. Each one suspected the other and all suspected the "woman."

It was Captain Lewis's scheme. Papa only helped to carry it out. . . .[1]

There was no blockading vessel at the mouth of the Rappahannock when the prizes came in. Suppose she had gone for provisions.

Tuesday July 2nd 1861

The clothes for Mr. Hill's party are finished and packed in a clothes basket ready to be sent up to Citizen's Hall. They look very neat and substantial and comfortable.

Wed. July 3rd 1861

Will went to Richmond this Morning. Papa wrote word last night that he was suggesting him for Prize Commissioner. Some legal proceedings have to be gone through with whenever a prize is brought

[1] Prof. J. Russell Soley, U. S. N., gives an account of this exploit of June 29 in *Battles and Leaders*, II, 143.

in, I believe. Do not know whether Will would like to have the place.

There are not more than thirty soldiers in the Hospital. The rest have been taken to private houses.

Fourth of July—1861

Not a gun was heard this morning. I hope our old National holidays will not be dropped by the Southern Confederacy.

Will returned from Richmond yesterday. Whether he got the appointment as Prize agent, or whether he would accept it if it was offered to him, or what he did in Richmond, I have not the most remote idea. I asked him to tell me where he went and what he did? He answered: "Oh! I went everywhere" and then told me he had tomatoes for dinner and that Jordan had a puppie for Nannie Belle. The rest he thought above my comprehension and reserved for some more fortunate male friend. Everybody gives me credit for more sense than my husband does.

Papa has gone to Norfolk. Do not know what for. . . .

Wed. July 10th 1861

Papa came yesterday evening. His secret mission failed, but I am so thankful that he has gotten back safe that I care very little about the failure. He went down to Sewells Point to blow up some of the ships that are at the mouth of the James river. Five noble vessels he says are there. He aimed for the two flag ships—the *Minnesota* and the *Roanoke*—Commodores Stringham[1] and Pendergrast.[2]

Friday night and Saturday night he sent an officer in a boat to reconnoiter. But there was a little steamer flying round and round the vessels keeping watch. Sunday as he was spying them through a glass and noting their relative positions he saw the church flag up on two of them. It is a white flag with a cross on it. The stars and stripes are lowered a little and that put above it. When he thought that those men were worshiping God in sincerity and in truth and no doubt think their cause as righteous as we feel ours to be, his heart softened towards them, for he remembered how soon he would be the means of sending many of them to eternity.

That night the party consisting of five skiffs, set off about ten o'clock. Papa was in the first boat with the Pilot and four oarsmen. Each of the other boats manned by an officer and four men, carried a magazine with thirty fathoms of rope attached to it.

[1] Silas H. Stringham, afterward rear-admiral.
[2] Lieutenant-Commander Austin Pendergrast.

The magazines were thick oak casks filled with powder in each of which there is a fuse. Two of these barrels, joined by the rope, were stretched across at the ebb tide and when directly ahead of the ship, let go. The rope then catching across the cable, the magazines would drift down under the ship—when the strain upon the rope would pull a trigger that would ignite the fuse. . . .

After putting the magazines under one ship, the boats that carried them were ordered back, and Papa went with the other two to plant the magazines under the other vessel.

They then rowed to some distance, and waited for the explosion, but it never came, thank God, for if it had Pa would have been hung long before now. At the first explosion the calcium light at Fortress Monroe would have been lit and the little steamer—whose steam was up—they could hear her—would have caught them within a few minutes. It took them an hour to get back.

If Papa's going again would ensure the destruction of every ship in the Yankee Navy, I would not have him go. If he had been lost then it would have been an everlasting stain upon the Southern Government that allowed so celebrated, valuable and clever a man as my father to risk his life in such an expedition. Europe would cry shame upon them.

Are not his brains worth more than two ships? He might have gone to the boats to see that all was right, but not in them to plant the magazines.

The Yankees would never have let him go. They appreciate his services better than that. Papa says, he was very much struck with the culpable negligence of the enemy. That he could have gone up and put his hand on those vessels with impunity.

Thur. July 11th

. . . Captain Thomas, the one who assisted in taking the *St. Nicholas,* has been captured in Washington.

Fri. July 12

William Blackford passed through here a few days ago with his cavalry company from Southwestern Virginia. He dined with us and gave us a very amusing account of their attempts at cooking. Said they bought half a bushel of rice one day. They nearly filled a pot with it and added a little water to boil. It soon commenced to swell, and they filled first one vessel and then another until every vessel that they had in camp was full, even their tin cups.

Monday 15—July 1861

Mamma has gone to Farley Vale with the children. I have undertaken the housekeeping. We have no cook since the old woman we had in Fanny's place, left us. Rebecca has been doing her best in that capacity, and we do the chamber work.

Thur. 16. July, 1861

The seceded counties in Western Virginia sent several members to the Congress at Washington. They elected a Governor some time ago —Governor Pierpont. There are between twenty and thirty disaffected counties, I believe.

Sat. July, 20—

Hurrah! we have beat the Yankees. The enemy was repulsed three times with considerable loss, 5 or 6 hundred, at Bull Run.[1] Our loss was not more than sixty.

Cousin Nanny and the children arrived last night. Cousin Dabney will be up tonight with Papa. They left Santa Fe the twenty sixth of May and did not stop one day on the way. They were forty days in crossing the plains in an *uncovered* wagon and camped out every night. They look like Indians they are so burned. Cousin Nanny tells us they had no wood on the plains, but used "buffalo-chips."

The Confederate Congress met today.

Sunday July 21

Distant firing has been heard all day.

Mon. July 22, 1861

There was an officer here last night who was in the fight at Bull Run. He says that the South Carolinians after firing threw down their muskets and charged with their bowie knives, seizing the Yankees by the collar and cutting them down.

Papa saw a gentleman yesterday, just from Washington. He said that many members of Congress and others went in carriages to see the fight last Thursday.

[1] There had been a small clash along the line of the Run on the eighteenth, which the Confederates called the Bull Run fight as distinguished from the big Battle of Manassas on the twenty-first.

A company of five hundred cavalry are to pass through here, today, on their way to Manassas—The Hampton Brigade of South Carolina.

I2 M

More news! More good news. Will has just come to tell me. The battle yesterday was more extensive than we thought. It extended along our whole line. The enemy is routed and we are in hot pursuit. Thank God, thank God. . . .

Thursday, July 25
Uncle Charley and many gentlemen from here have been up to Manassas to see the battle field. He returned this evening, says that many of the soldiers (Yankees) are still lying upon the field: our men are burying them.

Sunday, July 28, 1861
The more we learn of the victory last Sunday the greater it seems to be. We took fifty odd cannon and four hundred wagons each one filled with stores and provisions of various kinds and several stands of arms—new in their cases which were brought to arm the loyal citizens of Richmond. Their army was most completely equipped in every respect. They had blacksmiths shops and medicine wagons along. They never seemed to contemplate a defeat, and the arrogance and heartlessness of their preparations for victory are almost beyond conception. Many gentlemen and *ladies* came from Washington to witness the battle. Elegant dinners had been prepared at Fairfax C.H. and Centreville by French cooks, where they meant to regale themselves after their victory. Our soldiers found the tables set and many baskets of champagne and wine.

Abraham Lincoln professes to conduct this war on the most humane and merciful principles yet he has declared all medicines and surgical instruments contraband of war, a thing never before heard of among civilized people. And now having deprived us, as far as in his power, of all means of attending to our own sick and wounded, he leaves his poor soldiers to our care. They have never sent back for any of their wounded, or to bury their dead. Our soldiers buried them in trenches, fifty and sixty at a time.

Uncle Charley says that not one of the bodies he saw had shoes on. Our men took them. They were right. We have no leather. . . .

3. MARY BOYKIN CHESNUT—"A BATTLE
HAS BEEN FOUGHT AT MANASSAS"

The best-known of Confederate women diarists was born Mary Boykin Miller, March 31, 1823. Her father, Stephen Decatur Miller, was in turn congressman, Governor of South Carolina, senator. At seventeen she married James Chesnut, Jr., member of a prominent family and graduate of Princeton, whose home was at Mulberry plantation near Camden, S.C. He was active in politics and she in society. He was the first Southerner to resign from the U.S. Senate and in July 1861 was a provisional member of the Confederate Senate, He became aide to General Beauregard at Fort Sumter, and then served on the staff of President Davis, who greatly esteemed his advice, took the Chesnuts into his intimate circle and made him a sort of liaison officer between the Confederacy and South Carolina. While he traveled back and forth, his wife, when she did not accompany him, stayed at the Spotswood Hotel, a favorite place for official families in Richmond. In April 1864 he was appointed brigadier-general.

After the war the Chesnuts lived in a new house, Sarsfield. Mary died there November 22, 1886, and was buried beside her husband in the family cemetery at Knight's Hill. They had no children.

On December 6, 1861, Mrs. Chesnut wrote on the first page of a new diary—the one we have—"I have always kept a journal after a fashion of my own. . . . From today forward, I will tell the story in my own way." It is a charming, vivacious way. "The printed text," says Dr. Douglas S. Freeman, "is a remarkable human document. Of the complete devotion of Mrs. Chesnut to the Southern cause, there could be no question, but occasionally the reader hears champagne corks pop while boys are dying in the mud. Then again there is all the poignancy of woman's understanding of the sorrows of her sisters." To illustrate, he quotes the entries on the death of the gallant, impetuous Francis S. Bartow. He adds: "Her qualities are oddly gallic: One has to pinch oneself to realize that she is writing of hungry Richmond and of the Anglo-Saxon South." [1]

[1] *The South to Posterity*, pp. 123-128. New York: Charles Scribner's Sons, 1951.

By war's end the diary consisted of forty-eight slim volumes, nearly 400,000 words with entries dated at Charleston, Montgomery, White Sulphur Springs, Columbia, Richmond, Camden. Mrs. Chesnut bequeathed it to her friend Isabella D. Martin.

When writing his popular novel House Divided, *Ben Ames Williams based the character of Cinda Dewain largely on Mrs. Chesnut. Afterward he edited, under the title* A Diary from Dixie, *the most complete edition of her journals in print.*

Richmond, Virginia

July 22d. [1861]—Mrs. Davis came in so softly that I did not know she was here until she leaned over me and said: "A great battle has been fought. Joe Johnston led the right wing, and Beauregard the left wing of the army. Your husband is all right. Wade Hampton is wounded. Colonel Johnston of the Legion killed; so are Colonel Bee and Colonel Bartow. Kirby Smith[1] is wounded or killed."

I had no breath to speak; she went on in that desperate, calm way, to which people betake themselves under the greatest excitement: "Bartow, rallying his men, leading them into the hottest of the fight, died gallantly at the head of his regiment. The President telegraphs me only that "it is a great victory." General Cooper[2] has all the other telegrams."

Still I said nothing; I was stunned; then I was so grateful. Those nearest and dearest to me were safe still. She then began, in the same concentrated voice, to read from a paper she held in her hand: "Dead and dying cover the field. Sherman's battery taken. Lynchburg regiment cut to pieces. Three hundred of the Legion[3] wounded."

That got me up. Times were too wild with excitement to stay in bed. We went into Mrs. Preston's[4] room, and she made me lie down on her bed. Men, women, and children streamed in. Every living soul had a story to tell. "Complete victory," you heard everywhere. We had been such anxious wretches. The revulsion of feeling was almost too much to bear. . . .

[1] For Edmund Kirby Smith, see page 177 *infra.*
[2] The senior Confederate officer, adjutant and inspector-general.
[3] General Wade Hampton's Legion had arrived from South Carolina in time for the infantry portion to participate in the most severe fighting of the battle, in which he was wounded. He was forty-three years old, six feet in height, broad-shouldered, deep-chested, a magnificent figure of a man.
[4] Wife of General John S. Preston and mother of Sally Buchanan ("Buck") Preston, the famous beauty whose ill-fated love affair with General John B. Hood is mentioned on so many of Mrs. Chesnut's pages.

A woman from Mrs. Bartow's county was in a fury because they had stopped her as she rushed to be the first to tell Mrs. Bartow her husband was killed, it having been decided that Mrs. Davis should tell her. Poor thing! She was found lying on her bed when Mrs. Davis knocked. "Come in," she said. When she saw it was Mrs. Davis, she sat up, ready to spring to her feet, but then there was something in Mrs. Davis's pale face that took the life out of her. She stared at Mrs. Davis, then sank back, and covered her face as she asked: "Is it bad news for me?" Mrs. Davis did not speak. "Is he killed?" Afterwards Mrs. Bartow said to me: "As soon as I saw Mrs. Davis's face I could not say one word. I knew it all in an instant. I knew it before I wrapped the shawl about my head."

Maria, Mrs. Preston's maid, furiously patriotic, came into my room. "These colored people say it is printed in the papers here that the Virginia people done it all. Now Mars Wade Hampton had so many of his men killed and he wounded, it stands to reason that South Carolina was no ways backward. If there was ever anything plain, that's plain."

Tuesday.—Witnessed for the first time a military funeral. As that march came wailing up, they say Mrs. Bartow fainted. The empty saddle and the led war-horse—we saw and heard it all, and now it seems we are never out of the sound of the Dead March in Saul. It comes and it comes, until I feel inclined to close my ears and scream.

Yesterday, Mrs. Singleton[1] and ourselves sat on a bedside and mingled our tears for those noble spirits—John Darby,[2] Theodore Barker, and James Lowndes.[3] To-day we find we wasted our grief; they are not so much as wounded. I dare say all the rest is true about them—in the face of the enemy, with flags in their hands, leading their men. "But Dr. Darby is a surgeon." He is as likely to forget that as I am. He is grandson of Colonel Thomson of the Revolution, called, by way of pet name, by his soldiers, "Old Danger." Thank Heaven they are all quite alive. And we will not cry next time until officially notified.

[1] Mrs. Mat Singleton, mother of Mrs. Alexander Cheves Haskell.
[2] Surgeon of the Hampton Legion; he lived to go to Europe and get General Hood's wooden leg; married Mary Preston.
[3] "Toady" Barker and Captain James Lowndes, "the best of good company," old friends from South Carolina.

July 24th.—Here Mr. Chesnut opened my door and walked in. Out of the fulness of the heart the mouth speaketh. I had to ask no questions. He gave me an account of the battle as he saw it (walking up and down my room, occasionally seating himself on a window sill, but too restless to remain still many moments); and told what regiments he was sent to bring up. He took the orders to Colonel Jackson, whose regiment stood so stock still under fire that they were called "a stone wall." Also, they call Beauregard, Eugene, and Johnston, Marlboro. Mr. Chesnut rode with Lay's[1] cavalry after the retreating enemy in the pursuit, they following them until midnight. Then there came such a fall of rain—rain such as is only known in semitropical lands.

In the drawing-room, Colonel Chesnut was the "belle of the ball"; they crowded him so for news. He was the first arrival that they could get at from the field of battle. But the women had to give way to dignitaries of the land, who were as filled with curiosity as themselves—Mr. Barnwell,[2] Mr. Hunter,[3] Mr. Cobb, Captain Ingraham,[4] etc.

Wilmot DeSaussure[5] says Wilson[6] of Massachusetts, a Senator of the United States, came to Manassas, *en route* to Richmond, with his dancing shoes ready for a festive scene which was to celebrate a triumph. The New York Tribune said: "In a few days we shall have Richmond, Memphis, and New Orleans. They must be taken and at once." For "a few days" maybe now they will modestly substitute "in a few years."

They brought me a Yankee soldier's portfolio from the battlefield. The letters had been franked by Senator Harlan.[7] One might shed tears over some of the letters. Women, wives and mothers, are the same everywhere. What a comfort the spelling was! We had been willing to admit that their universal free-school education had put them, rank and file, ahead of us *literarily,* but these letters do not attest that fact. The spelling is comically bad.

---

[1] Captain John F. Lay.
[2] Robert W. Barnwell, of South Carolina, first Chairman of the Provisional Congress. Mr. Davis offered him the office of Secretary of State, but he declined it.
[3] R. M. T. Hunter, of Virginia, was named Secretary of State on this very day.
[4] Captain Duncan Nathaniel Ingraham.
[5] A friend from Charleston; Colonel Chesnut later gave him a position on the South Carolina Council.
[6] Henry Wilson, who was to be Vice-President of the United States in Grant's second administration (1872-1876).
[7] James Harlan, of Iowa.

July 27th.—Mrs. Davis's drawing-room last night was brilliant, and she was in great force. Outside a mob called for the President. He did speak—an old war-horse, who scents the battle-fields from afar. His enthusiasm was contagious. They called for Colonel Chesnut, and he gave them a capital speech, too. As public speakers say sometimes, "It was the proudest moment of my life." I did not hear a great deal of it, for always, when anything happens of any moment, my heart beats up in my ears, but the distinguished Carolinians who crowded round told me how good a speech he made. I was dazed. There goes the Dead March for some poor soul.

Today, the President told us at dinner that Mr. Chesnut's eulogy of Bartow in the Congress was highly praised. Men liked it. Two eminently satisfactory speeches in twenty-four hours is doing pretty well. And now I could be happy, but this Cabinet of ours are in such bitter quarrels among themselves—everybody abusing everybody.

Last night, while those splendid descriptions of the battle were being given to the crowd below from our windows, I said: "Then, why do we not go to Washington?" "You mean why did they not; the opportunity is lost." Mr. Barnwell said to me: "Silence, we want to listen to the speaker," and Mr. Hunter smiled compassionately, "Don't ask awkward questions."

Kirby Smith came down on the turnpike in the very nick of time. Still, the heroes who fought all day and held the Yankees in check deserve credit beyond words, or it would all have been over before the Joe Johnston contingent came. It is another case of the eleventh-hour scrape; the eleventh-hour men claim all the credit, and they who bore the heat and brunt and burden of the day do not like that.

Everybody said at first, "Pshaw! There will be no war." Those who foresaw evil were called ravens, ill-foreboders. Now the same sanguine people all cry, "The war is over"—the very same who were packing to leave Richmond a few days ago. Many were ready to move on at a moment's warning, when the good news came. There are such owls everywhere.

But, to revert to the other kind, the sage and circumspect, those who say very little, but that little shows they think the war barely begun. Mr. Rives[1] and Mr. Seddon[2] have just called. Arnoldus Van

---

[1] William Cabell Rives, of Virginia, member of the Confederate Congress, formerly U. S. Minister to France and U. S. Senator.

[2] James A. Seddon, Member of Congress from Virginia; to become Secretary of War November 20, 1862.

der Horst[1] came to see me at the same time. He said there was no great show of victory on our side until two o'clock, but when we began to win, we did it in double-quick time.

Arnold Harris told Mr. Wigfall the news from Washington last Sunday. For hours the telegrams reported at rapid intervals, "Great victory," "Defeating them at all points." The couriers began to come in on horseback, and at last, after two or three o'clock, there was a sudden cessation of all news. About nine, messengers with bulletins came on foot or on horseback—wounded, weary, draggled, footsore, panic-stricken—spreading in their paths on every hand terror and dismay. That was our opportunity. Wigfall can see nothing that could have stopped us, and when they explain why we did not go to Washington I understand it all less than ever. Yet here we will dilly-dally, and Congress orate, and generals parade, until they in the North get up an army three times as large as McDowell's, which we have just defeated.

Trescot[2] says this victory will be our ruin. It lulls us into a fool's paradise of conceit at our superior valor, and the shameful farce of their flight will wake every inch of their manhood. It was the very fillip they needed. There are a quieter sort here who know their Yankees well. They say if the thing begins to pay—government con-tracts, and all that—we will never hear the end of it, at least, until they get their pay in some way out of us. They will not lose money on us. Of that we may be sure. . . .

There seems to be a battle raging at Bethel, but no mortal here can be got to think of anything but Manassas. Mrs. McLean[3] says she does not see that it was such a great victory, and if it be so great, how can one defeat hurt a nation like the North.

John Waties[4] fought the whole battle over for me. Now I under-stand it. Before this nobody would take the time to tell the thing consecutively, rationally, and in order. Mr. Venable[5] said he did not see a braver thing done than the cool performance of a Columbia negro. He carried his master a bucket of ham and rice, which he had cooked for him, and he cried: "You must be so tired and hungry, marster; make haste and eat." This was in the thickest of the fight, under the heaviest of the enemy's guns.

[1] Descended from the Governor of South Carolina in 1792, who bore the same name.
[2] William Henry Trescot, from Columbia, S. C.
[3] Née Sumner, from the North, one of the clever women in Mrs. Davis' circle.
[4] The Waties were a well-known South Carolina family; William Waties signed the South Carolina Ordinance of Secession.
[5] Charles S. Venable, later on General Lee's staff.

The Federal Congressmen had been making a picnic of it; their luggage was all ticketed to Richmond. Cameron[1] has issued a proclamation. They are making ready to come after us on a magnificent scale. They acknowledge us at last foemen worthy of their steel. The Lord help us, since England and France won't, or don't. If we could only get a friend outside and open a port.

One of these men told me he had seen a Yankee prisoner who asked him "what sort of a diggins Richmond was for trade." He was tired of the old concern, and would like to take the oath and settle here. They brought us handcuffs found in the debacle of the Yankee army. For whom were they? Jeff Davis, no doubt, and the ringleaders. "Tell that to the marines." We have outgrown the handcuff business on this side of the water.

Dr. Gibbes[2] says he was at a country house near Manassas, when a Federal soldier, who had lost his way, came in exhausted. He asked for brandy, which the lady of the house gave him. Upon second thought, he declined it. She brought it to him so promptly he thought it might be poisoned; his mind was; she was enraged, and said: "Sir, I am a Virginia woman. Do you think I could be so base as that? Here, Bill, Tom, disarm this man. He is our prisoner." The negroes came running, and the man surrendered without more ado.

Another Federal was drinking at the well. A negro girl said: "You go in and see Missis." The man went in and she followed, crying triumphantly: "Look here, Missis, I got a prisoner, too!" This lady sent in her two prisoners, and Beauregard complimented her on her pluck and patriotism, and her presence of mind. These negroes were rewarded by their owners. . . .

4. ROSE O'NEAL GREENHOW—"MY HOME WAS CONVERTED INTO A PRISON"

Mrs. Greenhow, a native of Maryland, was the widow of Robert Greenhow, prominent Washingtonian and friend of President Buchanan, John C. Calhoun, Martin Van Buren and other political leaders of ante-bellum days. Shortly after the war began, she became a leading figure in the Confederate espionage system. The record book of "Old Capitol Prison" in Washington listed her as "a dangerous, skillful spy."

[1] Simon Cameron, of Pennsylvania, U. S. Secretary of War.
[2] Dr. Hampton Gibbes, of Columbia, S. C., active in the medical service.

From Washington she sent two messages in code to General Beau-
regard, and on this information he based his defense at First Manas-
sas. After the battle the Federal War Department instructed Allan
Pinkerton, head of the Federal Secret Service, to keep Mrs. Green-
how under surveillance. Pinkerton reported that she had "alphabets,
numbers, ciphers, and various other ways of holding communication
with the Confederate officials." Mrs. Greenhow's home, where she was
imprisoned, was at 398 16th Street. In 1861 she was forty-four years
old and the mother of four daughters.

On the morning of the 16th of July, 1861, the Government papers
at Washington announced that the "grand army" was in motion and
I learned from a reliable source (having received a copy of the order
to McDowell) that the order for a forward movement had gone forth.

There was great commotion amongst the military men. Officers
and orderlies on horse were seen flying from place to place; the
tramp of armed men was heard on every side—martial music filled
the air. "On to Richmond" was the war cry. So with drums beating
and flying colours, and amidst the shower of posies thrown by the
Yankee maidens, the grand army moved on into Virginia.

At twelve o'clock on the morning of the 16th of July, I dispatched
a messenger to Manassas, who arrived there at eight o'clock that
night.[1] The answer received by me at mid-day on the 17th will tell
the purport of my communication—

"Yours was received at eight oclock at night. Let them come: we
are ready for them. We rely upon you for precise information. Be
particular as to description and destination of forces, quantity of
artillery etc."
          Signed, "THOMAS JORDAN, ADJT GEN."

On the 17th of July, I dispatched another message to Manassas,
for I had learned of the intention of the enemy to cut the Winchester
railroad, so as to intercept Johnston and prevent his reinforcing

---

[1] This messenger was Betty Duvall, a Maryland girl. Disguised as a farm woman,
she rode across the Chain Bridge out of Washington in a farm cart. On the Virginia
side of the Potomac, she secured riding clothes and a horse from friends, and galloped
for Fairfax County Courthouse, where she ran into a Confederate picket commanded
by General Milledge R. Bonham. From what he said was the longest, most beautiful
roll of hair he had ever seen "she took a small packet, not larger than a silver dollar,
sewed up in silk." He promised to convey it to General Beauregard.

Beauregard who had comparatively but a small force under his command at Manassas.[1]

On the night of the 18th news of a great victory by the Federal troops at Bull Run reached Washington. Throughout the length and breadth of the city it was cried. The accounts were received with frantic rejoicings, and bets were freely taken in support of Mr. Seward's wise saws—that the rebellion would be crushed out in thirty days. My heart told me that the triumph was premature yet, O my God! how miserable I was for the fate of my beloved country which hung trembling in the balance.

On Sunday (21st) the great battle of Manassas was fought—— which ended in the total defeat of the entire "Grand Army." In the world's history such a sight was never witnessed: statesmen, Senators, Congressmen, generals and officers of every grade, soldiers, teamsters—all rushing in frantic fright, as if pursued by countless demons. For miles the country was thick with ambulances, accoutrements of war etc. The actual scene beggars description so I must relinquish the effort to portray it. The news of the disastrous rout of the Yankee army was cried through the streets of New York on the 22nd. The whole city seemed paralysed by fear.

For days the wildest disorder reigned in the Capitol. The streets of Washington were filled with stragglers, each telling the doleful tale.

It would be idle to recount the gasconade of those who fled from imaginary foes, or to describe the forlorn condition of the returning "heroes" who had gone forth to battle flushed with anticipated triumph and crowned in advance with the laurel of victory. Alas! their plight was pitiable enough. Some were described as being minus hat or shoes. Amongst this latter class was Colonel Burnside,[2] who on the morning that he sallied forth for Virginia is said to have required two

---

[1] "About July 10th 1861, Miss Duvall of Washington brought to Fairfax Court House, Headquarters for General Bonham, the first message from Mrs. Rose Greenhow telling of the intended positive advance of the Union Army across the Potomac. On the night of July 16, 1861, I received by special messenger (a Mr. Donnellan) the second dispatch (in cipher also) of Mrs. Greenhow telling of the Union Army, 55,000 strong, would positively commence that day to advance from Arlington and Alexandria on Manassas via Fairfax C. H.

"G. T. BEAUREGARD"

(*Official Records of the Union and Confederate Armies.*)

[2] In April 1861 Ambrose E. Burnside had organized the 1st Rhode Island Regiment at the request of the governor, and become its colonel; it was among the first regiments to reach Washington.

orderlies to carry the flowers showered upon him by the women of
Northern proclivities. The Northern troops had been taught to believe that a bloodless victory awaited them, and so possessed were
they with the idea of their philanthropic mission as liberators of an
oppressed people that many officers took far more pains to prepare
white gloves and embroidered vests for "the balls" to be given in
their honor in Richmond than in securing cartridges for their muskets.

When consulted on the subject I said "No doubt they would receive a great many balls, but I did not think that a very recherché
toilet would be expected."

The fanatical feeling was now at its height. Maddened by defeat,
they sought a safe means of venting their pent up wrath. The streets
were filled with armed and unarmed ruffians; women were afraid to
go singly in the streets for fear of insult; curses and blasphemy rent
the air and no one would have been surprised at any hour at a general massacre of peaceful inhabitants. This apprehension was shared
even by the better class of United States army officers.

On Friday Aug. 23, 1861, as I was entering my own door on returning from a promenade, I was arrested by two men, one in citizens
clothes and the other in the dress of an officer of the United States
Army. This latter was called Major Allen, and was the chief of the
detective police of the city. They followed close upon my footsteps.
As I ascended my steps the two men ascended also before I could
open the door and asked "Is this Mrs. Greenhow?" I answered
"Yes". "Who are you and what do you want?" "I come to arrest
you"—"By what authority?" The man Allen, or Pinkerton (for he
had several aliases) said: "By sufficient authority." I said: "Let me
see your warrant." He mumbled something about verbal authority
from the War and State Department and then they followed me into
the house. By this time the house had become filled with men, and
men also surrounded it outside like bees from a hive. An indiscriminate search now commenced throughout my house. Men rushed with
frantic haste into my chamber. My beds, my wardrobes were all upturned. My library was taken possession of and every scrap of paper
was seized.

As the evening advanced I was ordered upstairs accompanied by
my friend, Miss Mackall, a heavy guard of detectives being stationed
in the room with us. I was never alone for a moment. Wherever I
went a detective followed me. If I wished to lie down he was seated

a few paces from my bed. If I desired to change my dress or anything else, it was obliged to be done with open doors, and a man peering in at me. But, alas! I had no alternative but to submit, for when I remonstrated with detective Captain Dennis, I was met by the answer that it was the order of the Provost Marshal.

The work of examining my papers had commenced. I had no reason to fear of the consequences from the papers which had as yet fallen into their hands. I had a right to my own political opinions. I am a Southern woman, born with Revolutionary blood in my veins, Freedom of speech and of thought were my birthright, guaranteed, signed and sealed by the blood of our fathers.

The search went on. I desired to go to my chamber, and was told that a woman was sent for to accompany me. It did not, even then, flash upon my mind that my person was to be searched. I was, however, all the more anxious to be free from the sight of my captors for a few moments; so feigning the pretext of change of dress etc. as the day was intensely hot, after great difficulty and thanks to the slow movements of these agents of evil, I was allowed to go to my chamber and I then resolved to destroy some important papers which I had in my pocket, even at the expense of my life. (The papers were my cipher, with which I corresponded with my friends at Manassas.) Happily I succeeded without such a painful sacrifice.

The detective Dennis rapped at my door, calling Madam! Madam! and then opened it, but seeing me apparently legitimately employed he withdrew.

Shortly after the female detective arrived. Like all detectives, she had only a Christian name, Ellen. Well, I was ushered into my chamber, a detective standing guard outside to receive the important papers believed to be secreted on my person.

I was allowed the poor privilege of unfastening my own garments, which, one by one, were received by this pseudo-woman, and carefully examined until I stood in my linen. After this I was permitted to resume. I now began fully to realize the dark and gloomy perils which environed me.

The chief of detectives having gone out, several of the subordinates left in charge now possessed themselves of rum and brandy which aided in developing their brutal instincts: and they even boasted in my hearing of the "nice times" they expected to have with the female prisoners.

As every evil is said to be checkmated by some corresponding good, I was enabled by this means to destroy every paper of consequence. I had placed them where they could be found by me at any hour of the day or night, and was not slow to avail myself of the state of inebriation in which the guards were plunged. Stealing noiselessly to the library in the dark, I mounted up to the topmost shelf, took, from the leaves of a dusty folio, papers of immense value to me at that moment, concealing them in the folds of my dress, and returned to my position on the bed without my gaolers having missed me. The papers were more numerous than I imagined and the difficulty was how to dispose of them. I remembered, however, that in the search of my person in the morning my boots and stockings had not been removed; so Miss Mackall, who was held in durance but had been assured she would be released that night, concealed the papers in her stockings and boots. Between the hours of three and four on the 24th Miss Mackall was permitted to depart under escort of a detective guard who were then stationed around her house for the following day.

A very large sum had been offered for my cipher. This stimulated the zeal of the employees of the Government to a very remarkable degree. The tables were filled with fragments of old letters and scraps in cipher, in several languages, from early morning till late at night. For seven days they puzzled over them. I had no fear.—One by one they allowed the clue to escape them. Only once was I frightened. Miss Mackall, who like myself was always on the alert, abstracted from a heap of papers a sheet of blotting paper upon which was the whole of my dispatch to Manassas on July 16.

On Friday the 30th of August I was informed that my house was to be converted into a prison.

One morning as I opened my chamber door to pass to the library I saw the detective Allen taking an old lady up the stairs. It was the venerable mother of the martyr Jackson[1] killed in Alexandria, and I honored her gray hairs as being his mother. She was placed in an adjoining room to mine and kept until about twelve oclock at night when she was released. . . .

I received a visit from my sister, Mrs. James M. Cutts, and my niece, Mrs. Stephen A. Douglas, accompanied by Colonel Ingolls, U.S.A.,[2] the permit to see me making the presence of an officer obligatory and limiting the visit to fifteen minutes. . . .

---

[1] See page 36 *supra*.
[2] General Rufus Ingalls, chief quartermaster of the Army of the Potomac.

5. VARINA HOWELL DAVIS—OUR NEW HOME

When Mrs. Davis, with the children and her young sister Margaret Howell, came to Richmond the city gave her lavish welcome. The elegant, spacious house which it purchased for the President's family had been built, as Judith McGuire mentioned, By Dr. John Brockenbrough, onetime president of the Bank of Virginia. To go with it were a handsome carriage and four white horses.

The newspapers were eloquent. "Mrs. Davis," said the Dispatch, *is* "a tall, commanding figure, with dark hair, eyes and complexion, and strongly marked characteristics, which lie chiefly in the mouth. With firmly-set yet flexible lips there is indicated much energy of purpose and will, but beautifully softened by the usually sad expression of her dark, earnest eyes. Her manners are kind, graceful, easy, and affable, and her receptions are characterized by the dignity and suavity which should very properly distinguish the drawing-room entertainments of the Chief Magistrate of a republic."*

An Englishman, the Reverend William Malet, who visited the Executive Mansion, summed up the general verdict. "Mrs. Davis," he wrote, "is the right lady in the right place."

In July [1861] we moved to the "old Brockenbrough house," and began to feel somewhat more at home when walking through the old-fashioned terraced garden or the large airy rooms in the seclusion of family life.

The mansion stands on the brow of a steep and very high hill, that is sharply defined against the plain at its foot through which runs the Danville railway that leads to the heart of Virginia.

The house is very large, but the rooms are comparatively few, as some of them are over forty feet square. The ceilings are high, the windows wide, and the well-staircases turn in easy curves toward the airy rooms above. The Carrara marble mantels were the delight of our children. One was a special favorite with them, on which the whole pilaster was covered by two lovely figures of Hebe and Diana, one on either side in bold relief, which, with commendatory taste, were not caryatides. The little boys, Jefferson and Joe, climbed up to the lips of these "pretty ladies" and showered kisses on them. The entablature was Apollo in his chariot, in basso relievo. Another was a charming conception of Cupid and Psyche, with Guido's Aurora for the entablature. . . .

Every old Virginia gentleman of good social position who came to see us, looked pensively out on the grounds and said, with a tone of tender regret, something like this: "This house was perfect when lovely Mary Brockenbrough used to walk there, singing among the flowers;" and then came a description of her light step, her dignified mien, sweet voice, and the other graces which take hold of our hearts with a gentle touch, and hold them with a grip of steel. At first it seemed odd, and we regretted our visitor's disappointment, but after a while Mary came to us, too, and remained the tutelar goddess of the garden. Her name became a household word. "Whether Mary would approve," was a question my husband playfully asked, when he liked the arrangement of the drawing rooms.

Mrs. James Grant lived in another fine old house next door to us, and with her we formed a lasting friendship, which was testified on her part by every neighborly attention that kind consideration could suggest. If Mr. Davis came riding up the street with General Lee, and their staff officers clattering after them, Mrs. Grant heard them and sent some dainty which her housewifely care had prepared, or fruit from her farm on the outskirts of Richmond. If our children were ill, she came full of hope and kind offices to cheer us by her good sense and womanly tenderness. The very sight of her handsome face brought comfort to our hearts. She fed the hungry, visited the sick, clothed the naked, showed mercy to the wicked, and her goodness, like the city set upon the hill, "could not be hid." . . .

On my first introduction to the ladies of Richmond, I was impressed by the simplicity and sincerity of their manners, their beauty, and the absence of the gloze acquired by association in the merely "fashionable society." They felt the dignity attached to personally conducting their households in the best and most economical manner, cared little for fashionable small-talk, but were full of enthusiasm for their own people, and considered wisely and answered clearly any practical question which would tend to promote the good of their families or their country.

I was impressed by a certain offishness in their manner towards strangers; they seemed to feel that an inundation of people perhaps of doubtful standards, and, at best, of different methods, had poured over the city, and they reserved their judgment and confidence, while they proffered a large hospitality. It was the manner usually found in

English society toward strangers, no matter how well introduced, a wary welcome. In the more southern and less thickly settled part of our country, we had frontier hospitality because it was a necessity of the case. In Virginia, where the distances were not so great, and the candidates for entertainment were more numerous, it was of necessity more restricted.

We were fortunate in finding several old friends in Richmond. The Harrisons, of Brandon, and the handsome daughters of Mr. Ritchie, who had been for many years dear and valued friends. During our stay there we made other friends. . . .

6. LEORA SIMS—"OUR CAUSE WE KNOW IS JUST"

When war came fire-eating, hospitable Leora Sims of Columbia, South Carolina, was nineteen, a recent graduate of the Barhamville School for young ladies. When the first cavalry company was raised in Columbia her mother gave it her carriage horses, and Leora gave her favorite saddle horse, which was later killed on a Virginia battlefield.

At Appomattox the morning of April 9, 1865, it was Leora's father, Captain Robert Moorman Sims, who carried General Lee's message from Longstreet to Gordon to cease fire as a truce would be asked. Longstreet spoke of him as "Captain Sims, of the Third Corps staff, serving at my headquarters since the fall of A.P. Hill." [1] *According to family tradition, his white handkerchief was used as the flag of surrender. After the war Leora married Richard O'Neale of Columbia, who had spent five birthdays in the Confederate Army and was with General Lee at Appomattox.*

Leora wrote frequently to her dear school friend, Mary Elizabeth Bellamy of Wilmington, North Carolina.

> Home
> Columbia, South Carolina
> November 14, 1861.

My dear dear Mary

. . . Since we last interchanged communications what an increase in this mighty revolution. Virginia, the home of our loved Washing-

[1] D. S. Freeman, *Lee's Lieutenants*, III, 733. New York: Charles Scribner's Sons, 1937.

ton, the resting place of many great and noble, has been laid waste, and in the midst of the true and gallant, we find, thickly woven, traitors and Yankees of the blackest dye, if that race will admit of comparison. I cannot realize that our loved Carolina is now the abiding place of our enemies. You have the invaders at Cape Hatteras and we at Port Royal. Our people have acted nobly; some cotton has fallen into the hands of the enemy; and for my part, and it is so with nearly every one in this state—we would rather have lost our men, than that the Yankees should have been gratified. . . . Some of our men did daring deeds on that battle field [Port Royal] but you have heard them, twice told, ere this. I do love the noble people of the Southern Confederacy. When we look over all the innumerable deeds of magnanimity & self denial, every true heart bounds with pleasure. Though our cause we know is just, and will eventually triumph, it may be sealed in blood or bathed in blood more properly. How many beloved ones have "fought their last battle, and now sleep their last sleep." . . . Pa was in the Battle of Manassas. We have a good many trophies from the battle field. . . .

Mary, if you all conclude to leave Wilmington, Ma & every one in the house and me especially, beg and insist that you come right to us. In these days of confusion, we never know one day what will be the circumstances of the next. I want our people to whip the Yankees badly & I do not care how they do to accomplish that end, for an invader so hateful cannot be dealt with as other enemies. Our people are not going to stop for the want of guns, they are being armed (or some) with spikes, knives, saws & anything that will do to kill and cut the Yankees to pieces. The women are getting ready for any emergency. I am going to get me a bowie knife or look for some weapon of defense. We do not feel afraid of the Yankees but we must be ready for anything. "Booty & Beauty" for their watch word, the women may expect no quarter, and if I ever fall into their hands, I earnestly pray I may be enabled to give them one "fire eater" to deal with. . . . We have but one motto—Determination. And with God as our guide we will eventually overcome all these heart rending trials. I do not think this war will last long but you know I am always looking on the bright side. Now my dear friend, do come and stay with us, your Mother and all the children, and anyone else of your family or friends. We would ever welcome citizens from our Sister state to a home in our midst, but now we feel especially near to you all, and nothing would gratify us more than for you all to seek a safe retreat in our Home. Come one and all. Every body sends much love to you. Give my love to your dear Mother. Write soon to your old classmate and your companion in these times of uncertainty & confusion.

I am as ever your devoted friend.

BABE

7. MRS. DORIAN HALL—"I HOPE THIS STATE OF AFFAIRS WILL NOT LAST LONG"

Mrs. Hall was a member of an affluent Alabama family and the mistress of a large plantation at Lowndesboro. When her eldest son, Dr. William Hall, enlisted, she took over the added responsibility of his near-by plantation. She wrote these letters to him when he was stationed at Wilmington, North Carolina. Lieutenant-General Braxton Bragg commanded the Army of Pensacola.

January 6th, 1862

My dear William.

Your letter from Wilmington was received on last Friday. It was a long time getting here. You did not say anything about your health. I felt anxious as I had understood you was complaining while at the plantation. I was very much astonished when hearing you had remained down there that you did not write a line to let me know what detained you, and particularly when I was told you was not well.

They are all well at the Valley but there are quite a number of cases at big Swamp of sore throat. We have had the finest weather for picking cotton I ever saw. I hope we will soon finish if this weather continues. Last week it was very warm. Some persons have lost their meat, but today it is turning cold, so much so we are expecting to kill some hogs this afternoon altho I dont like to kill in the afternoon but its late in the season, and probably we should embrace it.

Such a December I dont recollect ever to have seen; so dry & pleasant. During the Christmas it was equally pleasant. There was quite a fine congregation at the Episcopal Church—the sermon good. The church looked very pretty. By the way did you tell Mr. Powers to send a wagon load of corn to the minister for me. I dont wish to send one if he has already had one. My last cotton only brought me 6½ cts & one dollar and a quarter profit. I was glad after I found cotton had gone down that you did not send any up—letters come here for you that I could have sent to you had we but known where you were. . . .

I will get Capt. Clowndes to sell 20 bales of your cotton as soon as it will bring anything, but dont wish to sell it at 6½ cts. . . .

I am very anxious to hear from you   goodby My dearest Son
YOUR MOTHER

January 9th 1862

My dear William:

Capt. Clowndes sold 20 bales of your cotton at 6¾ cts   sent the proceeds to me   he wrote me that good cotton was selling at 7⅛ cts but yours only brought 6¾ a quarter of a cent more than mine & it was good. We will wait now & see if the times will not change for the better. Judge Bragg thinks we will be able to sell by the first of May. I sincerely hope we will. It is a very destructive state of affairs now. Ruinous to us & our country. . . . I am engaged in setting out & transplanting tins of various lines of fruit and shade trees. Judge Bragg is suffering very much from dyspepsia worse than usual. I am anxious to hear from you very anxious. It is painful to hear of so much sickness & death among our Soldiers in various parts of the country but I hope the state of affairs will not last long & those who are away from their homes will soon return not to be called out again on such a mission. There has been a petition sent on to Richmond by the Mobile people for Gen. Bragg to move his headquarters to Mobile. They feel pretty badly scared about their safety. Mrs. Bragg, Miss Mary Ellis,[1] are at Pensacola now I suppose.

With a Mothers love   Good bye   I hope to hear from you soon.

8. MARY BYSON—HARD TIMES IN TEXAS

Mary lived with a young member of her family, Bettie Hooks, and her husband at Red River, Texas. Letters to her friend Margaret Butler, at her plantation home near St. Francisville in West Feliciana Parish, Louisiana, give a glimpse of economic conditions.

Red River   January 16th 1862

My dear Margaret

You must excuse my not writing sooner as Bettie sent me up to

[1] Mrs. Bragg's sister, from Louisiana. She lived to be a hundred years old.

Paris to get her some things for house-keeping, before they were all gone and I was absent nearly three weeks and only expected to be gone three days. . . .

I bought me one common calico in Paris, light purple. Bettie says too light for winter, gave twenty-five cents a yard, and not very thick. It was the darkest one I could find. I think the merchants must have packed away their goods and bring out a piece at a time. I would have got some last summer if I had thought they would have been so scarce. In hunting around for things for Bettie I chanced upon a pair of Congress gaiters, very soft and nice, just as good as I could find in the City, for three dollars so I shall not be barefooted for some time yet. There is an old Dutch shoemaker near here makes very nice shoes, but not very fashionable so they are comfortable. I do not mind the style. He told Mr. Hooks he had some very nice calfskin to make ladies shoes.

A regiment of infantry passed through Paris while I was there on their way to Kentucky. They had measles and typhoid fever, some died there. Poor fellows they say they are very much neglected when they are sick. They had orders from headquarters to get to Kentucky as soon as possible. . . .

Meat and bread are very plentiful here. Mr. Hooks will make enough meat this year for his own use. He was very much afraid of losing it at one time, but the weather turned cold in time to save it, and they will make one hundred & forty or fifty Bales of Cotton, but it will neither pay debts or buy groceries at this time. I thank you very much for thinking of me. I was in hopes I could go down this Spring, but no one can raise any money. Turkey gobblers were selling from thirty to fifty cents, eggs ten cents, sometimes five, can't get any paper money changed but can take it out in goods. Confederate bonds are not much thought of up here. Sugar & Tea are very scarce. Bettie let her Mother have some of her white sugar, and I am afraid it will give out before she can get it up from New Orleans. White Sugar is selling for twenty-five cents a pound. . . . Hard times is all the talk, besides the war. I expect I will have to give up tea as there is none in the country. I sent by Mr. Wright for some, but I am afraid we will not get any as they say everything is so scarce in New Orleans. I wish I was with you going to church. Sometimes I am afraid I shall become quite heathenish. I will try and write regularly as long as my paper lasts. . . .

My best love to your Mother and all the family and remember me to all inquiring friends. I was in hopes of going down but I think I might as well give it out as the stage has quit running.

God bless you all
Yours truly M. Byson

9. ROSE O'NEAL GREENHOW—Old Capitol Prison

Mrs. Greenhow was a prisoner in her own house in Washington for six months. It became known as "Fort Greenhow." Despite the carefully guarded area, information sent by Mrs. Greenhow continued to reach Confederate lines. Allan Pinkerton reported: "She has not ceased to lay plans, to attempt the bribery of officers having her in charge, to make use of signs from the windows of her house to her friends on the streets. . . ."

A letter written in code by Mrs. Greenhow on December 26, 1862, was found in the archives of the Confederate War Department when Richmond was evacuated. It was deciphered and published in the Official Records of the Union and Confederate Armies.

The Miss Poole to whom Mrs. Greenhow refers in the following passage from her book was a fellow prisoner in the Greenhow house.

On Saturday, January 18th [1862] at two o'clock, I learned incidentally, that I was to be removed from my house to another prison. I was sitting in my library reading. I immediately sent for the officer of the guard to know the facts. He told me he had orders not to communicate with me on the subject, but he would go to the Provost Marshal and obtain further instructions. He returned with orders fixing the hour for my removal. Detective Allen had the ordering and regulations of the arrangements. A covered wagon surrounded by a file of soldiers was ordered by Allen to be my conveyance to my prison. Believing that I should feel humiliated by this indignity, Lieutenant Sheldon however positively refused to obey this order.

Miss Poole, at this time, took the oath of allegiance, and fifty dollars in gold from the Yankee Government, and went on her way rejoicing. The woman Baxley also applied to be released upon similar terms which was refused and she was sent to the Old Capitol Prison upon which occasion I saw her for the first time. About four o'clock I turned my back upon what had been a happy home.

I reached the Old Capitol Prison[1] just at dark; the whole guard were under arms to receive me; a general commotion was visible in all directions and it was evident that a great deal of interest and curiosity was felt as to the destination of "so noted a rebel."

After the lapse of some half-hour I was taken up to the room which had been selected for me by General Porter.[2] It was situated in the back building of the prison on the northwest side, the only view being that of the prison yard and was chosen purposely so as to exclude the chance of my seeing a friendly face. It is about ten feet by twelve and furnished in the rudest manner—a straw bed with a pair of newly-made unbleached cotton sheets, a small feather pillow—a few wooden chairs, a wooden table and a glass six by eight inches completed my adornment; soldiers rations being only allowed me by this magnanimous Pennsylvanian. . . .

I have been one week in my new prison. My letters now all go through the detective police who subject them to a chemical process to extract the treason.

My existence is now a positive blank. Day glides into day, with nothing to mark the flight of time and hope paints no silver lining to the clouds which hang over me. . . .

10. MARY H. JOHNSTONE—PERSONAL OBSERVATIONS
AT SOME OF THE CAMPS AND HOSPITALS

Mrs. Johnstone, of Savannah, Georgia, at the request of Vice-President Stephens, made a survey of medical conditions at camps and hospitals in Virginia.

Savannah   Feby 3rd, 1862

To Alexander H. Stephens
   Private

Sir

In compliance with a request made by Mr. Duncan in *your* name to my adopted son, Cap Waring, I committ to paper the result of

[1] The dingy brick building at the corner of First and A streets had been erected for the use of Congress in 1815, while the noble edifice across the parkway, burned by British soldiers, was being restored. Before it was turned into a military prison it had been a boardinghouse. Rose Greenhow's idol, John C. Calhoun, had lived there. See *Reveille in Washington, 1860-1865*, by Margaret Leech, p. 134. New York: Harper & Brothers, 1941.

[2] Andrew J. Porter, Provost-Marshal.

my personal observation at some of the camps & hospitals in Va. No doubt to the emergency, & to a want of practical experience in the organization & management on a large scale of this very necessary appendage to an army in war, may be attributed much that is reprehensible, but no great improvement can be expected so long as surgeon appointments remain a political preferment, and are consequently made with so little reference to the most important qualifications to the position.

The man's life in the Army is not sufficiently valued—though it is there of so great moment, and most recklessly in some cases have the scales of life been intrusted to inexperienced, if not incompetent hands. Surely, where neither Patient nor friend has a choice in the medical adviser, & the one freely offers his life for his country, the other more than life! Common justice requires a judicious selection by those in authority; above all, that power for good or for ill should not be confided to the Intemperate; Without desiring to make a charge, I simply ask, in the name of those being thus sacrificed, that professional men of more experience be chosen, and that a more rigid examination into their habits be instituted. This one vice of Intemperance ought to be sufficient to condemn any applicant for the post, and be a reason for dismissal when already appointed. . . .

. . . There should be local hospitals. Camp fevers, it is said, are incurable under canvass, & the camp Hospitals, where even under roof, are devoid of comfort, even necessaries, & yet to remove an ill person any distance is death in most cases. Supposing it be not possible to procure a suitable building in the direct vicinity of the encampment to form a proper hospital, then it remains but to permit friends, or persons willing to receive a few patients, to do so. . . .

It is a fact which came under my own knowledge that the private medicine chest of a company, recently arrived at Manassas, was in request immediately for the whole regiment to which it was attached. . . .

The few observations I was enabled to make upon my recent sojourn at Manassas are such as would strike any kind of practised eye, but many valuable suggestions might occur to one habitually a visitor, whose business it might be to investigate matters, & to be responsible for the faithful discharge of duty in every department. An Inspector General whose character & experience in his profession should command respect from his fellow surgeons, and of kindliness of heart not to consider the smallest matter that might contribute to the poor soldiers comfort beneath his notice.

This supervision should extend, not only over nurses & the minutiae of their duties, but also over surgeons themselves, and he should be invested with authority in turn, should be cashiered in default of moral courage to exercise this discretion.

Wishing you success in the beautiful & important work to which you are so charitably devoting your attention, I am, Sir, one most earnestly interested in the same cause.

MARY H. JOHNSTONE

11. LOUISA FREDERIKA GILMER—"MY HUSBAND WAS A PRISONER AT FORT HENRY"

In 1861 Mrs. Gilmer, a native of Georgia and the mother of two young children, was living in San Francisco where her husband, Jeremy F. Gilmer, was stationed with the United States Army. When war broke out he promptly resigned his commission and they returned to Georgia, to make their home in Savannah. Then Mr. Gilmer was appointed major of engineers in the Western army under General A. S. Johnston and departed for Tennessee. He was at Fort Henry when it fell to General Grant. In a letter to her father, A. L. Alexander of Washington, Georgia, Mrs. Gilmer gives the news she had from Tennessee.

Savannah   Feb. 10th   1862
Monday night

My dear Father.

I suppose you have seen in the papers the telegraphic account that Mr. Gilmer was a prisoner at Fort Henry & also from Maj. Rains' account that he afterwards escaped. Maj. Rains had the first intimation to that effect & was kind enough to telegraph me to that effect on Sat. morning—too late this to save me from a dreadful nervous headache from which I am but just coming out.

Sat. night I had a telegram from Mr. G. dated in Clarksville, Tenn. telling me he had reached there safely—but giving no further particulars—and today I had another dated at Fort Donelson, where he is now gone & expects to remain I presume until the fight is over there. I felt sure when I first heard Friday night that Fort Henry was taken that he was in all probability either a prisoner or killed. He was just starting there when his last letter to me was mailed and I was in such a state by the time I recd Maj. Rains telegraph that

I could not hold my head up. I have been in bed ever since. It seems a dreadful state of affairs there. That the Tennessee country is in possession of the enemy & if they have as stated pushed all the way into Alabama, then it is simply disgraceful to our people. I feel too sick to write but only thought you would feel anxious & wanted you to know all I know.

All seems quiet here yet.

Affectionately

L

12. MISS A. M. B.—THE UNION FLAG WAS RAISED IN NASHVILLE

The sensitive observer who is known only by these initials lived near Nashville. After the occupation her home and the countryside about it were to remain in enemy hands throughout the war. Miss A. M. B. served in the hospitals of Nashville and Murfreesboro. Once she was arrested, charged with being a "Rebel letter carrier."

General John B. Floyd and General Gideon J. Pillow, the ranking officers, escaped across the Cumberland River with Floyd's Virginia brigade. This left the third officer, General Simon Bolivar Buckner, to yield Fort Donelson to his old West Point friend, General Grant.

Saturday, the 15th of February, was a rainy, drizzling, sleeting, chilly day, when the bell tolled from our market house, ordering the citizens to assemble in solemn conclave. One old marketer on hearing its mournful echoes said, "I have done bin cummin' to this market for these twenty years and I never heard that bell make such a queer noise before!" We told him our forces at Donelson would have to retreat and we would be in the hands of the enemy. The following Sabbath was a day long to be remembered by those in and around Nashville. The Confederate forces were retreating South, and no citizen was allowed to cross the bridge until the army were over. Hurried words of parting were said by the young men who stopped at their homes, while many mothers pressed the manly forms of their sons to their hearts for the last time, and printed the good-bye kiss on their lips, while the tears choked their utterance. Everything was in a state of confusion, commissary stores were thrown open to the citizens, and stalwart women commenced rolling flour barrels, shouldering sides of bacon, and gathering up clothing until they had sufficient supplies to open a neighborhood store. Gens. Floyd and Pillow after the army had crossed ordered the suspension and railroad bridges over the Cumberland destroyed as a strategic move for a successful retreat of their forces.

Every day we expected to see the Federal army; but a week passed when, on Sabbath morning, the 23rd of February, Buell's[1] advance of a hundred cavalry entered the suburbs of Edgefield and camped. The citizens were much excited, but our apprehensions for safety were quieted when a friend told us the Federals "were having their horses shod, paying for the work in gold, and behaving themselves very well."

No attempt was made by the enemy to cross the river for another week, when thirty transports under protection of ten gun-boats, commanded by Gen. Nelson,[2] came crawling up the Cumberland slowly as though each bluff was a masked battery, and every mile of water a net work of torpedoes. The skies, as if in sympathy, covered the whole face of the country with water. What remained to grace the triumph of a conqueror was only some old men, women and children, with a few Confederate soldiers, too sick to follow their commands. It was a silent surrender with no exclamations of triumph or display of pageant. The Union flag was raised on the capitol building. . . .

13. CONSTANCE CARY—THE INAUGURATION OF JEFFERSON DAVIS AS PERMANENT PRESIDENT

Constance Cary spent her girlhood at "Vaucluse," a plantation near Alexandria, Virginia. When the Federals came that way they destroyed the house and turned the site into an army camp. Constance, her mother and her aunt fled to Richmond where they found lodgings in an overcrowded, dilapidated hotel. After some months they moved to a pleasant house on Franklin Street. It soon became the gathering place for a wide circle of friends and acquaintances, who made talented, vivacious, sixteen-year-old Constance a great favorite. She took leading roles in tableaux vivants *and amateur theatricals; her performance as Lydia in* The Rivals *captured all hearts, including that of Burton N. Harrison, the handsome private*

---

[1] Brigadier-General Don Carlos Buell, in command of the Federal Army of the Ohio at Louisville, had been ordered toward Nashville with 50,000 men.

[2] Brigadier-General William Nelson, in command of the 4th Division of Buell's Army of the Ohio, called "Bull" because of his stature and roaring manner.

secretary of President Davis. Mrs. Chesnut spoke of her as "the clever Conny," and said she had "a classically perfect profile."

That 22d of February [1862] was a day of pouring rain, and the concourse of umbrellas in the square beneath us had the effect of an immense mushroom-bed. As the bishop and the President-elect came upon the stand, there was an almost painful hush in the crowd. All seemed to feel the gravity of the trust our chosen leader was assuming. When he kissed the Book a shout went up; but there was no elation visible as the people slowly dispersed. And it was thought ominous afterwards, when the story was repeated, that, as Mrs. Davis, who had a Virginia negro for coachman, was driven to the inauguration, she observed the carriage went at a snail's pace and was escorted by four negro men in black clothes, wearing white cotton gloves and walking solemnly, two on either side of the equipage. She asked the coachman what such a spectacle could mean, and was answered, "Well, ma'am, you tole me to arrange everything as it should be; and this is the way we do in Richmond at funerals and sich-like." Mrs. Davis promptly ordered the out-walkers away, and with them departed all the pomp and circumstance the occasion admitted of. In the mind of a negro, everything of dignified ceremonial is always associated with a funeral!

About March 1st marital law was proclaimed in Richmond, and a fresh influx of refugees from Norfolk claimed shelter there. When the spring opened, as the spring does open in Richmond, with a sudden glory of green leaves, magnolia blooms, and flowers among the grass, our spirits rose after the depression of the latter months. If only to shake off the atmosphere of doubts and fears engendered by the long winter of disaster and uncertainty, the coming activity of arms was welcome! Personally speaking, there was vast improvement in our situation, since we had been fortunate enough to find a real home in a pleasant brown-walled house on Franklin street, divided from the pavement by a garden full of bounteous greenery, where it was easy to forget the discomforts of our previous mode of life. The gathering of many troops around the town filled the streets with a continually moving panorama of war, and we spent our time in greeting, cheering, choking with sudden emotion, and quivering in anticipation of what was yet to follow. We had now finished other battle-flags begun by way of patriotic handiwork, and one of them was bestowed upon the "Washington Artillery" of New Orleans, a body of admirable soldiers who had wakened to enthusiasm the daughters of Virginia in proportion, I dare say, to the woe they had created among the daughters of Louisiana in bidding them good-bye. One morning an orderly arrived to request that the ladies would be out upon the veranda at a given hour; and, punctual to the time fixed, the travel-stained battalion filed past our house. These were no holiday soldiers. Their gold was tarnished and their scarlet faded by sun and wind and gallant service—they were veterans now on their way to the front, where the call of duty never failed to find the flower of Louisiana. As they came in line with us, the officers saluted with their swords, the band struck up "My Maryland," the tired soldiers sitting upon the caissons that dragged heavily through the muddy street set up a rousing cheer. And there in the midst of them, taking the April wind with daring color, was our flag, dipping low until it passed us.

A few days later, on coming out of church—it is a curious fact that most of our exciting news spread over Richmond on Sunday, and just at that hour—we heard of the crushing blow of the fall of New Orleans and the destruction of our iron-clads.[1] As the news came directly from our kinsman, General Randolph,[2] the Secretary of War, there was no doubting it; and while the rest of us broke into lamentation, Mr. Jules de St. Martin, the brother-in-law of Mr. Benjamin,[3] merely shrugged his shoulders, with a thoroughly characteristic gesture, making no remark.

"This must affect your interests," some one said to him inquiringly.

"I am ruined, *voilà tout!*" was the rejoinder—a fact too soon confirmed.

[1] The forts surrendered on April 28. The next day Farragut took formal possession of the city.

[2] George W. Randolph, Secretary of War from March to November 1862.

[3] Judah P. Benjamin, having first been Attorney-General, and then Secretary of War, became Secretary of State on March 17, 1862.

III

A FRIGHTING SPRING

March—May 1862

On March 8, 1862, the Confederate ironclad Virginia *attacked the fleet of Federal blockading vessels at Hampton Roads, Virginia. At the end of the day the* Cumberland *was sunk, the* Congress *was burned, the* Minnesota *had run aground and the rest of the fleet was scattered. The next day the first great battle between ironclads was fought when the* Monitor *engaged the* Virginia *in a drawn battle tactically, with strategic victory going to the* Monitor.

On the Western front the first really great land battle of the war was fought April 6 and 7 at Shiloh Church, Tennessee. On the sixth Albert Sidney Johnston drove back the Union army under Generals Grant and Sherman and had it in jeopardy, but lost his own life. Before the battle he had urged his men to show themselves "worthy of the women of the South whose noble devotion in this war has never been exceeded in any time." After his death General Beauregard was placed in command. The evening of the sixth large Union reinforcements under Buell arrived and the second day things did not go well for the Confederates. Beauregard withdrew the army to its base at Corinth in northern Mississippi. More than 4,000 men from North and South were killed at Shiloh, and 16,000 wounded; compared with these losses, First Manassas was a skirmish. The waters of Bloody Pond were dyed crimson with blood.

On April 8 the loss of Island No. 10, the Confederate fort where the Mississippi makes a long S at the Tennessee-Kentucky border, opened the upper stretches of the river to the Union fleet. On the twenty-fourth, after five days of bombardment, Forts St. Philip and Jackson, guarding New Orleans, were passed by Admiral Farragut and his fleet. That day portended the fall of the greatest port of the Confederacy.

In Virginia on April 16 the Confederate Congress passed the first Conscription Act, calling into military service all between eighteen and thirty-five. Martial law was proclaimed in Richmond, Norfolk, parts of South Carolina and other threatened areas.

The operations of General George B. McClellan, in command of the Army of the Potomac, constituted the greatest threat. The hazard from his naval attack on Richmond increased with the coming of May. Yorktown had fallen and Williamsburg, and on the ninth Norfolk with its great naval yards was evacuated. Mrs. Davis' levee at the Executive Mansion was interrupted that evening by a message to the President: "The enemy's gunboats are ascending the river." While the enemy fleet steamed toward Richmond, Mrs. Davis and the children were hurried off to Raleigh. The advance up the James was repulsed at Drewry's Bluff, eight miles below Richmond, on the fifteenth, and the Confederate capital saved from naval bombardment. But McClellan's mighty army kept working its slow way up the Peninsula between the York and the James rivers. Stonewall Jackson's First Valley Campaign was in progress—but what Cornelia McDonald saw of that is reserved for Section IV.

1. ALICE READY—"THE DARING, RECKLESS CAPTAIN MORGAN VISITS MURFREESBORO"

Alice Ready was the younger daughter of Charles Ready, sometime Member of Congress from Murfreesboro, Tennessee. After graduating from Patapsco Institute, near Baltimore, she came home in the summer of 1860, and took her place in Murfreesboro and Nashville society. That year also she began a diary. "Whoever reads a single line without the writer's permission forfeits her love and friendship forever," she wrote in a childish scrawl.

War brought both Confederate and Federal troops to Murfreesboro, and the Ready house was intermittently the scene of gay social activities and a place of drawn blinds and heartsickness. After the Battle of Murfreesboro or Stone's River (December 31, 1862-January 2, 1863) the Ready family was separated. Alice accompanied her sister Mattie, lovely bride of dashing John Hunt Morgan, in flight from the occupied town, and for the next two years she was her devoted companion in Tennessee, Virginia and Georgia. Finally she wrote the bitter entry: "I am growing thin hating the Federals."

The diary, which she kept for some three years, with lapses of many weeks, began as the hurried, headlong, hit-or-miss, spelling-punctuation-syntax-go-hang record of a wide-eyed, keenly observing girl. It is filled with dramatic excitement and with romance yielding to tragedy as the shadows lengthened over the fair world she knew.

    After the fall of Nashville, General Albert Sidney Johnston's army encamped near Murfreesboro. The Ready family—father, mother and the young-lady daughters, Mattie (the "Sister" of the diary) and Alice—offered hospitality to the officers.

                                   Murfreesboro, Tennessee,
                                  Monday March 3, 1862

On last Thursday we all went out to witness a review of Gen. [William J.] Hardee's troops, or at least a portion of them. While there we saw Gen [John C.] Breckinridge who told us he would have a review in a day or two, and invited us out, we promised of course to go, we invited the two Generals with Hardee's "staff" to spend the evening with us. They accepted, Gen H—— came into town with us, we have seen a great deal of him, a day has not passed without our seeing him and some member of his staff—his evenings are always spent with us, and we have found him charming—he is a tall, fine looking man, quite militarie between 45 & 50 years of age, he is very unassuming and affable in his manners, perfectly at home here calls for whatever he wants, pets Ella and me a good deal seems to regard me as a child—Sister as a young lady. After digressing to describe the General, I will say they were all here to spend the evening except Gen B—— as soon as they came told they had orders to leave next day. It sent a chill to my heart, for besides bidding them, whom I had known to like so well, farewell, Brother must now leave us with greater surrounding dangers than ever before. I was sad and quiet all evening. . . .

    The next day the General came around with one of his aids, just as we finished dinner, had not left the table, so they took their seats and dined with us. After dinner we had the carriage after they had insisted very much, and drove out to the Generals Camp. The army was moving and had only stopped for the night. I think the Generals was the only tent pitched, we drove up to it, found Major Shoup and Capt White there to receive us, though not intentionally as they were not expecting us. There was a large log fire in front of the door; we went in the tent to see how things were arranged, found a goods box inverted for a table, with dishes on it, the Generals bed rolled up in a bundle—and one large arm chair completed the furniture. We took our seats by the fire and had a delightful time, the scene was picturesque in the extreme. Whilst we were there Col Adams' Cavalry regiment passed—the band playing a beautiful, heart stirring piece. It was just dark or growing dark, all around far as we could see were bright camp fires, with figures standing round, distinguishable as men from the light thrown out from the fires. The effect of the whole was equal to the most beautiful picture ever painted by my imagination.

The General went to his trunk and brought forth, as a trophy of our visit to his Camp, an elegant blue satin Mouchoir case with his initials embroidered in white, we only waited then for a cup of thin coffee, which I must confess was not worth waiting for. We concluded we should find some better at home, so the General and Capt White came in with us. We found Brother and Hugh[1] all waiting supper for us. The General and Aid only remained until half past nine. Brother retired, I went to the dining room to assist Mama in packing provisions for her "pets" to eat on their march, which must begin in the morning. General gave Brother leave to remain with us until 10 or 11 oclock, said perhaps he would come in and breakfast with us. . . .

Saturday morning after we had bid our *Brothers* a sad sad farewell, the General came, we had breakfast for him, he staid until 2 oclock. Whilst here the already celebrated Capt. John H. Morgan came to see him, with Col Wood,[2] both of whom had just returned from a scout near Nashville, when they came upon a party of Federals, killed a Captain and five or six others—we saw the sword belonging to the Capt, there were many valuable papers found on his person, which were of course given to the General. Morgan is an extremely modest man, but very pleasant and agreeable, though one to see him would scarcely imagine him to be the daring reckless man he is. An immense crowd collected at the front door to see him, two or three actually came in and stood before the parlor door to see him. He and Col Wood, who is a grandson of Gen Taylor's, will be left here with a few cavalry probably until they are driven back by the enemy. Col W—— has promised to make Sister and I his confidants of military matters, so long as he remains. Before the General left he took the comfort from his neck, which he had worn during the bombardment of Bowling Green and tied it around my neck, asking me to "wear a Soldier's comfort." Bless his old heart.[3] I love him

[1] Hugh Gwyn, friend of Alice's brother Horace; a young lieutenant who had escaped from Donelson.

[2] Lieutenant-Colonel Wood belonged to Wirt Adams' cavalry regiment.

[3] General Hardee was in his forty-seventh year—so Alice had made a good guess.

dearly. Yesterday morning soon after breakfast a courier came from the General with a note to me, very sweet of course. I replied to it immediately. . . . We returned from Church and found a note from Brother, also one from Hugh—which is very sweet and precious . . . .

The Minister made a most touching appeal to the congregation to provide for the sick soldiers, at the Hospital, who were greatly in need of attention. I was under the impression that the sick had all been removed. But came home had some chicken water made and Sister and I went to the Hospital with it and other little delicate things nourishing for the sick. I was shocked to find the place in such a condition men dying all around and no more notice taken of them than if they had been dogs—as if they had neither feeling or soul. . . . I came home with a heavy sad heart, to see human creatures, suffering. . . .

We have done nothing today except think and talk of the absent Soldiers. How it rained on them last night. Gen. Hardee says "The Heavens have been weeping at our misfortunes." There is very great dissatisfaction among the troops against Gen Johnston. Officers and all censure him very severely for the course he has taken. Some accuse him of not being true, that I think is a gross slander.

I must stop my writing for the present Albert has just brought me several notes from "headquarters" brought by Col Wood and Capt Morgan who are down stairs, and I must see them. . . .

Wednesday, March 5th 1862

Monday night after I laid my journal aside sat up until two oclock writing notes—the courier left next morning at nine, so every thing had to be done that night. I was much surprised to find among my notes or "dispatches" as Papa calls them one from Capt White enclosing one to Alice Martin in N—— which he wanted me to send. The one from the General was like all of his very sweet and precious. Sister had one from Brother. They are near Shelbyville and will be for several days. The General said I need not be surprised to see him some night at 11 oclock. We all thought he would be here tonight, but were doomed alas! to disappointment, owing perhaps to the fact that the "Feds" have commenced pursuit—they are 12 or 13 miles from N—— in this direction. Mama has been packing up *from* them ever since our army left. . . .

Yesterday the Texan Rangers, which Gen. Hardee had sent back to support Morgan, arrived. . . . We were at the Hospital again

yesterday, met Col Wood who would not allow us to go in the wards.
. . . I am really disappointed at not receiving a single note today—
was sure the General would come, and he did not, Wood returned
from his Camp today said they were all well. Tonight there was
quite a number of soldiers around the house who said they had orders to guard it. . . . I am tired scribbling Oh! that the soldiers were
back again.

Thursday March 6th 1862

Awoke this morning and found the ground covered with snow. My
first thought was of the Soldiers exposed to the bitter cold. This has
been a dreadful day for them, cold and gloomy with the sharp March
winds, and many of the Soldiers I have no doubt with insufficient
clothing. . . .

Friday March 7th 1862

. . . This evening, young Mr Buckner of Nashville came for a letter which he had given Papa to send to N—— for him, there was a
young man with him who intended going down tomorrow. I availed
myself of his offer, to send Major White's letter to his "ladye love."
It has lain like a weight upon my mind ever since it has been in my
possession. While the gentlemen were waiting, the bell rang and a
"dispatch" was handed me from the General. he does not forget his
young friend, although so much harrassed with business. . . .

Saturday March 8th 1862

. . . My first act after breakfast was to reply to the General's
letter, which of course gave me pleasure. I sent him a geranium leaf
with some violets. . . . Sister and I went out to walk this afternoon.
It was delightful to breath the fresh air once more. We met White
Jetton, and asked him to carry some letters for us to Shelbyville,
leaves in the morning. There is a good deal of anxiety felt this evening for Col Wood and Capt Morgan, who went out yesterday with
30 men to make a reconnoissance. At first I did not attach much
importance to it, remembered how seriously "the Captn" (as his men
all call him) said to the General, "Sir, it would be an impossibility
for them to catch me," and I was willing to trust to Woods luck, of
which he thinks he possesses a pretty good share.

After supper Mr Wallace a Texan Ranger called to see me, and
expressed his fears of the safety of our Marion, and his comrades,

giving some very good reasons, one was that they had not been gone an hour before every body, for 8 or 9 miles knew where they had gone, and for the purpose of catching a General to exchange for Buckner. I think by morning we must hear something of them. The loss of Morgan the best scout in the service, the Marion of the war, would be an irreparable loss, it is such men as he is that we want, bold, daring and fearless.

Sunday March 9th 1862

. . . The feeling and anxiety for Morgan and Wood had reached the highest pitch this morning, about nine oclock one of Morgans men came in and said he was afraid he had been taken, that Wood was safe. Papa was very anxious yet said he knew they were all safe. White Jetton called for our letters just before we started to Church. Had not been seated in Church more than a very few minutes, when a lady came in and took her seat just behind us, whispered to me that Morgan was safe with 10 prisoners, there was of course great rejoicing. I sent a silent prayer of thanksgiving, to a kind and merciful God. Just before the minister commenced reading the first lesson, the Sexton brought a note and handed it to me, from Capt Morgan and Col Wood, who said "in accordance with their promise they would present us in about an hour with thirty eight Yankee prisoners." It excited us very much, we felt it would be mockery to remain in Church and pretend to hear the sermon, so we left, something which I do not remember ever to have done before, had we been in any condition to listen to a sermon, we might have remained, as they did not come until some time after Church was over. We stopped a good many coming from Church and told them so there was quite a crowd collected at our door, to witness the triumphal entrance of Morgan and Wood into town, with their 38 prisoners. The first signal of their approach was a number of Texan Rangers, galloping by here on horseback to the first street crossing this one below. In a much shorter time than I can write it the grand cavalcade appeared from that street, there was I suppose 60 or 70 horsemen including prisoners and all, with Morgan and Wood at the head. As soon as they came in sight, it seemed impossible for any one to restrain their enthusiasm, There was heart felt cheers and waving of handkerchiefs. They moved on until about the middle of the procession were opposite our door, when they were halted, and the two braves rode back to the stepping stone, without dismounting they raised their hats, and said to Sister and me, "Ladies I present you with your prisoners, what disposal shall be made of them?"

We replied, "You have performed your part so well, we are willing to intrust it all to you." I suppose they remained before the door for 15 or 20 minutes. The prisoners were well dressed, most of them Germans. One old grey haired fellow rode up with his guard and asked for a glass of water, while the servant was getting it, he made quite a little speech, asked the ladies to interceed with Captain Morgan to have him released, said he was not fighting, but was a teamster, was compelled to do it, to keep his family in Cincinatti from starving. When the water came he raised it to his lips, saying "ladies here is to your health in water."

I have not attempted a description of the two "great men," nor shall I for it would be worse than useless. I only know that in my admiration and pride for them, I lost control of myself, and must have acted almost as a crazy person. Papa invited them to come back and dine with us. The Captain was too unwell, and fatigued. Col Wood however came, just before dinner. Puss Ready came in to spend the night with us, regreted very much not being here to see the Yankees, was speaking of it after dinner, when Col W—— proposed we should go to the Court House, where they were—said he would go up and see if things were arranged so that we could go. I did not think it by any means proper, though he seemed to think it was and of course I did not say anything. Just before he left the old man who made the speech came down with his guard to ask Mama for an old quilt, seemed very grateful that he was not shot which he and all of them fully expected. He said "when the Captain went up to him he so skeered he just liked to have dropped." They all seem to be cowards. I feel assured that [if] the army at Nashville 65,000. would only come out and give our men battle they would be whipped, such material as it is composed of could never stand before our army, which embraces all the chivalry and worth of the entire south, who if they have the proper leaders must be successful.

Wood was very much engaged getting information from one of the prisoners, and could not come back for us himself, so he sent young Buckner, who seemed happy as possible that the Capt'n had returned, all of his men are equally delighted. I never saw such devotion to a leader in my life. . . . Buckner had a Yankee pistol, which the "Captn" had given him, and a pair of spurs which he said "he gave them a quarter for."

Papa received a note from Gen Hardee asking for information of the absent scouting party, he was very anxious about them, I wanted Papa to allow me to reply to it, which he would not consent to, so I wrote a short note myself, and told the Courier to tell him to open it first. I wanted to be the first to give him the good news. . . .

Tuesday March 11th 1862

I did not write yesterday because I was really quite unwell, and then there was nothing to write. Except in the morning Capt Morgan sent us the Louisville Journal to read the first newspaper I have seen for three weeks. . . . Papa told us last night that Morgan and Wood would leave this morning for Shelbyville to confer with Gen Hardee, respecting that expedition to Gallatin, they go in person, hoping to gain his consent. The Capt' called this morning for any letters we might have to send. . . .

The troops have almost all left Shelbyville—the General goes tomorrow, and so far that we can hold no communication. . . . My heart is so full and sad tonight that I can scarcely write at all. . . . With that army went all whom I held dear. . . .

I hear they are making men, women and children take the oath in Nashville. I dont think it would be binding, and should feel no scruples in breaking it, when I had the opportunity. . . .

Wednesday March 12th 1862

. . . I expected to have had a ride of horseback this afternoon with Cousin Kate but was disappointed, and very fortunately too or I would have missed Col Wood and Capt Morgan who had just returned from Shelbyville and came down to ask us to make them a flag of truce, which they wanted to go for their four men who are missing. . . .

Thursday March 13th 1862

Last night just after I had retired—Sister was still writing—the front door bell was pulled very hurriedly. Margret went down and found a servant waiting with a letter from our darling Brother, which was written from Fayettville. When I discovered what it was I jumped out of bed very quickly—but Sister got the letter first. I was too impatient to wait until she had finished it, and wanted her to tear it in two, so I could read one half, while she read the other—however she would not consent to this, and I had to wait. . . .

The last troops left Shelbyville today for Huntsville. Morgan leaves here Saturday. The Rangers left this morning. . . .

Col Wood called, they were going to leave at 2 o'clock with the flag of truce. He spoke very feelingly and indignantly about Gen Johnston—said he had defended him as long as he could, but believed now that he was either a fool or a traitor, left Gen Hardee to bring up the rear of the retreat blindfolded, took no notice of the many and important dispatches which were sent to him, said that it was not the silence of wisdom, but the wisdom of silence. . . .

Saturday March 15th 1862

. . . Capt' Morgan called last night and remained quite late, so late that I prefer seeking the bed, rather than my pen to make a record in my journal. He returned yesterday after a successful trip with his flag of truce his four men taken prisoners two of them wounded—shot after they were taken. Had it not been for that flag of truce our town might now have been in ashes with Morgan and his men prisoners, or killed. About fourteen miles from here they met 3,000 Federals commanded by Gen Mitchell[1] coming up to attempt his capture, which must have been certain, 50 men brave and daring as ours are could but poorly have coped with 3000 cravens as they are. . . .

Captain Morgan was more agreeable last night than ever before. I think all of his powers were called into play to be as charming as possible—related a number of amusing incidents that occured on Green river Ky. when he would be out scouting—he would become excited, his eyes flash, and cheek flush he is very modest and personally, is truly appreciated only after an acquaintance of some length. He spoke highly of the Federal officers except Col Kennet[2]—said they were all nice gentlemen. . . .

Miss Putnam reached this place last night from Nashville where she says exists a most complete military despotism. The houses are all being searched. they entered one for that purpose, the lady was sick, quite so, regardless as usual of the sanctity of a lady's chamber, they went in and striped the bed where she lay of each piece of covering, looking for Texan Rangers and arms. The former with Morgans squadron they hold in perfect terror, say M has 5,000 men here numbering each of his men as 100, Capt Morgan and Col Wood called

[1] General Ormsby M. Mitchel.
[2] Colonel H. G. Kennett, who became Chief of Staff to General Rosecrans.

just before they left town, their hopes in regard to taking Andy
Johnson are disappointed, he has already reached N—— with his
100 body guard. No one knows of the expedition on foot except our
family. Papa went out of town several miles to show them the way.
As he was shaking hands with Capt Morgan he said "tell the young
ladies I will bring them a trophy on my return"—O! for a dozen
Morgan's. . . .

Monday March 17th 1862

. . . I was seated in my own quiet room reading when some of the
servants came rushing in, "The Yankees have come." What an
excitement ensued, my first thought was of the gallant Morgan, and
then to have all the front window blinds closed. . . . We all went
to the windows to *peep* through the closed blinds. There were not
more I think than 100, who came into town, though they are said to
be in force at the river they were a fine looking body of men well
mounted and uniformed—the 4th Ohio Regiment, the same from
which those prisoners brought into town last week were taken. . . .
Papa thinks it may not be safe for him to remain here for a day or
two. He is going tonight with some of the negro men & horses, to
the Country. . . .

Wednesday March 19th 1862—

. . . Cousin Kate and Puss were spending the night with us,
sometime, after supper, we were all sitting around the fire in my
room, when Ella came in and announced that Morgan was safe in
Shelbyville, having accomplished his object in Gallatin, taken 18
prisoners a Colonel among the number. . . . We had just retired.
. . . All at once I scarcely know how I found myself in Sisters
room, where she and Cousin K and Puss had their heads out the
window talking to a solitary horseman, who wanted he said to see
Mr. Ready, upon Sisters suggestion he dismounted to come in and
communicate his intelligence to her, we had quite a scene then to get
her dressed and a candle, for her to go down. We had burnt ours till
there was not a piece of wick left in the socket. We all felt he was
a courier from Morgan nor were we disappointed, he was the bearer
of a note from Capt. Morgan asking if it would be safe for him to
pass through town, he was then at Lascasses about 8 or 10 miles
from here, Papa was not at home, Mama asleep, so we had to act

on our own responsibility. Sister wrote "They are eight miles from here, come in haste." . . .

After the courier left and Mama who had been aroused by the noise, had learned the cause of it and been informed of our reply, she became very much excited, said "we were sacrificing the lives of some of our best men—that now the town would certainly be shelled, the enemy were not so far as we supposed." . . . Sister and I still sat up. In the lone hour of the night when nothing was heard save the roaring of the fire in the grate and my own breathing, Sister and I sat before the fire. . . . Sister hastened into the other room and raised the window. I jumped up, and away she and I flew down stairs—for the horseman whom she had spoken to from the window was no other than our gallant Morgan himself. We reached the front door and found him there with Col Wood. Both dismounted and stood on the steps talking for at least a half hour. . . . While we were talking Puss came down, said she must see Capt Morgan. We talked until day began to dawn and then came the sad goodbye. . . . Both mounted their horses and joined the men on the square, when they all stood and sang in the sweetest tones I ever heard, "Cheer boys, cheer." I think it must have been "little Tom Morgan" who sang the solo, in the chorus all joined heartily—and clearest above the other voices was heard the Captains. . . . It was so thrilling and sad that the tears were only restrained by an effort. We watched them till there was none to be seen, and with them went a blessing from true southern womans heart—and a prayer that God would bless them. . . . We have the pleasant, yet melancholy satisfaction of having seen the last, of the gallant Morgan, who endears himself to all, and the last of our Army. . . .

2. LOULIE GILMER—"WRITE ME WHAT YOUR HORSE IS NAMED"

Loulie was ten when she wrote this letter to her father, Major Jeremy F. Gilmer, who had escaped from Fort Henry and Fort Donelson and was somewhere in Tennessee with Albert Sidney Johnston. Later on he was to be chief of the Engineer Bureau in Richmond, with the rank of major-general. We have met Loulie's mother, Louisa F. Gilmer.

March 16, 1862
Savannah, Georgia

My Dear Dear Father

I do want to see you so much. I do miss you so much in the evenings, when I come in and no one is in, and I am so lonesome by myself and if you were here you would tell me stories and so I would not be so lonesome. I wish you would tell one in your letter to me for I want you to write to me what your horse is named. Give my love to James and tell him I hope he is well. Auntee sends her love and hopes you are well and I hope so too. The Yankees have not got near the city yet. The other day some heavy firing was heard and it was them firing into one of our Boats. . . . Mother and Auntee had the headache day before yesterday and they got up yesterday. . . .

I go almost every morning to Mr. H.'s printing office but I have no more to say. I am your loving child

LOULIE GILMER

3. CORNELIA PEAKE McDONALD—WINCHESTER IS OCCUPIED BY THE ENEMY

Mrs. Cornelia Peake McDonald, the daughter of Humphrey Peake and Anne Linton Lane Peake, was born in Alexandria, Virginia, on June 14, 1822. The family moved to Missouri and lived for a while in Palmyra and in Hannibal. As a young lady Cornelia visited at Jefferson Barracks in St. Louis where she met and danced with Ulysses S. Grant, James Longstreet and other officers. In 1847 she married Angus McDonald, a lawyer of Winchester, Virginia.

At the outbreak of war Mrs. McDonald was the mother of seven children: Harry, thirteen; Allan, twelve; Kenneth, nine; Ellen, seven; Roy, five; Donald, two; and Hunter, born June 12, 1860. She was described by one who knew her well as tall and slender, with dark hair always simply dressed; a lady of great dignity, courage and intelligence.

The night before he rode off with the Stonewall Brigade in the spring of 1862 Colonel McDonald urged his wife to keep a diary. "With the expectation that the town would be immediately occupied by the enemy," she said, "he wished to be informed of each day's

*events." He was prescient. No town changed hands so suddenly and
so often as Winchester.*

Winchester, March, 1862.—On the night of March 11th, 1862, the
pickets were in the town; part of the army had already gone, and
there were hurried preparations and hasty farewells, and sorrowful
faces turning away from those they loved best, and were leaving,
perhaps forever. At one o'clock the long roll beat, and soon the
heavy tramp of the marching columns died away in the distance.

The rest of the night was spent in violent fits of weeping at the
thought of being left, and of what might happen to that army before
we should see it again. I felt a terrible fear of the coming morning,
for I knew that with it would come the much dreaded enemy.

I laid down when the night was almost gone, to sleep, after securing all the doors, and seeing that the children were all asleep. I took
care to have my dressing gown convenient in case of an alarm, but
the night passed away quietly, and when the morning came, and all
was peaceful I felt reassured, dressed and went down.

The servants were up and breakfast was ready. The children
assembled and we had prayers.

I felt so thankful that we were still free, and a hope dawned that
our men would come back, as no enemy had appeared. We were all
cheerfully despatching our breakfasts, I feeling happy in proportion
to my former depression; the children were chatting gaily, Harry
and Allan rather sulky at not having been permitted to leave with
the army, as they considered it degradation for men of their years
and dimensions to be left behind with women and children. Suddenly a strain of music! Every knife and fork was laid down and
every ear strained to catch the faint sounds. The boys clap their
hands and jump up from the table shouting, "Our men have come
back!" and rushed to the door; I stopped them, telling them it must
be the Yankees. Every face looked blank and disappointed.

I tried to be calm and quiet, but could not, and so got up and went
outside the door. Sure enough that music could not be mistaken, it
was the "Star Spangled Banner" that was played. A servant came
in. "They are all marching through the town, and some have come
over the hill into our orchard."

I made the children all sit down again, and began to eat my
breakfast, but felt as if I should choke with anger and mortification.

Tears of anger started from Harry's eyes, while Allan looked savage enough to exterminate them if he had the power. Kenneth looked very wretched, but glanced occasionally out of the window, as if he would like, as long as they had come, to see what they were like. Nelly's face was bent in the deepest humiliation on her plate, as if the shame of defeat was peculiarly hers. Roy's black eyes were blazing, as if he scented a fight but did not exactly know where to find it. While Donald, only two and a half years old, turned his back to weep silently, in sympathy I suppose with the distress of the rest. Presently a trampling was heard around the house, loud voices and the sounds of wheels and horses' hoofs. Suddenly a most unwonted sound! A mule braying; Nelly looked up from her plate where her eyes had been fixed in shame and distress: "Even their very old horses are laughing." That was irresistible. I was compelled in spite of all to join the horses in their laugh.

I was obliged to attend to my household affairs, and in passing to and fro on the porch and through passages, encountered them often, but took no notice, just moved on as if they were not there. Donald was sitting on a step very disconsolate looking, when one blue coat passed near him, and laying his hand on his head, said "How d'ye do Bub." He did not look up, but sullenly said, "Take your hand off my head, you are a Yankee." The man looked angry, but did not try to annoy us because the small rebel scorned him.

Ten o'clock had come, and we were still undisturbed. Only men passing through the yard to get water from the spring; so I put on my bonnet and went to town to see what had befallen my friends, and to attend to some necessary business. As I approached Mrs. Powell's house, I saw a group of officers standing at the gate, brilliantly dressed men who, as I could not help seeing as I advanced, were regarding me very curiously. I was obliged to pass very near them, but did so without being, or seeming to be aware of their presence. When I had gone by, I heard behind me a "Whew" and a little quiet laugh. I knew they were laughing at my loftiness, but tried to smother my resentment.

As I came near the town I encountered throngs of soldiers of different parts of the army. The pavements were lined with them, the doorsteps and front yards filled, and they looking as much at home, and as unconcerned as if the town and all in it belonged to them, and they were quietly enjoying their own.

Conspicuous above the rest were Banks'[1] bodyguard. A regiment

[1] Major-General N. P. Banks, commanding the Union forces in the Shenandoah.

of Zuaves, with scarlet trousers, white leather gaiters, and red fez. I would not look at them, though I saw them distinctly.

As I passed Mrs. Seevers' beautiful house that was her pride and delight, I saw an unusual stir. More Zuaves were on the pavement in front, many stretched on the beautiful lawn or smelling the flowers that were just budding out. Two stood, straight and upright at each side of the door, while sentinels walked back and forth outside the gate. That I afterwards heard was Banks' headquarters.

I passed some friends who looked at me with unspoken mortification and distress. All houses were shut, and blinds down.

Occasionally at a door might be seen an excited woman talking resentfully to one, or a group of men. I hated the sight of the old town, as it looked with strangers meeting me at every step, their eyes looking no friendliness; only curiosity or insolence. I finished my business, and without exchanging a word with any one, set out for home.

As I turned in at the gate at the end of the avenue, I beheld a sight that made my heart stand still. A number of horses were tied on the lawn, and in the porch was a group of men. I went straight up to the house, as I came near saw they were U. S. officers. There they stood in all the glory of their gold lace and epaulettes, but I felt neither awed by their martial appearance, or fascinated by their bravery of apparel. I walked deliberately up the steps until I reached the top one, as I felt that I could be less at a disadvantage in an encounter if on a level with them. When there I stood still and waited for them to speak. One took off his cap and came towards me colouring violently. "Is this Mrs. McDonald," said he. I bowed stiffly, still looking at him.

He handed me a card, "De Forest, U. S. Army."[1] I bowed again and asked if he had any business with me, knowing well that he had, and guessing what it was. Another then came forward as if to relieve him, and said that they had been sent by General Williams[2] to look at the house, with a view to occupying it as headquarters, and asked if I had any objection to permitting them to see the rooms. I told him that I had no objection to them seeing the rooms, but that I had very many objections to having it occupied as headquarters. (This was said very loftily.) But that as I could not prevent it, they must,

[1] John William DeForest, brevetted major in July 1863; author of *Miss Ravenel's Conversion* and *Kate Beaumont*.
[2] General Alpheus S. Williams.

if they chose do it. This was meant to be indignant, but at the end, angry tears would come. One or two seemed sorry for me, but the others looked little moved. I went and opened a room for their inspection, but they declined looking in, and asked what family I had, and how many rooms the house contained. I told them there were seven children, and that the two youngest were ill.

They bowed themselves out but Maj Wilkins, the one who was the second to speak, turned back and coming close to me said, "I will speak to Gen. Williams and see if they cannot be accommodated elsewhere." Then they all left, but in a few hours a note came from Maj. Wilkins, saying that in consideration of sickness in my family, Gen. Williams would not inconvenience me. I was very grateful at being left to myself, but not glad to be obliged to feel grateful to these intruders.

For a week or more I was annoyed but little, though every day would hear tales of the arrest of citizens, and occupation of houses belonging to them, while their families were obliged to seek quarters elsewhere, so of course there was nothing like quietness or peace of mind. These outrages roused all our indignant feelings, but when we had a closer acquaintance with war, we wondered how such things could have disturbed us so much.

One morning, very early I observed a U. S. flag streaming over Mr. Mason's house. Found out that it was occupied as headquarters by a Massachusetts regiment. . . .

March, 1862.—The *Baltimore American,* the only paper we see, is full of the amazing success of the "National Army" over the rebels. "The traitor Jackson is fleeing up the valley with Banks in hot pursuit. The arch rebel suffers not the grass to grow under his flying feet. There is perfect confidence in his speedy downfall."

Gen. Shields[1] is in command; Banks has gone—with nearly two-thirds of the army. Those that are here make a great display of their finery, and the grandeur of their equipments, but the people take no notice of them. I meet the gorgeous officers every day in our hall, but I never raise my eyes.

As I came up the avenue a few days since, I noticed one of the beautiful ornamental trees cut down for fuel. I was greatly disturbed by it; and as I entered the hall, still angry and excited, I met rather a fine looking officer coming out. He was a large man, handsomely

[1] Brigadier-General James Shields.

dressed, and seemed inclined to be courteous. He raised his cap, and held the door open for me to pass, but remained standing after I had entered. I took the opportunity to speak of the trees and asked that no more be allowed to be destroyed. He said he would do his best to prevent it and as he still stood and wished to say something else, I waited to hear what it was. First he said he was astonished to see so much bitterness manifested toward them by the people, especially by the ladies of Winchester. "I do not think," he said, "that since I have been here I have seen a pleasant countenance. I always notice that the ladies on the street invariably turn away their faces when I look at them, or if they show them at all, have on all their sour looks. Do they always look sour and do they always dress so gloomily in black?" "As for the dress," said I, "many of them are wearing black for friends killed in battle, and others are not inclined to make a display of dress when those they love are in hourly danger; and they cannot look glad to see those they would like to have drowned in the sea, or overwhelmed with any calamity that would take them from our country." He said no more but passed on.

One day Maj. Wilkins called to bring me a written protection for the house and ground, consigning to death any who should violate it. Gen. Shields had given it. He also offered to take for me any letters to friends in the Stonewall Brigade, as he was to set out that day for the upper valley, and could communicate by flag of truce. I soon wrote one or two while he waited, putting nothing in them but that we were well, and in quiet, but anxious for intelligence of their well-being.

He sealed them in my presence, and when I asked him if it would not occasion him trouble he only laughed and said carelessly that it might cost him his commission, but that he would see that it did not.

I expressed great concern lest it should be a cause of trouble to him, and felt so grateful for his kindness, that I told him if he was ever sick or otherwise in need of a kind office to apply to me; he thanked me, and mounting his horse, galloped off to join Banks in his advance up the valley.

The *Baltimore American* still continues to publish flaming accounts of the advance of the Union Army up the valley, and having no means of knowing their resources, or ability as a military body, except from their own boastful accounts, I was filled with apprehension. A feeling of utter despair would take possession of me when I saw their great army moving, or marshalled in all its pomp for parade or review. My heart would be filled with indignation and even rage, all the more violent because of its impotence.

Had I forgotten the gallant array and brave appearance of Gen. Johnston's army as they passed our house on their march to their great victory at Manassas? The exulting strains of "Dixie" or the "Bonnie Blue Flag" almost giving wings to their feet as they moved triumphantly on, keeping step to the joyous music.

I could not recall any triumph of a former time in the humiliation of the present, and the apprehensions for the future which their power and strength would awaken. To hear their bands playing, as they constantly did, in our streets as if to remind us of our captivity and insult our misery was distracting, but Oh! the triumph of their faces when they had a slight advantage! It was maddening to see.

Though their papers were so noisy and boastful, it was observable that they continued to hover near Winchester, and as we could every day hear the sound of cannon not very far off, it was not easy to persuade us to believe that our troops were frightened away altogether.

For two or three weeks, on successive Sundays there was brisk cannonading near the town, and an evident commotion among the troops. One bright Sunday morning I was standing on the porch listening to the sounds of the cannon in the distance, when a Yankee approached and asked me if I expected "Old Jack" that day, saying that "Sunday was the day he usually selected to come."

But a day came, a Sunday, when the cannonading did not cease after the usual annoyance of the enemy in the distance, but as the day wore on it thundered louder and louder, and came nearer and nearer. All the troops left the town, and we soon became aware that a battle was being fought very near us. An intervening hill shut out the sights but not the fearful sounds, which, as the right of the enemy met our left, became more and more dreadful and deafening till two o'clock in the afternoon; then the cannon ceased, and in its place the most terrible and long continued musketry firing, some said, that had been heard since the war began, not volley after volley, but one continued fearful roll, only varied in its distinctness by the swaying of the battle, now nearer and now farther away, as each combatant seemed to gain or lose ground. Harry and Allan had begged me to let them go to the top of the hill early in the morning to see what was going on. I had given permission, thinking of no danger other than occurred every day; but now, how I repented having let them go, and sat all that fearful afternoon in terror for fear my boys had come to harm.

I remained during all those miserable hours with my baby on my lap, and the four little ones clustered round, listening to the dreadful storm of battle, and feeling, Ah! how bitterly, that at each shot some one of the flower of our youth was perishing (for that Stonewall Brigade comprised the very pride and flower of the upper counties of Virginia), that they were being cut down like the grass. Oh, the anguish of those hours! My little boys! How could I have suffered them to go away from me so thoughtlessly when nearly every moment brought danger?

At last the gloomy hours had all rolled by, and with the darkness came silence. All the turmoil had ceased, and in its place a dreary pattering rain was the only sound I heard.

As I sat there in the darkness my imagination painted the scenes behind that hill. The dead, the dying, the trampling horses, the moans, the ghastly forms of those that some of us loved, the cries for help when no help was near. I cried out in my terror, "Where are my boys?" and ran down to the kitchen in the hope of seeing some face that looked natural and reassuring. Aunt Winnie sat there by the fire with Tuss. He was the picture of terror. His poor ugly face was ghostly, his eyes and mouth wide open and his hands clasping each other nervously. He looked up at me and asked in a husky voice, "Whey is dem boys?" I could not answer but went back and sat in the dining room with the little children and poor little Kenneth, who was grieving about the boys. About nine o'clock they came in, very grave and sad looking. Indeed they seemed not like the same boys, so sad and unnatural was their expression. Everything that fearful day seemed unreal. I felt as if a new and terrible existence had begun, as if the old life was over and gone, and one had opened, from the threshold of which I would if I could, have turned away, and lived no longer.

All the careless happiness had gone from the faces and manner of the boys, and though there was no sign of fright or of excitement, they were very grave and sorrowful; disappointed, too, as we had lost the battle, and they had been compelled to see the Southern troops sullenly withdraw after the bloody struggle. I could see that they had comprehended the situation of the contending forces, and had given a correct account of what had transpired under their observation.

They told of the prolonged fight behind the stone wall, of the repeated onsets of our men, and the rolling back of the blue columns,
as regiment after regiment was repulsed by the Confederates, till at
last, outnumbered and borne back, they had retired from the field,
leaving behind the dead and dying, and even their wounded. When
the boys told of the retreat their anger and mortification found relief
in tears, but they were tears of pity when they told of the wounded.
They remained for a while to give water to some, and would have
gladly done more, but were hurried away by the sentinels. "I was
mortified all the time," said Allan, "because we had to stay on the
Yankee side."

They had a position in the beginning of the battle near where a
body of the Federals were awaiting an attack, and they, the boys,
were perched on a fence for a better view, but the attack was made,
and a man's head rolled close to where they were, and they prudently
retreated to a more secure position.

Next morning, a worn and weary, ragged and hungry train of
prisoners came in town under a strong guard. Throngs of ladies and
poor women greeted them and cheered them with comforting words.
Mothers at the doors of elegant houses waited to give these poor boys
food. They were not allowed to stop, but were hurried out of sight
without a word to the parents whose darlings they were. No one had
been allowed to go to the battlefield the night before, though many
had begged to be permitted to carry relief to the wounded.

No one knew who was dead, or who was lying out in that chilly
rain, suffering and famishing for the help that was so near, and
would have been so willingly given but for that barbarous order that
no relief should be sent from the town. No eyes closed during those
nights for the thought of the suffering pale faces turned up under the
dark sky, or for the dying groans or helpless cries of those they were
powerless to relieve.

Not until the Federal dead were all buried on the field, and their
wounded brought in, which occupied nearly two days, were our
people allowed to go to the relief of their wounded. Then, no doubt,
many had perished who could have been saved had timely relief been
given. Our people buried their own dead. Though, as we had no conveyances, the authorities had our wounded brought in.

Every available place was turned into a hospital, the courthouse
was full, the vacant banks, and even the churches. I went with some
refreshments as soon as I heard they were coming in. I first went to

the Farmer's Bank, where I saw some ladies standing by several groaning forms that I knew were Federals from their blue garments. The men, the surgeon said, were dying, and the ladies looked pityingly down at them, and tried to help them, though they did wear blue coats, and none of their own were there to weep over or help them.

I went from there to the courthouse; the porch was strewed with dead men. Some had papers pinned to their coats telling who they were. All had the capes of their great coats turned over to hide their still faces; but their poor hands, so pitiful they looked and so helpless; busy hands they had been, some of them, but their work was over.

Soon men came and carried them away to make room for others who were dying inside, and would soon be brought and laid in their places. Most of them were Yankees, but after I had seen them I forgot all about what they were here for. I went on into the building intending to find our own men and give them what I had brought.

A long line of blue clad forms lay on each side as I passed up the room. I had not gone far before I saw a pair of sad looking eyes intently regarding the pitcher the servant carried. I stooped and offered him some: it was lemonade; he could not raise his head to drink, so I poured it into his mouth with a tablespoon. He looked up at me so thankfully. "It is a beautiful drink," he said, "for a thirsty man," and the poor fellow looked after me as I walked away.

The next day when I went he was past all succor in this world; he still lay in the same place and in the same position, with his head bent far back; he was breathing painfully and heavily, and after I had spent some time in another part of the room and was going out, I saw them carrying his corpse towards the door.

Many, many poor sufferers were there, some so dreadfully mutilated that I was completely overcome by the sight.

I wanted to be useful, and tried my best, but at the sight of one face that the surgeon uncovered, telling me that it must be washed, I thought I should faint. It was that of a Captain Jones, of a Tennessee regiment. A ball had struck him on the side of the face, taking away both eyes, and the bridge of his nose. It was a frightful spectacle. I stood as the surgeon explained how, and why he might be saved, and the poor fellow not aware of the awful sight his eyeless face was, with the fearful wound still fresh and bleeding joined in the talk, and raising his hand put his finger on his left temple and said, "Ah! if they had only struck there, I should have troubled no one." The surgeon asked me if I would wash his wound. I tried to say yes, but the thought of it made me so faint that I could only stagger towards the door.

As I passed my dress brushed against a pile of amputated limbs heaped up near the door. My faintness increased, and I had to stop and lean against the wall to keep from falling. Just then Mrs. Magill stopped by me on the way in, and asked me what was the matter. I told her about the poor man whose wound I could not wash. "I'll wash him," she said, and with her sweet cheerful face she went in, and I saw her leaning over him as he laid propped up by a bench.

Another poor man I saw who was well known to my family. Townes was his name. He told me his wife was away in Missouri and he should not see her ever again, as the doctor had told him that he could not live till night. It seemed dreadful to hear him say that when his face was full, and his eyes bright as if in health. His wound was in his neck or spine. He shook my hand as I left him and begged me to give his regards to my husband and family.

The regards of a dead man! But he was so polite, and such a gentleman he must send a message of remembrance even though when it could be delivered he would be in another world. He did not like me to see how he suffered, but tried to talk pleasantly, never mentioning his wound. He said he would love to hear some of the church prayers, but there was no book at hand, and it would have been impossible to read among all those sounds of war, for all the amputations were being performed in the room where the wounded lay.

The afternoon of the next day I went by the courthouse, the scene of so much anguish and despair. I could not believe my own eyes when I saw a flaming banner flying from the porch gaily painted and inscribed with the words, "Theatre here tonight." A gentleman told me that they had spent the night before removing the wounded and dying to make way for the theatre, as they said the men must be amused.

Soon after, the *Baltimore American* contained a paragraph to the effect that the ladies of Winchester evinced a very great unconcern for their people and the army as well as for their own situation as prisoners, as the theatre was nightly thronged. It was thronged with negro women and Yankee soldiers.

Some days after the battle of Kernstown[1] I noticed unusual preparations going on by the officers in the house, and soldiers outside.
Sleek, splendid horses were brought from the stables, and gorgeously
dressed officers came out and mounted them. The band was playing
"Hail Columbia" on the lawn. I felt curious to know what was the
occasion of so much parade, and raised the windows to ask a soldier.

The Col. saw me, and after the patriotic strain was ended spoke to
a soldier to play "Dixie," which was done, but always spoiled by in-
troducing parts of other pieces, for fear that we, I suppose, should
enjoy our rebellious pleasure unalloyed. So as the strains of "Dixie"
floated on the air, the Col. and his officers rode down the avenue,
their horses curvetting and prancing, as if to keep time to the music.

About sunset the bright cavalcade returned, and after dismounting, seated themselves on the front porch. I went and stood in the
door, as I was consumed with anxiety to know the occasion of their
gay expedition in the afternoon. Col. Candée, after saying good evening, soon remarked that they had had a most delightful time. Mr.
Seward and his daughter had come from Washington to see the
battlefield, that all the troops had been ordered out to meet them at
the depot, and escort them to the scene of their great victory.

The thought of their triumph, and of the glee of the heartless old
schemer whose intrigues and falsehoods had done so much for our
undoing, was more than I could bear. "Ah!" said I, forgetting prudence, "we can well excuse him for rejoicing as it is the first time
he has had occasion to do so, but I must tell you what crossed my
mind as you told me of his visit to the battlefield. It was a short
poem of Lord Byron's wherein he relates how Mr. Seward's great
prototype once visited a battlefield:

> "Then next he paused upon his way
> To look upon Leipsic plain,
> And so sweet to his eyes was the sulphury glare,
> And so soft to his ears was the cry of despair,
> That he perched on a mountain of slain
> And gazed with delight on its growing height
> Not often on earth had he seen such a sight,
> Or his work done half so well."[2]

Some of them laughed, but the Col., with a very red face, sat silent
for some time. I began to repent what I had done, as I felt that I

[1] The Confederates suffered a slight repulse at Kernstown on March 23, 1862.
[2] "The Devil's Drive," quoted from memory.

might have to pay a severe penalty for my rashness, but soon the
Col., addressing the Major, said, "Did the General give the order
concerning the hospitals today?" And turning to me, "You will probably have to seek other quarters, Madam, for whenever I leave this
house as I may do in a few days, it is quite likely it will be occupied
as a hospital."

My courage had all oozed out by that time, so I silently withdrew
into the hall, and standing by the window tried, tried to realize the
probable consequences of what I had done.

Two days afterwards, preparations were on foot for a march, and
the Col. asking to see me for a moment after breakfast, I went out
and found them all waiting to take leave of me before mounting their
horses. All were politely and smilingly standing, and offered their
hands which I was not quite sure I ought to take, but could not be
rude enough to refuse.

The Col. thanked me for the civility I had shown him during his
stay under my roof, regretting being obliged to leave his pleasant
quarters, but they had orders to push on up the valley with the rest
of their army. After they had mounted and were touching their caps
gallantly as they turned their horses, I spoke to the Col. "I shall be
very glad to see you Col. Candée on your way back if you have time
to stop."

That last piece of impudence was cowardly, as he could not, as
I thought, reply, but he did, saying, "Madam, Jackson is now pushed
to extremities—three columns are now converging to crush him."
My heart sank, and as usual my courage melted away in a fit of
weeping.

4. MARGARET LEA HOUSTON—"MY BOY
IS GONE FROM ME"

*A schoolgirl with violet eyes, Margaret Lea had seen the heroic
General Houston when New Orleans greeted the victor of San
Jacinto. They met in 1839 when he called on her brother-in-law
William Bledsoe at Spring Hill near Mobile; fell passionately in love
and were married on May 9, 1840.*

*Strongly attached to the Union and bitterly opposed to secession,
the general was deposed as Governor of Texas. Sam, Jr., eldest of*

the seven children, enlisted as a private in Ashbel Smith's company of the 2nd Texas.

After the death of her husband on July 26, 1863, Mrs. Houston moved with her children to Independence, Texas. During a yellow-fever epidemic in 1867 she volunteered as a nurse, was stricken and died. Her grave is at Independence.[1]

Cedar Point [Texas]
March 17th 1862

My beloved Mother,

Since Gen'l Houston's return, I have had no spirit to write to any of you, on account of my deep affliction from my dear boy being sent to Missouri. My heart seems almost broken. . . . I left nothing undone that was in my power, to prevent his going, but my weakness gave him an opportunity of displaying traits of character that made his father's heart swell with pride. . . . When I first heard the news, I thought I would lie down and die, but it is strange how life will cling to such a poor emaciated frame as mine. I want one of the girls to write a letter for you and just give me your words. Reprove me as sharply as you please. It will do me good. I deserve it all. I find now that I had really enshrined an idol in my heart. I did not love him more than the rest of my children, but he absorbed all my anxiety, all my hopes and fears. . . . I believe it is a settled thing now, that Galveston is not to be attacked. I am teaching the little ones at home. They are all learning very well. Beg my Christian friends all to pray for Sam. Tell Bro. Ross, when the sun is setting, it is my custom to pray for those who are near and dear to me, and I want him and his wife to meet me at that time at a throne of grace, and plead for my poor boy.

Gen'l Houston and the children unite with me in love to all the kindred and friends.

Ever thy affectionate daughter
M. L. HOUSTON

5. KATE CUMMING—THE AFTERMATH OF SHILOH

In her childhood Kate Cumming came from Scotland with her family to Mobile, Alabama. When the war started, her brother en-

---

[1] See *The Raven*, by Marquis James, p. 457 (Indianapolis: The Bobbs-Merrill Company, Inc., 1929).

*listed in the famous 21st Alabama. Kate, then twenty-eight, espoused
the Confederate cause with equal enthusiasm. On the second day of
Shiloh she and other women from Mobile who had volunteered for
service in the hospital division of the Army of Tennessee left for
Corinth, the Confederate base some twelve miles from the battlefield.
She carried with her comforts and delicacies of all kinds, provided
by the good people of her home town.*

*Kate Cumming's journal is an astute, authoritative account of
events and conditions.*

Corinth, Mississippi

April 11 1862. Miss Booth and myself arrived at Corinth to-day.
It was raining when we left Mrs. Henderson's, and as her carriage
was out of repair, she sent us to the depot in an open wagon. We
enjoyed the novel ride, and began to feel that we were in the *service*
in reality. My heart beat high with expectation as we neared Corinth.
As I had never been where there was a large army, and had never
seen a wounded man, except in the cars, as they passed, I could not
help feeling a little nervous at the prospect of now seeing both. When
within a few miles of the place, we could realize the condition of an
army, immediately after a battle. As it had been raining for days,
water and mud abounded. Here and there were wagons hopelessly
trying to wade through it. As far as the eye could reach, in the midst
of all this slop and mud, the white tents of our brave army could be
seen through the trees, making a picture suggestive of any thing but
comfort. . . .

The crowd of men at the depot was so great that we found it impossible to get to our place of destination by ourselves. Mr. Miller
was not there to meet us. I met Mr. George Redwood of Mobile, who
kindly offered to pilot us. We found Mr. Miller and all the ladies
busy in attending to the wants of those around them. They had not
been assigned to any particular place, but there is plenty for them to
do. We are at the Tishomingo Hotel, which like every other large
building, has been taken for a hospital. The yellow flag is flying from
the top of each. Mrs. Ogden tried to prepare me for the scenes which
I should witness upon entering the wards. But alas! nothing that I
had ever heard or read had given me the faintest idea of the horrors
witnessed here. I do not think that words are in our vocabulary expressive enough to present to the mind the realities of that sad scene.
Certainly, none of the glories of the war were presented here. But I

must not say that; for if uncomplaining endurance is glory, we had plenty of it. If it is that which makes the hero, here they were by scores. Gray-haired men—men in the pride of manhood—beardless boys—Federals and all, mutilated in every imaginable way, lying on the floor, just as they were taken from the battle-field; so close together that it was almost impossible to walk without stepping on them. I could not command my feeling enough to speak, but thoughts crowded upon me. O, if the authors of this cruel and unnatural war could but see what I saw there, they would try and put a stop to it! To think, that it is man who is working all this woe upon his fellow-man. What can be in the minds of our enemies, who are now arrayed against us, who have never harmed them in any way, but simply claim our own, and nothing more! May God forgive them, for surely they know not what they do.

This was no time for recrimination; there was work to do; so I went at it to do what I could. If I were to live a hundred years, I should never forget the poor sufferers' gratitude; for every little thing, done for them—a little water to drink, or the bathing of their wounds—seemed to afford them the greatest relief.

The Federal prisoners are receiving the same attention as our own men; they are lying side by side. Many are just being brought in from the battle-field. The roads are so bad that it is almost impossible to get them moved at all. A great many ladies are below stairs; so I thought that I had better assist them. The first thing which I did was to aid in giving the men their supper, consisting of bread, biscuit, and butter, and tea and coffee without milk. There were neither waiter, nor plates; they took what we gave them in their hands, and were glad to get it. I went with a lady to give some Federal officers their supper, who were in a room by themselves; only one or two of them were wounded. One, a captain from Cincinnati had a broken arm. Before I went in, I thought that I would be polite, and say as little as possible to them; but when I saw them laughing, and apparently indifferent to the woe which they had been instrumental in bringing upon us, I could not help being indignant; and when one of them told me he was from Iowa, and that was generally called out of the world, I told him that was where I wished him, and all like him, so that they might not trouble us any more.

April 12—I sat up all night, bathing the men's wounds, and giving them water. Everyone attending them seemed completely worn out.

Some of the doctors told me that they had scarcely slept since the battle. As far as I have seen, the surgeons are very kind to the wounded, and nurse as well as doctor them.

The men are lying all over the house, on their blankets, just as they were brought from the battle-field. They are in the hall, on the gallery, and crowded into very small rooms. The foul air from this mass of human beings at first made me giddy and sick, but I soon got over it. We have to walk, and when we give the man any thing kneel, in blood and water; but we think nothing of it at all. There was much suffering among the patients last night; one old man groaned all the time. He was about sixty years of age, and had lost a leg. He lived near Corinth, and had come there the morning of the battle to see his two sons, who were in the army, and he could not resist shouldering his musket and going into the fight. I comforted him as well as I could. He is a religious man, and prayed nearly all night.

Another, a very young man, was wounded in the leg and through the lungs, had a most excruciating cough, and seemed to suffer awfully. One fine looking man had a dreadful wound in the shoulder. Every time I bathed it he thanked me, and seemed grateful. He died this morning before breakfast. Men who were in the room with him told me that he prayed all night. I trust that he is now at rest, far from this dreary world of strife and bloodshed.

Other ladies have their special patients, whom they never leave. One of them, from Natchez, Miss., has been constantly by a young man, badly wounded, ever since she came here, and the doctors say that she has been the means of saving his life. Many of the others are doing the same. Mrs. Ogden, and the Mobile ladies are below stairs. I have not even time to speak to them. Mr. Miller is doing much good; he is comforting the suffering and dying; and has already baptised some.

This morning when passing the front door, a man asked me if I had any thing to eat, which I could give to some men at the depot awaiting transportation on the cars. He said that they had eaten nothing for some days. Some of the ladies assisted me, we took them hot coffee, bread, and meat. The poor fellows ate eagerly, and seemed so thankful. One of the men, who was taking care of them, asked me where I was from. When I replied Mobile, he said that Mobile was the best place in the Confederacy. He was a member of the Twenty-first Alabama Regiment. I have been busy all day, and can scarcely tell what I have been doing; I had not taken time even to eat, and certainly not time to sit down. There seems to be no order. All do as they please. We have men for nurses, and the doctors complain very much at the manner in which they are appointed; they are detailed from the different regiments, like guards. We have a new set every few hours. I can not see how it is possible for them to take proper care of the men, as nursing is a thing that has to be learned, and we should select our best men for it—the best, not physically, but morally—as I am certain that none but good, conscientious persons will ever do justice to the patients.

Sunday, April 13—Enjoyed a very good night's rest upon some boxes. We all slept below stairs, in the front room—our baggage separating us from the front part of it, which is the clerks' office, and sleeping apartment of some dozen men. It was a laughable sight to see Father Miller fixing some beds for us. Poor man! He tried so hard to make us comfortable. Some slept on shelves. I slept so soundly that I did not even dream, as I was completely worn out with the labor of the day. I could realize how, after a hard days' marching or fighting, a soldier can throw himself upon the ground, and sleep as soundly as if he was on a bed of down. A number of persons arrived last night, looking for their relations. One very pretty lady, with her parents, is in search of her husband, a colonel, who is reported badly wounded. I have since heard that she has found him at a farm-house, and he is much better off than she had been informed. Her mother, on leaving, presented me with some very nice sperm-candles.

I have just seen my brother. He looks rather the "worse for wear." But, thank God, he is safe. This was his first battle, and I have been told that "he was brave to a fault." The company distinguished itself on that eventful day; and Mobile may well be proud of the gallant men who compose it.

I have been told by a friend that the night of the first day's battle he passed by a wounded Federal, who requested him to bring him some water from a spring nearby. On going to it, he was much shocked to see three Federals lying with their heads in it. They had dragged themselves to the spring to slake their thirst, and there they had breathed their last. There is no end to the tales of horror related about the battle-field. They fill me with dismay.

The confusion and want of order are as great as ever. A great many doctors are here, who came with the men from the different regiments. The amount of good done is not near what it might be, if things were better managed. Some one is to blame for this state of affairs. Many say it is the fault of Dr. Foard, the medical director. But I suppose that allowance must be made for the unexpected number of wounded. I trust that in a little time things will be better.

One of the doctors, named Little of Alabama, told me to-day that he had left his young wife on his plantation with more than a hundred negroes upon it, and no white man but the overseer. He had told the negroes, before he left, if they desired to leave, they could do so when they pleased. He was certain that not more than one or two would go.

I have conversed with some of the wounded prisoners. One of them, quite a young man, named Nott, is very talkative. He says that he dislikes Lincoln and abolitionism as much as we do; declares that he is fighting to save the Union, and nothing more. All of them say the same thing. What a glorious Union it would be!

Quite a number of bunks arrived today, and we are having the most severely wounded placed on them. I am so glad, as we can have some of the filth taken off the floors. A doctor requested me to go down stairs and see if there was a bunk with a Federal upon it, and if so have him taken off, as he had a badly wounded man that needed one. I went and asked Mrs. Royal, from Mobile, whom I had heard talk very bitterly. She knew of one, but would not tell me where it was. Her true woman's nature showed itself, in spite of her dislike. Seeing an enemy wounded and helpless is a different thing from seeing him in health and in power. The first time that I saw one in this condition every feeling of enmity vanished at once. I was curious to find out who the Federal was, and, as Mrs. R. would not tell me, I went in search of him. I found him with but little trouble; went to the men who were upon the bunks, and asked them where they were from. One, quite a youth, with a childish face, told me he was from Illinois. I knew in a moment that he was the one. I asked him about his Mother, and why he had ever left. Tears filled his eyes, and his lips quivered so that he was unable to speak. I was deeply moved myself, spoke a few words of comfort, and left him. I would not have had him give up his bunk for the world. Poor child! there will be a terrible day of reckoning for those who sent you on your errand, and who are the cause of desolating so many hearts and homes.

As I was passing one of the rooms, a man called me, and begged me to do something for him and others who were with him. No one had been to see them that morning, and they had had no breakfast. I gave them something to eat, and got a nurse to take care of them. About eight were in the room, among them Mr. Regan of Alabama and Mr. Eli Wasson of Texas, both of whom had lost a leg. I paid these special attention as they were worse than the others. They were very grateful, and thanked me all the time. Mr. W. said that he knew that he would get well now. They are both unmarried, and talk much of their mothers and sisters, as all men do now. "Home, sweet home," is the dearest spot on earth to them, since they are deprived of its comforts. Mother, wife, and sister seem to be sweeter to them than any words in the English language.

We eat in the kitchen, surgeons and all. It is not the cleanest place in the world, and I think, to use a Scotch phrase, would make even Mrs. McClarty "think shame." Hunger is a good antidote for even dirt. I am aware that few will think so except those who have tried it.

April 15.—Enjoyed a very good night's rest in a crowded room. Had part of a mattress upon the floor, but so many were upon it that for half of the night I was under a table.

My patients are doing well. My own health is excellent. While I was down stairs this morning a gentleman requested me to give him something to eat for some fifty or sixty wounded men whom he had in his care. He had nothing for them, but was expecting something from his home in Tennessee. It would be some days before he could get it. Mrs. Ogden gave him what she could. He informed us that his name was Cannon; that he was a doctor and a clergyman of the Episcopal Church. He said that if our men were not better treated than at the present time, it would be the means of demoralizing them more than the enemy's cannon balls.

Mr. Wasson is cheerful, and is doing well; tells me much about his home in Texas and the nice fruit there; says that I must go home with him, as his family would be so glad to see me.

Mrs. Lyons is sitting up day, and night, attending to some eight or nine patients. One of them is shot in the face, and has it covered with a cloth, as it is so lacerated that it presents a most revolting aspect. Mrs. L. is also taking care of some prisoners. There is a Federal surgeon named Young waiting on them. I have been told that Dr. Lyle, one of our surgeons, refused to attend them, as he had just

lost two brothers in the war, and has heard that his father is a prisoner. His feelings are such that he is fearful he might not do justice
to the sufferers. If there were no other surgeons here, he would
endeavor to do his duty by them.

April 16.—Mrs. Miller, Mrs. Ogden, and nearly all the ladies from
Mobile left for Columbus, Miss. I remained, with Mrs. Glassburn,
from Natchez. My brother is here, and I have become so much interested in some of the wounded that I could not leave them. Mrs.
Ogden was completely worn out; and it is not much to be wondered
at, as she, with the rest of us, has had to sleep in any and every
place; and as to making our toilet, that was out of the question. I
have not undressed since I came here.

I dislike very much to see some of the ladies go, as they have been
very kind to the sufferers, and I know that they will miss them very
much. They go to Columbus, Miss., where are a great many of the
wounded. I daily witness the same sad scenes—men dying all around
me. I do not know who they are, nor have I time to learn.

April 17.—I was going round as usual this morning, washing the
faces of the men, and had got half through with one before I found
out that he was dead. He was lying on the gallery by himself, and had
died with no one near him. These are terrible things. . . . I thought
that my patients were all doing well. Mr. Wasson felt better, and
knew that he would soon go home. I asked the surgeon who was
attending him about his condition, and was much shocked when I
learned that neither he nor Mr. Regan would live to see another day.
This was a sad trial to me. I had seen many die, but none of them
whom I had attended so closely as these two. I felt toward them as
I do toward all the soldiers—as if they were my brothers. I tried to
control my feelings before Mr. W., as he was so hopeful of getting
well, but it was a hard task. He looked at me once and asked me
what was the matter; was he going to die? I asked him if he was
afraid. He replied no; but he was so young that he would like to live
a little longer, and would like to see his mother and father once
more. . . . I could not muster courage to tell him that he was going
to die. Poor Mr. Regan was wandering in his mind. I managed to get
him to tell me of his mother's address. He belonged to the Twenty-
second Alabama Regiment. . . .

April 18.—I remained with Mr. Wasson all night. A child could not have been more composed. . . . About 4 o'clock A.M. he insisted that I should leave him, as I required rest. He begged so hard that I left him for a little while. When I returned he had breathed his last. One of his companions was with him, and was very attentive—told me that he died as if he was going to sleep. . . .

Mr. Regan died this morning; was out of his mind to the last. . . .

Mrs. Lyons left this morning for home. She was very sick; and one of the doctors informed her, if she did not leave immediately, she would certainly die. I know the men whom she has been nursing will miss her very much, as she has been so attentive to them.

Dr. Smith has taken charge of this hospital. I think that there will be a different order of things now. He is having the house and yard well cleaned. Before this, it was common to have amputated limbs thrown into the yard, and left there.

Mrs. Glassburn and myself started to go to College Hospital, when we met the doctor who spoke to my patient last night, and he went with us. His name is Hughes—is from Lexington, Ky. The walk was very pleasant. Met a general and his staff. The doctor thought it was General Polk[1]—our bishop-general, as he is called. We called at a shed on the way; found it filled with wounded, lying on the floor; some men attending them. All were in the best of spirits. Mrs. G. promised to send them some of our good things. When we arrived at the hospital, we were charmed with the cleanliness and neatness visible on every side. The Sisters of Charity have charge of the domestic part, and, as usual with them, everything is *parfait*. We were received very kindly by them. One was a friend of Mrs. G. She took us through the hospital. The grounds are very neatly laid out. Before the war it was a female college. I saw, as his mother requested, Mr. John Lyons, who is sick; he is a member of Ketchum's Battery. The wounded seem to be doing well. One of the surgeons complained bitterly of the bad management of the railroad, and said that its managers should be punished, as they were the cause of a great deal of unnecessary suffering. They take their own time to transport the wounded, and it is impossible to depend upon them. That is the reason why we see so many sick men lying around the depot. Crossing the depot upon our return, we saw a whole Mississippi regiment sick,

[1] Leonidas Polk, Bishop of Louisiana and major-general, C. S. A., had been called in with his garrison from Columbus, Ky., to General A. S. Johnston's concentration before Shiloh and fought bravely there.

awaiting transportation. They looked very badly, and nearly all had a cough. . . .

April 22.—All the patients are being sent away on account of the prospects of a battle; at least, those who are able to be moved.

We have had a good deal of cold, wet weather lately. This is the cause of much sickness. Dr. Hereford, chief surgeon of Ruggles'[1] brigade, has just informed me, that nearly our whole army is sick, and if it were not that the Federals are nearly as bad off as ourselves, they could annihilate us with ease. . . .

Everyone is talking of the impending battle with the greatest indifference. It is strange how soon we become accustomed to all things; and I suppose it is well, as it will do no good to worry about it. Let us do our duty, and leave the rest to God.

April 23.—A young man whom I have been attending is going to have his arm cut off. Poor fellow! I am doing all I can to cheer him. He says that he knows that he will die, as all who have had limbs amputated in this hospital have died. It is said that the reason is that none but the very worst cases are left here, and they are too far gone to survive the shock which the operation gives the frame. The doctors seem to think that the enemy poisoned their musket balls, as the wounds inflame terribly. Our men do not seem to stand half so much as the Northerners. Many of the doctors are quite despondent about it, and think that our men will not be able to endure the hardships of camp-life, and that we may have to succomb on account of it, but I trust that they are mistaken. None of the prisoners have died; this is a fact that can not be denied; but we have had very few of them in comparison with the number of our own men.

April 24.—Mr. Isaac Fuquet, the young man who had his arm cut off, died to-day. He lived only a few hours after his amputation. . . .

It is reported that an engagement is going on at Monterey. A wounded man has just been brought in.

The amputating table for this ward is at the end of the hall, near the landing of the stairs. When an operation is to be performed, I keep as far away from it as possible. To-day, just as they had got through with Mr. Fuquet, I was compelled to pass the place, and the sight I there beheld made me shudder and sick at heart. A stream of

[1] Brigadier-General Daniel Ruggles of Louisiana.

blood ran from the table into a tub in which was the arm. It had been taken off at the socket, and the hand, which but a short time before grasped the musket and battled for the right, was hanging over the edge of the tub, a lifeless thing. . . .

6. BETTY HERNDON MAURY—ABRAHAM LINCOLN WAS IN FREDERICKSBURG

Betty was in Fredericksburg when Confederate forces evacuated the town in the early spring of 1862. With her were little Nannie Belle, her sister Sally and her mother. Will was in Richmond, and so was Betty's father Commodore Maury, now heading the Confederate naval laboratories. Betty longed to be with them. She didn't like Will's leaving her to the oncoming Yankees one bit. Her brothers Johnny and Dick were with their regiments in the field. A cousin, Ellen Herndon, had married Chester A. Arthur, inspector-general and quartermaster-general of New York troops, and so was in disgrace with the family. The young Yankee officer whom Betty met on the street with exclamation points of scorn was to be President of the United States from 1881 to 1885.

Fredericksburg, Virginia
Good Fri. April 18—62

While we were dressing, we saw great columns of smoke rising from the river and soon learned that the enemy were in strong force, that our troops had retreated to this side of the river and fired the bridges.

I went down to the river and shall never forget the scene there. Above were our three bridges all in light blaze from one end to the other and every few minutes the beams and timbers would splash into the water with a great noise. Below were two large steamboats, the *Virginia* and the *Nicholas*, and ten or twelve vessels all wrapt in flames. There were two or three rafts dodging in between the burning vessels containing families coming over to this side with their negroes and horses.

The streets have been filled with waggons and drays and men and women in carriages and buggies leaving the town. But all have gone now and the streets are deserted. The stars and stripes are floating

in Falmouth about five miles North. Some say the enemy is eight and
some say ten thousand strong. . . .

No cars came up this morning of course. It will be dreadful to be
cut off from all tidings of those that are nearest and dearest to
us. . . .

Easter Sunday April 20

. . . We can see the Yankees and their tents across the river.
They received a reinforcement of ten thousand last night. One can
scarcely realize that the enemy is so near and that we are in their
hands. I heard the Yankees this evening with their full brass band
playing "Yankee Doodle" and "The Star Spangled Banner." I could
not realize that they were enemies and invaders. The old tunes
brought back recollections of the old love for them. It was a sad and
painful feeling.

Friday April 25th 1862

Five steamboats and twenty canal boats came up here this evening.
We suppose the canal boats are to make a bridge of.

The negroes are going off in great numbers and are beginning to be
very independent and impudent. We hear that our three are going
soon. I am afraid of the lawless Yankee soldiers, but that is nothing
to my fear of the negroes if they should rise against us.

Nanny came back yesterday. She left Farley Vale with Mr.
Corbin on Friday and went to Richmond. Papa and Mr. Corbin
induced her to come back here and stay with Mamma. Mr. Corbin
had been ordered to Norfolk. His arm is still in a sling.

Ten of Mr. Corbin's servants ran off last Friday. The farm, servants, stock, and all are now in the hands of the enemy.

Wed. April 30th

Went down yesterday evening to see the bridge of canal boats
that the Yankees are building at the lower wharf. The boats are laid
close together side by side. The length of the boat being the width
of the bridge. Eight boats are in place and it already reaches more
than half way across the river. The soldiers on the bridge and the
surrounding boats were shouting and talking to the colored men and
women on the wharf. There are several artillery companies stationed
on the hill above the bridge to protect it.

May 1st. 1862

Just before dusk, as we were all seated around the fire in Mamma's room, we heard a light tap at the door, and in walked Johnny, my dear brother Johnny. Cousin Dabney has applied for him as his aide de camp. He expects to start for the West in a day or two—and came to tell us good bye. He looks so handsome. It was a precious visit but at such a risk. The enemy have had guards out for the last few days in search of stragglers. He came in with five others, but they stopped on the outskirts of town. One can realize what the enemy is and how near he is, when our own dear ones are in danger of their lives when they come to their *homes* and have to hide around corners and steal away after dark like guilty wretches.

Sunday May 4, 1862

Gov. Seward, Secretary Stanton[1] and two or three Senators were in town yesterday evening with several Generals. McDowell among the number. The enemy are building a second pontoon bridge above the old Chatham bridge.

General Van Rennselaer was at church today. He sat in the Mayor's pew and the Mayor sat in the gallery.

Mr. Randolph has omitted the prayer for our President and for the success of our cause ever since the enemy have been here. Papa and Will say that such time serving is unworthy of the place and the people. I think there is something to be said on both sides.

Received letters yesterday. Johnny has gotten back safe. . . .

Tuesday May 13th, 1862

. . . I am much struck by the superior discipline of these Yankee soldiers over ours. I have not seen a drunken man since they have been here. They are much healthier too and are not coughing constantly during drill as our Dixie boys used to do.

Friday May 16th, 1862

Matters are getting worse and worse here every day with regard to the negroes. They are leaving their owners by the hundreds and demanding wages. The citizens have refused to hire their own or

---

[1] William H. Seward, Lincoln's Secretary of State, had been Governor of New York. Edwin M. Stanton of Pennsylvania had succeeded Simon Cameron of the same state as Secretary of War on January 15, 1862.

other peoples slaves, so that there are numbers of unemployed negroes in town. Old Doctor Hall agreed to hire his servants, but the
gentlemen of the town held a meeting and wrote him a letter of re-
monstrance telling him that he was establishing a most dangerous
precedent, that he was breaking the laws of Virginia and was a traitor of his state. So the old man refused to hire them and they all left
him. Ours have gone except one girl about 15—Nanny's Molly. We
clean up and take it by turns to assist and direct the cooking. It is
a great relief to get rid of the others. They were so insolent and idle,
and Jinny was a dangerous character. She *boasted* that she had
brought the soldiers here to get the swords and threatened to tell that
our name was Maury and that we brought things here from the
Observatory.

Sat. May 17th, 1862

General!!! Arthur, Ellen Herndon's husband, was in town yesterday. I met him in the street, but did not speak to him. I could not
shake hands with a man who came as an invader to desolate our
homes and kill our brothers and husbands. Besides the soldiers, there
are many Yankee citizens and Dutchmen in town.

Sun. May 18th, 1862

This afternoon we saw a Confederate officer on horseback blindfolded, led by a mounted Federal officer and surrounded by a guard
on his way to headquarters. He came under a flag-of-truce. We cannot hear what for. It was so refreshing to see him and to see our gray
uniform again. Mamma wanted to say "God Bless you," but was
afraid to venture.

Thursday May 22, 1862

Received a long letter from my dear husband yesterday of the
14th telling me of Tom's safe arrival in Richmond and of his adventures while in the enemy's lines. After the battle of Williamsburg
Tom went with several other surgeons, under a flag of truce to attend
to our wounded that had fallen into the enemy's hands. He was
treated with great courtesy and took several juleps with General
McClelland who sent his love to cousin Dabney Maury. A Yankee
General (Hancock)[1] told Tom that immortality ought to be inscribed

---

[1] Winfield S. Hancock, brigade commander in McClellan's army.

upon the banners of the 24th (Dick's) and the 5th North Carolina for their great bravery in that charge at Williamsburg.

Nannie Belle was playing on the pavement yesterday evening when a soldier accosted her and asked if she would not go down the street with him and let him buy her some candy. She replied "No I thank you, Yankee candy would choke me." He seemed much amused.

Sunday, May 25th, 1862

Abraham Lincoln was in town on Friday. Our Mayor did not call on him and I did not hear a cheer as he passed along the streets. The streets are full of wagons and soldiers. A large portion of the army advanced towards Richmond this afternoon. They came over different bridges and advanced over different streets. The Yankees are building their fifth bridge across the Rappahannock. . . .

7. SARAH MORGAN—ENEMY SHIPS
PASS THE FORTS BELOW NEW ORLEANS

Sarah, one of Judge Thomas Gibbes Morgan's nine children, was born in Baton Rouge, in 1841. Her father died in '61. Of her several brothers: Henry was killed in a duel in the early days of secession. Philip, a judge in New Orleans, adhered to the Union. Thomas Gibbes, Jr., married Lydia, daughter of General A. G. Carter and a cousin of Mrs. Jefferson Davis; he was a captain in the 7th Louisiana, serving under Stonewall Jackson. George was a captain in the 1st Louisiana, also with Stonewall. He and Gibbes lost their lives in '64. James, the youngest, resigned from Annapolis and hurried home to enlist in the Confederate Navy.

Sarah began her diary on March 9, 1862. When she wrote the following entry her sister Eliza or "Lilly"—wife of J. Charles La Noue— with her five children was with Sarah in Baton Rouge. Miriam was the other sister.

Baton Rouge, Louisiana
April 26th, 1862

There is no word in the English language that can express the state in which we are, and have been, these last three days. Day before yesterday, news came early in the morning of three of the enemy's boats passing the Forts, and then the excitement began. It increased rapidly on hearing of the sinking of eight of our gunboats in the engagement, the capture of the Forts, and last night, of the burning of the wharves and cotton in the city [New Orleans] while the Yankees were taking possession. To-day, the excitement has reached the point of delirium. I believe I am one of the most self-possessed in my small circle; and yet I feel such a craving for news of Miriam, and mother, and Jimmy, who are in the city, that I suppose I am as wild as the rest. Nothing can be positively ascertained, save that our gunboats are sunk, and theirs are coming up to the city. Everything else has been contradicted until we really do not know whether the city has been taken or not. We only know we had best be prepared for anything. So day before yesterday, Lilly and I sewed up our jewelry, which may be of use if we have to fly. I vow I will not move one step, unless carried away. Come what will, here I remain.

We went this morning to see the cotton burning—a sight never before witnessed, and probably never again to be seen. Wagons, drays,—everything that can be driven or rolled,—were loaded with the bales and taken a few squares back to burn on the commons. Negroes were running around, cutting them open, piling them up, and setting them afire. All were as busy as though their salvation depended on disappointing the Yankees. Later, Charlie sent for us to come to the river and see him fire a flatboat loaded with the precious material for which the Yankees are risking their bodies and souls. Up and down the levee, as far as we could see, negroes were rolling it down to the brink of the river where they would set them afire and push the bales in to float burning down the tide. Each sent up its wreath of smoke and looked like a tiny steamer puffing away. Only I doubt that from the source to the mouth of the river there are as many boats afloat on the Mississippi. The flatboat was piled with as many bales as it could hold without sinking. Most of them were cut open, while negroes staved in the heads of barrels of alcohol, whiskey, etc., and dashed bucketsful over the cotton. Others built up little chimneys of pine every few feet, lined with pine knots and loose cotton, to burn more quickly. There, piled the length of the whole levee, or burning in the river, lay the work of thousands of negroes for more than a year past. It had come from every side. Men stood by who owned the cotton that was burning or waiting to burn. They either helped, or looked on cheerfully. Charlie owned but sixteen bales—a matter of some fifteen hundred dollars; but he was the head man of the whole affair, and burned his own, as well as the property of others. A single barrel of whiskey that was thrown on the cotton, cost the man who gave it one hundred and twenty-five dollars. (It shows what a nation in earnest is capable of doing.) Only two men got on the flatboat with Charlie when it was ready. It was towed to the middle of the river, set afire in every place, and then they jumped into a little skiff fastened in front, and rowed to land. The cotton floated down the Mississippi one sheet of living flame, even in the sunlight. It would have been grand at night. But then we will have fun watching it this evening anyway; for they cannot get through to-day, though no time is to be lost.

Hundreds of bales remained untouched. An incredible amount of property has been destroyed to-day; but no one begrudges it. Every grog-shop has been emptied, and gutters and pavements are floating with liquors of all kinds. So that if the Yankees are fond of strong drink, they will fare ill. . . .

April 27th

What a day! Last night came a dispatch that New Orleans was under British protection, and could not be bombarded; consequently, the enemy's gun-boats would probably be here this morning, such few as had succeeded in passing the Forts; from nine to fifteen, it was said. And the Forts, they said, had *not* surrendered. I went to church; but I grew very anxious before it was over, feeling that I was needed at home. When I returned, I found Lilly wild with excitement, picking up hastily whatever came to hand, preparing for instant flight, she knew not where. The Yankees were in sight; the town was to be burned; we were to run to the woods, etc. If the house had to be burned, I had to make up my mind to run, too. So my treasure-bag tied around my waist as a bustle, a sack with a few necessary articles hanging on my arm, some few unnecessary ones, too, as I had not the heart to leave the old and new prayer books father had given me, and Miriam's, too;—pistol and carving-knife ready, I stood awaiting the exodus. I heaped on the bed the treasures I wanted to burn, matches lying ready to fire the whole at the last minute. . . . People fortunately changed their minds about the *auto-da-fé* just then; and the Yankees have not yet arrived, at sundown. So, when the excitement calmed down, poor Lilly tumbled in bed in a high fever in consequence of terror and exertion.

8. JULIA LeGRAND—NEW ORLEANS HAS FALLEN

"The Journal of Julia LeGrand," *wrote Dr. Freeman in his delightful book* The South to Posterity,[1] *"was kept by a woman of thirty-two who embodied all the elements of romance that an early Victorian novelist would have desired for a heroine." Her grandfather, of the* petite noblesse, *had come to Maryland not long before the French Revolution. Her father, educated in France, a wealthy planter in Maryland, bought a large estate in Louisiana and moved his family there when Julia was a child. He surrounded his daughters Julia and Virginia—Ginnie—with every luxury. He would take them with a staff of servants to the St. Charles in New Orleans for the opera season, and in summer to the Virginia springs. A contemporary portrait of Julia reveals a lovely girl in a long white gown, a big dog at her side. She played the harp and was "full of romantic fancies." A lover, too poor to press his suit, was killed in a wagon train somewhere in the west of Mexico, presumably by Indians. Julia made him the hero, under the name of Guy Fontenoy, of an unpublished novel.*

Colonel LeGrand lost all his money and all his estate. When he died the destitute girls sought a modest competence by keeping a "select school for girls" in New Orleans. Their only brother, Claude, left them there when he went off to Virginia with the first Louisiana volunteers. There they stayed until a few months after the city was occupied. Julia refused to take the oath of allegiance, "but," she wrote, "how can an outsider ever know what a temptation it was to take that oath?" They became refugees—in various parts of Louisiana, in Mississippi, Georgia and Alabama—and nursed the sick and wounded of Joe Johnston's army. Their journeys ended in Galveston, Texas, where in 1867 Julia married a young German, Adolph Waitz, "a gentleman of fine ability and attainments."

Her diary was written without expectation of publication. Much of it was destroyed. What survives covers succinctly the period from December 1861 through December 1862 and fully the early spring season of 1863. It ends abruptly in the middle of a sentence.

All the details of her life, as Dr. Freeman says, would make the reader expect a slushy, sentimental diary—"which is distinctly what it is not. It is an intelligent, direct and honest narrative . . . the

---

[1] Charles Scribner's Sons, New York, 1939, 1951.

*story of neighbors' woes, of personal hardship stoically endured . . .
of hopes raised one day and dashed the next by reading the
newspapers."*

New Orleans, May 9th, 1862. . . . Lovell,[1] a most worthless
creature, was sent here by Davis to superintend the defense of this
city. He did little or nothing and the little he did was all wrong.
Duncan,[2] the really gallant defender of Fort Jackson, could get nothing that he needed, though he continually applied to Lovell. Only
a few guns at the fort worked at all, but these were gallantly used
for the defense of the city. The fort is uninjured and could have held
out till our great ram, the *Mississippi,* was finished, but a traitor
sent word to the commander of the Federal fleet to hasten, which he
did, and our big gun, our only hope, was burned before our eyes to
prevent her from falling into Federal hands. First and last then, this
city, the most important one in the Confederacy, has fallen, and
Yankee troops are drilling and parading in our streets. Poor New
Orleans! What has become of all your promised greatness! In looking through an old trunk, I came across a letter to my father from
my Uncle Thomas, in which, as far back as 1836, he prophesied a
noble future for you. What would he say now to see you dismantled
and lying low under the heel of the invader!

Behold, what has now come to the city! Never can I forget the
day that the alarm bell rang. I never felt so hopeless and forsaken.
The wretched generals, left here with our troops, ran away and left
them. Lovell knew not what to do; some say he was intoxicated,
some say frightened. Of course the greatest confusion prevailed, and
every hour, indeed almost every moment, brought its dreadful rumor.
After it was known that the gunboats had actually passed, the whole
city, both camp and street, was a scene of wild confusion. *The
women only* did not seem afraid. They were all in favor of resistance,
no matter how hopeless that resistance might be.

The second day matters wore a more favorable aspect, and the
Mayor and the City Council assumed a dignified position toward the
enemy. Flag Officer [David] Farragut demanded the unconditional
surrender of the town. He was told that as brute force, and brute
force only, gave him the power that he might come and take it. He
then demanded that we, with our own hands, pull down the flag of
Louisiana. This I am happy to say, was refused.

[1] Major-General Mansfield Lovell.
[2] General J. K. Duncan.

Four days we waited, expecting to be shelled, but he concluded to waive the point; so he marched in his marines with two cannons and our flag was taken down and the old stars and stripes lifted in a dead silence. We made a great mistake here; we should have shot the man that brought down the flag,[1] and as long as there was a house-top in the city left, it should have been hoisted. The French and English lay in the Gulf and a French frigate came up the river to protect French subjects.

Farragut allowed the women and children but forty-eight hours to leave the city, but the foreign consuls demanded a much longer time to move the people of their respective nations. If we had been staunch and dared them to shell, the Confederacy would have been saved. The brutal threat would never have been carried out, for England and France would never have allowed it. The delay would have enabled us to finish our boat, and besides a resistance would have showed the enemy and foreign nations too, what stuff we were made of and how very much we were in earnest. I never wished anything so much in my life as for resistance here. I felt no fear—only excitement.

The ladies of the town signed a paper, praying that it should never be given up. We went down to put our names on the list, and met the marines marching up to the City Hall with their cannon in front of them. The blood boiled in my veins—I felt no fear—only anger. I forgot myself and called out several times: "Gentlemen, don't let the State Flag come down," and, "Oh, how can you men stand it?" Mrs. Norton was afraid of me, I believe, for she hurried me off.

I have forgotten to mention—at first, the Germans at the fort mutinied and turned their guns on their officers. In the first place, several gunboats had passed the fort at night because a traitor had failed to give the signal. He was tried and shot, and Duncan telegraphed to the city that no more should pass—then came a report that the Yankee vessels were out of powder and coal and they could not get back to their transports which they had expected to follow them. We were quite jubilant at the idea of keeping them in a sort of imprisonment, and this we could have done but for the German mutineers. The wives of these men were allowed to visit the fort, and they represented the uselessness of the struggle, because the city had

---

[1] As a matter of fact, a man named William B. Mumford did tear down the flag that was raised over the U. S. Mint. Governor Ben Butler had him hanged for it, and perhaps nothing except his famous—or infamous—"women's order" contributed so much to "Beast" Butler's ill fame in New Orleans and throughout the South.

already surrendered. They were told, too, that Duncan intended to blow up the fort over their heads rather than surrender. So they spiked their cannon and threatened the lives of their officers and then the Yankee fleet poured up.

These people have complimented us highly. To quell a small "rebellion," they have made preparations enough to conquer a world. This is a most cowardly struggle—these people can do nothing without gunboats. Beauregard in Tennessee can get no battle from them where they are protected by these huge block steamers. These passive instruments do their fighting for them. It is at best a dastardly way to fight. We should have had gunboats if the Government had been efficient, wise or earnest.

We have lost our city, the key to this great valley, and my opinion is that we will never, never get it more, except by treaty. Many think otherwise.

The most tantalizing rumors reach us daily (though the papers are not allowed to print *our* news, we hear it). We have heard that Stonewall Jackson has surprised and taken Washington City; that Beauregard has had a splendid victory in Tennessee; and our other generals have annihilated the enemy in Virginia. Sometimes we are elated, but most generally depressed. . . .

This is a cruel war. These people are treated with the greatest haughtiness by the upper classes and rudeness by the lower. They know how they are hated and hang their heads. Shopkeepers refuse to sell to them, and the traitor who hurried them up the river has to have guard. Public buildings have been seized by the troops, but so far the civil government has not been interfered with. I think their plan is to conciliate if possible. The cotton and sugar have been burned; that is one comfort, and the work of destruction still goes on on the plantations. I shall never forget the long, dreadful night when we sat with our friends and watched the flames from all sorts of valuables as the gunboats were coming up the river. . . .

I am told that a stand will be made at Vicksburg. They are working hard at batteries there. They will at least delay the gun-boats until we can do something that we wish. About their having the whole river, that is of course only a question of time. Fort Pillow will fall, if it has not already done so. Our only hope now is from our soldiers in the field, and this brings me to my dear brother again and all he will have to endure. Sometimes I feel that nothing is worth such sacrifice. These States may divide and fight one another, too, sometime. This war has shaken my faith. Nothing is secure if the passions and follies of men can intermeddle. Often, though, I feel that these insolent invaders with their bragging, should be conquered —come what will. Better to die than to be under their rule.

The Yankees have established strict quarantine. The people of the town are frightening them terribly with tales about the yellow fever. We are compelled to laugh at the frequent amusing accounts we hear of the way in which they are treated by boys, Irish women, and the lower classes generally. Mr. Soulé[1] refused General Butler's hand (they were old friends), remarking that their intercourse must now be purely official. Our Mayor[2] has behaved with great dignity. Butler says he will be revenged for the treatment he and his troops have received here—so he will, I expect, if matters go against us in other places. There is some fear that the city will need provisions very much. The country people won't send in anything; they are so angry about the surrender. The Texas drovers who were almost here as soon as they heard of it, sold their cattle for little or nothing just where they were and went home again. I wish we were all safe back there again. I don't think Texas will ever be conquered.

9. SARAH MORGAN—THE ENEMY
COMES TO BATON ROUGE

Sarah gave as a reason for keeping a diary "I had to find some vent for my feelings, and I would not make an exhibition of myself by talking, as so many women did." She turned to this outlet when Baton Rouge was occupied. She had the pen of a ready and accustomed writer and more and more disclosed her independence of judgment. Naturally these qualities were suspended at this time by the strength of her feeling, which led her into some extravagances of expression. But it was just as well that the carving knife had been abandoned.

Baton Rouge, Louisiana
May 9th 1862

Our lawful (?) owners have at last arrived. About sunset day before yesterday, the *Iroquois* anchored here, and a graceful young

[1] The Hon. Pierre Soulé, a leading citizen and member of the Committee of Safety.
[2] John T. Monroe.

Federal stepped ashore, carrying a Yankee flag over his shoulder, and asked the way to the Mayor's office. I like the style! If we girls of Baton Rouge had been at the landing, instead of the men, that Yankee would never have insulted us by flying his flag in our faces! *We* would have opposed his landing except under a flag of truce; but the men let him alone, and he even found a poor Dutchman willing to show him the road!

He did not accomplish much; said a formal demand would be made next day, and asked if it was safe for the men to come ashore and buy a few necessaries, when he was assured the air of Baton Rouge was very unhealthy for Yankee soldiers at night. He promised very magnanimously not to shell us out if we did not molest him; but I notice none of them dare set their feet on *terra firma*, except the officer who has now called three times on the Mayor, and who is said to tremble visibly as he walks the streets.

Last evening came the demand: the town must be surrendered immediately; the Federal flag Must be raised; they would grant us the same terms they granted New Orleans. Jolly terms those were! The answer was worthy of a Southerner. It was, "The town was defenseless; if we had cannon, there were not men enough to resist; but if forty vessels lay at the landing,—it was intimated we were in their power, and more ships coming up,—we would not surrender; if they wanted, they might come and Take us; if they wished the Federal flag hoisted over the Arsenal, they might put it up for themselves, the town had no control over Government property." Glorious! What a pity they did not shell the town! But they are taking us at our word, and this morning they are landing at the Garrison.

"All devices, signs, and flags of the Confederacy shall be suppressed." So says Picayune Butler. *Good.* I devote all my red, white, and blue silk to the manufacture of Confederate flags. As soon as one is confiscated, I make another, until my ribbon is exhausted, when I will sport a duster emblazoned in high colors, "Hurra! for the Bonny blue flag!" Henceforth, I wear one pinned to my bosom—not as duster, but a little flag; the man who says take it off will have to pull it off for himself; the man who dare attempt it—well! a pistol in my pocket fills up the gap. I am capable, too. . . .

May 10th

Last night about one o'clock I was wakened and told that mother and Miriam had come. Oh, how glad I was! I tumbled out of bed

half asleep and hugged Miriam in a dream, but waked up when I
got to mother. They came up under a flag of truce, on a boat going
up for provisions, which, by the way, was brought to by half a dozen
Yankee ships in succession, with a threat to send a broadside into
her if she did not stop—the wretches knew it *must* be under a flag of
truce; no boats leave, except by special order to procure provisions.

What tales they had to tell! They were on the wharf, and saw the
ships sail up the river, saw the broadside fired into Will Pinckney's
regiment, the boats we fired, our gunboats, floating down to meet
them all wrapped in flames; twenty thousand bales of cotton blazing
in a single pile; molasses and sugar thrown over everything. They
stood there opposite to where one of the ships landed, expecting a
broadside, and resolute not to be shot in the back. I wish I had been
there! And Captain Huger[1] is not dead! They had hopes of his life
for the first time day before yesterday. Miriam saw the ball that had
just been extracted. He will probably be lame for the rest of his life.
It will be a glory to him. For even the Federal officers say that never
did they see so gallant a little ship, or one that fought so desperately
as the *McRae*. Men and officers fought like devils. Think of all those
great leviathans after the poor little "Widow Mickey"! One came
tearing down on her sideways, while the *Brooklyn* fired on her from
the other side, when brave Captain Warley[2] put the nose of the
Manassas under the first, and tilted her over so that the whole broadside passed, instead of through, the *McRae,* who spit back its poor
little fire at both. And after all was lost, she carried the wounded and
the prisoners to New Orleans, and was scuttled by her own men in
port. Glorious Captain Huger! Brave, dare-devil Captain Warley is
prisoner, and on the way to Fort Warren, that home of all brave,
patriotic men. We'll have him out. . . .

And this is WAR! Heaven save me from like scenes and experiences
again. I was wild with excitement last night when Miriam described
how the soldiers, marching to the depot, waved their hats to the
crowds of women and children, shouting, "God bless you, ladies! We
will fight for you!" and they, waving their handkerchiefs, sobbed
with one voice, "God bless you, Soldiers! Fight for us!"

We, too, have been having our fun. Early in the evening, four
more gunboats sailed up here. We saw them from the corner, three

[1] Thomas B. Huger, in command of the Confederate steamer *McRae,* was mortally
wounded by fire from the U. S. S. *Iroquois.*

[2] Alex F. Worley fought his Confederate ram *Manassas* until she was helpless, then
drove her into the swamp and abandoned her.

squares off, crowded with men even up in riggings. The American flag was flying from every peak. It was received in profound silence, by the hundreds gathered on the banks. I could hardly refrain from a groan. Much as I once loved that flag, I hate it now! I came back and made myself a Confederate flag about five inches long, slipped the staff in my belt, pinned the flag to my shoulder, and walked downtown, to the consternation of women and children, who expected something awful to follow. An old negro cried, "My young missus got her flag flyin,' anyhow!" Nettie[1] made one and hid it in the folds of her dress. But we were the only two who ventured. We went to the State House terrace, and took a good look at the *Brooklyn*[2] which was crowded with people, who took a good look at us, likewise. . . .

May 11th

I—I am disgusted with myself. Last evening, I went to Mrs. Brunot's,[1] without an idea of going beyond, with my flag flying again. They were all going to the State House, so I went with them; to my distress, some fifteen or twenty Federal officers were standing on the first terrace, stared at like wild beasts by the curious crowd. I had not expected to meet them, and felt a painful conviction that I was unnecessarily attracting attention, by an unladylike display of defiance, from the crowd gathered there. But what was I to do? I felt humiliated, conspicuous, everything that is painful and disagreeable; but—strike my colors in the face of the enemy? Never! Nettie and Sophie[1] had them, too, but that was no consolation for the shame I suffered by such a display so totally distasteful to me. How I wished myself away, and chafed at my folly, and hated myself for being there, and every one for seeing me. I hope it will be a lesson to me always to remember a lady can gain nothing by such display.

I was not ashamed of the flag of my country,—I proved that by never attempting to remove it in spite of my mortification,—but I was ashamed of my position; for these are evidently gentlemen, not the Billy Wilson's crew we were threatened with. Fine, noble-looking men they were, showing refinement and gentlemanly bearing in every motion. One cannot help but admire such foes! They come as visitors without either pretensions to superiority, or the insolence of con-

---

[1] Nettie, Sophie and Mrs. Brunot were neighbors.

[2] One of Farragut's frigates. Opposite the forts the *Manassas* had torn a great hole in her side.

querors; they walk quietly their way, offering no annoyance to the
citizens, though they themselves are stared at most unmercifully, and
pursued by crowds of ragged little boys, while even men gape at
them with open mouths. I came home wonderfully changed in all my
newly acquired sentiments, resolved never more to wound their feelings, who were so careful of ours, by such unnecessary display. And
I hung my flag on the parlor mantel, there to wave, if it will, in the
shades of private life; but to make a show, make me conspicuous and
ill at ease, as I was yesterday,—never again!

There was a dozen officers in church this morning, and the psalms
for the 11th day seemed so singularly appropriate to the feelings of
the people, that I felt uncomfortable for them. They answered with
us, though.

May 17th

Four days ago the Yankees left us, to attack Vicksburg, leaving
their flag flying in the Garrison without a man to guard it, and with
the understanding that the town would be held responsible for it. It
was intended for a trap; and it succeeded. For night before last, it
was pulled down and torn to pieces.

Now they will be back in a few days, and will execute their threat
of shelling the town. If they do, what will become of us? All we
expect in the way of earthly property is as yet mere paper, which will
be so much trash if the South is ruined, as it consists of debts due
father by many planters for professional services rendered, who, of
course, will be ruined, too, so all money is gone. That is nothing, we
will not be ashamed to earn our bread, so let it go.

But this house is at least a shelter from the weather, all sentiment
apart. And our servants, too; how could they manage without us?
The Yankees, on the river, and a band of guerrillas in the woods, are
equally anxious to precipitate a fight. Between the two fires, what
chance for us? They say the women and children must be removed,
these guerrillas. Where, please? Charlie says we must go to Greenwell.[1] And have this house pillaged? For Butler has decreed that no
unoccupied house shall be respected. If we stay through the battle,
if the Federals are victorious, we will suffer. It is in these small cities
that the greatest outrages are perpetrated. What are we to do?

A new proclamation from Butler has just come. Butler says,
whereas the so-called ladies of New Orleans insult his men and offi-

[1] The Morgans' summer cottage.

cers, he gives one and all permission to insult any or all who so treat them, then and there, with the assurance that the women will not receive the slightest protection from the Government, and that the men will all be justified. These men our brothers? Not mine! Come to my bosom, O my discarded carving-knife, laid aside under the impression that these men were gentlemen. . . .

May 21st

I have had such a search for shoes this week that I am disgusted with shopping. I am triumphant now, for after traversing the town in every direction and finding nothing, I finally discovered a pair of *boots* just made for a little negro to go fishing with, and only an inch and a half too long for me, besides being unbendable; but I seized them with avidity, and the little negro would have been outbid if I had not soon after discovered a pair more seemly, if not more serviceable, which I took without further difficulty. Behold my tender feet cased in crocodile skin, patent-leather tipped, low-quarter boy's shoes, No. 2! "What a fall was there, my country," from my pretty English glove-kid, to sabots made of some animal closely connected with the hippopotamus! *A dernier ressort, vraiment!* for my choice was that, or cooling my feet on the burning pavement *au naturel;* I who have such a terror of any one seeing my naked foot! And this is thanks to war and blockade! Not a decent shoe in the whole community! *N'importe!* "Better days are coming, we'll all"—have shoes —after a while—perhaps!

May 27th

The cry is "Ho! for Greenwell!" Very probably this day week will see us there. I don't want to go. If we were at peace, and were to spend a few months of the warmest season out there, none would be more eager and delighted than I; but to leave our comfortable home, and all it contains, for a rough pine cottage seventeen miles away even from this scanty civilization, is sad. It must be! We are hourly expecting two regiments of Yankees to occupy the Garrison, and some fifteen hundred of our men are awaiting them a little way off, so the fight seems inevitable. . . .

May 30th, Greenwell

After all our trials and tribulations, here we are at last, and no limbs lost! How many weeks ago was it since I wrote here? It seems very long after all these events; let me try to recall them.

Wednesday the 28th,—a day to be forever remembered,—as luck would have it, we rose very early, and had breakfast sooner than usual, it would seem for the express design of becoming famished before dinner. I was packing up my traveling-desk with all Harry's little articles that were left to me, and other things, and I was saying to myself that my affairs were in such confusion that if obliged to run unexpectedly I would not know what to save, when I heard Lilly's voice downstairs, crying as she ran in—she had been out shopping— "Mr. Castle has killed a Federal officer on a ship, and they are going to shell—" Bang! went a cannon at the word, and that was all our warning.

Mother had just come in, and was lying down, but sprang to her feet, and added her screams to the general confusion. Miriam, who had been searching the libraries, ran up to quiet her; Lilly gathered her children, crying hysterically all the time, and ran to the front door with them as they were; Lucy saved the baby, naked as she took her from her bath, only throwing a quilt over her. I bethought me of my "running-bag" which I had used on a former case, and in a moment my few precious articles were secured under my hoops, and with a sunbonnet on, I stood ready for anything.

The firing still continued; they must have fired half a dozen times before we could coax mother off. What awful screams! I had hoped never to hear them again, after Harry died. Charlie had gone to Greenwell before daybreak, to prepare the house, so we four women, with all those children and servants, were left to save ourselves. I did not forget my poor little Jimmy; I caught up his cage and ran down. Just at this moment mother recovered enough to insist on saving father's papers—which was impossible, as she had not an idea of where the important ones were. I heard Miriam plead, argue, insist, command her to run; Lilly shriek, and cry she should go; the children screaming within; women running by without, crying and moaning; but I could not join in. I was going I knew not where; it was impossible to take my bird, for even if I could carry him, he would starve. So I took him out of his cage, kissed his little yellow head, and tossed him up. He gave one feeble little chirp as if to ascertain where to go, and then for the first and last time I cried, laying my head against the gate-post, and with my eyes too dim to see him. Oh, how it hurt me to lose my little bird, one Jimmy had given me, too!

But the next minute we were all off, in safety. A square from home, I discovered that boy shoes were not the most comfortable things to run in, so I ran back, in spite of cannonading, entreaties, etc., to get another pair. I got home, found an old pair that were by no means respectable, which I seized without hesitation; and being perfectly at ease, thought it would be nice to save at least Miriam's and my tooth-brushes, so slipped them in my corsets. These in, of course we must have a comb—that was added—then how could we stand the sun without starch to cool our faces? This included the powder-bag; then I must save that beautiful lace collar; and my hair was tumbling down, so in went the tucking-comb and hair-pins with the rest. By this time, Miriam, alarmed for me, returned to find me, though urged by Dr. Castleton[1] not to risk her life by attempting it, and we started off together.

We had hardly gone a square when we decided to return a second time, and get at least a few articles for the children and ourselves, who had nothing except what we happened to have on when the shelling commenced. She picked up any little things and threw them to me, while I filled a pillow-case jerked from the bed, and placed my powder and brushes in it with the rest. Before we could leave, mother, alarmed for us both, came to find us, with Tiche.[2] All this time they had been shelling, but there was quite a lull when she got there, and she commenced picking up father's papers, vowing all the time she would not leave. Every argument we could use was of no avail, and we were desperate as to what course to pursue, when the shelling recommenced in a few minutes. Then mother recommenced her screaming and was ready to fly anywhere; and holding her box of papers, with a faint idea of saving something, she picked up two dirty underskirts and an old cloak.

As we stood in the door, four or five shells sailed over our heads at the same time, seeming to make a perfect corkscrew of the air,— for it sounded as though it went in circles. Miriam cried, "Never mind the door!" mother screamed anew, and I stayed behind to lock the door, with this new music in my ears. We reached the back gate, that was on the street, when another shell passed us, and Miriam jumped behind the fence for protection. We had only gone half a square when Dr. Castleton begged us to take another street, as they were firing up that one. We took his advice, but found our new street worse than the old, for the shells seemed to whistle their strange songs with redoubled vigor.

[1] A neighbor.
[2] Mrs. Morgan's maid, Catiche.

We were alone on the road,—all had run away before,—so I thought it was for our especial entertainment, this little affair. I cannot remember how long it lasted; I am positive that the clock struck ten before I left home, but I had been up so long, I know not what time it began, though I am told it was between eight and nine. We passed the graveyard, we did not even stop, and about a mile and a half from home, when mother was perfectly exhausted with fatigue and unable to proceed farther, we met a gentleman in a buggy who kindly took charge of her and our bundles. We could have walked miles beyond, then, for as soon as she was safe we felt as though a load had been removed from our shoulders; and after exhorting her not to be uneasy about us, and reminding her we had a pistol and a dagger, she drove off, and we trudged on alone, the only people in sight on foot, though occasionally carriages and buggies would pass, going towards town. One party of gentlemen put their heads out and one said, "There are Judge Morgan's daughters sitting by the road!" —but I observed he did not offer them the slightest assistance. . . .

While we were yet resting, we saw a cart coming, and, giving up all idea of our walking to Greenwell, called the people to stop. To our great delight, it proved to be a cart loaded with Mrs. Brunot's affairs, driven by two of her negroes, who kindly took us up with them, on the top of their luggage; and we drove off in state, as much pleased at riding in that novel place as though we were accustomed to ride in wheelbarrows. Miriam was in a hollow between a flour barrel and a mattress; and I at the end, astride, I am afraid, of a tremendous bundle, for my face was down the road and each foot resting very near the sides of the cart. These servants were good enough to lend us their umbrella, without which I am afraid we would have suffered severely, for the day was intensely warm.

Three miles from town we began to overtake the fugitives. Hundreds of women and children were walking along, some bareheaded, and in all costumes. Little girls of twelve and fourteen were wandering on alone. I called to one I knew, and asked where her mother was; she didn't know; she would walk on until she found out. It seems her mother lost a nursing baby too, which was not found until ten that night. White and black were all mixed together, and were as confidential as though related. All called to us and asked where we were going, and many we knew laughed at us for riding on a cart; but as they had walked only five miles, I imagined they would like even these poor accommodations if they were in their reach.

The negroes deserve the greatest praise for their conduct. Hundreds were walking with babies or bundles; ask them what they had saved, it was invariably, "My mistress's clothes, or silver, or baby." Ask what they had for themselves, it was, "Bless your heart, honey, I was glad to get away with mistress's things; I didn't think 'bout mine."

It was a heart-rending scene. Women searching for their babies along the road, where they had been lost; others sitting in the dust crying and wringing their hands.

Presently we came on a guerrilla camp. Men and horses were resting on each side of the road, some sick, some moving about carrying water to the women and children, and all looking like a monster barbecue, for as far as the eye could see through the woods, was the same repetition of men and horses. They would ask for the news, and one, drunk with excitement or whiskey, informed us that it was our own fault if we had saved nothing, the people must have been—— fools not to have known trouble would come before long, and that it was the fault of the men, who were aware of it, that the women were thus forced to fly. In vain we pleaded that there was no warning, no means of foreseeing this; he cried, "*You* are ruined; so am I; and my brothers, too! And by —— there is nothing left but to die now, and I'll die!" "Good!" I said. "But die fighting for us!" He waved his hand, black with powder, and shouted, "That I will!" after us.

Lucy[1] had met us before this; early in the action, Lilly had sent her back to get some baby-clothes, but a shell exploding within a few feet of her, she took alarm, and ran up another road, for three miles, when she cut across the plantations and regained the Greenwell route. It is fortunate that, without consultation, the thought of running here should have seized us all.

May 31st

I was interrupted so frequently yesterday that I know not how I continued to write so much. First, I was sent for, to go to Mrs. Brunot, who had just heard of her son's death, and who was alone with Dena.

To return to my journal.

Lucy met mother some long way ahead of us, whose conscience was already reproaching her for leaving us, and in answer to her "What has become of my poor girls?" ran down the road to find us,

[1] A servant.

for Lucy thinks the world can't keep on moving without us. When she met us, she walked by the cart and it was with difficulty we persuaded her to ride a mile; she said she felt "used" to walking now. About five miles from home, we overtook mother. All the talk by the roadside was of burning homes, houses knocked to pieces by balls, famine, murder, desolation; so I comforted myself singing, "Better days are coming" and "I hope to die shouting, the Lord will provide"; while Lucy toiled through the sun and dust, and answered with a chorus of "I'm a-runnin', a-runnin' up to glo-ry!"

IV

THEY CALLED THEM "GREAT DAYS"

May-September, 1862

Now in the face of danger the Confederate military genius was afire.

Stonewall Jackson and his incredible "foot cavalry" of some nineteen thousand men fought five battles, defeated four separate commands and marched nearly four hundred miles within a month. He defeated Milroy at McDowell on May 8; routed Banks's army at Front Royal on May 23—Belle Boyd helped there—defeated him again at Winchester on the twenty-fifth and drove him out of the Shenandoah Valley the next day; held off Frémont on June 8 at Cross Keys and repulsed Shields at Port Republic on the ninth. Now he held firmly all the upper Valley. On the twenty-first he could leave the scene to confer with General Lee near Richmond.

> "Ah! Maiden, wait and watch and yearn
>   For news of Stonewall's band!
> Ah! Widow, read, with eyes that burn,
>   That ring upon thy hand.
> Ah! Wife, sew on, pray on, hope on;
> Thy life shall not be all forlorn;
> The foe had better ne'er been born
>   That gets in "Stonewall's way."[1]

McClellan had pushed his campaign up the Peninsula until his advance could see the church spires and hear the church bells of Richmond. On May 31 and June 1 Joe Johnston struck him at Seven Pines, a clump of trees near Fair Oaks Station. On the second day of fierce struggle General Johnston was wounded, and Robert E. Lee was placed in command.

Lee's victories in the Seven Days' fighting, from June 26 at Mechanicsville to dark on July 1 at bloody Malvern Hill, raised the siege of Richmond. McClellan—a great organizer and always im-

---

[1] From "Stonewall Jackson's Way," by John Williamson Palmer (1825-1906). *The Home Book of Verse,* ed., Burton Egbert Stevenson. New York: Henry Holt and Company, 1912.

mensely popular with his men, but a timid offensive leader always overestimating the number of his foes—was forced back to the protection of his gunboats on the James.

The whole South rejoiced over the deliverance, except Lee who had not accomplished what he sought—the destruction of the enemy army; it was still intact, and mighty. The whole South rejoiced, but many women wept. The losses amounted to over 20,000, including 3,286 dead, whom the South could not afford to lose.

Then Lee's genius shone again. On the last days of summer, with valiant help from Stonewall Jackson and James Longstreet, he gave the boastful General John Pope, McClellan's successor, a grand licking at Second Manassas. But more than 7,200 Confederates were killed or wounded.

The early summer had seen the first of General J. E. B. ("Beauty") Stuart's cavalry raids around the entire Union army.

In the Central South it was mostly an affair of cavalry. John Hunt Morgan, another beau sabreur, *made his first Kentucky raid, with fights in July at Tompkinsville, Lebanon, Cynthiana and at Gallatin, Tennessee. The Ready family were breathlessly happy over his successes. Nathan Bedford Forrest, natural genius, master of skill and bluff, captured the Union garrison at their city of Murfreesboro on July 13, and rode on to scare the daylights out of the large Union garrison at Nashville.*

In the Mississippi Valley Beauregard skillfully evacuated his army from Corinth at the end of May and drew back to Tupelo. Braxton Bragg took over from the ailing Beauregard and, making Chattanooga his new base, assembled there a noble army. From Chattanooga he marched on August 28 to the invasion of Kentucky.

An attempt by General John C. Breckinridge to recapture Baton Rouge by land and river in early July failed—a fact of decided interest to Sarah Morgan.

The blockade continued its slowly strangling coils, while the diplomats of the Confederacy were seeking recognition by England and France.

1. CORNELIA PEAKE McDONALD—STONEWALL DEFEATS
BANKS AT WINCHESTER

In occupied Winchester Cornelia had had no news from her husband since he left home in March. She did not know that Stonewall

had opened his First Valley Campaign on May 4, defeated Banks at
Front Royal on the twenty-third and at Middletown and Newton on
the twenty-fourth, and was now rapidly driving the "huge mass of
blue" toward Winchester in confusion.

Winchester, May, 1862. May had come, and the trees were showing their young leaves, the lawn was a bright, vivid green, and the
flowers were all out in the garden, and but for marching troops, and
strains of martial music from the regimental bands, we might have
felt like ourselves again.

One rainy afternoon, I was looking from my chamber window at
the lovely fresh green of the grass and the dripping trees, and thinking how beautiful everything was, and how they seemed to rejoice at
the refreshing rain. Smooth as velvet was the turf, and neat and trim
the walks and drive.

As I stood by the window, the large gate opened and troop after
troop of cavalry entered and wound along through the cedars that
lined the drive. They did not keep to the drive, but went on over the
grass in any direction they saw fit to take. Fifteen hundred horsemen
rode into the grounds and dispersed themselves, tying their horses
to the trees and pouring out grain for them to eat. As I looked a
party tore off the light ornamental wooden railing on top of the
stone wall to kindle their fires. A crowd soon collected around the
house demanding admittance.

I told the servants to close every door and bolt it, and to answer
no knocks or calls, that no one must go to a door but myself. For
some time I took no notice of any knock or summons to open the
door, but at last the calls became so imperative, that I, fearing the
front door would be broken in, went and opened it. I only opened it
a very small space, but saw three men holding another up between
them, they requested permission to bring in a sick comrade. I suspected a trick and closed the door again. They retired, but soon
another party came, and more earnest and determined than the
other, as their man was hurt, and was their Captain. His horse had
fallen down a stone wall with him as he rode to the stables, and had
broken his leg. It was no use to refuse permission as I was sure they
would take it. So I had to open the door, and they brought him in
and laid him on a lounge in the dining room.

From that moment such confusion reigned that it was impossible
for me to do anything to stem the tide of those crowding in. The hall,

the rooms and even the kitchen was thronged. I tried to get into the kitchen to get some supper for the children, but had to give it up. So Mary and I took our little ones and went up stairs for the night, leaving the invaders possession of the lower floor.

The next morning I went down, determined at all hazards to have some breakfast for my family. My heart sunk as I beheld the scene that waited me down stairs. Mud, mud, mud—was everywhere, over, and on, and in everything. No colours were visible on the carpets, wet great coats hung dripping on every chair and great pools of water under them where they hung. I went to the hall door and looked out at the lawn. I would never have recognized it; a sea of deep mud had taken the place of the lovely green—horses and mules were feeding under the trees, many of which had been stripped of bark as far up as the animals could reach; wagons were tilted up with lazy men around them laughing and joking. I turned from the sight and went into the dining room where was a scene almost as irritating and wretched.

Stretched on a lounge, pale and ill, lay the man who had been hurt; the lounge was drawn close to the fire, and seated around were several more men who never moved or looked up at my entrance. One had hung his great coat on the back of a large rocking chair before the fire to dry, and another was scraping the mud from his boots over the handsome bright carpet, or what had been so the day before.

I knew it would not do to give them quiet possession, so I took the great coat, and threw it out on the back porch, turned the chair around and seated myself in it by the fire.

The men, upon this, got up one after the other and left the room.

After a moment's silence the man on the sofa spoke and attempted to express his regret at my being so incommoded; saying that after his own admittance he tried to keep the others out, but that he could do nothing with them as they did not belong to his own company.

After some days we become accustomed to the condition of things around us, and began to pick up a few crumbs of comfort in a state of existence that at first seemed unbearable. Pratt was still there, though his regiment had left. The surgeons said he ought not to be moved, and for fear he would be too comfortable, I would not give him a chamber up stairs, but still permitted him to occupy the lounge in the dining room.

He was therefore present at the family gathering around the fireside, and as our talk was unreserved, he acquired some knowledge of our feelings for Yankees in general, though he hoped we did not entertain the like kindly sentiments for him in particular. We gave him to understand, however, that though as a man we might show him kindness, as a Yankee we would feel it our duty to withhold from him our mercy, should an occasion arise when we had the opportunity so to do.

One morning in May, Pratt rode away to join his regiment. He took leave very politely, and hesitatingly offered me a crisp bank note. It had "United States" on it very conspicuously, as I could see at a glance, but I proudly ignored the note and the offer also, and merely shook hands with him.

The town was now emptied of troops, all having pushed on up the valley after Jackson, but in a few days a regiment from Maine, very fresh and clean, with perfect neatness displayed in all their appointments, occupied the town.

Comparative quiet reigned, and but for the separation from our friends and family, and the remembrance that those in the army were hourly surrounded by dreadful dangers we might have had some happiness. Our church, Christ's, was occupied by Yankee preachers, so we went to the Kent Street Presbyterian Church, where we could have the comfort of hearing God's word from the lips of a friend, and of knowing that every heart there joined in the prayers for the safety of our army, and the success of our cause, though their lips must be silent on that subject.

Of our army we knew nothing except what we could learn from the papers of our enemies, and they with exulting joy and great flourishing of trumpets published flaming accounts of the advance of their conquering hosts, and of our poor, ill-clad rabble, humbled, flying, disheartened, and in a short time to be wiped off the face of the earth.

But though sometimes our hearts sickened, they did not altogether fail for we believed in our people, and trusted in God to deliver us.

On the evening of May 22nd, 1862, a guard of soldiers from that triumphant army rode into town at a gallop.

Orders were hurriedly given, and preparations for something important set on foot. I had been in town on business and was hurrying home when I first saw the commotion. As I came up to Mr. Patrick Smith's house, an officer was dismounting at the gate. I do not know what prompted me to do it, but I stopped and asked him where Gen.

Banks was. He looked at me for a moment very angrily and suspiciously, but in a little while said that he was near the town and would be in that night. I never could imagine why he told me unless he thought I was a Union woman. His information was sufficient. I knew from it that they were retreating because they were beaten, and I went on home quietly, and slowly, with an air sad and subdued, but those I passed could see the triumph of my heart in my face and manner. I got home, whispered it to Mary, and quietly sat down to supper without a word of what I had heard to the boys and children.

Soldiers were constantly passing about near the house as if to observe what went on.

I sent all the children to bed early, put out the lights, and fastened the doors in the lower story, then took my seat up stairs by my chamber to await whatever might come. . . .

At dawn the next morning we were awakened by cannon close to the town.

Through the early morning hours the din of the musketry and cannon increased and came nearer and nearer. Federal troops were moving in all directions, some scudding over the hills toward a point opposite to the place where the battle raged.

Mr. Mason's house had been long occupied as headquarters by the Maine Regiment, and their camp was in the grounds. Those gallant fellows had fled early in the morning, leaving their breakfasts cooking on the stoves, savory dishes that the hungry rebels enjoyed greatly. Harry and Allan ran in to say that they could see our flag coming up from behind the hill to the south, from the top of the house, where they had posted themselves.

I could see from the front door the hill side covered with Federal troops, a long line of blue forms lying down just behind its crest, on the top of which just in their front a battery spouted flame at the lines which were slowly advancing to the top. Suddenly I saw a long even line of grey caps above the crest of the hill, then appeared the grey forms that wore them, with the battle flag floating over their heads! The cannon ceased suddenly, and as the crouching forms that had been lying behind the cannon rose to their feet they were greeted by a volley of musketry from their assailants that scattered them. Some fell where they had stood but the greatest number fled down the hill side to swell the stream of humanity that flowed through every street and by way, through gardens and over fences, toward the Martinsburg turnpike, a confused mob of trembling, fainting objects that kept on their mad flight till they were lost in the clouds of dust their hurrying feet had raised. Nothing could be distinguished, nothing but a huge moving mass of blue, rolling along like a cloud in the distance.

At different points the battle continued, and through the streets the hurrying masses still rushed. Occasionally a few would pause to fire at their pursuers, but all were making frantically for the one point of egress that was left open to them. Arms, accoutrements, clothes, everything was thrown away as they sped along, closely followed by their victorious foes, who never paused except to give a word or smile to the friends who were there to greet them.

I put on my bonnet and went in town, and the scenes I there witnessed I could not describe to do them justice. Old men and women, ladies and children, high and low, rich and poor, lined the streets. Some weeping or wringing their hands over the bodies of those who had fallen before their eyes, or those who were being brought in by soldiers from the edge of the town where the battle had been thickest, and others shouting for joy at the entrance of the victorious Stonewall Brigade, and exultation at the discomfiture of the flying enemy. All were embracing the precious privilege of saying what they chose, singing or shouting what they chose.

My husband did not come. He wrote saying that he was on duty in Richmond and could not leave then; but if our army held the lower valley he could come in a few weeks. . . .

2. CONSTANCE CARY—IN RICHMOND
DURING AND AFTER SEVEN PINES

Constance the Witty and the other young ladies of the threatened Confederate capital had no time for tableaux, private theatricals or any other form of gaiety as May ended and June began in 1862. These were grave days. While the Battle of Seven Pines, or Fair Oaks, was raging outside Richmond they prepared to receive the wounded and the dead.

And now we come to the 31st of May, 1862, when the eyes of the whole continent turned to Richmond. On that day General Joseph E. Johnston assaulted the portion of McClellan's troops which had been advanced to the south side of the Chickahominy, and had there been cut off from the main body of the army by the sudden rise of the river, occasioned by a tremendous thunder-storm. In face of recent reverses, we in Richmond had begun to feel like the prisoner of the Inquisition in Poe's story, cast into a dungeon with slowly contracting walls. With the sound of guns, therefore, in the direction of Seven Pines, every heart leaped as if deliverance were at hand. And yet there was no joy in the wild pulsation, since those to whom we looked for succor were our own flesh and blood, standing shoulder to shoulder to bar the way to a foe of superior numbers, abundantly provided as we were not with all the equipments of modern warfare, and backed by a mighty nation as determined as ourselves to win. Hardly a family in the town whose father, son, or brother was not part and parcel of the defending army.

When on the afternoon of the 31st it became known that the engagement had begun, the women of Richmond were still going about their daily vocations quietly, giving no sign of the inward anguish of apprehension. There was enough to do now in preparation for the wounded; yet, as events proved, all that was done was not enough by half. Night brought a lull in the cannonading. People lay down dressed upon their beds, but not to sleep, while their weary soldiers slept upon their arms. Early next morning the whole town was on the street. Ambulances, litters, carts, every vehicle that the city could produce, went and came with a ghastly burden; those who could walk limped painfully home, in some cases so black with gunpowder they passed unrecognized. Women with pallid faces flitted bareheaded through the streets, searching for their dead or wounded. The churches were thrown open, many people visiting them for a sad communion-service or brief time of prayer; the lecture-rooms of various places of worship were crowded with ladies volunteering to sew, as fast as fingers and machines could fly, the rough beds called for by the surgeons. Men too old or infirm to fight went on horseback or afoot to meet the returning ambulances, and in some cases served as escort to their own dying sons. By afternoon of the day following the battle, the streets were one vast hospital. To find shelter for the sufferers a number of unused buildings were thrown open.

I remember, especially, the St. Charles Hotel, a gloomy place, where two young girls went to look for a member of their family, reported wounded. We had tramped in vain over pavements burning with the intensity of the sun, from one scene of horror to another, until our feet and brains alike seemed about to serve us no further. The cool of those vast dreary rooms of the St. Charles was refreshing; but such a spectacle! Men in every stage of mutilation lying on the bare boards with perhaps a haversack or an army blanket beneath their heads,—some dying, all suffering keenly, while waiting their turn to be attended to. We passed from one to the other, making such slight additions to their comfort as were possible, while looking in every upturned face in dread to find the object of our search. The condition of things at this and other improvised hospitals was improved next day by the offerings from many churches of pew-cushions, which, sewn together, served as comfortable beds. To supply food for the hospitals the contents of larders all over town were emptied into baskets; while cellars long sealed and cobwebbed, belonging to old Virginia gentry who knew good Port and Madeira, were opened by the Ithuriel's spear of universal sympathy. There was not much going to bed that night, either. There was a summons to my mother about midnight. Two soldiers came to tell her of the wounding of one close of kin; but she was already on duty elsewhere, tireless and watchful as ever. Up to that time the younger girls had been regarded as superfluities in hospital service; but on Monday two of us found a couple of rooms where fifteen wounded men lay upon pallets around the floor, and, on offering our services to the surgeons in charge, were proud to have them accepted and to be installed as responsible nurses, under direction of an older and more experienced woman. The constant activity our work entailed was a relief from the strained excitement of life after the battle of Seven Pines. When the first flurry of distress was over, the residents of those pretty houses standing back in gardens full of roses set their cooks to work, or better still, went themselves into the kitchen to compound delicious messes for the wounded, after the appetizing old Virginia recipes. Flitting about the streets in the direction of the hospitals were smiling white-jacketed negroes, carrying silver trays with dishes of fine porcelain under napkins of thick white damask, containing soups, creams, jellies, thin biscuit, eggs à la crème, broiled chicken, etc., surmounted by clusters of freshly gathered flowers.

From one scene of death and suffering to another we passed during those days of June. Under a withering heat that made the hours preceding dawn the only ones of the twenty-four endurable in point of temperature, and a shower-bath the only form of diversion we had time or thought to indulge in, to go out-of-doors was sometimes worse than remaining in our wards.

Day after day we were called to our windows by the wailing dirge of a military band preceding a soldier's funeral. One could not number those sad pageants: the coffin crowned with cap and sword and gloves, the riderless horse following with empty boots fixed in the stirrups of an army saddle; such soldiers as could be spared from the front marching after with arms reversed and crape-enfolded banners; the passers-by standing with bare, bent heads. Funerals less honored outwardly were continually occurring. Then and thereafter the green hillsides of lovely Hollywood were frequently upturned to find resting-places for the heroic dead. So much taxed for time and attendants were the funeral officials, it was not unusual to perform the last rites for the departed at night. A solemn scene was that in the July moonlight, when, with the few who valued him most gathered around the grave, we laid to rest one of my own nearest kinsmen, about whom in the old service of the United States, as in that of the Confederacy, it was said, "He was a spotless knight."

During all this time President Davis was a familiar and picturesque figure on the streets, walking through the Capitol square from his residence to the executive office in the morning, not to return until late in the afternoon, or riding just before nightfall to visit one or another of the encampments near the city. He was tall, erect, slender, and of a dignified and soldierly bearing, with clear-cut and high-bred features, and of a demeanor of stately courtesy to all. He was clad always in Confederate gray cloth, and wore a soft felt hat with wide brim. Afoot, his step was brisk and firm; in the saddle he rode admirably and with a martial aspect. His early life had been spent in the Military Academy at West Point and upon the then northwestern frontier in the Black Hawk War, and he afterwards greatly distinguished himself at Monterey and Buena Vista in Mexico; at the time when we knew him, everything in his appearance and manner was suggestive of such a training. He was reported to feel quite out of place in the office of President, with executive and administrative duties, in the midst of such a war. General Lee always spoke of him as the best of military advisers; his own inclination was to be with the army, and at the first tidings of sound of a gun, anywhere within reach of Richmond, he was in the saddle and off for the spot—to the dismay of his staff-officers, who were expected to act as an escort on such occasions, and who never knew at what hour of the night or of the next day they should get back to bed or a meal.

When on the 27th of June the Seven Days' strife began, there was none of the excitement attending the battle of Seven Pines. People had shaken themselves down, as it were, to the grim reality of a fight that must be fought. "Let the war bleed, and let the mighty fall," was the spirit of their cry.

3. LUCY LOWE—"I WANT TO SEE YOU SO BAD"

Lucy Lowe, wife of John Lowe of Lowndes County, Alabama, gave four sons and a husband to the Confederacy. During their absence she managed the crops, fed and clothed the small children at home and prayed for her husband "nearly every breath she drew."

lounds County June 1 1862

Dier husban I know take my pen in hand drop you a few lines to let you no that we are all well as common and I am in about the same helth that I was when you left I hopes these lines may find you the same I received a leter from you the 29 of May and you sed that you had not got many leters from me yet I have sent you fore leters besides this one George has got home he got hear the end of May he is very lo yet the boys has come home to sea me on a furlow and stade 10 days they started back yestrday to the camp they dont no whare they wil git to from their they are station at arbon [Auburn] above Mongary [Montgomery] John my corn is out know and I have not drawed any thing yet but I hop I wil my crop is nice but pane hes quit and left my crop in bad fix but the neighbors ses they will help us you sed you wanted me to pray for you as for prayers I pray for you all of the time I pray for you nearly every breth I draw and I want you to pray for your self I have give the bys 13 dollars and I bought some 9 bushels of corn and that is all that I give him for his work and I have got 20 dolars yet George is very bad yet and he dont no whether he wil ever get able to go back the sargent give him furlo to stay at home til he was able to rejoin his company and he ses for you to try to get him a discharge from the head one for he never will be able to go back agane and I want you to get one if you can George ses that you can get one any time you want to Sister ses she wants to sea you and

kis you Your baby is the pertyest thing you ever saw in your life
She can walk by her self and your little gran son is perty as a pink
and growes the fastest in the world you must come home and sea
all of your babyes and kis them I have got the ry cut hook sent and
cut it for nothing Your old mare is gone blind in one eye and something is the matter with one of her fet so she cant hardly walk your
hogs and cows is coming on very wel I want you to come home for
I want to sea you so bad I dont no what to do I must come to a
close by saying I remane your loveing wif until deth You must write
to me as soon as you get this leter goodby to you

    Lucy lowe to John P. lowe

4. BETTY HERNDON MAURY—"JACKSON IS DOING GREAT THINGS"

Enemy occupation of Fredericksburg did not prevent Betty Maury from paying a brief visit to her husband beyond the lines. Neither did it prevent her mother from attending the twice-postponed wedding of Dick to Sue Crutchfield on July 17. Brother Dick had been wounded at the Battle of Seven Pines and later was again wounded and imprisoned.

Fredericksburg
Thursday June 12, 1862

Jackson is doing great things. He is somewhere between Winchester and Staunton. We got our information from the Yankee papers and they give a very subdued and confused account of things. Say that they were outnumbered five to one. Had to retire, etc. etc. And we interpret it that they were *well whipped*.

When the enemy first came to Fredericksburg we put all of our silver, including the New York service presented to Papa at Mr. Goolrick's, the English Vice Consul, that it might be under the protection of the British flag. Since our new military Governor came, the house has been searched and the flag and several boxes taken away. Fortunately ours escaped them. Nanny and I went there today, opened the box and smuggled the contents away under our shawls and in a basket. They were informed by a negro woman. The Governor! says that Mr. Goolrick is not an authorized Vice Consul.

Sun. June 22nd, 1862

The town is intensely Yankee and looks as though it never had been anything else. Yankee ice carts go about selling Yankee ice. Yankee newsboys cry Yankee papers along the streets. Yankee citizens and Yankee Dutchmen have opened all the stores on Main Street. Some of them have brought their families and look as if they had been born and bred here and intended to stay here until they died. One man has built him a house!

The different currencies are very confusing. A pair of shoes are worth so much in Specie, so much more in Yankee paper, and double their real value in Virginia money.

General Stuart made a most daring dash the other day with two thousand of our Cavalry. They passed *through the enemy lines to their* rear, burnt several loaded transports on the Pamunky and many loaded wagons, took many horses and mules and prisoners. We lost one man killed and two wounded and were gone between two and three days. They were greeted with shouts and cheers by the country people as they galloped along. One old woman rushed out to her gate and shouted out above all the clatter and din, "Hurrah, my Dixie boys, you drive the blue coated varmints away."

Wed. June 25th
At Mr. White's—twelve miles from
Fredericksburg

Monday afternoon Willie White came to our house to say that my dear husband was at his father's and he had come to take me out to him. In less than half an hour Nannie Belle and I were ready to start. When we had gotten about three miles from town we were overtaken by a party of Yankee cavalry that had pursued us to search for letters. They asked my name, where I came from and where I was going. And when I gave my word of honor that we had no letters or papers of any kind they allowed us to go on.

We were out in a dreadful storm and got wet through and through. Had to ford a river. The bridge had been burned by our army on its retreat. The descent to the river was perpendicular. It seems a miracle that we got down safely.

When we arrived I was much relieved to find that Will had gone to Uncle Jourdan Woolfolk's. Mr. White thought he would be running a risk to stay here all night and had persuaded him to go, promising that he would send me down the next day. But the storm of that night has caused such a freshet in the rivers that it will be impossible for us to go for several days yet. All the bridges have been destroyed and we can only cross by fording.

Sat. 28th June
Uncle Jourdan's

Here I am at last safe and sound with my dear husband. Oh! how thankful I am to be with him again once more. Had many difficulties and adventures in getting here. Left Mr. White's Thursday afternoon but when we reached the Matapony—a distance of seventeen miles we found that it was impossible to ford it. Willie White and I concluded that we would have to ask the hospitality of some people in the neighborhood for the night. Mr. Gravitt received us most kindly and hospitably. Found a party of gentlemen there who had been waiting for two days to cross the river. Spent a very pleasant day at Mr. Gravitts and forded the river in the afternoon in the Marylander's wagon. It was higher and safer than our buggy.

Will looks horrid in a dark calico shirt and a heavy beard.

Sunday June 29th

Will has shaved off the beard and looks handsome again. I do not object to the shirt.

Wednesday July 9th

Will has gone back to Richmond to that most disheartening of all occupations, waiting and waiting and trying to get something to do. But I will not complain so many blessings have been granted us lately. We have passed a happy, happy ten days together and ought to feel strengthened and elevated and ready for the work set before us.

Thursday July 10, 1862

Heard yesterday that Mamma and Sue are at Ridgeway. The old woman was determined not to be outdone by her daughters. Bless her heart. I should have liked to see her running the blockade. What a happy meeting they will all have up there. I suppose Dick was married yesterday evening.

July 29, 1862

My husband is thirty years old today. God grant him many happy returns.

Mon. Aug. 18, 1862

Hurrah for domestic manufactures, and a fig for the Yankees. We can do without them. Have just completed a hat of plaited wheat-straw for Mr. Maury. I made it every bit myself and it looks elegant. I've been hard at work on it for the last three days.

Sunday Aug. 31st, 1862

I've been deep in the mysteries of wool dying, spinning and weaving lately. Am trying to have the cloth made for a suit of winter clothes for Mr. Maury. Cousin Anne Morris said she would like to see Mother's shocked look when he makes his appearance in Washington in a homespun hat.

Aunt Betsy replied: "Well she ought n't to look shocked. She ought to think he has a jewel of a wife to be able to turn her hand to such things, when necessary."

5. AMIE KELLY—"what cannot be cured must be endured"

Amie Kelly was the mother of four small children and the wife of Samuel Camp Kelly who was fighting with the Army of Northern Virginia. The responsibility of their plantation in Calhoun County, Alabama, rested on her shoulders.

Calhoun County, Alabama
At home, July 8th, 1862

My dearest S.

. . . Bro. James has sold your corn. There were only 60¼ bu. He paid me yesterday at 1$ a bu. and I paid Stipes. . . . You say I must sell a mule if I am out of money. I had rather buy than sell. I have plenty of money so far, and keep getting a little along. What has become of your Mexican blanket? Have you lost it with your clothes? I should be sorry for you to lose it. I heard before that some of the Reg. were lousy. Is it the case? Do try to keep them off you. I would hate it so bad for you to get lousy. I heard this morning that you were elected Major. Is that so? I do not believe it. I had rather you were a good soldier than Major, there is not so much danger. We are listening for a fight at Chattanooga. Oh, may the God of Battles shield your precious self. How could I bear to hear that you had fallen and no one near to close your eyes or wipe the death damp from your brow. May God sustain us all and keep us in the way we should go. We are needing rain. The weather is dry and hot and I feel like it is for our sins that these things come upon us. Truly these are trying times and who will be able to stand. I will leave half of this sheet for you to write back on. I send it with Mother's. But for this cruel war you would be at home, but be a good soldier and maybe it will not be long till we can sit at home together. Write often, my dear one. Good bye. AMIE

At Home, July 17, 62

My dearest S.

. . . God grant to send us peace on honorable terms and that speedily! All the soldiers write that peace will soon be made. For my part I wish soon, but do not see anything to justify the conclusion, for England and France are both uncertain and Lincoln has called for 300,000 more troops. Bro. Smith was here day before yesterday. He looks badly and limps a little. He says we did not near whip the Yanks at Richmond, they are reinforcing for another fight. We heard that your Reg. was ordered to Richmond, but I did not believe it. . . . I am sorry you dislike your Captain, but it has turned out as I feared. He thinks he knows it all. . . . H. Steel will start back next Monday night. I do not knew whether to send your jeans pants and some shoes or send you the money and let you buy for yourself. I could send the money easier than the things unless you are on the railroad. I wish it were so I could come and see you or you me! I do want to see you so bad I can scarcely bear it, but what cannot be cured must be endured and I will have to wait, as bad as I hate to. The boys are done plowing and the corn looks better than other corn in the neighborhood. We had roasting ears day before yesterday that we got out of the garden. We have a big peach pie every day and how I do wish my dearest had some. I never sit down to eat but I think of you and wish you were here to help us enjoy what we have. . . .

The ambulances and wagons of Van Dorn's[1] army passed this week going to Chattanooga. They had some of the finest mules I ever saw. There were not many men with them. They went by Atlanta. They looked stout and rough, the Yanks may run when they get after them. There is no news now. All quiet at R. and I am afraid the next

---

[1] Generals Earl Van Dorn and Sterling Price had brought the Army of the West across the Mississippi to Beauregard's concentration after Shiloh.

big fight will be in Tennessee, and you will be in it. I have not got any wool yet and will have to pay 75 cents in the dirt when I do, which is rather tough. I sent you some paper and envelops this morning by Griffin and will send this by B. Pike tonight, and will write again by H. S. next Monday, if I can. You say you have a notion of having 2 teeth pulled but thought you would consult me. I would dislike to have them pulled unless they ached. Could you have them plugged and save them? . . .

I like the plan of your writing back on my letters, particularly when written with ink but when written with pencil, it is hard to make out. Sometimes I think you improve in writing very much. Go on improving and you will make your mark some day. May God help you so to live that you will not be ashamed in a coming day. I want you to be a meek follower of the Savior and a useful one too to your fellow men. I would not do all the work and not study any. I would let the Capt. do his part. May God direct you and keep you from harm.

Amie

6. ELIZABETH McGAVOCK HARDING—"i am proud to be your wife"

The Belle Meade plantation near Nashville was famous throughout the South for its hospitality, its fine blooded horses and its many servants. Its mistress, the wife of General William G. Harding, was a woman of beauty and charm, a great lady who put honor first.

General Harding was arrested after the occupation of Nashville for refusing to take the demanded oath of allegiance. He was then fifty-four years old. He was sent to Fort Mackinaw in northern Michigan and imprisoned till 1866. Meanwhile Mrs. Harding ran the plantation with the help of the overseer, Mr. Hague. Having bravely and steadfastly done her full duty, she died soon after her husband's return.

Her letters to him in the summer of 1862 give a vivid picture of life in Nashville under Yankee possession, and at Belle Meade, with all its problems. She was forty-four, the mother of two daughters, Mary Elizabeth and Selene.

Belle Meade, Thursday, July 17th, 1862

My Dearest Husband,

I wrote you on Sunday last, stating the facts in regard to a skirmish that occurred during the day in Murfreesboro[1]; on Monday I went in, and prevailed on your Father to leave the City, at least until the excitement subsided, and intend using my best efforts to get him to stay here, during my absence. . . .

His health is very good. He looks more robust than in the spring, and if you were only at home, would be perfectly content and happy. I cannot tell you how often he repeats the question, "Daughter, when do you think William will be at home?" and what benefit to the Union cause in Tenn. to be gained by his incarceration in a distant prison, the *policy* is *bad,* and will never result in any good. I am not able to answer either question satisfactorily, but as regards the first, I hope the autumn will find you in the enjoyment of home, and the inestimable blessing of liberty. Surely you will not be overlooked, when a general exchange of prisoners is made. We have political or state prisoners, who are expecting an exchange, and it seems very unjust they should be denied the same consideration accorded prisoners of war; I cannot think it will be so, and many friends agree with me in opinion.

I told you in several preceeding letters, I should leave, probably the 22nd, (next Tuesday) and am still determined to go, if possible, but the whole country is in a state of excitement, particularly between this place and Louisville; the trains have been stopped several times this week, and forced to return, each way, after securing the persons, or property desired. John Morgan[2] has created all the disturbance in Ky. so the "Journal" says, and Colonel Forrest commanded at Murfreesboro. To show the state of excitement here, *among certain persons*, on Monday last, John Trimble, Gov. Campbell,[3] Jordan Stokes and brother, and several others of the same stamp, took the train for Louisville, all having sudden pressing business to transact, not known of on Saturday. They passed through safe, as I

[1] Colonel N. B. Forrest captured Murfreesboro and its Union garrison on July thirteenth. He was commissioned brigadier-general on the twenty-first.

[2] Colonel J. H. Morgan was on his first raid in Kentucky, with fights at Tompkinsville on the ninth, Lebanon on the twelfth, and Cynthiana on the seventeenth.

[3] William Bowen Campbell, elected in 1851, was the last Whig governor of Tennessee. He strenuously opposed secession and was the most distinguished of those in Middle Tennessee who remained Unionists. For a brief period he held a brigadier-generalship in the Union Army.

saw their names in the list of arrivals in Louisville, en route to New York. What do you think of it?

When Gov. J.[1] heard of Gov. C's. hasty exit, he became furious, and remarked, "Gov. C. has just applied for a Brigadiership, at his solicitation I backed him, now at the first approach of danger he deserts his post. I consider his action indefensible and open to the charge of cowardice." Pretty plain spoken for a politician, was it not? I think he prides himself in his candor and blunt mode of speaking, but tis said he was greatly excited at the time. Gen. [Wm.] Nelson and his brigade of five hundred men arrived here from Huntsville night before last, and today left for Murfreesboro. Forrest took two thousand prisoners, fifty wagons, and numerous stores and arms, so the papers say; paroled upwards of nineteen hundred privates, and sent the officers to Chattanooga, among them two Generals, Crittenden and Duffield,[2] of Indiana.

You can understand now why it may not be possible for me to get off the day appointed, though I will strive to do so. I have concluded to take Mr. Hague for an escort, as Brother John finds it impossible to leave home. . . .

If anything occurs to prevent my going at the appointed time, I will write, every few days, until I do start. Farewell, my beloved; I trust we will meet *very soon.*

Your loving wife,
E.

Belle Meade, July 24th, 1862

My Dearest Husband;

I hoped ere this to have been on my road to Mackinaw, but events have transpired *immediately around us,* of a nature to stop all regular communication between this and Louisville. I wrote you on Sunday last to say that we could start on the 22nd as appointed, as Mr. Hague went in town Saturday on some business, and was told to report himself at the Provost's office Tuesday, the very day we were to have started. Of course I had no fears of *his* detention *long,* but it prevented our starting that day, and it was well, for the cars were taken above Gallatin by Forrests or Starnes[3] Cavalry, and the

---

[1] Andrew Johnson, Military Governor of Tennessee.

[2] The Union force at Murfreesboro was under command of General T. T. Crittenden of Indiana. Duffield was colonel of the 9th Michigan.

[3] Colonel John W. Starnes.

passengers forced to return; on the same day ninety-three federal pickets were taken prisoners eight miles from Nashville on the Murfreesboro Pike, and two bridges destroyed on the railroad, thus cutting off communication between Nelson's brigade at Murfreesboro and this place.

Immediate preparations were made to defend Nashville (from some of her own sons) by the Federal forces; cannon planted on Capitol hill; at the mouths of all the streets, and on College hill; some of the principal streets, leading in the direction of Murfreesboro and Lebanon, were barricaded by wagons chained together, and the cannon placed behind them, rendering it perfectly impossible to get in, or out.

Our road too was blocked at the depot in the same manner, and the Charlotte Pike was the only unobstructed passway in this direction, though the cannon on Capitol hill perfectly commanded it; in short, the preparations made proved they expected an attack, and were determined to resist it; some threats were made by the federals to burn the city, though it was understood to be Gen. Buell's order, if they could not hold it, to surrender, as we had done to them; in answer, it is said, Gov. Johnson remarked "No, we will defend it to the last extremity, and if defeated, leave it in a heap of smouldering ruins, not one stone shall remain to mark the spot where our proud Capitol now stands." Whether he said it, or intends carrying out his threat, it is certain he and Gen. Buell do not get on well, as is evidenced by Gov. J's wish to get rid of Gen. B. in Tenn; his popularity here did not please the Gov.

It is certain the officers here, belonging to Buell's staff, do not harmonize at all with the Gov. They all disapprove of the arrests made in direct violation of Gen. Buell's promise, yours among the number and *particularly;* and a gentleman, a Union man, told me, if Buell had been here, he would not have permitted your removal from Tenn. nor indeed your arrest at all, after the assurances given you; if this be so, oh how I wish he had never left, or had the power to rescind Gov. J's. decrees.

It is said, and believed here, Gen. Buell is falling back on Nashville, as his supplies are cut off near Chattanooga; Lebanon is in the hands of the Confederates, and day before yesterday a picnic party went to the "Hermitage" and there met with a large body of Forrest's men, who escorted them back to Mount Olivet, taking sixteen Federal pickets on the way, paroled them, and sent them in with the pleasure party. Yesterday Gov. J. had the gentlemen of the company up, to know if they were aware, beforehand, who they would meet, but as some good unionists happened to be among the numbers, and they affirmed their utter ignorance of the proximity of Forrest, he let them off, with a lecture about being found in *bad company*.

You can see from what I have written, we are almost surrounded by the Confederates, and yet, I do not think they seriously intend to attack Nashville now; if so, they could have taken it easily last Thursday, as the federal force was then small and inadequate to hold the city, and a perfect panic prevailed, as news of the approach of the cavalry with artillery was brought in by the pickets, on the Murfreesboro and Lebanon Pikes, to stop the artillery. They left town about five o'clock, had a skirmish in front of Mr. Weaver's residence, near the Asylum, and near Mill Creek Bridge, on the Lebanon Road; they did not succeed in burning either bridge, and came in next morning, paroled by *Forrest*.

The soldiers in Nashville slept on their arms Monday and Tuesday nights, but yesterday reinforcements arrived from Huntsville, and they breathe more freely; I assure you, *we* are made to suffer for all these alarms.—I mean in a petty way.—For instance, on Tuesday morning last, I went in town, not knowing the state of excitement pervading the whole community, to bring Father Harding out, and to see Gov. J. in regard to your being paroled to stay with me at the Hotel, while in Mackinaw; when I arrived on "Capitol Hill" the formidable preparations for war alarmed me, and I determined to write to, instead of seeing Gov. Johnson; did so, he sent word to call at five o'clock, and the *letter* would be *ready*. I sent Miles for the letter at five, and he told him to come in the morning, as he had been too busy to attend to the letter.

Just as I was starting home, Cousin Frank and Amanda Cheatham drove up, both looking much excited and informed me they had been turned back from Cockrill's Spring, because they refused to take the "oath," though they had a "pass" signed by the Provost Marshal; the pickets had not acted so before, and we began to suspect *the new order* was designed to catch all unwary country men then in town. Cousin F. determined to remain all night, and as Mr. Cheatham was in town to take care of Amanda, I hurried on, not dreaming of being stopped, as the children only were with me; as we passed Elliston's, Joe hailed the carriage, and said we could not pass, as Mrs. John Williams had just been turned back, with no gentlemen in, only a small son, and begged we would stay all night with them. I had left Sister entirely alone, of course could not; as we neared the spring, one stood in the middle of the road, and called to Miles to halt; an inferior officer of Johnson's precious body guard stepped up, took the "Pass" from Miles and remarked to me, "I suppose you have read the oath, on the back of this pass, Madam." I replied, "I have, Sir." "Have you any objection to taking this oath." "I have most decidedly." "Pray, what objections?" "They are numerous, and insuperable, Sir, but why do you ask? My pass is correct, and renewed a few days since?" He replied, "My orders are to let no one through, unless they take the oath, or have taken it." I asked him why he did not inform people of that as they went in the city; because he had no orders to that effect, beside they were surrounded with dangers, and must be very strict with both women and men. Just then Miles spoke up and said "I showed Gov. Johnson my pass this evening, and asked him if it would take us home, and he said Yes." The man looked at me earnestly for a moment, and said "Madam, if you will give me your word you will not give any information to any Confederate Cavalry that may visit your house, tonight or tomorrow, detrimental to us?" "I will certainly promise *that,* as I have no information to give." He then called on Selene, to know if she promised also, she answered very coldly, "I know nothing to communicate," then, Mary's turn came; the answer was quite as brief, and we were then permitted to pass; but if Miles had not mentioned the "all powerful name" we would have been turned back, as *every other* was. I knew nothing of his application till just before we left town, he told me not to be uneasy, as "his pass was good sure." I asked why, and he told me Gov. J. had approved it.

Next morning early, I sent in for the promised letter; the servant waited one—two hours, at last the servant that waits on him confessed he was not up, and he did not know what hour he would, as he *sat up late* the night before. The truth is, he was afraid to lie down, lest the rebels should catch him napping. When he did rise, he sent the servant to the Capitol, saying his secretary would give him the letter; he did so, and when I opened the unsealed envelope, it contained the *self same complimentary* letter of introduction to the "Officer Commanding the Post" I referred to in several of my previous letters.

What a bitter *disappointment* it was to me, you can well imagine, after promising so much, and I am at a loss to determine whether he intended it, or, in the excitement of the preceeding twenty-four hours it was entirely overlooked; but why not say so, and ask me to call, or send again, instead of enclosing a formal note, "hoping the enclosed will be satisfactory"? "Put not your faith in Princes" sayeth the Bible, but I have almost lost faith in all politicians & Union Governors.

I *will* go to see you *yet,* and tell you what he said to me, when I asked him why you were in a distant prison, and Gov. at liberty to enjoy *home* and *freedom;* his answer made my heart thrill with pride for my husband. Yes, I was proud to be your wife, the loved one of that noble heart,—but I must reserve this until we meet, and it will not be long, I trust, but I must wait patiently until the times are more settled.

One danger I have not hinted at, and that is, John,[1] from going back and forth, as he will be compelled to do, and to get permits, runs the risk of being required to take the —— what he does not wish or intend to do, Since the excitement commenced he has remained close at home, and as yet has not been molested. Well my eighth page is nearly full, and I have said nothing about home affairs. Ask Capt. Wormer to excuse my *war details,* but I have told nothing the newspapers have not published, therefore tis not contraband. . . .

Farewell my darling husband,
E.

Belle Meade, Sunday morning, July 27th

My dearest,

I cannot resist slipping in a little scrap to give you a faint idea of the present state of affairs and account for my detention; Mr. Hague was refused a pass to come home yesterday, unless he took the oath; and David[2] was arrested late last evening, to report at ten o'clock this morning; we fear John's arrest every hour, and tis said they will give no more passes to come and go, unless the person takes "the oath," or is a union man. If I leave *now,* John will be compelled to stay part of his time at home, as it *requires his presence more than usual;* he cannot do so, even if he is not arrested, without a pass,—

[1] John McGavock, Mrs. Harding's older brother, who inherited Cairnton, her birthplace.
[2] David Turner McGavock, a first cousin.

and then the troops here daily look for Forrest or Starnes to turn up near the city, consequently the reins are tightened with us all.

Tis said the renowned Bull Nelson intends calling on the people of Davidson County to furnish one thousand negroes to work upon fortification *here,* and the newspaper called the "Union," edited by a man named Mercer from Ky., advocated it strongly and *urges* that the negroes shall subsist, while so employed, on the secessionists around. . . . All the regular army officers, almost without an exception, disapprove this, and are the most conservative men we have among us, but our Governor, I fear, will use his influence against us. . . .

Oh, how this state of uncertainty worries me, but the hardest of all to bear is the thought of your *disappointment,* after looking for me to say when I can start, and I fear I cannot be spared long from our dear old home; but let it be long or short, I will assuredly go to see you *if I can,*—but until we know whether John is to be arrested, I cannot leave; if he is not to be taken up, we will know it in a few days.

. . . If you should fail to hear frequently from home, do not be uneasy, as the mails are, and have been, interrupted in *both* Ky. and Tenn.

Your Father is in usual health now, had a little spell this week of a few hours duration, caused by eating too much fruit, but has perfectly recovered. All the rest in usual health. Farewell, my beloved husband, that we may meet soon is my intense desire and prayer.

Yours,

E.

Belle Meade, August 5th, 1862

My Beloved Husband,

Again I sit down to chronicle another disappointment about leaving here, after writing you on Sunday last that we would certainly start Thursday, 7th. In your last letter to John (the last recd.) you said you appreciated the slight manner in which he referred to the causes of my detention, and other troubles, but would prefer the *whole facts,* even if it increased your anxiety in regard to us. It is useless for me to dwell on the pain these repeated disappointments give me, but I feel it on your account so much more keenly than my own, for I know you are looking every day to see us, but my dearest,

I strive to act as *you* would advise me, if cognizant of the situation of affairs at the present time.

You know, John had consented to stay at Belle Meade until my return, and go back and forth home; unfortunately he has had a good deal of trouble of late about keeping his servants away from town, the camps, and running about generally; of course his presence is required often, and he expected to go up two or three times a week; in order to do so, of course a "pass" is requisite; within the last few days this is denied, unless the person asking one goes up and proves his loyalty by taking the oath.

This deters hundreds from leaving home, and if that were *all*, it could be borne patiently, but arrests *at home* are of hourly occurrence, and they are hurried off immediately, without a hearing, not to the prison, but out of the state, and to a northern place of confinement. *All the ministers,* except Dr. Sehon, are at Jeffersonville, Ind., in the state prison, and the Dr. leaves tomorrow, accompanied by your old friend Jo Edwards, and thirty other prominent citizens from Sumner [County], living near Saunderville. Col. Watson is another you know, and probably all, but I cannot give the list; if you can procure a "Louisville Journal," that will inform you.

I looked for John and family this evening, but rec'd. a note only, begging me not to start *just yet,* and giving the reasons mentioned. . . . It is the intention of Gov. Johnson to get up about one thousand horses in this county for the cavalry, batallion of Col. Jordan Stokes, and in requiring persons to furnish their quota, the men sent wish to choose the horses themselves. David feels very solicitous about your blooded stock, as he well may, and begs me to defer my departure for a time, until this matter be settled, as well as a probable call on us to furnish hands to work on fortifications to be commenced here soon.

I think it is my duty to heed their advice, but, oh my husband, how my heart yearns to be with you, if only for a short time. . . .

I went to Gov. Johnson this day, to get a protection for the place until my return, he promised to send me tomorrow a paper worded somewhat in this wise, *as I understood him,* "No person shall molest or take anything away from Gen. H's plantation, without first coming to me." What this will be worth, I cannot tell. I represented to him how unprotected the place was, and that you had valuable and favorite horses, unfit for cavalry purposes, and yet I feared were in danger. He said when persons were called on to furnish horses, certificates would be given attesting their value, to be paid at a *"proper time."* I told him your blooded animals were all too valuable to be used for such purposes, and I hoped he would not permit to be molested in my absence.

He asked how long I wished to stay, I replied, "Until my husband returns with me," he smiled, shook his head, and asked me if I knew Col. Guild was coming home? I was never more surprised and scarcely knew how to believe it, yet he assured me it was so; it is spoken of on the streets as a hoax, and few persons credit it.

Have you heard anything of political prisoners being exchanged? I heard the Louisville Journal contained a paragraph, saying, they too, would be, very soon. God grant it may be so.

It is growing very late, and I must close, with the assurance I will do all in my power to insure the safety of your *favorites,* and hope my next will tell you certainly when to expect us. All the family in usual health. Every servant wants to send a present by me, and wish to be remembered. . . .

> Farewell,
>   Your loving wife.

Belle Meade, August 29th, 1862

My Dearest Husband,

For seventeen days we have not received a through mail from Louisville; of course, our letters to you cannot reach you, nor can we hear from you. For six weeks I have expected to visit you. . . . I have at last abandoned the idea, and as Gov. Johnson seems willing to parole you, that you may come home and judge for yourself in regard to the present state of affairs, I deem it best to send Mr. Hague with the parole, as it is impossible to communicate with you by mail.

You know, my dear husband, I would never have applied to Gov. J. to parole you, if in my own judgement your acceptance of it could compromise your honor, dearer to you and myself then life itself; but I have consulted with many of your dearest friends, and they all agree with me in thinking you should accept, come home and examine the condition of things, with the distinct understanding that you are at liberty to surrender it, when you see fit, and place yourself in the same position you occupy at present.

I tried hard to procure your release on your simple bond, with security, but Gov. J. said no such paroles were given, and the one sent only bound you so long as you kept it in possession. I endeavored to procure the release of your companions on the same terms, but failed, though I think *their friends* could do if they were to make application.

I understand, through a not perfectly reliable source, that *our* and every one else's negroes about here, that are now working on the fortifications, are to be sent to Cairo to work there. When our men were pressed, the understanding was they should not be sent out of the county. The runaways are the negroes to send, and not those who have staid at home and behaved themselves, as *all ours* have done. . . .

But all this is of small importance to the object of Mr. H's mission, and only speak of it to show what little control we have of our property, and it is no better as regards *all* other kinds. Gov. Johnson told me to write you plainly, so that you might have a correct idea of the state of things, as they now exist, and I have told both Randall [1] and Sister to do so.

If you conclude to come home (I pray God you may), you had best purchase your winter clothing either in Canada or some of the northern cities. Almost nothing can be procured here, and what there is, at enormous prices. Mr. Hague has a little list of things I want that cannot be procured here at all. If you decide *not to come,* I can only say I will do all in my power to take your place, as I have done, but I am feeble substitute for you, though I believe your place has suffered less than if you had been here. My unprotected position, as well as the knowledge of your imprisonment, have prevented some encroachments made upon others.

Mr. Hague is waiting to start, and I must close. May God direct you, *but I say come.*

Yours ever,
E.

7. LUCY SMITH—"we appeal to you as our friend"

The son of Mrs. Smith of Oak Hill, Georgia, had recently been killed while fighting under General Magruder before Richmond in the Seven Days' battles. On behalf of all bereaved mothers, she wrote

---

[1] Randall M. Southall, Mrs. Harding's nephew.

a letter of protest to the officials of the Confederate government in Richmond—criticizing the Conscription Act passed by the Confederate Congress on April 21, 1862, and the conduct of Confederate generals and surgeons.

John Bankhead Magruder, of Virginia, was a colonel when he turned back the Federals at Big Bethel. He became a major-general in October 1861. "Prince John" had been most energetic in building defenses against McClellan's advance. On June 29 he attacked gallantly at Allen's Farm and at Savage Station. Of Malvern Hill on July 1, where he marched on the wrong road, General D. H. Hill said, "I never saw anything more grandly heroic than the advance of the nine brigades under Magruder's orders. Unfortunately they did not move together, and were beaten in detail." The carnage was awful.

Mrs. Smith is not an elegant writer, but there is no mistaking her meaning.

Oak Hill, [Georgia]
August the 20 [1862]

To President Davis, Ex President Alex H. Stephens and the
War department

Dear Sirs   We appeal to you as our friend   Please read pardon and consider and act accordingly   It is with great emotion that we women of the Southern Confederacy and striving to maintain ourselves as patriotic mothers are almost driven to subjugation and almost preferring the tyranny of Lincoln to the tantalizing inhumane treatment to our soldiers by our head leading Generals and regimental surgeons   We have born it long and silently with all the fortitude we could hoping that they would certainly amend after awhile what we speak of is the tyranny of our generals and surgeons. Look at Magruder when he ordered my poor sons charge when they knew it was death inevitable under the circumstances but he [was] so drunk [he] dident have no care as is the case with the drunk but cursed them and ordered again which proved a failure of accomplishing anything but dreadful slaughter on one side in which my poor child fell   the name of Butler is more agreeable in this bereaved neighborhood than Magruder   Butler never drove out our sons head long into a slaughter pen   Magruder did it and it is the case with the most of our big generals to gallop off to the hospitals to drink up the wines that are sent in for the sick   now dont we have great encouragement to contribute to the sick when [they] rarely if ever get sight of the dainties that are sent them tell us what is more despotic and more disgusting when they write to us mother wife or sister you said you sent us jellies fruit and so forth but we never saw any of it the head ones eats the dainties sent to the sick themselves all that is overbearing enough but next comes something still worse the conscript now we have no objections to the conscript and think it a blessed thing to take some of the stout cowards or lazy men but here is the point they say all under and over such an age none excepted all to report themselves well now here and there is a man that has a big lingering disease which the least exposure will kill still he must go out when he could hardly keep up at home with all the attention of a wife and not half his time able to cut his own firewood still he was a great help to that wife who took all the hardships on herself to prolong her husbands life to aid her in raising her little family Still the conscript (for all it says able boddied men) takes him along the surgeon merely thumps his breast and grasp his arm tells him he has a good mussle wishes he had a regiment like him and sends him on through then he must travel day and night perhaps on open cars take the rain night air and heat of the sun as it comes without a place hardly to sit down for 3 and 4 or 5 days at a time then when he lands to walk perhaps 10 or 12 miles a thing which his constitution never could bear then camp out without even a tent let the weather be as it may now the loss of sleep the fatigue of traveling the damp night are all unaccustomed and diseased lungs or liver to contend with who could stand it you will admit none but stout sound men no they dont stand it we hear directly they are sick next news they are dead but a trifle over there but it is a serious damage to us here is a little group of children a broken hearted mother to maintain and raise now as little as you may make of this that is the case in these parts no less than 10 of our neighbor men taken off by conscript failing to get a discharge when we all knew that the poorest surgeon in the world could tell they were infirm men by the complexion if nothing else are burried over at Richmond after having been there only 3 weeks 10 widows in one neighborhood made so in the course of 3 weeks when apt as not if the surgeon had rightfully examined them he would have known they couldnt of stood it if he had of discharged them and let them return home they perhaps would have lived to raised their families by being prudent that is the main thing we say conscript and take all the able boddied men but let the infirm remain if you want to abate the distress among the women and children   these lines can be vouched for   Our Surgeons are savage   unprincipled men   especially in Atlanta   they regard not ours as their interest   and tell me what use is a man lying on a couch in a hospital to the government when he carried the disease with him there   do you expect to have a new man made out of him why not let him remain where there is room for him

A patriotic mother and wife

LUCY SMITH

8. SARAH MORGAN—"GONE WAS MY SMALL PARADISE!"

When things in Baton Rouge quieted down, the Morgans moved back home. Acting on General Earl Van Dorn's proclamation of July 10, advising all persons within eight miles of the Mississippi to withdraw into the interior, they fled for the second time. Sarah, her mother and her sister Miriam found temporary refuge on near-by plantations. Mr. LaRoue established sister Lilly and their five small children in Clinton, Louisiana. Sarah listened to the guns when General John C. Breckinridge made an unsuccessful attempt to re-capture Baton Rouge on August 5. She was then on Dr. Nolan's plantation some seven miles to the east of the city. Enemy shells drove them to Randallson's Landing and to Linwood, the home of General A. G. Carter, whose daughter Lydia had married Thomas Gibbes Morgan, Jr. When she heard reports of property destruction and pillage in Baton Rouge, Sarah wrote on August 20, "I am deter-mined to see my home. . . . I'll not cry." Instead she laughed—but there was bitterness in her laughter.

Illness and near starvation were to drive the Morgan family to the protection of Unionist Judge Philip Morgan in New Orleans. Sarah unwillingly took the oath of allegiance, comforting herself with the thought that "a forced oath is not binding."

After the war Sarah married a young Englishman in South Caro-lina, Francis Warrington Dawson, who had run the blockade to give his service to the Confederacy. Until his death in 1889 he was the brilliant and influential editor of the Charleston News and Courier. Sarah died in Paris in 1912, survived by a son, Warrington.

She wrote the last entry in her dairy on June 15, 1865. It was never intended for publication. Indeed, Sarah had directed that it be

burned, but at her son's plea it escaped oblivion. The year after her death it was issued under the title A Confederate Girl's Dairy.

[Linwood] *August 28th.* [1862]

I am satisfied. I have seen my home again. Tuesday I was up at sunrise, and my few preparations were soon completed, and before any one was awake, I walked over to Mr. Elder's, through mud and dew, to meet Charlie. He was very much opposed to my going; and for some time I was afraid he would force me to remain; but at last he consented, and with wet feet and without a particle of breakfast, I at length found myself in the buggy on the road home. . . . Four miles from town we stopped at Mrs. Brown's to see mother, and after a few moments' talk, went on our road.

I saw the first Yankee camp that Will Pinckney and Colonel Bird had set fire to the day of the battle. Such a shocking sight of charred wood, burnt clothes, tents, and all imaginable articles strewn around, I had never before seen. The next turn of the road brought us to two graves, one on each side of the road, the resting-place of two who fell that day. They were merely left in the ditch where they fell, and earth from the side was pulled over them. Beyond, the sight became more common. And one poor fellow lay unburied, just as he had fallen, with his horse across him, and both skeletons. Next to Mr. Barbee's were the remains of a third camp that was burned; and a few more steps made me suddenly hold my breath, for just before us lay a dead horse with the flesh still hanging, which was hardly endurable. Close by lay a skeleton,—whether of man or horse, I did not wait to see. Not a human being appeared until we reached the Penitentiary, which was occupied by our men. After that, I saw crowds of wagons moving furniture out, but not a creature that I knew. Just back of our house was all that remained of a nice brick cottage—namely, four crumbling walls. It really seems as though God wanted to spare our homes. The frame dwellings adjoining were not touched, even. The town was hardly recognizable; and required some skill to avoid the corners blocked up by trees, so as to get in at all.

Our house could not be reached by the front, so we left the buggy in the back yard, and running through the lot without stopping to examine the storeroom and servants' rooms that opened wide, I went through the alley and entered by the front door. . . .

I stood in the parlor in silent amazement; and in answer to Charlie's "Well?" I could only laugh. It was so hard to realize. The *papier-maché* workbox Miriam had given me was gone. The baby sacque I was crocheting, with all knitting needles and wools, gone also. Of all the beautiful engravings of Annapolis that Will Pinckney had sent me, there remained a single one. Not a book remained in the parlor, except "Idyls of the King," that contained my name also, and which, together with the door-plate, was the only case in which the name of Morgan was spared. Where they did not carry off articles bearing our name, they cut it off, as in the visiting-cards, and left only the first name. Every book of any value or interest, except Hume and Gibbon, was "borrowed" permanently. I regretted Macaulay more than all the rest. Brother's splendid French histories went, too; all except "L'Histoire de la Bastille."

The dining-room was *very* funny. I looked around for the cut-glass celery and preserve dishes that were to be part of my "dot," as mother always said, together with the champagne glasses that had figured on the table the day that I was born; but there remained nothing. There was plenty of split-up furniture, though. I stood in mother's room before the shattered armoir, which I could hardly believe the same that I had smoothed my hair before, as I left home three weeks previously. Father's was split across, and the lock torn off, and in the place of the hundreds of articles it contained, I saw two bonnets at the sight of which I actually sat down to laugh. One was mother's velvet, which looked very much like a football in its present condition. Mine was not to be found, as the officers forgot to return it. Wonder who has my imperial? I know they never saw a handsomer one, with its black velvet, purple silk, and ostrich feathers.

I went to my room. Gone was my small paradise! Had this shocking place ever been habitable? The tall mirror squinted at me from a thousand broken angles. It looked so knowing! I tried to fancy the Yankee officers being dragged from under my bed by the leg, thanks to Charles; but it seemed too absurd; so I let them alone. My desk! What a sight! The central part I had kept as a little curiosity shop with all my little trinkets and keepsakes of which a large proportion were from my gentlemen friends; I looked for all I had left, found only a piece of the *McRae,* which, as it was labeled in full, I was surprised they had spared. Precious letters I found under heaps of broken china and rags; all my notes were gone, with many letters. . . .

Bah! What is the use of describing such a scene? Many suffered along with us, though none so severely. All our handsome Brussels carpets, together with Lydia's fur, were taken, too. What did they not take? In the garret, in its darkest corner, a whole gilt-edged china set of Lydia's had been overlooked; so I set to work and packed it up, while Charlie packed her furniture in a wagon, to send to her father.

It was now three o'clock; and with my light linen dress thrown off, I was standing over a barrel putting in cups and saucers as fast as I could wrap them in the rags that covered the floor, when Mr. Larguier sent me a nice little dinner. I had been so many hours without eating—nineteen, I think, during three of which I had slept—that I had lost all appetite; but nevertheless I ate it, to show my appreciation.

As soon as I had finished my task, Charlie was ready to leave again; so I left town without seeing or hearing any one, or any thing, except what lay in my path. I cast many a longing look at the graveyard; but knowing Charlie did not want to stop, I said nothing, though I had been there but once in three months, and that once, six weeks ago. I could see where the fence had been thrown down by our soldiers as they charged the Federals, but it was now replaced, though many a picket was gone. Once more I stopped at Mrs. Brown's, while Charlie went on to Clinton, leaving me to drive mother here in the morning. Early yesterday we started off in the buggy, and after a tedious ride through a melting sun, arrived here about three o'clock, having again missed my dinner, which I kept a profound secret until supper-time.

By next Ash Wednesday, I will have learned how to fast without getting sick! Though very tired, I sat sewing until after sunset. . . .

9. MARY FRANCES BROOKS—"THE CHILDREN ALL WANT TO SEE YOU"

The wife of Rhodam Maxie Brooks of Meriwether County, Georgia, had four small children. While her husband was off fighting Yankees she managed the farm, taught the youngsters, and tried unsuccessfully to hire a "substitute" for him—a practice sanctioned by the Confederate conscript law. One hopes she got the pocketknife.

Georgia, Meriwether Co.
September 3, 1862

Dear Beloved Husband,

. . . I was very glad to hear from you and to hear that you are well. This leaves me and the family well but I am so tired for I never get any rest night or day, and I don't think I will last much longer, but I will try to write to you as long as you stay there, if I can raise a pen. . . . We have had a very fine rain at last, it came last Saturday, Sunday, and Monday, but we have fair weather now and all hands are pulling fodder. Mr. Andrews sent two hands two days so I reckon if they don't have any bad luck they will get through by frost.

My dear, when I wrote to you last I thought I would get a man in your place, but I have failed. The man I thought of getting had already hired himself to another man, I could get plenty of men if I knew what to do and how much you would be willing to pay. Mr. Brown wants me to hire him, and says he will go for fifty dollars for two weeks, and me to pay his way, but I thought that was more than you would be willing to pay. Lutron has n't been here yet so I got Mr. Brown to take your note . . . and if he gets the money, I will send to you forthwith, for I want you home the worst sort, for I can't get anything attended to with out the money, it is money for every thing so you may know it is getting low with me, and I have got to buy bacon, and have n't any salt, and no one to see to it with out pay.

You wrote that you wanted to know how much the children had learned, they are getting along tolerable well. Henrietta is reading, writing and studying geography, and dictionary, Buddy can spell in three syllables very well, and I do not think I ever saw children grow as fast in my life as they all do, they all want to see you and talk of you very often. I have n't weaned the baby yet but I think I shall soon. My dear, I want you to try to get me a little pocket knife from the Yankees as long as you have got to trading with them.

I must close for want of room to write more. So farewell my dear husband,

MARY F. BROOKS

10. BELLE BOYD—"I RECEIVED MY COMMISSION"

The most sensational of Southern spies, daughter of a well-known family of the Shenandoah Valley, was born at Martinsburg,

Virginia (now West Virginia), on May 9, 1843. After attending Mount Washington Female College in Baltimore from twelve to sixteen, she made her debut in Washington society in the winter of 1860-1861. Belle was an attractive, fair-haired, blue-eyed girl with a tall and charming figure. Promptly she became a favorite. With secession her father Ben Boyd enlisted in the 2nd Virginia and the family returned to Martinsburg. Belle nursed the wounded in Valley hospitals.

Inspired by the Manassas exploit of Betty Duvall, Rose Greenhow's assistant, and encouraged by the gallant Turner Ashby, the chief of Stonewall Jackson's cavalry and scouts, Belle Boyd became a Confederate courier. As she moved about on her missions to Jackson, Stuart, Beauregard and other generals, she soon fell under Union suspicion. She was arrested at Winchester and sent to Eutaw House in Baltimore, but General Dix kindly released her. Then she went to Front Royal in the Valley where her uncle and aunt kept a small hotel, which had been taken over by General Shields. She found this an ideal arrangement for espionage. While a council of war was being held in the dining room, Belle lay in the closet over it, her ear glued to a knothole which she had enlarged in the floor. As soon as the council was over she jumped on her horse, galloped fifteen miles to give her information to Ashby and was back home before dawn.

On May 23, 1862, came her opportunity to be of greatest service to the Confederacy. She had gathered all sorts of information about the several Union forces being concentrated against her "undaunted hero," Stonewall Jackson. By moving quickly he could save the bridges the Federals planned to wreck and keep the road open for an advance on Banks. Jackson was ten miles from Front Royal. Belle ran over open fields, under a cross fire from pickets of both armies, climbed fences, crawled along the tops of hills, till she drew close to the first line of Confederates. Frantically she waved her sunbonnet as a signal to advance. They caught on and did so. She succeeded in getting her full message to Jackson. A few days later he wrote her: "I thank you, for myself and for the Army, for the immense service that you have rendered your country."

Melodrama always attended Belle when she did not create it. A scout for the 5th West Virginia Cavalry, with whom she had fallen in love, betrayed her to the Union government. She was arrested on July 29, 1862, by order of Secretary of War Stanton, and carried to

Old Capitol Prison in Washington. Leslie's Weekly *said "the Secesh Cleopatra is caged at last." After a month she was released in an exchange of prisoners and returned to Virginia.*[1]

> September, 1862
> Martinsburg, Virginia

The very day after my return home I rode out to the encampment, escorted by a friend of my family, in order to pay a visit to General Jackson. As I dismounted at the door of his tent, he came out, and, gently placing his hands upon my head, assured me of the pleasure he felt at seeing me once more well and free. Our interview was of necessity short, for the demands upon his valuable time were incessant; but his fervent "God bless you, my child," will never be obliterated from my memory, as long as Providence shall be pleased to allow it to retain its power.

In the course of our conversation the General kindly warned me that, in the event of his troops being forced to retreat, it would be expedient that I should leave my home again, as the evacuation of Martinsburg by the Confederates would, as on former occasions, be rapidly followed by its occupation by our enemies and that it would be unwise and unsafe for me to expose myself to the caprice or resentment of the Yankees, and run the risk of another imprisonment. He added that he would give me timely notice of his movements, by which my plans must be regulated.

Very shortly after the interview I have just noted, the General rode into the village and took tea with us, and on the very day after his visit I received from him a message to the effect that the troops under his command were preparing for a retrograde movement upon Winchester, and that he could spare me an ambulance, by aid of which I should be enabled to precede the retreat of the army, and thus keep my friends between my enemies and myself.

Acting upon General Jackson's advice, I removed to Winchester; and it was there and then that I received my commission as Captain and honorary Aide-de-camp to "Stonewall" Jackson; and thenceforth I enjoyed the respect paid to an officer by soldiers.

Upon the occasion of the review of the troops in presence of Lord

---

[1] Belle Boyd's autobiography gives a lavishly detailed account of all her romantic and well-nigh incredible adventures. Indebtedness is acknowledged to *Dictionary of American Biography*, II, 524, for a convenient condensation, and to *Spies for the Blue and the Gray*, by Harnett T. Kane (Garden City: Hanover House, 1954) for a highly entertaining version.

Hartingdon and Colonel Leslie, and again, when General Wilcox's[1] division was inspected by Generals Lee and Longstreet, I had the honor to attend on horseback, and to be associated with the staff officers of the several commands. . . .

I went on to Charlottesville, where I remained some time.

At last, feeling very anxious to rejoin my mother, I determined to write to General Jackson and ask his opinion upon the step I so longed to take. I was prepared to run almost any risk; but, at the same time, I resolved to abide by the General's decision.

It was pronounced in the following note, which I transcribe verbatim:

> "Head-Quarters, Army of Virginia,
> "Near Culpepper Court-House.
>
> "My Dear Child,
> "I received your letter asking my advice regarding your returning to your home, which is now in the Federal lines. As you have asked for my advice, I can but candidly give it. I think that it is not safe; and therefore do not attempt it until it is, for you know the consequences. You would doubtless be imprisoned, and possibly might not be released so soon again. You had better go to your relatives in Tennessee, and there remain, until you can go with safety. God bless you.
>
> "Truly your friend,
> "T. J. JACKSON."

I lost no time in acting upon this sound advice, and was soon "on the road" once more.

[1] Major-General Cadmus M. Wilcox, C. S. A.

V

HIGH HOPES WANING

September 1862—May 1863

The armies of the Confederacy launched three offensives in the autumn of 1862.

On September 5 General Lee and the Army of Northern Virginia crossed the Potomac and invaded Maryland. On the sixteenth and seventeenth he fought at Antietam (or Sharpsburg) an indecisive battle with McClellan, who had been restored to command after Second Manassas. The seventeenth was the bloodiest day of the whole war. Out of less than 40,000 men Lee lost 8,000; out of 70,000 McClellan lost more than 12,000. His disproportionate force so hurt, Lee recrossed the Potomac into Virginia.

On September 7 General Braxton Bragg invaded Kentucky. He gave up a good position to go to Frankfort to inaugurate a Confederate Governor of Kentucky, letting General Don Carlos Buell acquire reinforcements at Louisville. Buell marched against Bragg's divided command, part of which he met and fought at Perryville on October 8. In a tactical victory Bragg lost 3,000 men out of 15,000; Buell nearly 4,000 out of more than 25,000 actively engaged. So depleted, Bragg drew back toward East Tennessee.

Early in October General Earl Van Dorn and Sterling Price made a desperate effort to retake the stronghold of Corinth, but were beaten off and driven back in Mississippi by General W. S. Rosecrans.

Lincoln, in his effort to find a general who could cope with the great Virginians, tried Ambrose E. Burnside, but the frightful decimation at Fredericksburg on December 13 proved he was not up to the mark. Betty Maury was one among Southern millions who rejoiced for a great victory. Several weeks before the battle, the message went out from the headquarters of the Army of Northern Virginia: "General Lee desires me to state, for the information of the Secretary of War, that of barefooted men there are in total 6466."

At the Battle of Stone's River, or Murfreesboro, in Tennessee (December 31, 1862-January 2, 1863) Braxton Bragg lost 10,000 men. *He withdrew to Tullahoma, and Rosecrans occupied Murfreesboro on January 4.*

The miscalled "Fighting" Joe Hooker was the next one to try things for Lincoln. He was terrifically outfought and defeated by Robert E. Lee at Chancellorsville, but Lee lost there his right arm—Stonewall Jackson—and more than 10,000 Confederates fell, dead or wounded.

So the Union of Southern States was being drained of its vital force, but not of its stanch determination. Undiscouraged, it fought on with hope deferred. Back home or in exile the women gave their thrift and love. Some of them, like young Emma Sansom down in Alabama, had active parts to play.

1. CASSIE SELDEN SMITH—"what shall i name the baby?"

Cassie, daughter of Samuel S. Selden of Lynchburg, Virginia, met thirty-seven-year-old Edmund Kirby Smith in August 1861 during his convalescence from a wound received at First Manassas. They were married on September 24.

Edmund Kirby Smith, born in St. Augustine, Florida, had distinguished himself in the Mexican War and risen rapidly in the Confederate Army from colonel to major-general. Early in 1862 he had been given command of the Department of East Tennessee. In June he invaded Kentucky, won the Battle of Richmond, and occupied Lexington. His force was united with Bragg's after the Battle of Perryville (October 8) and he commanded the rear guard as Bragg retired. Now a lieutenant-general, he was in Middle Tennessee when Cassie wrote him this letter from back home.

Some months later she joined him in Tennessee. When in February 1863 he was placed in command of the Trans-Mississippi Department she followed him to Shreveport. In the spring of 1864 she moved to Hempstead, Texas, for the rest of the war. On May 26, 1865, General Smith surrendered the last large military force of the Confederacy and sought refuge in Mexico and Cuba. Cassie went to Washington to secure permission for his return to the United States. He got back in November. For a short while the Kirby Smiths were in Kentucky where Edmund tried his hand running a military school. From 1870 to 1875 they were in Nashville where he was president

of the University. From then on they lived happily in Sewanee,
Tennessee, where he was professor of mathematics at the University
of the South. Edmund died in 1893, Cassie in 1905. She had five
sons and six daughters.

Lynchburg, Virginia Oct. 10th 1862

My dear Husband:

As I am unable to give an account of myself, I have employed
Nina to be my amanuensis. The day after *the baby* was born Mrs. B.
wrote to you. . . . All day Saturday I felt badly, as night grew on
the pains grew worse. I thought I had better make known my situation. Until then I kept it to myself, a silent sufferer. I could not
muster up courage to send for a Dr. so the boy went off post haste
for Mrs. B., the ladies' friend in such cases, with the information
that if I grew worse Dr. Owens should be sent for & chloroform
administered which however was not done, although I suffered great
pain all night Saturday and all day Sunday. I walked the floor (when
I could) in extreme agony & not until twelve o'clock at night was the
baby born—& after such a length of suffering Mrs. B. said I had a
good time. If mine was good what can the worst be?

At first, I regretted the baby was not a boy—as you were so
anxious that it should be so, but she is a dear little girl, & I feel
thankful it is all over. She is a little, fat creature, & only weighs six
pounds. Her eyes are very dark blue. I think they will be like yours.
Her mouth is beautiful, forehead fine, but I can't say much about
her nose. Everybody says it is a pity she is not a *Little General.* I
have one consolation—she is very good. Sleeps well & gives no one
any trouble. Our Mary is with me & is very faithful & kind—nurses
me well. Josephine was with me during all my trouble. I am doing
very well—am very prudent—dieting myself to try & get rid of
dyspepsia. I wish so much that you were with me & trust that you
can be relieved from duty sometime this fall.

What shall I name the baby? Can you not think of a pretty fancy
name—Spanish names are pretty—something uncommon as I consider her an *uncommon baby.*[1] You must come on as soon as you can
to have her christened. I am glad & proud of your success in Ky.

I lie in bed, look at your picture & the baby, & think of you all
the time. . . .

---

[1] They named the baby Frances.

I will give you continued assurances of mine & the baby's good health.

I recd. the letter sent by Genl. Marshall's[1] cousin. I have written every week since you have been in Ky., sending your letters to Knoxville. I recd. the box sent from Barboursville—which was very acceptable. I thank you very much for it. Write when you can to

Your devoted wife

CASSIE

2. CORDELIA LEWIS SCALES—"I NEVER WALK OR RIDE WITHOUT MY PISTOL"

Delia Scales was born on July 10, 1843, at the family home "Oakland," eight miles north of Holly Springs in northern Mississippi. Her brothers Dabney and Henry became officers in the Confederate Navy, and Joe was an aide to General Beauregard. All through the war there were movements of troops in and about Holly Springs. Oakland was repeatedly used as headquarters by officers of the invading armies and at intervals furnished hospitality to Confederates from near-by encampments.

Cordelia carried on a lively, slapdash correspondence with her old school friend Lou Irby, of Como Depot, some thirty miles away.

Home Sweet Home
Oakland Oct. 29 1862

My dear darling Loulie:

I have just received your letter of the 29th of September; & I do not blame you for thinking I had forsaken you after writing three letters & not hearing a word from me; but before I proceed farther, I must clear myself—in the first place I have received only two letters, & you remember the Yankees paid us a visit soon after the reception of the first, & after their departure I was taken very sick very sudden one morning. Oh! Loulie I cannot describe my sufferings, I had three attacks of conjestion. After that I was then taken with inflammation of the stomach. I had three Doctors (enough to kill any common person). They all gave me up. . . . Brother Joe ran the risk of losing his life to save mine by making two trips to

---

[1] Brigadier-General Humphrey Marshall, C. S. A.

Memphis for ice & lemons for me, & I do think the ice was the means of saving my life. . . . And Lou what do you think, they shingled my hair & it was so long & even & I had learned to braid & tuck it up like a grown lady. You do not know how becoming it was. I have enough to make me a beautiful braid. . . . I wish you could see me now with my hair parted on the side with my black velvet zouave on & pistol by my side & riding my fine colt, Beula. I know you would take me for a Guerilla. I never ride now or walk without my pistol. Quite warlike, you see. We have had the house full of our soldiers ever since the Yankees left. I suppose you know our Army is encamped almost in sight of us. I was down at Gen Tilghman's[1] headquarters yesterday & had the pleasure of dining with the officers, enjoyed myself so much. I sent some wine down to them (the General and other officers there) & thought we would brake up with a barn dance. Lou, I do wish you were here. We would have so much fun. Do please come up. I will go home with you. Now please come Loulie. I think we have about fifty soldiers with us every day. They are as thick as the flies used to be in the dining room of the old College. Speaking of the College reminds me to tell you that it is full of Federal soldiers & Dr. C. has taken the *oath*.

I do wish you could see the camps. The tents look so pretty. I must tell you about the Yankees as you are so anxious to know how they behaved. You may congratulate yourself, my dear friend, on being slighted by them. They came & stayed in our yard all the time. The camp was where our soldiers are now. And they use to order the milk to be churned any time & they took corn, fodder, ruined the garden & took everything in the poultry line. Hulberts[2] division, the very worst, stayed here with us nearly all the time. I never heard such profanity in all my life & so impudent, they would walk around the house & look up at the windows & say, "wonder how many Secesh gals they got up there." I did not have my pistol & Ma would not let me go where they were, but one evening she was so worn out she sent me down to attend to the skimming of some wines & other household matters, when she thought they had all left. Just as I got out in the yard, two Cavalry men & six infantry came up & surrounded me. Pa was not at home. Ma & Sis Lucy were looking on & were frightened very much for they knew I would speak my mind to them if they provoked me. The first Lt. asked me if we had any chickens. I told

[1] Brigadier-General Lloyd Tilghman, C. S. A.
[2] Major-General Stephen A. Hurlbut, U. S. A.

him, "no," "Any milk?" I said, "no,"—that some of his tribe had
been there that morning & got every thing in that line. He smiled &
said "they did not pay you for them?" I told him a few pretended to
pay by giving us federal money, that I preferred leaves to that. He
said "why federal money dont seem to be in demand." I said "not
down this way sure." The second Lt. a red-haired ugly pert thing
commenced to laugh about our men running from Holly Springs &
said "our men never run, miss." I told him, no, we all knew what a
orderly retreat they made from Bull Run, Manassas, & Leighsburg,[1]
that it did their army a great deal of credit & that I hope they felt
proud of it. One of the pickets remarked then "Oh! hush Tom you
dont know how to talk to Secesh gals." I turned to him & thanked
him that we were all ladies in the South. The 2nd. Lt. got very mad
at what I said about their men running—said, "I can inform you
miss, I was in the battle of Leighsburg & our men did not run far."
I told him I knew they did not, they ran as far as they could and then
jumped in the river. The first Lt. broke out in a laugh & said "Ah!
Tom shes got you now," & turned to me & said, "I admire your
candor very much. I had much rather see you so brave than for you
to pretend to entertain Union sentiments." I told him that there
wasnt a Union man, woman, or child in the state of Mississippi &
the first man that he was to shoot him right there for he did it only
to protect his property. He said he would & wanted to know if all
the ladies were that brave. I informed him they were & if they
whipped this part of our army that we had girls & boys enough to
whip them. One of the soldiers said, "I think you had better inspire
some of your men with your bravery." I told him that our men
needed no inspiration whatever. The Lt. then said to me "Now, Miss,
you southern ladies would not fight, you are too good natured." I
said we were very good natured but when our soil was invaded & by
such creatures as they were it was enough to arouse any one—he
wanted to know what I styled them. I told him Yankees or Negro
thieves. This made him very mad & he told me they were western
men. I told him I judged people by the company they kept, that they
fought with them & stayed with them that "birds of a feather would
flock together." He remembered & turned & left then. I wish you
could have seen me when I walked away just like the very ground
was polluted by them. The first Lt. asked me for some water when
he saw I was going, I told him there was a spring on the place if he

[1] Battle of Ball's Bluff on the Potomac, near Leesburg, Virginia, October 21, 1861.

wanted any. He then told me that such bravery should be rewarded —that nothing on the place should be touched. He made all the men march before him & he did not let them trouble anything. . . .I could write you a newspaper about them but I reckon you are tired now & it makes me mad to think about them. Write soon to your true friend,

DELIA

Excuse this scribbling I can get no pens fit to write with. If you read this it is more than I can do.

Your friend,
DELIA

3. MARY WILLIAMS PUGH—WE HOPE
TO REACH TEXAS

Mary, daughter of John Williams, was born at Leighton plantation, Assumption Parish, Louisiana. On February 7, 1861, she married Richard L. Pugh, son of the master of Dixie plantation near Thibodaux in Lafourche Parish. The next year Richard enlisted in the Washington Artillery' at New Orleans. He campaigned under General Bragg in Mississippi, Tennessee and Kentucky. When the Federal troops of General Godfrey Weitzel threatened the Bayou Lafourche late in October 1862 Mary joined her father and mother for a journey to Rusk, in east central Texas. They carried their many slaves with them, and their household and plantation equipment. It was hard, month-long travel. They stayed in Rusk till hostilities ceased.

Mary had five children. Three sons went to Virginia Military Institute. When Richard died in 1885 she bought Live Oaks plantation in Lafourche Parish and spent the rest of her days there, living on to a grand old age.

(According to Lyle Saxon in Old Louisiana *"there was an old Louisiana conundrum: Why is Bayou Lafourche like the aisle of a church? And the answer was: Because there are Pughs on both sides of it.")*

Between Opelousas & Alexandria [Louisiana],
Sunday night Nov. 9th 1862

My *dear dear* husband

How little did I dream when I last wrote you that my next letter would be written so far away from our dear old home yet here we are in this miserable country feeling very grateful & happy at our escape from the horrid wretches who are now doubtless enjoying themselves in that same old home. You will have heard long before receiving this of the Bayou being in their possession & I know have suffered great anxiety in not knowing what had become of us so I will go back two weeks & try to tell you as well as I can how this thing has all come about. On Saturday morning (two weeks ago yesterday) we heard Yankees were at Donaldsonville, but this being a common report caused no alarm. Judge then of our astonishment Saturday evening when we heard they were coming down the bayou & that our troops had fallen back twelve miles where they said they would make a stand. This quieted the people as they believed our troops would whip them back but no sooner did the Yankees show themselves again than our troops retreated to the piece of woods just above Mr. Littlejohn's where they did make a final stand but were badly defeated owing to miserable management. But for the pretense of Gen. M——[1] to fight above Napoleon many would have moved their negroes—as it was they were completely sold & caught.

At daylight Sunday morning Pa went up to the camp above Mr. L's & returned saying he did not believe our officers had any great desire to fight & thought it more than probable we would have to leave & advised us to begin packing immediately. At twelve oclock we were fully convinced we would have to go & in the evening after a long day spent in packing I rode up to Dixie, sent for all the negroes & told them there was a strong probability of the Yankees coming in which case it was your desire that I should move & take all of them—that you had plenty of money to support them until they could return home (a big story isn't it?) & that you would certainly take care of them as long as possible, &c. They all expressed great regret at leaving their "good fields" but said they were willing to do anything I said. I then sent them off to get their clothes ready in case we were forced to go. When I reached home about dark Pa and David [2] were there & had made up their minds to leave next morning at daylight as the Yankees were by this time nearly down to Mr. Littlejohn's & only waiting for the next morning to begin the fight.

About ten oclock that night Pa & David went up to Dixie & told the negroes they must be ready to start at daylight. They sat up all

[1] General Alfred Mouton, the Confederate commander.
[2] Mrs. Pugh's brother.

night cooking & getting ready & I met them all on the road next morning looking bright & happy. They have behaved as well as possible since we started notwithstanding they have had every example to do otherwise. The morning we started about 27 of Pa's had disappeared, amongst them Jim Bynum (Will you ever have faith in one again?), old Mary Nell & her husband, & old David & his family & old Virgil & his family. The first night we camped Sylvester left—the next night at Bayou B. about 25 of Pa's best hands left & the next day at Berwick Bay nearly all of the women & children started—but this Pa found out in time to catch them all except one man & one woman. Altogether he had lost about sixty of his best men. He bears his losses very cheerfully all things considered & says he thinks he was fortunate in saving what he has done. As I wrote you David started with us but turned back at Bayou Boeuf. Twelve of his best hands left him the morning we started & as many more at Bayou B. so this decided him to return as he was afraid of being left with only women & children. Your Mother started little Nathan with David but he left with the last twelve. He told some of the negroes he was going back to your Mother. Now all of this was going on around & about your negroes & of course they heard all the talk & had everything to induce them to behave badly & every opportunity to go if they wished—but they are all here still & as humble & respectful as possible. I really feel *grateful* to them for their good behavior & you have every reason to be proud of them as I have told them you would be. They are the talk of every neighborhood they pass through as they are such exceptions to other negroes. Even Aunt Tiby is along. I tried for some time to persuade her to stay—but she seemed so unwilling that I consented she should come. I thought too her staying might tempt Sharp to run off & as negroes are so much like sheep I did not desire any such example. I am very glad now I brought her as she would certainly have wanted something alone there. She looks ten years younger already & is *grinning* all the time. She talks a great deal about the sheep which I think is her only regret. I had cloth enough left from their clothes to make several cart covers—so they are very comfortable at night. I brought their winter clothes along in bundles—as I had not yet given them out I determined if any of them ran off they should go without any clothes. I will give them out in a day or two as we now think all danger is past.

Pa has at last determined after a great deal of thought to go into

Texas . . . *he thinks* about Polk county. There provisions can be had in any quantities and at a reasonable rate. We hear 40 cents a barrel for corn—12 to 18 dollars for beef &c. & as it is more than likely that we will be kept from home all winter it is of course very necessary to look to this. The distance from here is about two hundred miles & Pa expects to reach there certainly in two weeks. The roads & weather are splendid & we hope to get the negroes in comfortable quarters before the winter rains. Edward is along with his negroes—more have left him since he started but he left several families at home. Mrs. Young is along too & about eighty women & children which Pa has to look after as all of her men have run off with the exception of about twelve. Your Mother declined moving her negroes & said they were too many to attempt it. She would protect them there or nowhere & I think she was perfectly right. She was very well when we left. I had a note from her the day before we left.

We could hear distinctly the firing at Labadia as we drove from our gate—the fight had just then commenced so you see how narrowly we escaped as the Yankees were in Thibodaux[1] a few hours after. Oh Wretched [2] you can guess how sad it made me feel to say good-bye to all the things so dear to me. As I rode through the yard as I was leaving Dixie I felt as if I were saying good-bye again to you. Your sheep were quietly feeding with their many beautiful little lambs around them—your pretty colts and our little trees all looked so beautiful & were so dearly associated with you that it was hard to take what I know more than likely my last look at them. David engaged Mrs. Williams brother to look after & stay on the place & he said he would turn the sheep & two small colts in the fields & try & keep them hid until the Yankees left, but they find out everything so we may as well make up our minds never again to see anything left there—if we do find anything it will be an agreeable surprise. Ma brought nothing but her clothes & bedding—not a single piece of furniture—her glass & china are packed & sent to Mrs. S. hoping she might protect them. Pa left old Mr. R. his engineer to stay in the house & look after the place. He left old Uncle Punch & one or two other old negroes to assist him—but I am afraid the Yankees will carry them off.

Pa had sold all of his crop to the government but left your sugar

---

[1] They reached Thibodaux on October 27.
[2] A pun on her husband's name, Richard, used as a term of endearment.

all in his sugar house & some of it in the moulds—he says he could have sold it for sixty thousand dollars—but of course the Yankees will save him that trouble. We have heard all sorts of stories since leaving but don't know what to believe. One is that they have visited & stripped Gen. Bragg's place.[1] We saw Mr. Miles Taylor at Mr. Wilson's where we spent two days—they have been to his place & taken off everything that could walk—not even a chicken left. He borrowed a coat & came off with his daughter & they are spending some time with Mr. Wilson. The Yankees did not wait until they reached Thibodaux to begin their work of destruction but commenced as soon as they reached the bayou. I hear they have taken all of Mr. R.'s negroes—killed two who refused to go with them. Your brother Walter took his negroes off but I have not heard where to. Mr. Dillon, Jr. has overtaken us & says they have taken all of his father's & all of old Mr. Parkins—even old Lucinda. It is said they have made a camp of all of the negroes on Mr. Buxton's place until they can send them off but a great many they have already sent.

Frank poor fellow leaves on tomorrow morning. I have written this tonight to send by him as he promises me faithfully to go to see you if you are anywhere near. He seems much to prefer returning to his old company & I don't wonder at anyone being disgusted with the military doings here. We all feel very sorry to see him go again but God grant that he soon may return to us.

We hear nothing encouraging except rumors of intervention which we are afraid to believe. I have almost despaired of the war ever ending though many persons look for it by Spring & now Wretched that I have told you as well as I can in this hurried way all of our troubles of the past two weeks I must take a little time to pour out my heart to you which has been so full & so sad for the two past months. First of all I have not heard one word from you in all that time. My last letter was dated Sept. 6th. I knew all of this time that you were so situated it was impossible to get letters back to me. I should have been crazy long before now—*no one* has received a letter from Gen. Bragg's army since my last one came—not even Mrs. Bragg. I have kept myself alive from day to day hoping better things for tomorrow—expecting each day to bring up something which would permit me to go at least near enough to hear from you. When

[1] Braxton Bragg had married Elisa Brooks Ellis of Louisiana in 1849 and bought a plantation in Lafourche Parish after he resigned from the U. S. Army in 1856. He named it "Bivouac." From now on Mrs. Bragg was a refugee.

I look back & think of the long long time spent without news from you I look at myself in astonishment & wonder how I have stood it. . . . I have tried so hard to please you by bearing this patiently & cheerfully dear Wretched that surely now I deserve some reward. All of my cries have been taken in our dear old room so no one but you will ever know of them. Yesterday I must confess I did behave badly but I have been thinking for some time of going to Miss. with Frank & yesterday when he determined to go tomorrow & I knew I could not go with him it was more than I could bear. I expect he will tell you how much I *did* cry—but I know dear Wretched it would be wrong for me to leave the negroes now & I go with them most cheerfully once I knew twould be your wish but my good behavior now is all put on & will soon disappear unless I see something brighter ahead—the truth is Wretched you *must* come home. Pa says your interests demand that you should leave the army & *he* thinks it your duty to come if you possibly can. You can certainly find some way of getting off—either a substitute or this late exemption law which requires one white man to every twenty-five slaves. Many persons have been taking advantage of this & why cannot you?

Mr. Williams,[1] although he is with us now, is very much dissatisfied at having left his family & wishes to return now to see after them but I told him I could not consent to have him go until we arrived at our place of destination & got the negroes a little comfortable & straight—so he has agreed to go on—but of course he will not be contented to stay there & have his family on the bayou & it will be impossible for him to bring them over even if the Yankees would allow it. So I know when I once let him go I may make up my mind not to see him again for some time although he says he will return as soon as he sees that his family is comfortable—but it would be so much better Wretched if you could be yourself with your negroes— they are satisfield now but I don't know how long I can keep them so —besides Pa has more than he can attend to. Mrs. Young has attached herself on to him *for the war* & this with her women is no slight tax. Pa says you *ought* to come Wretched & you know he would never say this unless he believed it. Frank Nicholls & his wife are here. He has a furlough & speaks of resigning to take care of the G. family. I wish he would & relieve Pa. I have told your negroes that I thought as soon as you hear of this you would come & I think it has had a great deal to do with their good behavior. They look so

[1] The Pughs' overseer.

happy at the idea. Surely Wretched you have done enough now
to satisfy yourself & every one else so come now if only for the sake
of your little wife. . . . You must write to me immediately upon the
receipt of this if you are where you can possibly write. We know
nothing here except that Gen. Bragg has fallen back & can't even
find out where his army is.[1] Direct your letters to Opelousas, La.
care "William J. McCulloch, Surveyor General." Pa has made
arrangements with him to send my letters on—but heaven grant dear
Wretched you may yourself come. I have lost all hope of letters. I
sent you by Frank the shirts I have made for you. I have been very
happy in making them though I have buried my face in them &
taken many good cries. I know *you* will appreciate them & think
them nice & will acknowledge for *once* that you have a sweet little
wife—no one else has put a stitch on them. I did it all myself. Tell
Caesar when he washes them he must pull the *tails long* & the sleeves
wide else they will draw up & be uncomfortable. I have many other
little things I would like to send you & some things for Caesar but
Frank is uncertain about seeing you as he does not know where the
army is & as he may be forced to send the shirts by some one going
I am afraid to make too large a bundle.

It is very late & I am all alone writing this when I know I ought
to be in bed as we start very early tomorrow morning but it has been
such a long time since I have written you & I have so much to say
that I feel as if I would rather never stop. When you do come
Wretched (for you will come, *I know you will*) how much we will
have to tell each other—how many nights I will keep you awake—
but ah when, when will they come? You must remember me kindly
to Caesar. I have taken a boy to drive me that Mr. Williams calls
"Yellow Lewis." He is a very nice obedient fellow & gets on with the
carriage & horses as well as anyone. I am now driving Champ &
Inkey. Poor old John died at Mr. Nelson's with lock jaw fever
sticking a nail in his foot. . . .

I do sincerely pray that Frank will be able to see you my dear dear
Wretched. I know it will be such a satisfaction to you to see him. You
must ask him all you want to know. How sorry I am that he must go.
May we meet him soon at home. . . .

God bless & take care of you. Yours fondly & devotedly

MARY

[1] Bragg and his army had retired to Murfreesboro after the Battle of Perryville.

La. Near Sabine City
Tuesday night. Nov. 18th/62

My *dear dear* husband,

We reached this place this morning and will remain here at a comfortable house until tomorrow by which time the wagons will all be across Sabine river when we cross & begin our journey again. So far we have got on very well but for the last week rather slowly owing to bad roads & sometimes bad hills. However we hear now that these are all over with so we hope we get on more rapidly. We have had no break driving—no sick mules or sick negroes. Pa has only had a few slight breaks with his wagons. Mrs. Young has been in a *stew* from the time we started until now & I am afraid her troubles are not over—her mules all in a wretched condition & not able to haul all of the old plunder she has allowed her negroes to bring. Of course we have all tried to help her as much as possible but she seems to feel so little gratitude that master & overseer are all getting tired—so I think hereafter she will hardly be able to keep up. At first as she started with Pa he felt bound to assist her as she could not possibly get on without it, having been left with only sixteen men—so we all lent her mules & men who have worked hard at her wagons for two weeks *apparently* without her knowledge for not one word of thanks has anybody ever received—on the contrary a stranger would think *we* were the favored party. Her face is nearly a yard long & would give anyone the "horrors" out here in these piney woods when we travel on until day without seeing even a bird. You must not think the troubles have passed me for I *do* feel sorry for the poor woman as who would not? but then her troubles are no greater than other peoples & she ought sometimes to think of this. I often often think as I see her management of her negroes &c. of what you once said of her "that for a woman who prided herself on her common sense she had very little." There are many little scenes which I have stored away for your amusement. At first Mr. Williams at my request did every thing in his power for her—in fact as much almost as if he had been her overseer—but for the last few days he won't do anything & says "I would not mind helping her Madam Pugh if she did not look at me like she thought I was so damned contemptible"—and I must confess I agree with him. . . .

Edward is still with us & in fine spirits. He says camping out has improved his health wonderfully. Mr. Brady serves as his overseer.

Pa and all of the gentlemen stay at night with the wagons but we go on in our carriages to the nearest house. We have been living on beef & corn bread so we are almost as much delighted as the negroes are to get a little bacon—which we are beginning to find now at twenty five cents a pound. Pa bought a little for them yesterday & gave them all a treat. I don't think they were particularly well pleased when they first heard they were going to Texas—but I think the prospect of pork has quite reconciled them.

Your negroes continue to behave as well as one could wish & believe that every days travel takes them nearer to you. I often listen to their talk of this with a smile on my face but with a sad heart & wish so fervently I could believe as they do. I often speak to them of your coming as I think it encourages them to good behavior & Frederick says he has already commenced to look up the road for you—& I must tell you that you have one more negro than we started with which is more than every one can say. Two days ago Bill Roads wife Martha was taken sick soon after we started in the morning & in about an hour her son was born. Bill's cart fortunately was one that I had covered so Martha & Mattie took possession of that & got on finely without the cart ever being stopped. I brought all of the hospital beds & blankets of which I gave her a good supply for a bed & then had the cotton cover covered closely with blankets which will prevent her from taking cold. I give her every attention & suitable food & have no fears about her doing well. Bill is delighted & asked me to name the baby. I proposed "Louella" which they all think is splendid. Pa has had two born since we started & Mrs. McFall one & they all got on finely. Ma named one of hers "Tribulation." Pa has taken a great fancy to Jacob who has been invaluable ever since we started. Both of Pa's smiths ran off so Jacob has had his hands full as something or other is always breaking or coming loose.

Pa has not yet decided where he will settle but has decided to go higher up than Polk county as he thinks that too near Galveston & that Leon or some county there would be better—but nothing is decided as yet. Tomorrow he will leave us & go on ahead to look around & find places by the time we reach there. He will try to find some deserted farms if possible so as to have some cabins. At any rate he will get cleared land enough to raise corn, potatoes &c. in case we have to stay next year. Edward & his mother will try and get places in the same neighborhood but Pa will find places adjoining for himself & you. I think that would be much better than to have one large place as I know you would rather your negroes were kept & managed to themselves. Mr. Williams seems much better satisfied & does not seem in such a hurry to get back home although I have told him as soon as we were comfortably settled if he could find a good man to take charge of the negroes during his absence I was perfectly willing for him to go for three or four weeks. We can hear nothing from home except wild exaggerated stories & I suppose will hear nothing reliable until some one goes there. As soon as Pa finds a place & gets us to it he will leave to go to Chattanooga & will hire some man at Port Hudson to go in home & see what is going on there. Pa thinks we will be at the end of our trip in about ten days at farthest—so he will be on his way back in less than two weeks. Ah my dear dear Wretched I do wish the negroes were all comfortably provided for for the winter & that I might give all my thoughts to you & you only.

When you told me three months ago that you would be back Christmas how long the time seemed then—how much longer it has proven itself—but Christmas is about here & will or will it not be a happy one for me? I shall probably not find an opportunity of writing you again until Pa goes. He of course will come to see you when he crosses the river if he can possibly reach you—so you may look for him soon after receiving this.

Pa & Ma send their kindest love & the negroes send their usual "howdy's" & messages. Remember me to Robert & Caesar. I hope Pa will soon take you good news of us all & God grant you may soon bring us good news of yourself. In the meantime be happy & don't forget to love me or how much I love you.

Ten thousand kisses

Yours forever devotedly
MARY

4. MARY CAHAL—"ACCEPT MY BEST WISHES FOR YOUR HAPPINESS"

As a relative of the Ready family, Mary Cahal of Lebanon, Tennessee, had met General John Hunt Morgan when he was camped at Murfreesboro in the spring of 1862. She was not present at the wedding of twenty-one-year-old Martha Ready and the thirty-seven-year-old general Sunday evening, December 14, 1862. The exigencies of war prevented the sending of invitations far and wide. John's brother Tom was hurt that he had not been asked. But Mary Cahal soon heard about it—from the general himself.

It was a brilliant occasion. The Ready house was a two-story building with spacious halls and rooms, just off the public square. With Christmas near, it was decorated with holly and winterberries. Mattie wore a lace dress with a veil. Morgan was in his general's regalia. Bishop Polk performed the ceremony, with his vestments over his lieutenant-general's uniform. Hardee—Alice Ready's friend —Breckinridge and Cheatham, corps commanders, were groomsmen. There was a lavish supper, with wines from Colonel Ready's cellar for toast after toast to the happy couple. The pretty Tennessee girls and the officers danced to a late hour, to the music of two regimental bands.

Mary Cahal's fears that marriage might interfere with Morgan's "career of glory" were soon allayed. He rode off on his Christmas raid six days after the wedding.[1]

Lebanon
Dec. 16th. '62

My Dear Cousin Mattie

I have just received General Morgan's note informing me of your marriage.

I heard Sunday that it was to be on that day but was not certain until a few minutes since.

Tell the General I only excuse him for not sending the courier for the reason he gave, i.e., he was *so much in love* he forgot all but *you.*

Accept my best wishes my dear friend for your happiness and prosperity and present them to General Morgan.

I thought of you much on Sunday and wished that it might be a bright day and thus typical of a bright and happy life.

Uncle Robert wishes to be remembered and says he hopes your fondness for *matrimonial Union* will not make you *union* in a political sense. Also that you must remember your promise not to restrain the General in his career of glory, but encourage him to go forward. Perhaps it will be over soon.

My love to Alice & the General.

[1] See *Morgan and His Raiders,* by Cecil Fletcher Holland. New York: The Macmillan Company, 1942.

May God bless you my dear friend in all relations of life as I feel your affectionate heart deserves.

Very Affectionately your friend
MARY CAHAL

5. JULIA LeGRAND—"NEW ORLEANS IS FULL OF RUMORS"

Life in occupied New Orleans brought limitations and hardship to Julia and Ginnie LeGrand. The animosity toward Ben Butler had been largely due to his Order No. 28: "When any female shall, by word, or gesture, or movement, insult or show contempt for any officer or soldier of the United States, she shall be regarded and held liable to be treated as a woman of the town plying her avocation." The general indignation which that created, hardly "pent-up," found expression in a poem written at the time of his departure from New Orleans, "The Ladies' Farewell to Brutal Ferocity Butler." Julia copied it into her diary. It began:

We fill this cup to one made up
Of beastliness alone.

Banks replaced Butler on December 16.

New Orleans, December 20th, 1862. Butler, after his long, disgusting stay here has been compelled to yield his place, his sword, and much of his stolen property. Banks arrival and Butler's disgrace has created a vent for a long pent-up disgust.

General Banks has, so far, by equitable rule commanded the respect of his enemies. We know him as an enemy, it is true, but an honest and respectable one. Every rich man is not his especial foe, to be robbed for his benefit. Butler left on the steamer *Spaulding,* was accompanied to the wharf by a large crowd, to which he took off his hat. There was not one hurrah, not one sympathizing cry went up for him from the vast crowd which went to see him off—a silent rebuke. I wonder if he felt it!

Heard to-day of the existence of a negro society here called the "vaudo" (I believe). All who join it promise secrecy on pain of death. Naked men and women dance around a huge snake and the room is suddenly filled with lizards and other reptiles. The snake represents the devil which these creatures worship and fear. The existence of such a thing in New Orleans is hard to believe. I had read of such a thing in a book which Doctor Cartwright gave us, but he is so imaginary and such a determined theorist that I treated it almost as a jest. The thing is a living fact. The police have broken up such dens, but their belief and forms of worship are a secret. These people would be savages again if free. I find that no negroes discredit the power of the snake; those who do not join the society abstain from fear and not from want of faith.

December 31st, 1862. I write, this beautiful last day of December, with a heart filled with anxiety and sorrow; with my own sad history that of others mingles. Our side has gained again. The Confederate banner floats in pride and security, but who can help mourning over the details of that ghastly battle of the Rappahannock.[1] Oh, Burnside! moral coward to lead men, the sons of women, into such a slaughter-pen to gratify a senseless president and a tyrannical giver of orders!

Our town is filled with rumors. There has been a bloody fight at Port Hudson,[2] it is said, and the brazen cannon which we have so often seen dragged through these streets have all been taken by our Confederate troops. Banks has ordered the return of the Federal troops sent up the river so proudly and confidently a short while ago, but it is reported that they are so surrounded by the Confederates that they cannot extricate themselves. It is rumored that we are to have a negro insurrection in the New Year (New Year's Day). The Federal Provost-Marshall has given orders that the disarmed Confederates may now arm again and shoot down the turbulent negroes (like dogs). This after inciting them by every means to rise and slay their masters. I feel no fear, but many are in great alarm. I have had no fear of physical ill through all this dreary summer of imprisonment, but it may come at last. Fires are frequent—it is feared that incendiaries are at work. Last night was both cold and windy. The bells rang out and the streets resounded with cries. I awoke from sleep and said, "Perhaps the moment has come." Well, well, perhaps it is scarcely human to be without fear. I wonder my Ginnie and I

[1] Fredericksburg, December 13.
[2] Port Hudson and Vicksburg were the only places on the Mississippi then held by the Confederacy.

cannot feel as others do—whether we suffer too much in heart to fear in body, or whether we lack that realizing sense of danger which forces us to prepare for it. Mrs. Norton has a hatchet, a tomahawk, and a vial of some kind of spirits with which she intends to blind all invaders. We have made no preparations, but if the worst happen we will die bravely no doubt.

The cars passed furiously twice about midnight, or later; we were all awaked by sounds so unusual. There are patrols all over the city and every preparation has been made to meet the insurrectionists. I indeed expect no rising now, though some of the Federals preach to the negroes in the churches, calling on them to "sweep us away forever." General Banks is not like Butler; he will protect us. The generality of the soldiers hate the negroes and subject them to great abuse whenever they can. This poor, silly race has been made a tool of—enticed from their good homes and induced to insult their masters. They now lie about, destitute and miserable, without refuge and without hope. They die in numbers and the city suffers from their innumerable thefts.

Christmas passed off quietly, and, to us, sadly. The ladies gave a pleasant dinner to the Confederate prisoners of war now in the city. Rumors from Lafourche that Weitzel has been defeated. His resignation was sent on the *Spaulding*, but has not been received yet by the President. He resigns, they say, to marry an heiress, Miss Gaskett. She, a creole of Louisiana, consents to marry one who has spent months in command of soldiers who have been desolating her country.

6. SARAH L. WADLEY—"THE NEGROES ARE HAVING A MERRY TIME"

Sarah was one of the eight children of William Morrill Wadley of New Hampshire and Rebecca Everingham Wadley of Cockspur Island off Savannah. Her father was president of the Vicksburg, Shreveport & Texas Railroad. Sarah got her schooling from a governess who lived with the family—a convenient arrangement as the railroad man moved from one home to another in Louisiana and Mississippi. In December 1862 the Secretary of War nominated him to take supervision and control of transportation for the government on all railroads in the Southern states, but the Senate refused to con-

firm the appointment.[1] *After the war he became president of the Central Railroad of Georgia. He built "Great Hill," a house some twelve miles from Macon. Sarah lived there to an advanced age.*

She was seventeen when she penned these entries in her diary. Her "Oakland" is a different one from Delia Scales's.

"Oakland"
Near Monroe, Louisiana

Dec. 25/1862. Christmas night.

It has been a sad Christmas to us, Father was not here. We received a despatch Tuesday night saying that he must return to Richmond before coming home.

Friday-Dec. 26th/1862

Our turn has come at last. We heard this morning the Yankees had come as far as Delhi (on the railroad) burning everything in their track, and coming four miles an hour. We know nothing of their force, all suppose that they are coming to Monroe. I do not know whether our few troops will resist or not. Willie is gone in at full speed to ascertain the truth of the matter and to bring back our teams which went in this morning for corn. Oh if Father was here! I am determined, come what may, never to renounce my country, but what is before us!

The negroes are busy barbecueing and cooking for their party night. They may have to start before day but we shall let them enjoy themselves while they can.

Night. Willie returned this evening, bringing us no further news. Mr. McGuire thinks that the Yankees e'er this have gone back to their gunboats. It is true that they laid Delhi in ashes.

General Blanchard[2] has ordered all the men under forty five to meet at Cotton post tomorrow morning early, he purposes to make a stand at Monroe. I hope he will.

We have been watching the negroes dancing for the last two hours. Mother had the partition taken down in our old house so that they have quite a long ball room. We can sit on the piazza and look into it. I hear now the sounds of fiddle, tambourine and "bones" mingled with the shuffling and pounding of feet. Mr. Axley is fiddling for

[1] See *Victory Rode the Rails,* by George Edgar Turner. Indianapolis: The Bobbs-Merrill Company, Inc., 1953.
[2] A. C. Blanchard.

them. They are having a merry time, thoughtless creatures, they think not of the morrow.

I am sad, very sad, tonight. Last Christmas Father watched their dancing with us; where is he now? Where shall we all be next Christmas, and tomorrow Willie[1] must go, perhaps to battle. I do not feel a single complaint in my heart, but I am sad. . . .

7. BETTY HERNDON MAURY—"GOD BLESSED US WITH VICTORY AT FREDERICKSBURG"

Protected by 147 guns on the Stafford hills to the north of the Rappahannock, the attempts of General Burnside's grand army to cross the river, pass through the town of Fredericksburg and storm the Confederate position on Marye's Heights resulted in complete defeat and awful slaughter. Betty Maury overestimates the Union losses; still they amounted to 12,500 killed or wounded. All the great leaders of the Army of Northern Virginia were noble participants in that day of victory—Stonewall Jackson in a splendid new lieutenant-general's uniform, Jeb Stuart with his bright yellow sash and plumed hat. General Burnside was dazed by the defeat and grief-stricken for the loss of life.

Writing from Richmond where she was then living, Betty records in her diary what she had heard about the painful scene in the quaint old town she knew so well.

Richmond.   December 28, 1862

On the —— of November the whole of the Yankee Army moved down and occupied the heights opposite Fredericksburg. Our forces fronting them on this side of the Rappahannock.

In a few days General Burnside gave notice to the women and children to leave the town, that he would shell it in sixteen hours. Mamma and the children came down to Richmond in a cattle car and were put out at Milford depot, with five hundred others. The sick and aged were brought out of town on beds. Mrs. Randolph had a baby two days old when she was moved. The scene at the cars is described as very touching.

On the 13th of December God blessed us with a great victory at Fredericksburg. Upwards of eighteen thousand of the enemy were

[1] Sarah's brother.

killed. We lost but one thousand. Even the Yankees acknowledge it to be a terrible defeat. The battle took place in and around the town. The streets were strewn with the fallen enemy. The houses were broken open, sacked, and used for hospitals and their dead were buried in almost every yard.

Dr. Nichols was there. Came as an Amateur with his friend General Hooker.[1] He occupied Uncle John's house (where his wife had been entertained for weeks at a time), drank up Uncle John's wine, used his flour and ate up Ellen Mercer's preserves.

I cannot find words to express my disgust and horror of the man who is so lost to all sense of delicacy and so cold blooded and heartless as to come—not at the stern call of duty—but for the love of it to gloat over the desolated homes of people whom he once called friends and who are relations and connections of his wife.

Mr. Corbin was here last night and gave us some account of the appearance of things in Fredericksburg. Almost every house has six or eight shells through it. The doors are wide open, the locks and windows broken. Two blocks of buildings were burned to the ground.

Our house was a hospital. He says every vessel in our house, even the vegetable dishes and cups, are filled with blood and water. There are large pools of gore on the floor. The table in the parlor was used as an amputating table—and a Yankee (Byron Pearce of N. Y.) is buried at the kitchen door. . . .

8. MARTHA READY MORGAN—"COME TO ME, MY DARLING"

Three exciting weeks had passed since the wedding in Murfreesboro. In his two weeks of Christmas raiding General Morgan, master of the hit-and-run, had fought in Kentucky at Green's Chapel, Bacon Creek, Elizabethtown and Bacon Creek again. With Bragg's retreat Mattie and the lovely Alice had been forced to take flight from home. Under escort by members of General Hardee's staff, they reached the army at Winchester, Tennessee, fifty miles away.

This was a foretaste of what was to become habitual for Mattie— flights before the enemy, lonely vigils, brief intervals with her husband. On his most famous raid—into Indiana and Ohio, nearly into

---

[1] General Joseph Hooker commanded at this time one of the three grand divisions of the Federal army.

Pennsylvania, the Confederacy's "farthest north," in the summer of 1863—the general was captured and imprisoned in Columbus, Ohio. From the dreary old prison he wrote to Mattie two or three times a week in terms of cheer and confidence, but his concern for her steadily increased. Mattie and Alice were in Knoxville, in Augusta, in Knoxville again, in Danville with the Withers family. When they heard that their brother Horace was wounded at Chickamauga, Alice hurried off to take care of him. Alone and desperately anxious, Mattie grew seriously ill. Her baby was born dead.

The night of November 27, 1863, Morgan, always sensational, made his sensational escape with several fellow officers who dug through the cell floor into an air chamber, tunneled through a wall into the outer yard and scaled the outer wall. After various adventures he managed to reach Mattie in time for Christmas.

She accompanied him to Richmond for a great ovation on January 9, 1864. Mrs. Chesnut was on hand to hear General J. E. B. Stuart praise the hero to the crowd "with all his voice." Mattie told her: "At Covington, after the escape, General Morgan did not know where to turn or whom to trust. He decided upon Mrs. Ludlow. She gave him a warm welcome, and without a moment's hesitation or loss of time ordered two horses saddled for Morgan, and one for her son. She handed Morgan sixty dollars in gold, all she had in the house. 'Now go. Ride for your life.' She did not show any fear of the vengeance Yankees were sure to wreak upon her and hers if they knew the part she played in Morgan's escape." Mrs. Chesnut goes on to say: "Throughout Kentucky it was the same thing. Men and horses were at his command, and brave women tried to force their money on him and were mortified when he refused."

Her general was with Mattie in Abingdon, Virginia, in the summer of 1864.

Winchester [Tennessee] Jan. 6th/63

Come to me my own Darling quickly. I was wretched but now I am *almost* happy and will be quite when my precious husband is again with me. I can bear anything Darling when you are with me, and so long as I have your love—but when separated from you and I know that you are surrounded by so many dangers and hardships as you have been on your last expedition I become a weak nervous child. Have I not lived a great deal, love, in the last three weeks?

When I look back now at the time, it seems three years. But in each hour I have passed through, there has always been one dear face ever before me—and can you doubt whose face that was! If you do, I dont intend to enlighten you, at least until you come. So there is another inducement. I have so much to tell you, and so very much to hear from you. Although I have heard nothing from you since you left Glasgow, I *knew* you had accomplished what you had in view— but oh I was so anxious for your safety.

I had some dark days, dearest, and when the battle was raging around me in such fury, and everybody from the commander-in-chief to the privates were praying for "Morgan to come," I thanked God in the anguish of my heart that it was not for me to say where you should be. There was one continual inquiry at the front door— "When will Genl. Morgan be here?" Madame Rumor says you attacked Nashville last Monday and as a natural course *captured* it.[1] Genl. Bragg established his head Quarters at this place. We reached here today . . . and although an entire stranger to the people I am with, they received me, as the saying is, with open arms, because I am your Wife. We are comfortably, but very plainly accommodated. Alice is with me. Papa & Mama remained at home with Ella. I almost dread to hear from them. I am so impatient for tomorrow to come. When the Courier arrived Cols.—— & Johnston of Genl. Bragg's staff were calling upon us. Came with an invitation from the Genl. for us to join his Hd. Qts. but Gen. Hardee had a prior claim. I sent the papers giving an account of your expedition, or part of it, to Gen. B. Everybody is anxious to hear from you, and to see you, but none a thousandth part as much as your little wife.

I am at Mrs. McGee, just in the suburbs of the town, so you will know exactly where to find me. I love to write to you, Dearest, and your *sweet* letters always make me happy. It grieved me that I could send you no word of love from my pen while in Kty. Both because it would have been a relief to pour out my heart to you, and then, Darling, I feared you would forget me. You left me so soon. Genl. Hardee has just arrived, and regrets he will not be here when you come tomorrow. Alice sends love. . . . Good night, my *Hero*. My dreams are all of you.

Your affectionate
MATTIE

[1] It was only rumor.

9. AGNES—"THERE IS NOT A BONNET FOR SALE IN RICHMOND"

We owe to a lifelong friend the memory of the lively lady who preferred to be known only by her Christian name. When Mrs. Roger A. Pryor published her Reminiscences of Peace and War *she happily included many of Agnes' letters to her. "Being a lady of the old school," explained Sara Pryor, "she is averse from seeing her name in print." We gather that her husband had been a Member of Congress in Washington at the same time as Roger, and now was a colonel on service with the Confederate army near Richmond, while Agnes, like Mrs. Chesnut, lived at the Spotswood Hotel. Her letters are filled with gossip of the Confederate capital; of White House receptions; of activities of old friends of Washington days. Since paper was no longer available, she wrote on blank sheets torn from an old album.*

At this time Mrs. Pryor was a refugee near Suffolk, Virginia. Some of her own writing will appear later on.

Richmond, January 7, 1863

My Dearie: Have you no pen, ink, and paper on the Blackwater—the very name of which suggests ink? I get no news of you at all. How do you amuse yourself, and have you anything to read? I am sending you to-day a copy of Victor Hugo's last novel, "Les Miserables," reprinted by a Charleston firm on the best paper they could get, poor fellows, pretty bad I must acknowledge. You'll go wild over that book—I did—and everybody does.

Major Shepard must order some copies for the brigade. As he has plenty of meat and bread now, he can afford it. I have cried my eyes out over Fantine and Cosette and Jean Valjean. The soldiers are all reading it. They calmly walk into the bookstores, poor dear fellows, and ask for "Lee's Miserables faintin'!"—the first volume being "Fantine." I've worlds of news to tell you. Alice Gregory is engaged to Arthur Herbert, the handsomest man I know. Alice is looking lovely and so happy. Helen came to see me in Petersburg, and is all the time worried about Ben. Did you know that Jim Field lost a leg at Malvern Hills—or in the hospital afterwards? He was such a lovely fellow—engaged to Sue Bland—I never saw a handsomer pair. Well, Sue thinks as much as I do about good looks, and Jim wrote to release her. She had a good cry, and finally came down to Richmond, married him, and took him home to nurse him.

Do you realize the fact that we shall soon be without a stitch of clothes? There is not a bonnet for sale in Richmond. Some of the girls smuggle them, which I for one consider in the worst possible taste, to say the least. We have no right at this time to dress better than our neighbors, and besides, the soldiers need every cent of our money. Do you remember in Washington my pearl-gray silk bonnet, trimmed inside with lilies of the valley? I have ripped it up, washed and ironed it, dyed the lilies blue (they are bluebells now), and it is very becoming. All the girls intend to plait hats next summer when the wheat ripens, for they have no blocks on which to press the coal-scuttle bonnets, and after all when our blockade is raised we may find they are not at all worn, while hats are hats and never go out of fashion. The country girls made them last summer and pressed the crowns over bowls and tin pails. I could make lovely flowers if I had materials.

It seems rather volatile to discuss such things while our dear country is in such peril. Heaven knows I would costume myself in coffee-bags if that would help, but having no coffee, where could I get the bags?

The papers announce that General French[1] reports the enemy forty-five thousand strong at Suffolk. How many men has your General? Dear, dear!

But we are fortifying around Richmond. While I write a great crowd of negroes is passing through the streets, singing as they march. They have been working on the fortifications north of the city, and are now going to work on them south of us. They don't seem to concern themselves much about Mr. Lincoln's Emancipation Proclamation, and they seem to have no desire to do any of the fighting.

Your loving

AGNES

P.S.—I attended Mrs. Davis's last reception. There was a crowd, all in evening dress. You see, as we don't often wear our evening gowns, they are still quite passable. I wore the gray silk with eleven flounces which was made for Mrs. Douglas's[2] last reception, and by the bye, who do you think was at the battle of Williamsburg, on General

---

[1] Major-General William H. French, U. S. A.
[2] Wife of Senator Stephen A. Douglas.

McClellan's staff? The Prince de Joinville who drank the Rose wine with you at the Baron de Limbourg's reception to the Japs. Doesn't it all seem so long ago—so far away? The Prince de Joinville escorted me to one of the President's levees—don't you remember?— and now I attend another President's levee and hear him calmly telling people that rats, if fat, are as good as squirrels, and that we can never afford mule meat. It would be too expensive, but the time may come when rats will be in demand.

Dearly,

AGNES.

10. CORDELIA LEWIS SCALES—"I WORE MY PISTOL
ALL THE TIME!"

For the sixth time Northern officers had made headquarters at Cordelia Scales's Oakland!

Late in 1862 General Grant's main base was at Columbus, Kentucky. Thence he used the railroad line south to Holly Springs, eight miles below Oakland, and built it up as a great secondary base. His plan was to send his principal army down the railroad while General William Tecumseh Sherman's force would float the winding Yazoo River in a fleet of transports. The objective of the combined operation was the capture of Vicksburg, the Confederacy's great stronghold on the Mississippi.

Sherman got started. But Grant had to change all his conceptions in a hurry. On December nineteenth the secretive, indefatigable N. B. Forrest got on his line to Columbus and began tearing up track and creating general havoc. And on the twentieth Earl Van Dorn burst into Holly Springs like a tornado and wrecked all those vast Union stores.

Delia writes again to her friend Lou Irby.

Destruction Hollow
Mississippi
Jan. 27th 1863

My Dear Sweet little Friend:

I really thought some time ago that I never should have the pleasure of writing to you again, & you have no idea how sad it made me feel, to think, that I was in the Federal line, & would never have the pleasure of holding sweet communion with the dearest friend I have on earth. Oh! Lou, I hope you may never experience such feelings as I did the day the Yankee army passed our home—you will think no doubt as I had stood two raids, that I ought to have got use to them & I suppose I would, if I had not seen the manner in which our troops left Holly Springs & I am sorry to say it was shameful; I could not keep from crying to save my life, I felt as though my heart would break—just a few days before I had attended the "Grand review," & I felt so confident that our army intended making a stand, & that north Mississippi would be defended. But I soon found out it was a stampede instead of a stand, they anticipated making. Our soldiers were ready & anxious for a fight, & it was all owing to the bad generalship of Vandorn & Pemberton,[1] that we did not drive the last blue devil from the country. When I saw the federals coming in such force, I thought this portion of the country would be held for some time & not like they had formerly done—stay a week or two & then "skeedadle," so you may know how bad I felt.

The first skirmish I witnessed was in front of our house at the pickett stand; our men were surprised by McPherson's[2] Cavalry. They were near enough to use their pistols; I'll tell you what our pickets run like clever fellows, they made railroad time. After the fight was over three hundred of the Yankees came up to our house— one of the officers asked me, "Well, Miss, what made your men Skeedadle so." I told him that our men only wanted to show them that they would beat them at every game they tried, that they had beat them fighting so often, they wanted a little variety. Pa was out in the field soon after the skirmish took place & the Yankees on the hill in front of our house fired on him three times. One of the balls passed through his coat under his left arm, one by his ear, and the other through his hat—they knew he was an unarmed citizen too, Lou. I'll tell you what the cowardely rascals have no respect whatever, for age, nor sex.

The day the army came to Holly Springs, & when the waggon trains were passing thirty & forty of the Yankees would rush in at a time, take everything to eat they could lay their hands on, & break, destroy & steal everything they wanted to—all of our mules, horses & waggons were taken, 42 waggons were loaded with corn at our

---

[1] General John C. Pemberton, who had been in command of the Department of South Carolina and Georgia, was sent west by the government to supersede Van Dorn in November 1862.

[2] General James B. McPherson, U. S. A.

cribs, & a good many more after. I'll tell you what I thought we would certainly starve. One thousand black republicans, the 26th Ill., camped in our groves, for two weeks. We did have such a beautiful grove & place too, but you ought to see it now, it looks like some "banquet hall deserted"—all the gates and pailings are torn down & burnt & as for a rail it is a curiosity up here. Col. Gilmore was in command of the 26th. He made our house headquarters; he use to let his men go out foraging every day & one day while some of them were out stealing chickens & hogs about four miles from here at Thompsons' place, a company of our "guerillas" overhauled them— killing two & wounding two. I never saw such enraged men in my life as they were when those that were taken prisoners & paroled came in camp with the news.

The Col. took Pa's room for a hospital; when they were bringing the wounded in, I never heard men groan as they did in my life; all our sick & wounded in the hospital did not make as much noise as those two did. Gilmore searched our house for arms & I wore my pistol (a very fine six shooter) all the time & stood by my saratoga, would not permit them to search it. One said, "She's a trump."

I met with an old school mate of Dabney's from Annapolis, his name was Meriman, a first cousin of Meriman, the jeweller, in Memphis. I liked him as well as I could a Yankee; & surprising to say he was a gentleman. . . . They had a large flag waving in our grove & you could not see anything but blue coats & tents. The Col. made the band come up & play Dixie for me. After Mitchel's company killed those men they turned Mrs. Thompson out of doors & burnt her house. The Col. left our house with two companys & waggons, to plunder & destroy the widow Mitchel's. When they got there & asked her if the Captain was her son she told them "Yes, Billie Mitchel is my son & I am proud of him. He is doing nothing but his duty & I hope he'll continue, & sir as long as I have a crust of bread that crust will be shared with him & his company." The Yankees turned & left her & did not touch one thing. Her son is such a brave fellow. Capt. Meriman told me " if her sons lack bravery it wasnt their mothers fault."

The next set that camped on us was the 90th Ill. Irish Legion. They treated us a great deal better than the black republicans did— the Irish were all democrats. One of the officers' wives, Mrs. Steward, staid here. She was a very nice lady. By the way, she was almost a Secesh; she was begging me to play for her, & I told her I played nothing but Rebel songs. She said they were the very kind she wanted me to sing to' her—so I sang "My Maryland," "Bonnie Blue flag," "Mississippi Camp Song," "Cheer Boys Cheer," "Life on the Tented Field," & "Dixie." She said "Oh! they are beautiful, I dont blame you for loving them." She made me write them off for her.

The next day Capt. Flynn came up; he asked me if I knew what he came for. I told him no; he then said it was to beg a great favor of me & he hoped I would be so kind as to grant it, that he wanted me to sing "My Maryland" for him. At first I thanked him & told him I did not play for Federal officers but Pa said I must, that Capt. Flynn had kept us from starving & had been so kind to us so I consented. He was so much pleased with it that he got me to write the words off for him. I put a little Confederate flag at the top of it & wrote under it "no northern hand shall rule this land." He sent it on North to his wife.

I wish you could have seen the parting between Capt. Flynn & myself, the Major & him & a good many officers came up to tell me goodbye & the Major was saying he was going to reduce the south to starvation & then send us north. I said to him I had rather starve to death in the South than be a beggar in the North, Major. Capt. Flynn jumped up, caught me by the hand & said "Miss Scales, you are a whole-souled Rebel & I admire you so much for it. I do wish I could stay here & protect you while our army is retreating. I'd fight for you, God knows I would." That sounds strange for a Yankee, dont it?

The next we had were the "Grierson Thieves"[1] & the next the 7th Kan. Jay hawkers. I can't write of these; it makes my blood boil to think of the outrages they committed. They tore the ear rings out of the ladies ears, pulled their rings & brest pins off, took them by the hair; threw them down & knocked them about. One of them sent me word that they shot ladies as well as men, & if I did not stop talking to them so & displaying my Confederate flag, he'd blow my brains out. I sent him word by the lady that I did not expect anything better from Yankees, but he must remember two could play at that game. Capt. Bannett was telling me before they all left about Stonewall Jackson telling his men about the passage in the Bible where the South should drive the North in the sea.[2] I told him I hoped I would be at the jumping off place & see the last blue coat go under.

[1] The 6th Illinois Cavalry was commanded by Colonel Benjamin H. Grierson.
[2] See Daniel, XI.

Lou, I tell you what we've been through fiery trials, and if we did not exactly cuss, there is a great many of us *that thought* cuss mighty strong.

Oh! how I did shout when Vandorn came into Holly Springs. He made them "skeedaddle" shows you born. I was so glad I had the pleasure of seeing Mr. Yankee run; just the day before some of them asked me where our men were that they could not find any of them. . . . I would write more about it but Mr. Caldwell is waiting to start. He is going to mail it at Sardis. The girls are wearing such pretty garabaldies up here. . . .

Goodbye my dear Loulie, Your

Aff. friend

DELIA

11. BETTY HERNDON MAURY—"WE ARE TO BE TURNED OUT OF DOORS"

We have now some of the concluding entries in Betty's diary. That of February 18, 1863, is the last. The pitifulness of her situation becomes apparent. Her great father, accompanied by her young brother Mathy, was in England on behalf of the Confederate government. Her mother and sisters were scattered in various parts of Virginia. Dick was with the army in Virginia. John was with the army in the West and would lose his life at Vicksburg.

Her husband, Will, had not succeeded in getting an appointment. They lived in the back parlor at her Cousin Hite's.

After Betty was forced to leave Richmond she wandered about trying to find a place of safety within the Confederate lines. She managed finally to reach Charlottesville where her baby was born. There she stayed until Appomattox.

When the war was over she and her husband and children returned to Washington, where Will became prominent at the bar and Betty was known as a woman of "forceful character and intellect." She died on January 8, 1903.

It was after her death that her daughter Alice, now Mrs. James Parmalee, found her mother's wartime diary, until then unknown in the family. Written in a clear, legible hand, it filled two large composition books. Mrs. Parmalee gave it to the Library of Congress— one of the most colorful of all extant Civil War diaries.

Richmond, Virginia
January 30th, 1863

If I live until next May, I expect to have another little baby. Cousin Hite has been very kind in expressing her willingness to have me here then and to do what she can for me. I told her how grateful I felt and how highly I appreciated her kindness. Our board here is two hundred dollars a month!! but that is less than we would have to pay at any boarding house in town. I do not know where the money is to come from to meet all our additional expenses in the Spring. But the Lord will provide I feel sure. Will gets a little employment here sometimes through his friend Mr. Ould,[1] but nothing permanent or constant.

Jan. 31st. 1863

Mrs. Jarnette, of Caroline [County] has been on a visit to Washington (Ran the blockade of the Rappahannock at night) and through the influence of some Yankee friends was allowed to return with a quantity of baggage!

She brought a trunk from Mother, containing things for cousin Sally, cousin Martha and myself. She sent Nannie Belle a Christmas gift of the most beautiful crying doll I ever saw. It was dressed in white with red ribbon trimmings and red shoes and a red riding hood on.

Judge Hallyburton has allowed Will two thousand dollars for his services as Receiver while he was in Fredericksburg. It is a great comfort to feel we have that much ahead and owe no man anything.

We see through the Yankee papers that Papa and Matsy have reached England in safety. I miss Papa so much. I miss his guiding influence and advice in the family even though we were not always with him.

Feb. 1st 1863

The "Princess Royal," an English vessel, was captured a few days ago while attempting to run the blockade into Charleston. The papers say the Captain escaped with valuable despatches from Commodore Matthew Fontaine Maury. I hope he had letters for us. We fear that Papa sent us a box of goods by the same opportunity. We all gave him commissions to execute in England. . . .

[1] Robert Ould had charge of the exchange of prisoners.

Feb. 12-1863

We have received letters from Papa from London of dates to the
20th of December. He did send us a large case of goods by the Princess Royal. It cost between three and four hundred dollars in gold,
and is worth nearly *four times* as much in our money. If we had lost
as much two years ago, I would have thought it a great calamity,
but now we see and feel so much real trouble that we cannot let the
loss of a few dollars trouble us much, especially when we hear that
all of our dear ones are safe and well. . . .

Feb. 17-1863

Will received a written notice from Mr. McGruder yesterday to leave
at the end of the month. It is a great surprise and mortification to
us. We have had no falling out, no difficulty with him or cousin Hite
or anyone in the house. Everything has been smooth and pleasant
up to this time. I had an express understanding with her that we were
to remain until after May. It was at her suggestion that I engaged
a nurse and with her consent that I brought the furniture here from
Fredericksburg, and now when Richmond is crowded to excess and
it is impossible to get comfortable even decent lodgings at any price
—we are to be turned out of doors.

No one will be willing to take us when told that I expect to be
confined in a month or two.

Feb. 18, 1863

I have written Aunt Betsy Woolfolk telling her of our troubles—of
how homeless and forlorn I feel and asking her to let me come there
as a boarder. Of course Will will have to stay in town.

12. MISSOURI STOKES—MY BROTHER IS AN EXCHANGE PRISONER

*A young teacher of Decatur, Georgia, Missouri Stokes was the
half sister of Mary A. H. Gay. Her only brother Thomie had moved
to Texas before the war. He enlisted with the 10th Texas Infantry
and was killed at the bloody Battle of Franklin, Tennessee, November 30, 1864.*

Decatur, Georgia

March, 1863. On the 11th of January, 1863, Arkansas Post, the fort where Thomie was stationed, fell into the hands of Yankees. General Churchill's[1] whole command, numbering about four thousand, were captured, a few being killed and wounded. We knew that Thomie, if alive, must be a prisoner, but could hear no tidings from him. Our suspense continued until the latter part of March, when Ma received a letter from our loved one, written at Camp Chase (military prison), Ohio, February 10th. This letter she forwarded to me, and I received it March 21st, with heart-felt emotions of gratitude to Him who had preserved his life. A few weeks afterwards another letter came, saying he expected to be exchanged in a few days, and then for several weeks we heard no more. . . .

May 16, 1863. He seemd much changed, although only four years and a half had elasped since we parted. He looked older, thinner and more careworn, and gray hairs are sprinkled among his dark brown curls. His health had been poor in the army, and then, when he left Camp Chase, he, as well as the other prisoners, was stripped by the Yankees of nearly all his warm clothing. He left the prison in April, and was exchanged at City Point. How strange the dealings of Providence. Truly was he led by a way he knew not. He went out to Texas by way of the West, and returned home from the East. God be thanked for preserving his life, when so many of his comrades have died. He is a miracle of mercy. After their capture, they were put on boats from which Yankee small-pox patients had been taken. Some died of small-pox, but Thomie has had varioloid and so escaped. He was crowded on a boat with twenty-two hundred, and scarcely had standing room. Many died on the passage up the river, one poor fellow with his head in Thomie's lap. May he never go through similar scenes again!

Monday, June 15th. Thomie left. I rode with him a little beyond the schoolhouse, then took my books and basket, and with one kiss, and, on my part, a tearful good-bye, we parted. As I walked slowly back, I felt so lonely. He had been with me just long enough for me to realize a brother's kind protection, and now he's torn away, and I'm again alone. I turned and looked. He was driving slowly along —he turned a corner and was hidden from my view. Shall I see him

---

[1] Brigadier-General Thomas C. Churchill surrendered Fort Hindman at Arkansas Post and its garrison of 4,791 men, after a four hours' bombardment by ironclads, to Major-General John A. McClernand's army of 32,000.

no more? Or shall we meet again? God only knows. After a fit of weeping, and one earnest prayer for him, I turned my steps to my little school.

13. AUGUSTA JANE EVANS—"MY NEW NOVEL IS DEDICATED TO THE ARMY OF THE CONFEDERACY"

Augusta, the eldest of eight children, was born on May 8, 1835, in Columbus, Georgia; lived for four years in San Antonio, Texas; moved to Mobile, Alabama, in 1849. She wrote Inez: A tale of the Alamo *in 1855 and* Beulah *in 1859, both popular novels. A love affair with her New York editor ended with the outbreak of war when she volunteered for work in the army hospital near home. In recognition of her service there General Beauregard gave her his personal pen. After First Manassas she felt inspired to write a novel which might bring glory to the Confederacy and lift the South's morale.* Macaria; or, Altars of Sacrifice, *bound in wallpaper, was published in Richmond in 1863. Augusta sent a copy of it by a blockade-runner to her old New York publisher who brought out an edition there.* Macaria *was read with enthusiasm by Southern soldiers and civilians. Its value as propaganda was recognized by Northern leaders, who called it "contraband and dangerous," and banned it among Yankee troops.*

St. Elmo, *published in 1866, was the great best seller of its day. It was shaped to meet exactly the mood of the South. Hotels, steamboats, plantations and towns were named after it.*

In 1868 Miss Evans married Colonel L. M. Wilson of Mobile. Various novels flowed from her pen. She died at her home "Ashland" at seventy-four.

The letter that follows was answered by General Beauregard on March 24. "Reports of the Battles of Bull Run and Manassas," he wrote, were being forwarded. The novelist revised the thirtieth chapter of Macaria *to accord.*

President Davis took offense at some things Beauregard said in these reports. Thereafter his hostility was felt by the general to be watchful and adroit, neglectful of no opportunity.[1]

General Beauregard was ill after the Battle of Shiloh, and when the Western army retired from Corinth to Tupelo, General Bragg took over the command.

[1] See Beauregard's article in *Battles and Leaders of the Civil War*, I, 225.

In April 1861 Pierre Gustave Toutant Beauregard had secured the bloodless surrender of Fort Sumter. Two years later he was back in Charleston charged with the defense of all South Carolina, Georgia and Florida. He made new installations and arrangements for the defense of the city which withstood an assault by Admiral DuPont on April 7 and later and more formidable attacks. "In neither army," says Robert S. Henry in The Story of the Confederacy *"was there a military engineer more competent, nor one with a better eye to the uses of the artillery arm."*

Mobile Alabama March 17th 1863

General Beauregard

Fearful as I am of intruding upon your valuable time, especially at this juncture when you must be so constantly occupied, and hoping that the reasons I shall assign, will plead my pardon, you must permit me to express my earnest gratitude for your exceedingly kind and gratifying letter, and also for the confidence you repose in me, as manifested by the gift of a copy of your "Review," which it seems you deem inexpedient to publish at this crisis. As I read the analysis and complete refutation of the ill natured, venomous, ungenerous and jealous remarks, elicited by the presentation of that petition, which embodied the hopes and wishes of the entire Confederacy, and reflected upon the systematic injustice that had been heaped upon you, by the President, the blood tingled in my veins, and I could not forbear recalling the words of Tennyson:

> "Ah God! for a man with heart, head, hand,
>   Like some of the simple great ones gone
>   Forever, and ever by!
>   One still strong man in a blatant land,
>   Whatever they call him, what care I?
>   Aristocrat, democrat, autocrat,—one
>   Who can rule, and dare not lie." [1]

The day is not distant I trust, when all the facts connected with the infamous persecution of yourself, and General Price,[2] may be laid before an indignant and outraged people.

Apropos! of the Western Scipio, I recently had the pleasure of

---

[1] From *Maud*.

[2] General Sterling Price had been subordinated to General Van Dorn in the West by order of President Davis.

becoming acquainted with him, as he passed through Mobile en route for Vicksburg, and as I looked into his noble gentle face, beaming with generosity and enthusiasm while he spoke of *You* Sir, in terms of unmeasured admiration and exalted esteem; I felt the lines of the great Ode to Wellington, creeping across my lips:

> "Oh good gray head which all men knew;
> Ah face from which their omens all men drew!
> Oh iron nerve, to true occasion true!"

In alluding to your removal from Department No. 2, which he said he should never cease to deplore, and regarded as the most flagrant Administrative faux pas, of the war, he added with his genial smile, and humorous twinkle of the eye, "in fine, General Beauregard has certainly been treated with more *rank injustice* than any other man in the Confederacy, except *one* far less important individual." . . .

Allow me if you please to detail my reason for inflicting a letter upon you at this time, when any interruption must be annoying. You may perhaps remember that I mentioned to you, that I had a MS, novel containing a chapter relative to the Battle of Manassas, where one of my characters was killed. I was very anxious to read it to you but could find no appropriate opportunity. At the time that I spoke of it to you, I intended not to publish it until the close of the war, but recently circumstances have determined me to bring it out, as soon as I can finish copying the MS upon which I am now employed. The chapter to which I allude is the XXXth and before I copy it I am extremely desirous to know that I am entirely accurate in all my statements relative to the Battle. I am afraid to trust to my memory of the conversation I had with you concerning it, and to avoid the possibility of error, I beg permission most respectfully to propound the following inquiries. Am I correct in saying—

1. That you and Gen'l Johnston were not acquainted with the fact that McDowell had left Washington with the main Fed. army to attack you at Manassas Junction, until a young Lady of Washington (I give no name), disguised as a market woman, and engaged in selling milk to the Fed. soldiers, succeeded in making her way through their lines to *Fairfax Court House* and telegraphed you of the contemplated attack.[1]

[1] See footnote, page 62 *supra.*

2. That you immediately telegraphed to Gen'l Johnston, then at Winchester, and in consequence of this information he hastened to Manassas?[1]

3. At what hour did you learn that your order for an advance on Centreville by your right wing, had failed to reach its destination?[2]

4. Did you not *lead* in *person* the second great charge which recovered the *plateau* and took the Batteries that crowned it?[3] Could I satisfy myself of the correctness of my view or impression regarding, these points, *elsewhere* than by applying to you, believe me Sir, I would not annoy you, for I shrink from the thought of becoming troublesome to you, or imposing, upon your generosity. I regret exceedingly that I could not have submitted this chapter of my new novel to you, before sending it to press. It is dedicated to the *Army of the Confederacy*.

In view of the impending attack upon Charleston, your name is constantly on our lips, in our hearts, and believe me, *in our prayers*. Yet apprehension does not mingle with my interest in all the tidings that come from your Department; I rest in perfect assurance, that with the blessing of our God, victory will, as everywhere else, nestle upon your banner. Have you heard recently from Mrs. Beauregard?[4] Earnestly, most earnestly do I hope, that ere this, her health has been perfectly restored, and that the day, is not very distant, when in peace and prosperity, you may return laden with the love, and followed by the prayers of a redeemed and grateful people, to your rescued home, and the bosom of your beloved family. That God will shield you, from all the dangers that threaten, and preserve you to the country, which so demands your services, and rests its hopes upon you, is the *heartfelt* wish of,—

Yours most respectfully and gratefully
AUGUSTA J. EVANS

P.S. My Sisters desire me to tender you, their love and gratitude for your kind and gratifying remembrance. A.J.E.

---

[1] Beauregard sent the word of McDowell's movement at once to President Davis, who passed it on to General Joseph E. Johnston.

[2] It appears that this was about 8:30 A.M., Sunday, July 21, 1861.

[3] Beauregard says (*Battles and Leaders of the Civil War*, 1, 213): "For the recovery of the plateau I ordered a charge of the entire line of battle, including the reserves, which at this crisis I myself led into action."

[4] In 1860 the general had married Caroline, daughter of André Deslonde, a sugar planter of St. James's Parish, Louisiana. She died in the spring of 1864.

14. EMMA SANSOM—"GENERAL FORREST ASKED FOR A LOCK OF MY HAIR"

On a small farm by Black Creek in northern Alabama Emma Sansom, sixteen years old, was living with her widowed mother and a sister. Her only brother was with the 19th Alabama Infantry. Of a sudden she was caught up in the startling tides of war. General Nathan Bedford Forrest was hot on the track of Colonel Abel D. Streight, of Indiana, who with 2,000 picked horsemen was aiming to cut General Bragg's railroad supply line between Atlanta and Chattanooga. Forrest's force was only about a third as large. By leading him to the lost ford Emma helped materially in the pursuit which led to the capture of Streight and his whole force near Rome on May 3.

Her bold, dangerous ride with "Old Bed" was not unrewarded. That night he wrote: "My highest regards to Miss Emma Sansom for her gallant conduct while my posse was skirmishing with the Federals across Black Creek near Gadsden Alabama." And thirty-six years later the legislature of Alabama voted her, as a token of "admiration and gratitude," the gift of 640 acres of land.

On October 29, 1864, Emma married C. B. Johnson, of the 10th Alabama. They went to Texas after the war, where her husband died in 1887, leaving her with seven children. She died August 9, 1900, and her grave is at Little Mound, Upshur County, Texas.

We were at home on the morning of May 2, 1863, when about eight or nine o'clock, a company of men wearing blue uniforms and riding mules and horses galloped past the house and went on towards the bridge. Pretty soon a great crowd of them came along, and some of them stopped at the gate and asked us to bring them some water. Sister and I each took a bucket of water, and gave it to them at the gate. One of them asked me where my father was. I told him he was dead. He asked me if I had any brothers. I told him I had *six*. He asked where they were, and I said they were in the Confederate Army. "Do they think the South will whip?" "They do." "What do you think about it?" "I think God is on our side and we will win." "You do? Well, if you had seen us whip Colonel Roddey[1] the other

---

[1] Philip D. Roddey, the Confederate cavalry leader.

day and run him across the Tennessee River, you would have thought God was on the side of the best artillery."

By this time some of them began to dismount, and we went into the house. They came in and began to search for firearms and men's saddles. They did not find anything but a side-saddle, and one of them cut the skirts off that. Just then some one from the road said, in a loud tone: "You men bring a chunk of fire with you, and get out of that house." The men got the fire in the kitchen and started out, and an officer put a guard around the house, saying: "This guard is for your protection." They all soon hurried down to the bridge, and in a few minutes we saw the smoke rising and knew they were burning the bridge. As our fence extended up to the railing of the bridge, mother said: "Come with me and we will pull our rails away, so they will not be destroyed." As we got to the top of the hill we saw the rails were already piled on the bridge and were on fire, and the Yankees were in line on the other side guarding it.

We turned back towards the house, and had not gone but a few steps before we saw a Yankee coming at full speed, and behind were some more men on horses. I heard them shout, "Halt! and surrender!" The man stopped, threw up his hand, and handed over his gun. The officer to whom the soldier surrendered said: "Ladies, do not be alarmed, I am General Forrest; I and my men will protect you from harm." He inquired: "Where are the Yankees?"

Mother said: "They have set the bridge on fire and are standing in line on the other side, and if you go down that hill they will kill the last one of you."

By this time our men had come up, and some went out in the field, and both sides commenced shooting. We ran to the house, and I got there ahead of all. General Forrest dashed up to the gate and said to me: "Can you tell me where I can get across that creek?"

I told him there was an unsafe bridge two miles farther down the stream, but that I knew of a trail about two hundred yards above the bridge on our farm, where our cows used to cross in low water, and I believed he could get his men over there, and that if he would have my saddle put on a horse I would show him the way.

He said: "There is not time to saddle a horse; get up here behind me." As he said this he rode close to the bank on the side of the road, and I jumped up behind him.

Just as we started off mother came up about out of breath and gasped out: "Emma, what do you mean?"

General Forrest said: "She is going to show me a ford where I can get my men over in time to catch those Yankees before they get to Rome. Don't be uneasy; I will bring her back safe."

We rode out into a field through which ran a branch or small ravine and along which there was a thick undergrowth that protected us for a while from being seen by the Yankees at the bridge or on the other side of the creek. This branch emptied into the creek just above the ford. When we got close to the creek, I said: "General Forrest, I think we had better get off the horse, as we are now where we may be seen."

We both got down and crept through the bushes and when we were right at the ford I happened to be in front. He stepped quickly between me and the Yankees saying: "I am glad to have you for a pilot, but I am not going to make breastworks of you."

The cannon and the other guns were firing fast by this time, as I pointed out to him where to go into the water and out on the other bank, and then we went back towards the house. He asked me my name, and asked me to give him a lock of my hair. The cannon-balls were screaming over us so loud that we were told to leave and hide in some place out of danger, which we did. Soon all the firing stopped, and I started back home. On the way I met General Forrest again, and he told me that he had written a note for me and left it on the bureau. He asked me again for a lock of my hair, and as we went into the house he said: "One of my bravest men has been killed, and he is laid out in the house. His name is Robert Turner. I want you to see that he is buried in some graveyard near here." He then told me good-bye and got on his horse, and he and his men rode away and left us all alone.

My sister and I sat up all night watching over the dead soldier, who had lost his life fighting for our rights, in which we were overpowered but never conquered. General Forrest and his men endeared themselves to us forever.

15. MARY ANNA JACKSON—"THEY SAID MY HUSBAND
HAD BEEN WOUNDED"

Mrs. Jackson had been with Stonewall four times after he left Lexington that spring morning in 1861.

In September '61 she journeyed from her father's home in North

Carolina to visit the general at Camp Harman, his headquarters near Manassas.

The following winter, when he was stationed at Winchester, they lived at the home of their friend, the Reverend J. R. Graham. With the approach of the spring campaign in the Valley she went back to her father's again, and they did not meet for thirteen months. She wrote to him every day; knit his socks; made his pantaloons and caps with broad gilt bands—and for this he scolded her. "Please," he wrote, "do not have so much gold braid about them." She begged him to come for a visit, but he did not feel he could leave his command. On November 23, 1862, their daughter was born in Charlotte, North Carolina, and was named Julia—for the general's mother Julia Neale.

Next April Mrs. Jackson and the baby were with Stonewall at Mr. Yerby's a mile from the camp at Moss Neck outside Fredericksburg. The baby was baptized by the army chaplain and christened "Little Miss Stonewall" by the soldiers. Minis, the photographer, came from Richmond to take the general's picture. Mrs. Jackson curled his hair in ringlets and he sat stern and unsmiling, dressed in his new uniform, the gift of Jeb Stuart. Henry Kyd Douglas in I Rode with Stonewall *gives a charming picture of the family:*

"I do not forget my embarrassment when at the mischievous suggestion of one of the neighborhood ladies Mrs. Jackson handed me little Julia to hold for a space. The General walked in and his amusement increased the surrounding merriment, but he made the nurse come to the rescue. Little Julia grew up in her beauty and was very fair to look upon. She married young and died young, and two children take her place with her mother."[1]

After nine days Mrs. Jackson and the baby were hurried off before the onset of the Battle of Chancellorsville. They stayed in Richmond with their friend the Reverend Moses D. Hoge, Presbyterian minister and Confederate chaplain. She had been there only five days when the news came: her husband had been wounded in three places. On Saturday May 3, the second day of Chancellorsville, after a march across the front of Joe Hooker's army, he had completed his last and greatest flank attack, assuring Lee of victory against double the Confederate strength; then in the darkness and confusion of the fighting he had been fired on by his own men.

[1] Chapel Hill: The University of North Carolina Press, 1940.

*Mrs. Jackson reached him at Mr. Chandler's at Guinea Station,
where he had been brought in agony. On May 10 at quarter past
three in the afternoon, dying, he said: "Let us cross over the river
and rest under the shade of the trees."*

*Afterward they carried his body to lie by the side of his first wife,
Eleanor Junkin Jackson, and her daughter who had lived only a
week. Once more Mary Anna returned with Julia to her father's
house in North Carolina.*

*Through the rest of her life honors were showered on General
Jackson's widow. She shrank from publicity and accepted only those
attentions which did not require her to speak or to appear in public.
Her* Memoirs of Stonewall Jackson *was published in 1895, a valuable
contribution to our knowledge of his personal as well as his military
life. She died at her home in Charlotte, March 24, 1915.*

On Sunday morning [May 3, 1863], as we arose from family worship in Dr. Hoge's parlor, Dr. Brown informed me that the news
had come that General Jackson had been wounded. . . . On Tuesday my brother Joseph arrived to my great relief, to take me to my
husband, but my disappointment was only increased by his report
that it had taken him nearly three days to ride through the country
and elude the raiding enemy. It was not until Thursday morning that
the blockade was broken, and we went up on an armed train prepared to fight its way through.

A few hours of unmolested travel brought us to Guiney's Station,
and we were taken at once to the residence of Mr. Chandler, which
was a large country-house, and very near it, in the yard, was a small,
humble abode, in which lay my precious, suffering husband.

From the time I reached him he was too ill to notice or talk much,
and he lay most of the time in a semi-conscious state; but when
aroused, he recognized those about him and consciousness would
return. Soon after I entered his room he was impressed by the woe-
ful anxiety and sadness betrayed in my face, and said: "My darling,
you must cheer up, and not wear a long face. . . . My darling, you
are very much loved."

Early on Sunday morning, the 10th of May, I was called out of
the sick-room by Dr. Morrison, who told me that the doctors, having
done every thing that human skill could devise to stay the hand of
death, had lost all hope, and that my precious, brave, noble husband
could not live!

He now sank rapidly into unconsciousness. . . .

That night, after a few hours sleep from sheer exhaustion, I awoke, when all in my chamber was perfect stillness, and the full moon poured a flood of light through the windows, glorious enough to lift my soul heavenwards; but oh, the agony and anguish of those silent midnight hours, when the terrible reality of my loss and the desolation of widowhood forced itself upon me, and took possession of my whole being! My unconscious little one lay sweetly sleeping by my side, and my kind friend, Mrs. Hoge, was near; but I strove not to awaken them, and all alone I stemmed the torrent of grief which seemed insupportable, until prayer to Him, who alone can comfort, again brought peace and quietness to my heart.

The next morning I went once more to see the remains, which were now in the casket, and were covered with spring flowers. His dear face was wreathed with the lovely lily of the valley—the emblem of humility—his own predominating grace.

On Monday morning began the sad journey to Richmond. . . .

VI

HEARTBREAK

May 1863-April 1864

Independence Day 1863 marked the culmination of two great disasters to the Southern cause, and a third, not so great, followed hard upon them.

Having tried without success various ways of approaching and capturing Vicksburg, General Grant finally on April 30, 1863, managed to get an army across the river from the Louisiana side and land it down-river at Bruinsburg. He first marched northeast, placing his men between General Joe Johnston, at Jackson with a small force, and General John C. Pemberton's much larger force at Edward's Station on the railroad between Vicksburg and Jackson. Johnston, in general command of the whole southwest, wanted Pemberton, charged with the defense of the fortress city, to join him in fighting Grant in the open; Pemberton would attack the Union army from the rear while Johnston hit it in front. Pemberton wavered between doing what his immediate superior called for and what the commander in chief, President Davis, repeatedly ordered—to hold Vicksburg at all cost. He procrastinated, compromised—and was lost.

Grant, moving with fast determination, drove Johnston north out of Jackson and then turned toward the Mississippi to defeat three of Pemberton's divisions at Baker's Creek or Champion Hill on May 16. One of the Southern divisions—that of General William W. Loring ("Old Blizzards")—was cut off; the men from the other two poured across the Big Black River into Vicksburg, bedraggled but not in panic. Pemberton skillfully disposed them and the two divisions he had kept in the city along the fifteen miles of trenches and rifle pits.

Grant tried to take the city by direct assault on May 22 but was beaten back with dreadful loss and settled down to siege operations. Reckoning from the eighteenth, the siege lasted forty-seven days. Grant's army, heavily reinforced, now numbered 70,000 before Vicksburg, while 30,000 held off Johnston. It was bountifully sup-

plied. Pemberton's army of 28,000 was slowly reduced to a diet of horse, dog and rat. The people in the city lived in caves hurriedly dug into the sides of the steep hills. Finally on July 4 Pemberton surrendered. A Pennsylvanian by birth, he reckoned he could get better terms on the national holiday. He did: the garrison was paroled on the spot.

In late May and in June there had been three assaults on Port Hudson, the Confederacy's strong point on the Mississippi three hundred miles below Vicksburg. On July 8 General N. P. Banks ordered a fourth, but before this final attack got under way General Frank Gardner surrendered his starved and battered garrison after a six weeks' siege. The Mississippi was now open to Union shipping from St. Louis to New Orleans.

A thousand times the story of Gettysburg has been told, and it will be told as many more. A brief reference will be enough to recall the great current of events and to suggest what it must have meant to the Confederate women.

Lee in the early summer of 1863 decided to invade the North, partly for the military and political advantage of a decisive victory on Union soil, partly in the hope that it would bring recognition and material aid from Napoleon III. His army marched forth in three great corps, Ewell (who had succeeded Stonewall Jackson) in the lead, then Ambrose P. Hill, then Longstreet. Some of Heth's men of Ewell's corps came from the west into the town of Gettysburg in southern Pennsylvania looking for shoes and stumbled into soldiers of General Meade's Union army coming from the east—George Meade had succeeded Hooker—and so precipitated the greatest battle of the war on a field neither commander would have chosen.

The fortunes and failures of those first three days of July will never cease to be debated. The climax came on the third day of furious fighting—"Pickett's charge" of 15,000 down a slope, up a slope, two miles across open country, in full battle array, the men aligned, the ranking officers on horseback, winning to a brief struggle among the massed guns on Cemetery Ridge, the "dread heights of destiny," then falling back under murderous direct and cross fire through those sloping fields again—so magnificent, so forlorn.

The afternoon of the fourth, General Lee started his wounded back toward the Potomac. And that night the army followed, over the mud, in the driving rain, through the passes of South Mountain. Meade thought his army too used up for any vigorous pursuit.

The Confederates suffered more than 15,000 casualties out of 60,000 engaged in the battle. The Union loss was 25,000 out of 90,000. The Union could replace. The Confederacy could not.

On July 10 the Federals began a combined sea and land attack on Charleston—a bombardment that was to last with little respite through the summer and far into the autumn. Indeed, the port and city were in a state of virtual siege till near the end of the war when the Confederate troops were withdrawn for service elsewhere. A Union force was landed on Morris Island on the Southern side of the inlet to the harbor and on Folly Island farther south. Battery Wagner guarding the harbor portal was under constant shelling. Sumter was gradually reduced to a pile of ruins, but those ruins were still crowned with the Confederate flag and the heroic garrison resisted every attempt to land—a symbol of the South's will to survive.

General Bragg, who had evacuated Chattanooga, gave battle to General Rosecrans on September 19-20 at Chickamauga. Rosecrans and most of his men were driven in rout to Chattanooga, but General George H. Thomas hung on long after the rest had fled and won his sobriquet of the "Rock of Chickamauga." In this greatest battle of the West the Confederate casualties numbered 18,000. During the last week of November, in hard fighting around Chattanooga at Lookout Mountain, Orchard Knob and Missionary Ridge, Bragg was defeated by Grant who had replaced Rosecrans. This meant further loss to the Confederacy of about 6,500 men.

Active Union operations in the first third of 1864 were largely confined to the Mississippi Valley. General Banks undertook a grand expedition up through the Red River valley to Shreveport, headquarters of General Kirby Smith. As part of the strategy General Frederick Steele was to come down from Arkansas. Banks was badly mauled by General "Dick" Taylor at Mansfield, Louisiana, on April 8. Taylor struck again at Pleasant Hill the next day; his attack was repelled but Banks retreated to the Red. Meanwhile Steele had got below Camden, Arkansas. Kirby Smith went after him and, in a series of running fights which included one at Poison Springs on the eighteenth and a final Confederate victory at Jenkins' Ferry on the Saline

River the thirtieth, drove Steele back to Little Rock. Then Kirby Smith turned round to join Dick Taylor, but their juncture was too late to destroy Banks's "grand" army which, bedraggled, reached the Mississippi.

Through the twelve months of conflict, disappointment, poignant sorrow, from May 1863 through April 1864, the women of the Confederacy noted in heart's blood what they heard and saw and did.

1. MARY ANN LOUGHBOROUGH—IN A CAVE AT VICKSBURG

Mrs. Loughborough gives us a graphic picture of what the cave dwellers of Vicksburg endured.

An Arkansas girl, born Mary Ann Webster, she was living with her husband and small daughter in Jackson in 1861. On the eve of his departure with his regiment, she decided, with his approval, to follow him. Mother and child traveled to Memphis and other points in Tennessee and in April 1863 visited Mr. Loughborough in Vicksburg. When the Federals started shelling the city, they hurried back to Jackson only to find Union troops entering their home town. Back to Vicksburg again at the beginning of May—and there, in spite of Pemberton's order to evacuate all noncombatants, they stayed throughout the siege.

The next year Mrs. Loughborough's journal was published— oddly enough in New York—under the title My Cave Life in Vicksburg, with letters of trial and travel.

Sunday, the 17th of May, 1863, as we were dressing for church, and had nearly completed the arrangement of shawls and gloves, we heard the loud booming of cannon. Frightened, for at this time we knew not *what* "an hour would bring forth," seeing no one who might account for the sudden alarm, we walked down the street, hoping to find some friend that could tell us if it were dangerous to remain away from home at church. I feared leaving my little one for any length of time, if there were any prospect of an engagement. After walking a square or two, we met an officer, who told us the report we heard proceeded from our own guns, which were firing upon a party of soldiers, who were burning some houses on the penin-

sula on the Louisiana shore; he told us, also, it had been rumored
that General Pemberton had been repulsed—that many citizens had
gone out to attend to the wounded of yesterday's battle—all the
ministers and surgeons that could leave had also gone. Still, as the
bells of the Methodist church rang out clear and loud, my friend and
I decided to enter, and were glad that we did so, for we heard words
of cheer and comfort in this time of trouble. The speaker was a
traveller, who supplied the pulpit this day, as the pastor was absent
ministering to the wounded and dying on the battle field.

As we returned home, we passed groups of anxious men at the
corners, with troubled faces; very few soldiers were seen; some battery men and officers, needed for the river defences, were passing
hastily up the street. Yet, in all the pleasant air and sunshine of the
day, an anxious gloom seemed to hang over the faces of men: a sorrowful waiting for tidings, that all knew now would tell of disaster.
There seemed no life in the city; sullen and expectant seemed the
men—tearful and hopeful the women—prayerful and hopeful, I might
add; for many a mother, groaning in spirit over the uncertainty of
the welfare of those most dear to her, knelt and laid her sorrows at
the foot of that Throne, where no earnest suppliant is ever rejected;
where the sorrow of many a broken heart has been turned in resignation to His will who afflicts not willingly the children of men. And
so, in all the dejected uncertainty, the stir of horsemen and wheels
began, and wagons came rattling down the street—going rapidly one
way, and then returning, seemingly, without air or purpose: now and
then a worn and dusty soldier would be seen passing with his blanket
and canteen; soon, straggler after straggler came by, then groups of
soldiers worn and dusty with the long march. "What can be the
matter?" we all cried, as the streets and pavements became full of
these worn and tired-looking men. We sent down to ask, and the
reply was: "We are whipped; and the Federals are after us." We
hastily seized veils and bonnets, and walked down the avenue to the
iron railing that separates the yard from the street.

"Where are you going?" we asked.

No one seemed disposed to answer the question. An embarrassed,
pained look came over some of the faces that were raised to us;
others seemed only to feel the weariness of the long march; again we
asked:

"Where on earth are you going?"

At last one man looked up in a half-surly manner, and answered:

"We are running."

"From whom?" exclaimed one of the young girls of the house.

"The Feds, to be sure," said another, half laughing and half shamefaced.

"Oh! shame on you!" cried the ladies; "and you running!"

"It's all Pem's fault," said an awkward, long-limbed, weary-looking man.

"It's all your own fault. Why don't you stand your ground?" was the reply.

"Shame on you all!" cried some of the ladies across the street.

I could not but feel sorry for the poor worn fellows, who did seem heartily ashamed of themselves; some without arms, having probably lost them in the first break of the companies.

"We are disappointed in you!" cried some of the ladies. "Who shall we look to now for protection?"

"Oh!" said one of them, "it's the first time I ever ran. We are Georgians, and we never ran before; but we saw them all breaking and running, and we could not bear up alone."

We asked them if they did not want water; and some of them came in the yard to get it. The lady of the house offered them some supper; and while they were eating, we were so much interested, that we stood around questioning them about the result of the day. "It is all General Pemberton's fault," said a sergeant. "I'm a Missourian, and our boys stood it almost alone, not knowing what was wanted to be done; yet, fighting as long as possible, every one leaving us, and we were obliged to fall back. You know, madam, we Missourians always fight well, even if we have to retreat afterward."

"Oh!" spoke up an old man, "we would ha' fit well; but General Pemberton came up and said: 'Stand your ground, boys. Your General Pemberton is with you;' and then, bless you, lady! the next we see'd of him, he was sitting on his horse behind a house—close, too, at that; and when we see'd that, we thought 'tain't no use, if he's going to sit there."

We could not help laughing at the old man's tale and his anger. Afterward we were told that General Pemberton behaved with courage—that the fault lay in the arrangement of troops.

At dark the fresh troops from Warrenton marched by, going out to the intrenchments in the rear of the city about two miles; many of the officers were fearful that the fortifications, being so incomplete, would be taken, if the Federal troops pushed immediately on, following their advantage.

As the troops from Warrenton passed by, the ladies waved their handkerchiefs, cheering them, and crying:

"These are the troops that have not run. You'll stand by us, and protect us, won't you? You won't *retreat* and bring the Federals behind you."

And the men, who were fresh and lively, swung their hats, and promised to die for the ladies—never to run—never to retreat; while poor fellows on the pavement, sitting on their blankets—lying on the ground—leaning against trees, or anything to rest their wearied bodies, looked on silent and dejected. They were not to blame, these poor, weary fellows. If they were unsuccessful, it is what many a man has been before them; endurance of the long fasts in the rifle pits, and coolness amid the showers of ball and shell thrown at devoted Vicksburg afterward, show us that men, though unfortunate, can retrieve their character. . . .

What a sad evening we spent—continually hearing of friends and acquaintances left dead on the field, or mortally wounded, and being brought in ambulances to the hospital! We almost feared to retire that night; no one seemed to know whether the Federal army was advancing or not; some told us that they were many miles away, and others that they were quite near. How did we know but in the night we might be awakened by the tumult of their arrival!

The streets were becoming quiet; the noise and bustle had died out with the excitement of the day, and, save now and then the rapid passing of some officer, or army wagon, they were almost deserted. . . .

The next morning all was quiet; we heard no startling rumors; the soldiers were being gathered together and taken out into the rifle pits; Vicksburg was regularly besieged, and we were to stay at our homes and watch the progress of the battle. The rifle pits and intrenchments were almost two miles from the city. We would be out of danger, so we thought; but we did not know what was in preparation for us around the bend of the river. The day wore on; still all was quiet. At night our hopes revived: the Federal troops had not yet come up—another calm night and morning. At three o'clock that evening, the artillery boomed from the intrenchments, roar after roar, followed by the rattle of musketry: the Federal forces were making their first attack. Looking out from the back veranda, we could plainly see the smoke before the report of the guns reached us.

The discharges of musketry were irregular. At every report our hearts beat quicker. The excitement was intense in the city. Groups of people stood on every available position where a view could be obtained of the distant hills, where the jets of white smoke constantly passed out from among the trees.

Some of our friends proposed going for a better view up on the balcony around the cupola of the court house. The view from there was most extensive and beautiful. Hill after hill arose in the distance, enclosing the city in the form of a crescent. Immediately in the centre and east of the river, the firing seemed more continuous, while to the left and running northly, the rattle and roar would be sudden, sharp, and vigorous, then ceasing for some time. The hills around near the city, and indeed every place that seemed commanding and secure, was covered with anxious spectators—many of them ladies—fearing the result of the afternoon's conflict.

It was amid the clump of trees on the far distant hillside, that the Federal batteries could be discerned by the frequent puffings of smoke from the guns. Turning to the river, we could see a gunboat that had the temerity to come down as near the town as possible, and lay just out of reach of the Confederate batteries, with steam up.

Two more lay about half a mile above and nearer the canal; two or three transports had gotten up steam, and lay near the mouth of the canal. Below the city a gunboat had come up and landed, out of reach, on the Louisiana side, striving to engage the lower batteries of the town—firing about every fifteen minutes. . . .

From gentlemen who called on the evening of the attack in the rear of the town, we learned that it was quite likely, judging from the movements on the river, that the gunboats would make an attack that night. We remained dressed during the night; once or twice we sprang to our feet, startled by the report of a cannon; but after waiting in the darkness of the veranda for some time, the perfect quiet of the city convinced us that our alarm was needless.

Next day, two or three shells were thrown from the battle field, exploding near the house. This was our first shock, and a severe one. We did not dare to go in the back part of the house all day.

In the evening we were terrified and much excited by the loud rush and scream of mortar shells; we ran to the small cave near the house, and were in it during the night, by this time wearied and almost stupefied by the loss of sleep.

The caves were plainly becoming a necessity, as some persons had been killed on the street by fragments of shells. The room that I had so lately slept in had been struck by a fragment of a shell during the first night, and a large hole made in the ceiling. I shall never forget my extreme fear during the night, and my utter hopelessness of ever seeing the morning light. Terror stricken, we remained crouched in the cave, while shell after shell followed each other in quick succession. I endeavored by constant prayer to prepare myself for the sudden death I was almost certain awaited me. My heart stood still as we would hear the reports from the guns, and the rushing and fearful sound of the shell as it came toward us. As it neared, the noise became more deafening; the air was full of the rushing sound; pains darted through my temples; my ears were full of the confusing noise; and, as it exploded, the report flashed through my head like an electric shock, leaving me in a quiet state of terror the most painful that I can imagine—cowering in a corner, holding my child to my heart—the only feeling of my life being the choking throbs of my heart, that rendered me almost breathless. As singly they fell short, or beyond the cave, I was aroused by a feeling of thankfulness that was of short duration. Again and again the terrible fright came over in that night.

I saw one fall in the road without the mouth of the cave, like a flame of fire, making the earth tremble, and, with a low, singing sound, the fragments sped on in their work of death.

Morning found us more dead than alive, with blanched faces and trembling lips. We were not reassured on hearing, from a man who took refuge in the cave, that a mortar shell in falling would not consider the thickness of earth above us a circumstance.

Some of the ladies, more courageous by daylight, asked him what he was in there for, if that was the case. He was silenced for an hour, when he left. As the day wore on, and we were still preserved, though the shells came as ever, we were somewhat encouraged.

The next morning we heard that Vicksburg would not in all probability hold out more than a week or two, as the garrison was poorly provisioned; and one of General Pemberton's staff officers told us that the effective force of the garrison, upon being estimated, was found to be fifteen thousand men; General Loring having been cut off after the battle of Black River, with probably ten thousand.

The ladies all cried, "Oh, never surrender!" but after the experience of the night, I really could not tell what I wanted, or what my opinions were.

So constantly dropped the shells around the city, that the inhabitants all made preparations to live under the ground during the siege. M—— sent over and had a cave made in a hill near by. We seized the opportunity one evening, when the gunners were probably at their supper, for we had a few moments of quiet, to go over and take possession. We were under the care of a friend of M——, who was paymaster on the staff of the same General with whom M—— was Adjutant. We had neighbors on both sides of us; and it would have been an amusing sight to a spectator to witness the domestic scenes presented without by the number of servants preparing the meals under the high bank containing the caves.

Our dining, breakfasting, and supper hours were quite irregular. When the shells were falling fast, the servants came in for safety, and our meals waited for completion some little time; again they would fall slowly, with the lapse of many minutes between, and out would start the cooks to their work.

Some families had light bread made in large quantities, and subsisted on it with milk (provided their cows were not killed from one milking time to another), without any more cooking, until called on to replenish. Though most of us lived on corn bread and bacon, served three times a day, the only luxury of the meal consisting in its warmth, I had some flour, and frequently had some hard, tough biscuit made from it, there being no soda or yeast to be procured. At this time we could, also, procure beef. A gentleman friend was kind enough to offer me his camp bed, a narrow spring mattress, which fitted within the contracted cave very comfortably; another had his tent fly stretched over the mouth of our residence to shield us from the sun; and thus I was the recipient of many favors, and under obligations to many gentlemen of the army for delicate and kind attentions. And so I went regularly to work, keeping house under ground. Our new habitation was an excavation made in the earth, and branching six feet from the entrance, forming a cave in the shape of a T. In one of the wings my bed fitted; the other I used as a kind of a dressing room; in this the earth had been cut down a foot or two below the floor of the main cave; I could stand erect here; and when tired of sitting in other portions of my residence, I bowed myself into it, and stood impassively resting at full height—one of the variations in the still shell-expectant life. M——'s servant cooked for us under protection of the hill. Our quarters were close, indeed; yet I was more comfortable than I expected I could have been made under the earth in that fashion.

We were safe at least from fragments of shell—and they were flying in all directions; though no one seemed to think our cave any protection, should a mortar shell happen to fall directly on top of the ground above us. We had our roof arched and braced, the supports of the bracing taking up much room in our confined quarters. The earth was about five feet thick above, and seemed hard and compact; yet, poor M——, every time he came in, examined it, fearing, amid some of the shocks it sustained, that it might crack and fall upon us.

One afternoon, amid the rush and explosion of the shells, cries and screams arose—the screams of women amid the shrieks of the falling shells. The servant boy, George, after starting and coming back once or twice, his timidity overcoming his curiosity, at last gathered courage to go to the ravine near us, from whence the cries proceeded, and found that a negro man had been buried alive within a cave, he being alone at that time. Workmen were instantly set to deliver him, if possible; but when found, the unfortunate man had evidently been dead some little time.

Another incident happened the same day: A gentleman, resident of Vicksburg, had a large cave made, and repeatedly urged his wife to leave the house and go into it. She steadily refused, and, being quite an invalid, was lying on the bed, when he took her by the hand and insisted upon her accompanying him so strongly, that she yielded; and they had scarcely left the house, when a mortar shell went crashing through, utterly demolishing the bed that had so lately been vacated, tearing up the floor, and almost completely destroying the room.

That night, after my little one had been laid in bed, I sat at the mouth of the cave, with the servants drawn around me, watching the brilliant display of fireworks the mortar boats were making—the passage of the shell, as it travelled through the heavens, looking like a swiftly moving star. As it fell, it approached the earth so rapidly, that it seemed to leave behind a track of fire.

This night we kept our seats, as they all passed rapidly over us, none falling near. The incendiary shells were still more beautiful in appearance. As they exploded in the air, the burning matter and balls fell like large, clear blue-and-amber stars, scattering hither and thither.

"Miss M——," said one of the more timid servants, "do they want to kill us all dead? Will they keep doing this until we all die?"

I said most heartily, "I hope not."

The servants we had with us seemed to possess more courage than is usually attributed to negroes. They seldom hesitated to cross the street for water at any time. The "boy" slept at the entrance of the cave, with a pistol I had given him, telling me I need not be "afeared —dat any one dat come dar would have to go over his body first."

He never refused to carry out any little article to M—— on the battle field. I laughed heartily at a dilemma he was placed in one day: The mule that he had mounted to ride out to the battle field took him to a dangerous locality, where the shells were flying thickly, and then, suddenly stopping, through fright, obstinately refused to stir. It was in vain that George kicked and beat him—go he would not; so, clenching his hand, he hit him severely in the head several times, jumped down, ran home, and left him. The mule stood a few minutes rigidly, then, looking round, and seeing George at some distance from him, turned and followed, quite demurely.

Days wore on, and the mortar shells had passed over continually without falling near us; so that I became quite at my ease, in view of our danger, when one of the Federal batteries opposite the intrenchments altered their range; so that, at about six o'clock every evening, Parrott shells came whirring into the city, frightening the inhabitants of caves wofully.

The cave we inhabited was about five squares from the levee. A great many had been made in a hill immediately beyond us; and near us; and near this hill we could see most of the shells fall. Caves were the fashion—the rage—over besieged Vicksburg. Negroes, who understood their business, hired themselves out to dig them, at from thirty to fifty dollars, according to the size. Many persons, considering different localities unsafe, would sell them to others, who had been less fortunate, or less provident; and so great was the demand for cave workmen, that a new branch of industry sprang up and became popular—particularly as the personal safety of the workmen was secured, and money withal.

Even the very animals seemed to share the general fear of a sudden and frightful death. The dogs would be seen in the midst of the noise to gallop up the street, and then to return, as if fear had maddened them. On hearing the descent of a shell, they would dart aside —then, as it exploded, sit down and howl in the most pitiful manner. There were many walking the street, apparently without homes. George carried on a continual warfare with them, as they came about the fire where our meals were cooking.

The horses, belonging to the officers, and fastened to the trees near the tents, would frequently strain the halter to its full length, rearing high in the air, with a loud snort of terror, as a shell would explode near. I could hear them in the night cry out in the midst of the uproar, ending in a low, plaintive whinny of fear.

The poor creatures subsisted entirely on cane tops and mulberry leaves. Many of the mules and horses had been driven outside of the lines, by order of General Pemberton, for subsistence. Only mules enough were left, belonging to the Confederacy, to allow three full teams to a regiment. Private property was not interfered with.

The hill opposite our cave might be called "death's point" from the number of animals that had been killed in eating the grass on the sides and summit. In all directions I can see the turf turned up, from the shells that have gone ploughing into the earth. Horses or mules that are tempted to mount the hill by the promise of grass that grows profusely there, invariably come limping down wounded, to die at the base, or are brought down dead from the summit.

A certain number of mules are killed each day by the commissaries, and are issued to the men, all of whom prefer the fresh meat, though it be of mule, to the bacon and salt rations that they have eaten so long a time without change. There have already been some cases of scurvy; the soldiers have a horror of the disease; therefore, I suppose, the mule meat is all the more welcome. Indeed, I petitioned M—— to have some served on our table. He said: "No; wait a little longer." He did not like to see me eating mule until I was obliged to; that he trusted Providence would send us some change shortly.

It was astonishing how the young officers kept up their spirits, frequently singing quartets and glees amid the pattering of Minié balls; and I often heard gay peals of laughter from headquarters, as the officers that had spent the day, and perhaps the night, previous in the rifle pits, would collect to make out reports. This evening a gentleman visited us, and, among other songs, sang words to the air of the "Mocking Bird," which I will write:

" 'Twas at the siege of Vicksburg,
  Of Vicksburg, of Vicksburg—
  'Twas at the siege of Vicksburg,
  When the Parrott shells were whistling through the air.

"Listen to the Parrott shells—
  Listen to the Parrott shells:
  The Parrott shells are whistling through the air.

"Oh! well will we remember—
  Remember—remember
  Tough mule meat, June *sans* November,
  And the Minié balls that whistled through the air.
  Listen to the Minié balls—
  Listen to the Minié balls:
  The Minié balls are singing in the air."

News came that one of the forts to the left of us had been under-mined and blown up, killing sixty men; then of the death of the gallant Colonel Irwin, of Missouri; and again, the next day, of the death of the brave old General Green, of Missouri.

We were now swiftly nearing the end of our siege life: the rations had nearly all been given out. For the last few days I had been sick; still I tried to overcome the languid feeling of utter prostration. My little one had swung in her hammock, reduced in strength, with a low fever flushing in her face. M—— was all anxiety, I could plainly see. A soldier brought up, one morning, a little jaybird, as a plaything for the child. After playing with it for a short time, she turned wear-ily away. "Miss Mary," said the servant, "she's hungry; let me make her some soup from the bird." At first I refused: the poor little play-thing should not die; then, as I thought of the child, I half consented. With the utmost haste, Cinth disappeared; and the next time she appeared, it was with a cup of soup, and a little plate, on which lay the white meat of the poor little bird.

On Saturday a painful calm prevailed: there had been a truce pro-claimed; and so long had the constant firing been kept up, that the stillness now was absolutely oppressive.

At ten o'clock General Bowen passed by, dressed in full uniform, accompanied by Colonel Montgomery,[1] and preceded by a courier bearing a white flag. M—— came by, and asked me if I would like

[1] General John S. Bowen, division commander, and Colonel L. M. Montgomery, aide-de-camp to General Pemberton.

to walk out; so I put on my bonnet and sallied forth beyond the terrace, for the first time since I entered. On the hill above us, the earth was literally covered with fragments of shell—Parrott, shrapnell, canister; besides lead in all shapes and forms, and a long kind of solid shot, shaped like a small Parrott shell. Minié balls lay in every direction, flattened, dented, and bent from the contact with trees and pieces of wood in their flight. The grass seemed deadened —the ground ploughed into furrows in many places; while scattered over all, like giants' pepper, in numberless quantity, were the shrapnell balls.

I could now see how very near to the rifle pits my cave lay: only a small ravine between the two hills separated us. In about two hours, General Bowen returned. No one knew, or seemed to know, why a truce had been made; but all believed that a treaty of surrender was pending. Nothing was talked about among the officers but the all-engrossing theme. Many wished to cut their way out and make the risk their own; but I secretly hoped that no such bloody hazard would be attempted.

The next morning, M—— came up, with a pale face, saying: "It's all over! The white flag floats from our forts! Vicksburg has surrendered!"

He put on his uniform coat, silently buckled on his sword, and prepared to take out the men, to deliver up their arms in front of the fortification.

I felt a strange unrest, the quiet of the day was so unnatural. I walked up and down the cave until M—— returned. The day was extremely warm; and he came with a violent headache. He told me that the Federal troops had acted splendidly; they were stationed opposite the place where the Confederate troops marched up and stacked their arms; and they seemed to feel sorry for the poor fellows who had defended the place for so long a time. Far different from what he had expected, not a jeer or taunt came from any one of the Federal soldiers. Occasionally, a cheer would be heard; but the majority seemed to regard the poor unsuccessful soldiers with a generous sympathy.

After the surrender, the old gray-headed soldier, in passing on the hill near the cave, stopped, and, touching his hat, said:

"It's a sad day this, madam; I little thought we'd come to it, when we first stopped in the intrenchments. I hope you'll yet be happy, madam, after all the trouble you've seen."

To which I mentally responded, "Amen."

The poor, hunchback soldier, who had been sick, and who, at home in Southern Missouri, is worth a million of dollars, I have been told, yet within Vicksburg has been nearly starved, walked out to-day in the pleasant air, for the first time for many days.

I stood in the doorway and caught my first sight of the Federal uniform since the surrender. That afternoon the road was filled with them, walking about, looking at the forts and the head-quarter horses: wagons also filled the road, drawn by the handsome United States horses. Poor M——, after keeping his horse upon mulberry leaves during the forty-eight days, saw him no more! After the surrender in the evening, George rode into the city on his mule: thinking to "shine," as the negroes say, he rode M——'s handsome, silver-mounted dragoon-saddle. I could not help laughing when he returned, with a sorry face, reporting himself safe, but the saddle gone. M—— questioned and requestioned him, aghast at his loss; for a saddle was a valuable article in our little community; and George, who felt as badly as any one, said: "I met a Yankee, who told me: 'Git down off dat mule; I'm gwin' to hab dat saddle.' I said: 'No; I ain't gwin' to do no such thing.' He took out his pistol, and I jumped down."

So Mister George brought back to M—— a saddle that better befitted his mule than the one he rode off on—a much worn, common affair, made of wood. I felt sorry for M——. That evening George brought evil news again: another horse had been taken. His remaining horse and his only saddle finished the news of the day.

The next morning, Monday, as I was passing through the cave, I saw something stirring at the base of one of the supports of the roof: taking a second look, I beheld a large snake curled between the earth and the upright post. I went out quickly and sent one of the servants for M——, who, coming up immediately, took up his sword and fastened one of the folds of the reptile to the post. It gave one quick dart toward him, with open jaws. Fortunately, the length of the sword was greater than the upper length of body; and the snake fell to the earth a few inches from M——, who set his heel firmly on it, and severed the head from the body with the sword. I have never seen so large a snake; it was fully as large round the body as the bowl of a good-sized glass tumbler, and over two yards long. . . .

The Confederate troops were being marched into Vicksburg to

take the parole that the terms of the treaty of surrender demanded. In a few days they would leave the city they had held so long.

On Friday they began their march toward the South; and on Saturday poor George came to me, and said he had put on a pair of blue pants, and, thinking they would take him for a Federal soldier, had tried to slip through after M——, but he was turned back; so he came begging me to try and get him a pass: the effort was made; and to this day I do not know whether he ever reached M—— or not.

Saturday evening, Vicksburg, with her terraced hills—with her pleasant homes and sad memories, passed from my view in the gathering twilight—passed, but the river flowed on the same, and the stars shone out with the same calm light! . . .

2. ESTHER ALDEN—"WE DANCE AT FORT SUMTER"

Esther was sixteen when in June 1863 she returned home to cheerfulness and gaiety in resolute Charleston. The next month there was a new bombardment of the city, and of Fort Sumter, much more serious than the one in April. Women and children were advised to leave the city. Esther, her mother and sisters unwillingly departed for their plantation some miles away, and, when the safety of this region was threatened, they took refuge in western North Carolina.

Esther kept a war diary which ended abruptly on April 1, 1865. Few Southern women had the heart to record the fall of the Confederacy. Esther did not. But now, like Sally Pickett, she could dance as a crisis of life approached and so make the tragedy of life less dark.

Plantersville, S.C.

May 29, 1863.—Heigh ho! I am to leave school to-day never to return! I suppose I am grown up! The war is raging, but we, shut up here with our books, and our little school tragedies and comedies, have remained very ignorant of all that is going on outside. Now, I suppose I will know more of the exciting events taking place, as I am going to Charleston to-morrow and we will stay there as long as it is considered safe. We have had some hardships to endure this winter. Our fare has been very poor, but much better than that of poor C., who writes that at his school they have not had meat nor butter, tea nor coffee for a long time, but have lived entirely on squash and hominy! I do not think girls could stand that; they would rebel; but the boys all recognize that the master is doing his best for them. We have always had meat once a day; our supper consists of a huge tray of corn dodgers which is brought into the school-room and placed on the table, that we may help ourselves and the tray goes back empty. Most of us have been very quiet about it, but not long ago one of the girls left and it seems she had stowed away some dodgers in her trunk, which she displayed to sympathizing friends and relations when she got home, making a melancholy story of her sufferings. The dodgers, with age added to their actually adamantine character, were simply indestructible, and there was quite a stir made outside about our woes. We who remained at school, however, disapproved of her conduct as being very disloyal. In our own homes even there were many privations now, and we are rather proud to feel that we are sharing, at a very safe distance, some of the hardships borne by our brave soldiers.

Charleston, June 20.—It is too delightful to be at home! In spite of the war every one is so bright and cheerful, and the men are so charming and look so nice in their uniforms. We see a great many of them, and I have been to a most delightful dance in Fort Sumter. The night was lovely and we went down in rowing boats. It was a strange scene, cannon balls piled in every direction, sentinels pacing the ramparts, and within the casemates pretty, well-dressed women, and handsome well-bred men dancing, as though unconscious that we were actually under the guns of the blockading fleet. It was my first party, and the strange charm of the situation wove a spell around me; every man seemed to me a hero—not only a possible but an actual hero! One looks at a man so differently when you think he may be killed to-morrow! Men whom up to this time I have thought dull and commonplace that night seemed charming. I had a rude awakening as we rowed back to the city. When we came abreast of Fort Ripley, the sentinel halted us demanding the countersign, the oarsmen stopped, but Gen. R., who was steering the boat, ordered them to row on. Three times the sentinel spoke and then he fired. The ball passed over the boat and Gen. R. ordered his men to row up to the fort, called the officer of the day, and ordered the sentinel put under arrest! Of course I knew nothing about it, but it seemed to me frightfully unjust, and I was so indignant that I found it hard to keep quiet until we got home.

3. MRS. G. GRIFFIN WILCOX—YANKEES
PARADE IN NATCHEZ

A woman of Natchez left for posterity a glimpse of war in her day—the enemy occupation in the summer of 1863.

Natchez, Mississippi
July, 1863

Grand, exclusive, heroic Natchez, with her terraced hills and fragrant gardens, colonial mansions and prehistoric memories, was gorgeous in gala day attire.

The Stars and Stripes floated from the domes and windows of all public buildings, and were stretched over the street crossings.

General Tuttle,[1] mounted on his milk-white steed, and escorted by his staff, paraded the principal thoroughfares.

Handsomely-uniformed soldiers, arrayed in the paraphernalia and insignia of office, were moving hither and thither, reminding one of a vast assemblage of strange bright birds driven hence by terrific storms on foreign shores, but alas! the storm was in our own beautiful and loved Southland, and we were compelled, perforce, to look upon and admire the brilliant plumage of these strange, bright birds, who brought not the rich tidings of all glorious things, but sad disaster, on their starry wings.

When Natchez was first garrisoned by the Union troops it was deemed necessary by General Tuttle to erect fortifications on the site occupied by the Susette homestead, one of the most magnificent residences of the city. The mansion was situated in a famous grove of forest trees, among which were grand old live oaks, elms and magnolias, planted more than half a century ago. The grounds were surrounded by one of the handsomest iron fences in the State.

The interior of the Susette home was furnished with exquisitely hand-carved Italian marble mantels. There were cut-glass window panes and a rosewood stairway. Most of the expensive furniture had

---

[1] General James M. Tuttle had been in the fight against Johnston in the Vicksburg campaign.

come from Paris. Included in the dining-room appointments was silver plate of four generations back.

Federal soldiers had stripped the house of many of its costly furnishings. The edict had gone forth that the "Susette mansion must be blown up with gun-powder and other combustibles, to clear the way for the fort." Excavations were immediately made under and around the grand old edifice. These, together with the cellar, were filled with such immense quantities of powder that when the match was applied to the fuse the explosion was so terrific that half of the window panes in the town were shattered and broken.

Such is war.

4. LaSALLE CORBELL PICKETT—
"I MARRY MY GENERAL, THE HERO OF GETTYSBURG"

She was born at Chuckatuck in Nansemond County, south-eastern Virginia in 1843. When she was eight years old she met at Old Point Comfort a young lieutenant from Richmond, George E. Pickett, who was grieving over the recent death of his wife, Sally Minge Pickett. LaSalle found him fascinating and admitted that she loved him from the first day. After that their paths crossed at infrequent intervals. She went on to Lynchburg Academy and confidently prepared herself for the life of a soldier's wife. In the spring of 1863 General Pickett was encamped briefly near her home. She saw him daily, embroidered his cape, his slippers, the stars on his coat. She was being graduated in June when Lee's army was beginning the march to Pennsylvania that ended in Gettysburg.

Beautiful Sally Pickett was in Petersburg during the siege. Her baby was born there; she called him affectionately "the little general." When the Federals came into Richmond she was there, and that night fire destroyed the warehouse where all her wedding presents and other valuables were stored. The Picketts fled to Canada where they lived in one room in a boardinghouse under the assumed name of Edwards. A year later they came back to Virginia and occupied a cottage on the site of George Pickett's old home, which had been sacked and burned during the war

After the war he declined a commission as brigadier-general in the Egyptian Army, and the marshalship of Virginia which Grant ten-

dered him, accepted the Virginia agency of the Washington Life Insurance Company of New York. He died in 1875.

When she was a widow Sally wrote her reminiscences, Pickett and His Men.

The temperature of the summer of 1863 seemed to keep pace with the high tide of war. The heat was so excessive that the schools were closed early.

The first week in June I was graduated from my alma mater. I stopped in Richmond for a few days en route to my home within the Federal lines. The day after I arrived I received a letter dated at Culpeper Court-house, June 13, full of faith in a successful campaign, a short separation, and a "speedy termination of the difficulties." June 15 and 18 there came other letters, one written on the march to Winchester,[1] the other after reaching that place, breathing the same spirit of confidence and hope. Until the fatal third of July such letters came to me, expressing hope and trust—always hope and trust.

Then drifted to us rumors, faint and indefinite at first, of a great battle fought at Gettysburg. Gradually they grew stronger and brighter, and the mind of the South became inbued with the impression that a grand victory had been won. Thus the news first came to us, transmuted in the balmy air of the South from the appalling disaster it really was into the glorious triumph which our longing hearts hoped it might be. A few days of this glowing dream, and then—the heartbreaking truth.

I could hear nothing of the General except the vague rumor that he had been killed in the final charge. Our mail facilities were very meager, and our letters were smuggled through the lines by any trustworthy person who, having been given the privilege of going back and forth, happened to be at hand at the time. Many a mile I had ridden on mule-back, hoping to hear directly from the General, before I was rewarded.

"Reck," our old mule, had been a benefaction not only to us but to the whole country. Every other mule and every horse had been confiscated and taken by the Federals. But for his wonderful memory, "Reck" would have changed owners, too, like all his half-broth-

[1] Longstreet's army corps, to which Pickett's division was attached, started for Pennsylvania on June 3 from Fredericksburg, crossed the Rapidan, proceeded to Culpeper Court House and then to and up the Valley.

ers and sisters, for he was a fine-looking mule. When a colt his leg
had been broken in crossing a bridge, and all the powers of coaxing
and whipping and spurring after that accident could not make him
step on a plank, much less cross a bridge, unless you pretended to
mend the bridge, and first walked across it yourself in safety, and
then came back and led him over. My last ride on "Reck" brought
me as compensation a package of five or six letters. The first was the
letter which the General, as he went into battle, had handed to General Longstreet, with its sad superscription—"If Old Peter's nod
means death———." [1] The next was written on the second day after
the great catastrophe.

Later there came to me the following:

Williamsport, July 8, 1863.
. . . "I am crossing the river to-day, guarding some four thousand
prisoners back to Winchester, where I shall take command and try
to recruit my spirit-crushed, wearied, cut-up people. It is just two
months this morning since I parted from you, and yet the disappointments and sorrows that have been crowded into the interval make the
time seem years instead. My grand old division, which was so full of
faith and courage then, is now almost extinguished. But one field-
officer[2] in the whole command escaped in that terrible third of July
slaughter, and alas! alas! for the men who fearlessly followed their
lead on to certain death.

"We were ordered to take a height. We *took it,* but under the most
withering fire that I, even in my dreams, could ever have conceived
of, and I have seen many battles. Alas! alas! no support came, and
my poor fellows who had gotten in were overpowered. Your uncle,
Colonel Phillips, behaved most gallantly—was wounded, but not
seriously. Your cousins, Captain Cralle and C. C. Phillips, are among
the missing. But for you, I should greatly have preferred to answer
reveille on the fourth of July with the poor fellows over there, and
how I escaped it is a miracle; how any of us survived is marvelous,
unless it was by prayer.

"My heart is very, very sad, and it seems almost sacrilegious to

---

[1] It ended: "Now, I go; but remember always that I love you with all my heart
and soul, with every fiber of my being; that now and forever I am yours—yours, my
beloved. It is almost three o'clock. My soul reaches out to yours—my prayers. I'll
keep up a skookum tumtum for Virginia and for you, my darling.
                                                                 "YOUR SOLDIER.
"Gettysburg, July 3, 1863."
[2] Richard G. Garnett and Lewis Armistead, brigade commanders, and three of
Pickett's five regimental commanders were killed, the others wounded. (The third field
officer, who escaped, was James L. Kemper.) Of the supporting brigadiers, James J.
Archer was severely wounded, Isaac R. Trimble wounded and captured, Alfred M.
Scales wounded.

think of happiness at such a time, but let my need of your sweet womanly sympathy and comfort in these sad hours plead extenuation, and be prepared, I beseech you, at a moment's notice to obey the summons that will make you my wife."

Twe weeks later I received this letter:

Culpeper C. H. July, 1863

"The short but terrible campaign is over, and we are again on this side of the Blue Ridge. Would that we had never crossed the Potomac, or that the splendid army which we had on our arrival in Pennsylvania had not been fought in detail. If the charge made by my gallant Virginians on the fatal third of July had been supported,[1] or even if my other two brigades, Jenkins and Corse,[2] had been with me, we would now, I believe, have been in Washington, and the war practically over. God in his wisdom has willed otherwise, and I fear there will be many more blood-drenched fields and broken hearts before the end does come. . . .

"I thank the great and good God that he has spared me to come back and claim your promise, and I pray your womanly assistance in helping me to its *immediate* fulfilment. This is no time for ceremonies. The future is all uncertain, and it is impossible for me to call a moment my own. Again, with all the graves I have left behind me, and with all the wretchedness and misery this fated campaign has made, we would not wish anything but a very silent, very quiet wedding, planning only the sacrament and blessing of the church, and, after that, back to my division and to the blessing of those few of them who, by God's miracle, were left.

"I gave Colonel Harrison[3] a gold luck-piece which was a parting gift to me from the officers of the Pacific, and told him to have it made into a wedding-ring at Tyler's. I asked him to have engraved within 'G. E. P. and S. C. Married ——,' and to leave sufficient space for date and motto, which you would direct. . . ."

Perhaps no girl just out of school ever had a more difficult problem sprung upon her than that which confronted me. Had we been living under the old regime nothing would have been easier than to prepare for a grand wedding in the stately old Southern style. Times had changed very greatly in the past few years, and

---

[1] Pickett was supported by Pettigrew's division—a Tennessee and Alabama brigade, a North Carolina brigade, Joe Davis' Mississippians, Brockenbrough's Virginians—and W. D. Pender's division of two North Carolina brigades. But Pickett hoped for a great deal more support from the center and left.

[2] Generals Albert D. Jenkins and Montgomery D. Corse.

[3] The reference seems to be to Colonel Burton N. Harrison, President Davis' secretary and later Constance Cary Harrison's husband.

how was a trousseau to be made away up in the frozen North, where
all the pretty things seemed to have gone, and spirited through the
lines to make a wedding brilliant enough to satisfy the girlish idea
of propriety? And yet, how could a marriage take place without the
accompaniments of white satin, misty laces, dainty slippers, and
gloves, and all the other paraphernalia traditionally connected with
that interesting event in a young woman's life? However, if "Love
laughs at locksmiths," he has more serious methods of treating
other obstacles in his way, and all the difficulties of millinery were
finally overcome. But still there were lions in the path.

Longstreet lay under a tree at Culpeper Court-house, seeking repose from the burdens which would necessarily weigh upon the mind
of a man in whose care was the destiny of the leading corps of the
Army of Northern Virginia. As he leisurely reclined Pickett came
up and sat on the grass beside him.

"General," he said, "I am going to be married, and want a furlough. This little girl"—handing my picture to General Longstreet—
"says she is ready and willing to marry me at any minute, in spite
of the risks of war, and will go with me to the furthest end of the
earth, if need be."

The younger man had consulted the older about many things
since the day when he had rushed forward into the place made vacant by the wounding of his superior officer and carried the flag to
victory,[1] but he had never before confided to him an aspiration of
so soulful and sacred a character. Longstreet considered the matter
gravely for a time.

"I can't give it to you, Pickett. They are not granting any fur-
loughs now. I might detail you for special duty, and of course you
could stop off by the way and be married," said General Longstreet,
with a twinkle in his eye.

It was not a time for insisting upon minor details, even in regard
to very momentous subjects, and the General eagerly consented to be
detailed for "special duty." Then there arose the problem of how to
get the two necessary parties to the transaction within the essential
proximity to each other. If the General attempted to cross the lines

---

[1] During the storming of Chapultepec in the War with Mexico, September 13, 1847,
"Lieutenant James Longstreet . . . 'advancing, color in hand,' was shot down. The
flag he carried was caught up and carried on by a very young lieutenant, George E.
Pickett, hardly more than a year out of the Academy." *The Story of the Mexican
War*, by Robert Selph Henry. Indianapolis: The Bobbs-Merrill Company, Inc., 1950,
p. 361.

he might be arrested, and then not only would the wedding be indefinitely postponed, but one of the divisions of Longstreet's corps would lose its leader.

The General had purposed coming to meet me at the Blackwater River, which was the dividing line between the Federal and Confederate forces, but fortunately, through military exigencies, his plans were changed. As cautious as we had tried to be, the Federals, by some unknown power, caught a glimmering of what was expected, and some poor fellow en route to the Blackwater, as innocent of being the General as of committing matrimony, was ambushed and captured by a squad of cavalry sent out from Suffolk for the purpose, and, though he pleaded innocent to the charges against him, put into Suffolk jail, before he was recognized and released.

Thus, in the interests of the Confederacy, as well as of the marriage, it became necessary that I should be the one to cross the lines.

My uncle was a physician and because of his profession was permitted to go where he wished, and I had often accompanied him on his professional visits.

On the 17th of September, my father and I set out to cross the lines under the protecting wing of this good uncle. Just before we were ferried over the Blackwater River, we came upon the Federal cavalry, who looked at us somewhat critically but, recognizing Dr. Phillips, evidently assumed that he was bent upon a mission of mercy —as, indeed, was he not?—and did not molest us.

We reached the railway station in safety. "Waverley," it was called, and the romantic associations clustering around the name filled my youthful fancy with pleasure. There we were met by my uncle, Colonel J. J. Phillips, and his wife, and by the General's brother and his aunt and uncle, Miss Olivia and Mr. Andrew Johnston. Colonel Phillips was a warm personal friend of the General and commanded a regiment in his division. He had been wounded at Gettysburg and was just convalescing.

They accompanied us to Petersburg where, to my great delight, the General awaited me at the station. When we reached the hotel he and my father went out for the purpose of procuring the license. They soon returned with the sorrowful announcement that, owing to some legal technicality, the license could not be issued without a special decree of court, I not being a resident of that jurisdiction. Court could not be convened until the next day, and the General must report at headquarters that evening. He went away sorrowful, and

I fell into a flood of tears, thereby greatly shocking the prim, rigid maiden lady—a friend of my mother—who had accompanied me as monitor and bridesmaid, and who was intensely horrified by the expression of my impatience and the general impropriety of my conduct in fretting over the delay.

As I sat in my room, drowned in grief, I heard the newsboys crying the evening papers:

"All about the marriage of General Pickett, the hero of Gettysburg, to the beautiful Miss Corbell, of Virginia!"

You know, a girl is always "beautiful" on her wedding-day, whatever she may have been the day before, or will be the day after.

However, it was not my wedding-day, but only was to have been, and I had serious doubts as to whether my tear-washed eyes and disappointed, grief-stained face would be likely to answer anybody's preconceived convictions of the highest type of beauty. Again was my mother's "prunes and prisms" friend unnecessarily shocked, as I thought, because I had simply opened the window to buy a paper containing the account of *my own marriage*.

The next day the General returned to Petersburg, and the court graciously convened. The license was granted, and we were married[1] by the Rev. Dr. Platt in dear old St. Paul's Church before congregated thousands, for soldier and civilian, rich and poor, high and low, were all made welcome by my hero. We left for Richmond on the afternoon train amidst the salute of guns, hearty cheers, and chimes and bands and bugles.

It may not be supposed that, in those dark days of the Confederacy, we were likely to find a sumptuous banquet awaiting us in the capital, but we did. The river and the woods had given of their varied treasures to do honor to my General. It was in the sora season, and so plentifully was that game supplied that the banquet was afterward known as "the wedding-sora-supper." Had it required the expenditure of ammunition to provide this delicacy, it would probably have been lacking, for the South at that time could not afford to shoot at birds when there were so many more important targets to be found. They were killed at night with paddles, and many hundreds were sent as bridal presents by the plantation servants from Turkey Island. There were thousands of delicious beaten biscuit and gallons of terrapin stew made, and turkeys boned and made into salads, too, by the faithful old plantation servants under the supervision of

[1] September 15, 1863.

Mrs. Simms, the loyal old overseer's wife. Not having sugar, we had few sweets, but Mrs. Robert E. Lee had made for us with her own fair hands, a beautiful fruit-cake, the General's aunt-in-law, Mrs. Maria Dudley, the mother of the present Bishop, sent us as a bridal gift a black-cake that had been made and packed away for her own golden wedding, and some of our other friends had remembered us in similar ways. So we even had sweets at our wedding-supper.

It was a brilliant reception. The Army of Northern Virginia, then stationed around Richmond, came in uniform. Of the thousands present, only President Davis and his Cabinet, a few ministers, and a few *very* old men were in civilian clothes. The General and I greeted and welcomed them all as they came; then they passed on to the banquet and the dance—dancing as only Richmond in the Confederacy could dance. With a step that never faltered she waltzed airily over the crater of a volcano. She threaded graceful mazes on the brink of the precipice. The rumbling of the coming earthquake struck no minor tones into her merry music. If people could not dance in the crises of life the tragedy of existence might be even darker than it is.

So they danced through the beautiful, bright September night, and when the last guests were going my General and I walked out upon the veranda with them and, as they closed the outer gates, watched the stars of night fade away before the coming dawn and the morning star rise and shine gloriously upon a new, happy day.

5. MARIE RAVENEL DE LA COSTE—"SOMEBODY'S DARLING"

The author of what is perhaps the best-known Confederate poem spent her early days in Savannah where she was teaching French when hostilities began. Her father was Henri de la Coste and her mother Angèle Pérony d'Istria, natives of France. The inspiration of the poem came from the scenes she witnessed in Confederate hospitals. In 1910 she was living in Washington, D.C. "Somebody's Darling" was in every scrapbook and recited by many a school child in the Confederacy. It was published anonymously in 1864 by J. C. Schreiner & Son of Augusta, Georgia, as a song, with music by John Hill Hewitt. A later musical setting, by A. C. Matheson, was published by J. H. Snow of Mobile.[1]

[1] The version followed here is as printed in *The Home Book of Verse,* ed., Burton Egbert Stevenson. New York: Henry Holt & Company, 1912.

Into a ward of the whitewashed walls
　　Where the dead and the dying lay—
Wounded by bayonets, shells, and balls—
　　Somebody's darling was borne one day.
Somebody's darling! so young and so brave,
　　Wearing still on his pale sweet face—
Soon to be hid by the dust of the grave—
　　The lingering light of his boyhood's grace.

Matted and damp are the curls of gold
　　Kissing the snow of that fair young brow,
Pale are the lips of delicate mould—
　　Somebody's darling is dying now.
Back from the beautiful blue-veined brow
　　Brush the wandering waves of gold;
Cross his hands on his bosom now—
　　Somebody's darling is still and cold.

Kiss him once for Somebody's sake;
　　Murmur a prayer, soft and low;
One bright curl from the cluster take—
　　They were Somebody's pride, you know.
Somebody's hand hath rested there;
　　Was it a mother's, soft and white?
And have the lips of a sister fair
　　Been baptized in those waves of light?

God knows best. He has Somebody's love;
　　Somebody's heart enshrined him there;
Somebody wafted his name above,
　　Night and morn, on the wings of prayer.
Somebody wept when he marched away,
　　Looking so handsome, brave, and grand;
Somebody's kiss on his forehead lay;
　　Somebody clung to his parting hand;—

Somebody's watching and waiting for him,
　　Yearning to hold him again to her heart;
There he lies—with the blue eyes dim,
　　And the smiling, child-like lips apart.

Tenderly bury the fair young dead,
  Pausing to drop on his grave a tear;
Carve on the wooden slab at his head,
  "Somebody's darling slumbers here!"

6. ROSE O'NEAL GREENHOW—"CHARLESTON IS IN GREAT DANGER"

For six months Mrs. Greenhow and her youngest daughter, Rose, had seen degradation and misery in Old Capitol Prison in Washington. In June 1862 she was released and banished beyond the Federal lines. Richmond gave her a warm welcome. President Davis called to convey his thanks for her aid to the cause. "But for you," he said, "there would have been no battle of Bull Run."

Rose Greenhow continued as agent for the Confederacy, with her activities kept shrouded in secrecy. She arrived in Charleston in the summer of 1863 to look for a blockade-runner to take her to Europe as a sort of unofficial ambassador. Because of the bombardment Charleston was undergoing, she got ship from Wilmington, North Carolina, on August 5, carrying letters to John Slidell and James M. Mason, the Confederate Commissioners in Paris and London. She had been posted up to the minute on the economic situation. From Bermuda to England she sailed on a British man-of-war.

After placing young Rose in the Convent of the Sacred Heart in Paris she devoted herself to her special mission. She was cordially received by Napoleon III and by Queen Victoria. She did what she could to help the Commissioners and Commander Maury, who was trying to get ships. Her book My Imprisonment and the First Year of Abolition Rule in Washington *was published by Richard Bentley in London and greeted in rather agreeable fashion. She saw something of Robert Browning, who was friendly to Lincoln, and of Thomas Carlyle, who was not. She used all her accomplished arts of persuasion in government circles. She was feted. Lord Granville proposed and she was of a mind to accept him.*

The recognition which all the Confederate agents sought was really further away than ever after the reverses in 1863 and 1864, but Rose was still confident and highly exhilarated when she sailed for home, August 10, '64, on the blockade-runner Condor. *The morning of October 1 her fast ship was sighted by the* Niphon, *a Federal*

gunboat, off Cape Fear. Rose insisted, against the advice of the
commander of the Condor, *in being rowed to shore. A high wave*
overturned the boat, the men in it reached shore, but Rose, weighted
down with sovereigns, was drowned. According to legend she carried
her secret code with the money around her waist. Her body was
washed ashore and buried in Wilmington with military honors. The
grave bears a simple marble cross on which is carved: "Mrs. Rose
O'N. Greenhow, a bearer of dispatches to the Confederate Govern-
ment, Erected by the Ladies Memorial Association."

Carl Sandburg[1] describes her as "a tall brunette with slumberous
eyes . . . with gaunt beauty, education, manners and resourceful
speech. . . . Her proud loyalty to the South and her will and cour-
age set her apart as a woman who would welcome death from a
firing squad if it would serve her cause."

From Charleston Mrs. Greenhow writes to President Davis, and
to her old friend Colonel Alexander Robinson Boteler, former aide
to General Jackson and later to General J.E.B. Stuart.

Charleston July 16th 1863

To the President
My dear Sir

I arrived here yesterday (Wednesday) at noon after rather a
fatiguing travel from Richmond, not stopping by the wayside long
enough to wash my face.

The only thing to mark the journey was the excitement and
anxiety manifested by all classes to hear the news from Richmond,
and especially from Lee's army, and many a sigh of relief was
uttered when I spoke of his calm confident tone. I endeavored also
to impress upon every one your conviction as to the necessity of
reinforcing the army by the most rigorous means.

Just as I left Richmond news of the fall of Fort Hudson had been
received which was confirmed by the intelligence of the wayside.

On reaching Wilmington the situation of Charleston became the
engrossing subject of conversation and of interest, which has not
diminished by the accounts received from time to time by passengers who got on, the principal portion of whom were from Charles-

---

[1] *Abraham Lincoln, The War Years,* I, 326. New York: Harcourt, Brace & Company, Inc., 1939. For a full biography see *Rebel Rose,* by Ishbel Ross. New York:
Harper & Brothers, 1954.

ton or the vicinity. Doubt and anxiety as to the result was the general tone of the people, and occasionally severe animadversions upon the conduct of the military affairs, especially instancing the supineness in the construction of the defense. These I mention—nor do I attach importance to criticism of this nature but rather to show you the temper & spirit of the people.

Soon after getting upon the territory of S.C. handbills were distributed along the route setting forth the eminent peril of Charleston and calling upon the people for 3000 negroes to work on the defenses. On nearing the City the booming of the heavy guns was distinctly heard, and I learned that the attack had been going on with but little intermission for several days. I omitted to mention also that the cars coming out were laden with cotton and in many instances carriages & horses also being sent to the interior, & hence the sense of insecurity which very generally prevails. . . .

The impression here that Charleston is in great danger is sustained by the opinion of the Military Authorities. I saw Genrl Beauregard who came to call upon me, and had a long conversation with him, and he is deeply impressed with the gravity of the position. He says that three months since he called upon the planters to send him 2000 negroes to work upon the fortification at Morris Island and other points and that he could only get one hundred, and that they would not listen to his representations as to the threatened danger.—That he considered the late successes against the Yankee iron clads as a grave misfortune, as the people in despite of his protests to the contrary have been lulled with a fatal security.—That the Yankees are in force upon a portion of Morris Island from which it will be impossible to dislodge them, as they are protected by the sea and marsh on one side and by their iron clads on the other.—That we must eventually abandon the portion of the island which we now occupy, but that he is erecting works on James Island which will command those works—which he will destroy—and render it impossible for them to reconstruct. He says the fall of Charleston now depends upon his ability to carry out his plans. . . .

News reached here this morning that Johnston is still near Jackson [Mississippi] altho fighting was going on.[1] Vizitelli Frank of the

[1] "When Vicksburg fell, General Johnston's inadequate relieving force was between Grant's lines and the city of Jackson. Immediately upon the fall of the fortress, and even before Port Hudson surrendered, the indefatigable Grant sent Sherman to drive Johnston off. By July 9, with some slight fighting, Sherman arrived in front of Jackson, to which Johnston had retired, and sat down for serious attack against the

London News[1] who has been down there has just left me and given me some very interesting details of that region. He says that heavy responsibility rests some where for the fall of Vicksburg—and he gives me all that he gathers, altho under the seal of confidence as I told him that I should also tell you. He says the universal criticism is that had the Commissariat done his duty and properly provisioned the place that the greatest military move of modern times would have been accomplished.—But that instead of buying beef, bacon, corn &c. when offered at the most ridiculously low prices and urged upon him he had said he knew what was needed and refused. I then asked is any blame attached to Pemberton? No, not after the place was invested he did all that mortal man could do. That before the surrender his garrison had been five days on quarter rations and five days on mule meat which was then exhausted. He summoned his officers and men and put it to them whether they should cut their way out—he himself favored this—but it was found upon examination that not one out of a 100 of his garrison were able to march the eight miles even without equipments of any kind so exhausted were they from starvation—hence the surrender. He says had they been able to have held out twenty days that Grant's army would have been precisely in the position of Vicksburg—as Johnson, Smith and others were surrounding the avenues of his supplies. . . .

He thinks our people unduly depressed now by the events at Vicksburg & is writing a series of articles. . . . He says he is very glad that I am going to England as he knows I can be useful, and gives me some very good letters. . . .

The iron clads have been coming nearer all day, and now are firing at Sumter and Wagner and Moultrie which are returning the compliment. I have just returned from St. Stevens tower where I had a good view, and the shells are flying thick and fast and their gun boats are blackening the water—altho they have not yet got in reach of our torpedoes. All the vessels which come into the harbor are seized by Beauregard and torpedoes attached.

It is impossible to attempt to run the blockade from here—as there are no vessels. Mr. Trenholm[2] has just called upon me and told

city. On the sixteenth, after a week of scattered skirmishing, the Confederates for the second time gave up the capital of Mississippi." *The Story of the Confederacy*, by Robert Selph Henry, p. 293. Indianapolis: The Bobbs-Merrill Company, Inc., 1931.

[1] Frank Vizetelly represented the *Illustrated London News* in America during the war.

[2] George A. Trenholm, head of the firm of Fraser, Trenholm & Company in Charleston, who operated a fleet of blockade-runners.

me of the impossibility of getting out from this Port and tells me that there are a number of Gov. vessels now at Wilmington and advises me to go there so I have once more, my kind friend, to trouble you. Will you cause the necessary directions to be sent me here so that I may be enabled to go from Wilmington and together with the permit to ship cotton for my expenses, and if it be not possible to ship the whole amount required by any one vessel can be distributed amongst the number so as to enable me to take the necessary amount. I shall remain here until Wednesday or Thursday and shall hope to get a letter from you which I can frame as an heirloom for my children. . . .

ROSE O'NEAL GREENHOW

Mills House
Charleston   South Carolina
July 20   1863

To Alexander Robinson Boteler

Here am I, my friend, en route for the old world spell bound by fearful interest here. Perhaps at no time could I have visited this city under circumstances of deeper interest. The enemy have put forth every effort to capture it—and the skill and daring of our people will be taxed to the utmost to repell the brutal hoards who are now hovering around. For the last week the enemy has been attacking our batteries—having made a lodgment on Morris Island— one end of which we hold and upon which is planted Battery Wagner. This point commands the city, and it is here that all their energies have been put forth to get possession of the Battery. On Saturday they commenced a combined naval and land attack, and continued until dawn to shell this Battery. I witnessed the whole from St. Michael's tower and it was fearfully grand. At 6 o'clock they attempted to storm the Battery, the attack coming from the point we hold. Fort Sumter then opened upon them, in anticipation of which her guns had been ranged in the morning with fearful precision. The attacking party were driven off with heavy loss—but after dark it was renewed four times, and each time with fresh troops. At one time they succeeded in making a lodgment in the works and planted their banner upon one and also holding a gun for some little time. Talliaferro[1] here ordered the Charleston Battalion to bring down the flag and dislodge them—he leading. Not a man of the enemy got

---

[1] Brigadier-General William B. Taliaferro.

out alive—so they paid dearly for a momentary triumph—they were finally repulsed with great slaughter—their killed and wounded number 1500, eight hundred have already been buried. Our own one hundred in killed & wounded. Yesterday all day they were burying their dead whilst we were busy preparing further entertainment for them. It is possible that they may get possession of Battery Wagner—but it will be a dear bought and bootless triumph to them as Beauregard has prepared a better entertainment for them which will not aid their digestion.

General Beauregard is fully equal to his great reputation and still holds his place as the great captain of the age. He has just written me a note reminding me that the battle Saturday was fought on the anniversary of Bull Run, 18th July[1]—and has certainly added another leaf to the laurel which then bound his brow.

I will direct this to Richmond as I see by the papers that the Yankees have again paid their compliments to your region.

I shall go to Wilmington as it is possible that I may not be able to run the blockade from this port—in which case you shall hear from me. I have not had a line from you for a long time. Rose is here. Altho severely disturbed by the mosquitoes, the weather is delightful. I wish with all my heart that you were here. The day I left R. I had an opportunity of saying a kind thing for you. . . .

I am very unhappy. I have just got from Beauregard a permit to visit Sumter, although the enemies guns within the last half hour are again roaring. With best regards believe me always your friend,

ROSE O'N GREENHOW

7. BELLE BOYD—"AN ARROW STRUCK THE WALL OPPOSITE MY WINDOW"

While Belle was in Old Capitol Prison she had become engaged to a fellow prisoner, a Lieutenant McVay, but he was not exchanged when she was. Time and separation led to its being forgotten by both. On Stonewall Jackson's advice she left Virginia and traveled over the South. In June 1863 she came back home to Martinsburg, was again arrested, conveyed to Washington and confined in Carroll

[1] The allusion seems to be to the Bull Run campaign which began on the eighteenth. First Manassas was fought on the twenty-first.

Prison, not far from Old Capitol, where the following incidents occurred.

The typhoid fever which she incurred led to her release again on December 1. Again she was bundled off to Richmond with a dire injunction to stay out of Union lines forever. Her father died. For her health's sake doctors advised a trip to Europe. Then developed the climaxing romance. The blockade-runner Greyhound *on which she embarked was captured by the U.S.S.* Connecticut. *Ensign Samuel Hardinge of Brooklyn was put in charge of the prize crew. He and Belle fell desperately in love. After landing Belle made her way to Canada and from there to England. Sam, who had been arrested, tried and dismissed from the Navy for neglect of duty, followed her and they were married at St. James's Church in Piccadilly August 25, 1864. Converted to the Confederacy by his bride, Sam attempted to get to Richmond, was seized by Union officials, imprisoned at various points, grew seriously ill, was freed, rejoined Belle in England, in a short time died, and left "la belle Rebelle" a widow at twenty-one.*

Belle had sold her jewels and trousseau in her efforts to help Sam. Her book Belle Boyd: In Camp and Prison *was published in London in 1865, and the next year she returned to America to continue the theatrical career which had begun in England. In 1869 she married John Hammond who had been a British Army officer; she divorced him in 1885 and married Nathaniel Rue High of Toledo, Ohio. With him she toured the country giving dramatic recitals of her life as a Confederate spy. She died suddenly from a heart attack on June 9, 1900, at Wisconsin Dells, Wisconsin, where she was buried.*

Carroll Prison
Washington
August, 1863

When I arrived in Washington, tired and worn, I was immediately taken, not to my former quarters [Old Capitol Prison], but to Carroll Prison. This large, unpretending brick building, situated near the Old Capitol, was formerly used as a hotel, under the name of Carroll Place. But, since my first taste of prison life, it had been converted into a receptacle for rebels, prisoners of state, hostages, blockade-runners, smugglers, desperadoes, spies, criminals under sentence of death, and, lastly, a large number of Federal officers convicted of defrauding the Government. Many of these last were army contractors and quartermasters.

At the guarded gates of this Yankee Bastile, I bade adieu to my father; and once more iron bars shut me off from the outer world, and from all that is dear in this life. I was conducted to what was termed the "room for distinguished guests"—the best room which this place boasts, except some offices attached to the building. In this apartment had been held, though not for a long period of time, Miss Antonia F., Nannie T., with her aged mother, and many other ladies belonging to our best families in the South. Again my monotonous prison routine began.

Friends who chanced to pass the Carroll would frequently stop and nod in kindly recognition of some familiar face at the windows; unconscious that in so doing, they violated prison regulations. When noticed by the sentries, these good Samaritans were immediately "halted"; and, if riding or driving, were often made to dismount by the officious and impudent corporal of the guard, and forced to enter the bureau of the prison—there to remain until such time as it should please their tormentors to let them depart.

A few days after my arrival at the prison, I heard the "old familiar sound" of a grating instrument against the wall, apparently coming from the room adjoining mine. Whilst engaged in watching to see the exact portion of the wall whence it came, I observed the plaster give way, and next instant the point of a knife-blade was perceptible. I immediately set to work on my side, and soon, to my unspeakable joy, had formed a hole large enough for the passing of tightly rolled notes.

Ascertaining my unfortunate neighbors to be, beyond a doubt, "sympathizers," I was greatly relieved; for our prison was not without its system of espionage to trap the incautious. These neighbors were Messrs. Brookes, Warren, Stuart, and Williams; and from them I learnt that they had been here for nine months, having been captured whilst attempting to get South and join the Southern army.

But soon, alas! the little paper correspondence, that enlivened, whilst it lasted, a portion of my heavy time, was put to a stop by Mr. Lockwood, the officer of the keys, whose duty it was to secure our rooms, and who was always prying about when not otherwise engaged. Although it was well concealed on both sides, our impromptu post-office could not escape his Yankee cunning; and he at once had the gentlemen removed into the room beyond, and the mural disturbance closed up with plaster.

Several days subsequently I learned that I was to have a companion in a Miss Ida P., arrested on the charge of being a rebel mail-carrier. She did not remain here long, for, having given her parole . . . she was released. . . .

One evening, about nine o'clock, while seated at my window, I was singing "Take me back to my own sunny South," when quite a crowd of people collected on the opposite side of the street, listening. After I had ceased they passed on; and I could not help heaving a sigh as I watched their retreating figures. What would I not have given for liberty!

I was soon startled from this reverie by hearing something whiz by my head into the room and strike the wall beyond. At the moment I was alarmed; for my first impression was that some hireling of the Yankee Government, following the plan of Spanish countries, had endeavored to put an end to my life. I almost screamed with terror; and it was some minutes before I regained sufficient self-command to turn on the gas, so that, if possible, I might discover what missile had entered the room.

Glancing curiously round, I saw, to my astonishment, that it was an arrow which had struck the wall opposite my window; and fastened to this arrow was a letter; I immediately tore it open, and found that it contained the following words:—

"Poor girl, you have the deepest sympathy of all the best community in Washington City, and there are many who would lay down their lives for you, but they are powerless to act or aid you at present. *You have many very warm friends;* and we daily watch the journals to see if there is any news of you. If you will listen attentively to the instructions that I give you, you will be able to correspond with and hear from your friends outside.

"On Thursdays and Saturdays, in the evening, just after twilight, I will come into the square opposite the prison. When you hear some one whistling ' 'Twas within a mile of Edinbro' town,' if alone and all is safe, lower the gas as a signal and leave the window. I will then shoot an arrow into your room, as I have done this evening, with a letter attached. Do not be alarmed, as I am a good shot.

"The manner in which you will reply to these messages will be in this way: Procure a large india-rubber ball; open it, and place your communication within it, written on foreign paper; then sew it together. On Tuesdays I shall come, and you will know of my presence by the same signal. Then throw the ball, with as much force as you can exert, across the street into the square, and trust to me, I will get it.

"Do not be afraid. *I am really your friend.*

"C.H."

For a long time I was in doubt as to the propriety or safety of replying to this note; for I naturally reasoned that it was some Yankee who was seeking to gain evidence against me. But prudence at last yielded to my womanly delight at the really romantic way of corresponding with an unknown who vowed he was my friend; and I decided on replying.

It was an easy thing for me to procure an india-rubber ball without subjecting myself to the least suspicion; and by this means I commenced a correspondence which I had no reason to regret; for whoever the mysterious personage may have been, he was, without doubt, honorable and sincere in his profession of sympathy.

Through him I became possessed of much valuable information regarding the movements of the Federals; and in this unique style of correspondence I have again and again received small Confederate flags, made by the ladies of Washington City, with which I was only too proud and happy to adorn my chamber. . . .

On several occasions I fastened one of these ensigns to a broomstick, in lieu of a flag staff, after which I returned to the back part of the room, out of sight of the sentinel. In a short time this would attract his attention—for, when on watch, the sentinels generally were gazing heavenwards, the only time, I really believe, that such was the case—and he would roar out at the top of his voice some such command as—

"Take in that —— flag, or I'll blow your —— brains out!"

Of course I paid no attention to this, for I was out of danger, when the command would generally be followed up by the report of a musket; and I have often heard the thud of the Minié-ball as it struck the ceiling or wall of my room.

Just after this episode I was taken dangerously ill with typhoid fever. . . .

8. SUSAN BRADFORD—"MANY THINGS ARE BECOMING SCARCE"

It has been more than two years since Susan Bradford, now a young lady of seventeen, witnessed the signing of the Ordinance of Secession in the capital of Florida. The enemy's flag now waves over many points in her state—Jacksonville, St. Augustine, Appalachicola, Pensacola and Fort Pulaski. Her father has given his time, his money and the products of his land to the Confederacy; he has brought

*wounded soldiers to his home to be nursed and cared for by Susan
and her mother. The blockade of Florida ports has caused a scarcity
of many things, including salt.*

Pine Hill Plantation
Leon County, Florida

September 1, 1863.—We are busy spinning, weaving, sewing and
knitting, trying to get together clothing to keep our dear soldiers
warm this winter. Brother Junius writes that he has worn all his
under garments to shreds and wants to know if it would be possible
to get some flannel, or some kind of wool goods to make him some
new ones? We have tried but none can be had, so I am spinning some
wool into knitting yarn and with some big wooden needles I have I
am going to knit both drawers and shirts for him. I am so impatient
to get to work on them and see if my plan is feasible, that I spend all
the time I can at the spinning wheel. I know the shirts can be knit,
for I made some for father last winter which he found quite comfortable but I am somewhat doubtful as to the drawers. After awhile we
will learn how to supply most of our needs.

Cousin Rob did not have a hat when he was getting ready for
school, which opens today, so I plaited palmetto and sewed it into
shape and Aunt Robinson, who knows everything, pressed it on a
block and then I sewed a ribbon around it and there it was, a sure
enough hat and very becoming. He sat near and admired the braid
all the time I was making it. I had no shoes except some terribly
rough ones that old Mr. McDermid made and Cousin Rob tanned
some squirrel skins and made me a pair of really beautiful shoes,
nice enough to wear with my one and only silk dress. This dress, you
must know, is "made of Mammy's old one" like Jim Crack Corn's
coat—Little Diary, I am afraid you do not know very much of
Mother Goose.

October 27, 1863.—We went to the salt works today and, though
I am tired and dirty and have no good place to write, I am going to
try to tell you about it.

A year ago salt began to get scarce but the people only had to
economize in its use, but soon there was no salt and then Father got
Cousin Joe Bradford to come down from Georgia and take charge of
some salt works he was having installed on the coast. He had plenty
of hands from the plantation but they had to have an intelligent head

and then, too, it is a rather dangerous place to work, for the Yankee gunboats . . . . may try shelling the works.

Though they have been in operation quite awhile this is my first visit. Father brought us with him and we will stay three days, so he can see just how they are getting on. We are to sleep in a tent, on a ticking filled with pine straw. It will be a novel experience.

I am so interested in seeing the salt made from the water. The great big sugar kettles are filled full of water and fires made beneath the kettles. They are a long time heating up and then they boil merrily. Ben and Tup and Sam keep the fires going, for they must not cool down the least little bit. A white foam comes at first and then the dirtiest scum you ever saw bubbles and dances over the surface, as the water boils away it seems to get thicker and thicker, at last only a wet mass of what looks like sand remains. This they spread on smooth oaken planks to dry. In bright weather the sun does the rest of the work of evaporation, but if the weather is bad fires are made just outside of a long, low shelter, where the planks are placed on blocks of wood. The shelter keeps off the rain and the fires give out heat enough to carry on the evaporation. The salt finished in fair weather is much whiter and nicer in every way than that dried in bad weather, but this dark salt is used to salt meat or to pickle pork. I think it is fine of Father to do all this. It is very troublesome and it takes nine men to do the work, besides Cousin Joe's time; and Father does not get any pay whatever for the salt he makes.

We expected to have a grand time swimming and fishing. We are both good swimmers, but Father and Cousin Joe will not allow us to go outside of this little cove. Yankee gun-boats have been sighted once lately and there is no knowing when the salt works may be attacked. . . .

9. PARTHENIA ANTOINETTE HAGUE—DEPENDENT
   ON OUR OWN RESOURCES

Miss Hague, a native of Harris County, Georgia, was a teacher on a plantation near Eufaula in southern Alabama. Deprived of customary supplies and conveniences of daily life by the effectiveness of the Federal blockade, the plantation was forced to find all sorts of expedients and substitutes.

Most of the women of southern Alabama had small plots of ground for cultivating the indigo bush, for making "indigo blue," or "indigo mud," as it was sometimes called. The indigo weed also grew abundantly in the wild state in our vicinage. Those who did not care to bother with indigo cultivation used to gather, from the woods, the weed in the wild state when in season. Enough of the blue was always made either from the wild or cultivated indigo plant. We used to have our regular "indigo churnings," as they were called. When the weed had matured sufficiently for making the blue mud, which was about the time the plant began to flower, the plants were cut close to the ground, our steeping vats were closely packed with the weed, and water enough to cover the plant was poured in. The vat was then left eight or nine days undisturbed for fermentation, to extract the dye. Then the plant was rinsed out, so to speak, and the water in the vat was churned up and down with a basket for quite a while; weak lye was added as a precipitate, which caused the indigo particles held in solution to fall to the bottom of the vat; the water was poured off, and the "mud" was placed in a sack and hung up to drip and dry. It was just as clear and bright a blue as if it had passed through a more elaborate process.

The woods, as well as being the great storehouse for all our dyestuffs, were also our drug stores. The berries of the dogwood-tree were taken for quinine, as they contained the alkaloid properties of cinchona and Peruvian bark. A soothing and efficacious cordial for dysentery and similar ailments was made from blackberry roots; but ripe persimmons, when made into a cordial, were thought to be far superior to blackberry roots. An extract of the barks of the wild cherry, dogwood, poplar, and wahoo trees were used for chills and agues. For coughs and all lung diseases a syrup made with the leaves and roots of the mullein plant, globe flower, and wild-cherry tree bark was thought to be infallible. Of course the castor-bean plant was gathered in the wild state in the forest, for making castor oil.

Many also cultivated a few rows of poppies in their gardens to make opium, from which our laudanum was created; and this at times was very needful. The manner of extracting opium from poppies was of necessity crude. The heads or bulbs of the poppies were plucked when ripe, the capsules pierced with a large-sized sewing-needle, and the bulbs placed in some small vessel (a cup or saucer would answer) for the opium gum to exude and to become inspissated by evaporation. The soporific influence of this drug was not excelled by that of the imported articles.

Bicarbonate of soda, which had been in use for raising bread before the war, became "a thing of the past" soon after the blockade began; but it was not long ere some one found out that the ashes of corncobs possessed the alkaline property essential for raising dough. Whenever "soda" was needed, corn was shelled, care being taken to select all the red cobs, as they were thought to contain more carbonate of soda than white cobs. When the cobs were burned in a clean swept place, the ashes were gathered up and placed in a jar or jug, and so many measures of water were poured in, according to the quantity of ashes. When needed for bread-making, a teaspoonful or tablespoonful of the alkali was used to the measure of flour or meal required. . . .

All in our settlement learned to card, spin, and weave. Our days of novitiate were short. We soon became very apt at knitting and crocheting useful as well as ornamental woolen notions, such as capes, sacques, vandykes, shawls, gloves, socks, stockings, and men's suspenders. The clippings of lambs' wool were especially used by us for crocheting or knitting shawls, gloves, capes, sacques, and hoods. Our needles for such knitting were made of seasoned hickory or oakwood a foot long, or even longer. To have the hanks spotted or variegated, they were tightly braided or plaited, and so dyed; when the braids were unfolded a beautiful dappled color would result. Handsome mittens were knit or crocheted of the same lambs' wool dyed jet black, gray, garnet, or whatever color was preferred; a bordering of vines, with green leaves and rosebuds of bright colors, was deftly knitted in on the edge and top of the gloves. . . .

Our shoes, particularly those of women and children, were made of cloth, or knit. Some one had learned to knit slippers, and it was not long before most of the women of our settlement had a pair of slippers on the knitting needles. They were knit of our homespun thread, either cotton or wool, which was, for slippers, generally dyed a dark brown, gray, or black. When taken off the needles, the slippers or shoes were lined with cloth of suitable texture. The upper edges were bound with strips of cloth, of color to blend with the hue of the knit work. . . .

Sometimes we put on the soles ourselves by taking wornout shoes, whose soles were thought sufficiently strong to carry another pair of uppers, ripping the soles off, placing them in warm water to make them more pliable and to make·it easier to pick out all the old stitches, and then in the same perforations stitching our knit slippers or cloth-made shoes. We also had to cut out soles for shoes from our hometanned leather, with the soles of an old shoe as our pattern, and with an awl perforate the sole for sewing on the upper. . . . We used to hold our selfmade shoes at arm's length and say, as they were inspected: "What is the blockade to us, so far as shoes are concerned, when we can not only knit the uppers but cut the soles and stitch them on? Each woman and girl her own shoemaker; away with bought shoes; we want none of them!" But alas, we really knew not how fickle a few months would prove that we were. . . .

We became quite skilled in making designs of palmetto and straw braiding and plaiting for hats. Fans, baskets, and mats we made of the braided palmetto and straw also. Then there was the "bonnet squash," known also as the "Spanish dish-rag," that was cultivated by some for making bonnets and hats for women and children. Such hats presented a fine appearance, but they were rather heavy. Many would make the frame for their bonnets or hats, then cover it with the small white feathers and down of the goose, color bright red with the juice of poke berries, or blue with indigo mud, some of the larger feathers, and on a small wire form a wreath or plume with bright-colored and white feathers blended together; or, if wire was convenient, a fold or two of heavy cloth, or paper doubled, was used to sew the combination of feathers for wreath, plume, or rosette. . . .

One of our most difficult tasks was to find a good substitute for coffee. This palatable drink, if not a real necessary of life, is almost indispensable to the enjoyment of a good meal, and some Southerners took it three times a day. Coffee soon rose to thirty dollars per pound; from that it went to sixty and seventy dollars per pound. Good workmen received thirty dollars per day; so it took two days' hard labor to buy one pound of coffee, and scarcely any could be had even at that fabulous price. Some imagined themselves much better in health for the absence of coffee, and wondered why they had ever used it at all, and declared it good for nothing any way; but "Sour grapes" would be the reply for such as they. Others saved a few handfuls of coffee, and used it on very important occasions, and then only as an extract, so to speak, for flavoring substitutes for coffee.

There were those who planted long rows of the okra plant on the borders of their cotton or corn fields, and cultivated this with the corn and cotton. The seeds of this, when mature, and nicely browned, came nearer in flavor to the real coffee than any other substitute I now remember. Yam potatoes used to be peeled, sliced thin, cut into small squares, dried, and then parched brown; they were thought to be next best to okra for coffee. Browned wheat, meal, and burnt corn made passable beverages; even meal-bran was browned and used for coffee if other substitutes were not obtainable.

We had several substitutes for tea. Prominent among these substitutes were raspberry leaves. Many during the blockade planted and cultivated the raspberry-vine all around their garden palings, as much for tea as the berries for jams or pies; these leaves were considered the best substitute for tea. The leaves of the blackberry bush, huckleberry leaves, and the leaves of the holly-tree when dried in the shade, also made a palatable tea.

Persimmons dried served for dates. . . .

In place of kerosene for lights, the oil of cotton seed and ground peas, together with the oil of compressed lard, was used, and served well the need of the times. For lights we had also to fall back on moulding candles, which had long years lain obsolete. When beeswax was plentiful it was mixed with tallow for moulding candles. Long rows of candles so moulded would be hung on the lower limbs of wide-spreading oaks, where, sheltered by the dense foliage from the direct rays of the sun, they would remain suspended day and night until they were bleached as white as the sperm candles we had been wont to buy, and almost as transparent as wax candles. When there was no oil for the lamps or tallow for moulding candles, which at times befell our households, mother-wit would suggest some expedient by which the intricate problem of light could be solved.

One evening at a neighbor's, where we had gone to tea, when we took our seats at the supper-table we were diverted by the lights we were to eat by, the like of which, up to that time, we had not seen, nor even thought of.

In the absence of any of the ordinary materials for lighting, the good woman of the house had gone to the woods and gathered a basketful of round globes of the sweet-gum tree. She had taken two shallow bowls and put some lard, melted, into them, then placed two or three of the sweet-gum balls in each of the vessels, which, soon becoming thoroughly saturated with the melted lard, gave a fairylike light, floating round in the shallow vessels of oil like stars.

At other times rude lamps or candles were improvised, anything but attractive in appearance, though the light was fairly bright.

Medium-sized bottles were taken, and several strands of spun thread twisted together to form a wick two or three yards long were well steeped in beeswax and tallow, and coiled around the bottle from base to neck closely and evenly. When ready for lighting, one or more of the coils of thread would be loosed from the bottle, raised above the mouth an inch or so, and pressed with the thumb to the neck of the bottle. When the wick had burned to the bottle's mouth, the same process of uncoiling and pressing the wick to the bottle would be repeated. This gave a steady flame. When beeswax could not be had, tallow was used for steeping the strands.

Sewing societies were formed in every hamlet, as well as in our cities, to keep the soldiers of the Confederacy clothed as best we could. They met once every week, at some lady's house, if it was in the country. To such societies all the cloth that could be spared from each household was given and made into soldiers' garments. . . .

In many settlements there were spinning "bees." Wheels, cards, and cotton were all hauled in a wagon to the place appointed. On the way, as often as not, a long flexible twig would be cut from the woods, and attached to one of the spinning wheels; from the top of such flagstaff would play loosely to the wind, and jolts of the wagon, a large bunch of lint cotton, as our ensign. Sometimes as many as six or eight wheels would be whirring at the same time in one house. . . . We were drawn together in a closer union, a tenderer feeling of humanity linking us all together, both rich and poor; from the princely planter, who could scarce get off his wide domains in a day's ride, and who could count his slaves by the thousand, down to the humble tenants of the log-cabin on rented or leased land.

10. SARA RICE PRYOR—CHRISTMAS IN PETERSBURG

"Agnes'" friend Sara Pryor was the daughter of the Reverend Samuel Blair Rice of Halifax County, Virginia, who became a chaplain in the Confederate Army. At eighteen she married Roger A. Pryor, who came from the vicinity of Petersburg. In 1851 they moved to Washington, where Mr. Pryor was successively on the staff of the Union, The South *and the* States. *In 1855 he went to Greece as a special commissioner. He was elected to Congress in 1859, reelected in 1860, resigned March 3, 1861, to join the Confederacy.*

He stood beside the gun at Charleston that fired the first shot of

the war, enlisted and became colonel of the 3rd Virginia. After First
Manassas Sara determined to follow the regiment. She was in Rich-
mond during the Seven Days' battles, working as a volunteer nurse
in the hospitals. She was with Roger at Culpeper, and in the winter
of 1862 lived near his camp on the Blackwater. General Joe Johnston
had made Roger a brigadier-general for bravery on the battlefield of
Williamsburg, but feeling that he was a brigadier without a brigade
he gave up his rank on August 18, 1863, and served as a special
courier with Fitzhugh Lee's cavalry. From the fall of 1863 on Sara
was in Petersburg.

Having no longer a home of my own, it was decided that I should
go to my people in Charlotte County, Virginia. One of my sons,
Theo, and two of my little daughters were already there, and there
I expected to remain until the end of the war.

But repeated attempts to reach my country home resulted in
failure. Marauding parties and guerillas were flying all over the
country. There had been alarm at a bridge over the Staunton near
the Oaks, and the old men and boys had driven away the enemy.
I positively *could* not venture alone.

So it was decided that I should return to my husband's old district,
to Petersburg, and there find board in some private family.

I reached Petersburg in the autumn [1863] and wandered about
for days seeking refuge in some household. Many of my old friends
had left town. Strangers and refugees had rented the houses of some
of these, while others were filled with the homeless among their own
kindred. There was no room anywhere for me, and my small purse
was growing so slender that I became anxious. Finally my brother-
in-law offered me an overseer's house on one of his "quarters." The
small dwelling he placed at my disposal was to be considered temporary only; some one of his town houses would soon be vacant.
When I drove out to the little house, I found it hardly better than a
hovel. We entered a rude, unplastered kitchen, the planks of the floor
loose and wide apart, the earth beneath plainly visible. There were
no windows in this smoke-blackened kitchen. A door opened into a
tiny room with a fireplace, window, and out-door of its own; and
a short flight of stairs led to an unplastered attic, so that the little
apartment was entered by two doors and a staircase. It was already
cold, but we had to beat a hasty retreat and sit outside while a

colored boy made a "smudge" in the house to dislodge the wasps that had tenanted it for many months. My brother had lent me bedding for the overseer's pine bedstead and the low trundle-bed underneath. The latter, when drawn out at night, left no room for us to stand. When that was done, we had to go to bed. For furniture we had only two or three wooden chairs and a small table. There were no curtains, neither carpet nor rugs, no china. There was wood at the woodpile, and a little store of meal and rice, with a small bit of bacon in the overseer's grimy closet. This was to be my winter home.

Petersburg was already virtually in a state of siege. Not a tithe of the food needed for its army of refugees could be brought to the city. Our highway, the river, was filled, except for a short distance, with Federal gunboats. The markets had long been closed. The stores of provisions had been exhausted, so that a grocery could offer little except a barrel or two of molasses made from the domestic sorghum sugar-cane—an acrid and unwholesome sweet used instead of sugar for drink with water or milk, and for eating with bread. The little boys at once began to keep house. They valiantly attacked the woodpile, and found favor in the eyes of Mary and the man, whom I never knew as other than "Mary's husband." He and Mary were left in charge of the quarter and had a cabin near us.

I had no books, no newspapers, no means of communicating with the outside world; but I had one neighbor, Mrs. Laighton, a daughter of Winston Henry, granddaughter of Patrick Henry. She lived near me with her husband—a Northern man. Both were very cultivated, very poor, very kind. Mrs. Laighton, as Lucy Henry,—a brilliant young girl,—had been one of the habitués of the Oaks. We had much in common, and her kind heart went out in love and pity for me.

She taught me many expedients: that to float tea on the top of a cup of hot water would make it "go farther" than steeped in the usual way; also that the herb, "life everlasting," which grew in the fields, would make excellent yeast, having somewhat the property of hops; and that the best substitute for coffee was not the dried cubes of sweet potato, but parched corn or parched meal, making a nourishing drink. And Mrs. Laighton kept me a "living soul" in other and higher ways. She reckoned intellectual ability the greatest of God's gifts, raising us so far above the petty need of material things that we could live in spite of their loss. Her talk was a tonic to me. It stimulated me to play my part with courage, seeing I had been deemed worthy, by the God who made me, to suffer in this sublime struggle for liberty.

I had not my good Eliza Page this winter. She had fallen ill. I had a stout little black girl, Julia, as my only servant; but Mary had a friend, a "corn-field hand," "Anarchy," who managed to help me at odd hours. Mrs. Laighton sent me every morning a print of butter as large as a silver dollar, with two or three perfect biscuits, and sometimes a bowl of persimmons or stewed dried peaches. She had a cow, and churned every day, making her biscuits of the buttermilk, which was much too precious to drink.

A great snow-storm overtook us a day or two before Christmas. My little boys kindled a roaring fire in the cold, open kitchen, roasted chestnuts, and set traps for the rabbits and "snowbirds" which never entered them. They made no murmur at the bare Christmas; they were loyal little fellows to their mother. My day had been spent in mending their garments,—making them was a privilege denied me, for I had no materials. I was not "all unhappy!" The rosy cheeks at my fireside consoled me for my privations, and something within me proudly rebelled against weakness or complaining.

The flakes were falling thickly at midnight, when I suddenly became very ill. I sent out for Mary's husband and bade him gallop in to Petersburg, three miles distant, and fetch me Dr. Withers. I was dreadfully ill when he arrived—and as he stood at the foot of my bed I said to him: "It doesn't matter much for me, Doctor! But my husband will be grateful if you keep me alive."

When I awoke from a long sleep, he was still standing at the foot of my bed where I had left him—it seemed to me ages ago! I put out my hand and it touched a little warm bundle beside me. God had given me a dear child!

The doctor spoke to me gravely and most kindly. "I must leave yon now," he said, "and, alas! I cannot come again. There are so many, so many sick. Call all your courage to your aid. Remember the pioneer women, and all they were able to survive. This woman," indicating Anarchy, "is a field-hand, but she is a mother, and she has agreed to help you during the Christmas holidays—her own time. And now, God bless you, and goodby!"

I soon slept again—and when I awoke the very Angel of Strength and Peace had descended and abode with me. I resolved to prove to myself that if I was called to be a great woman, I *could* be a great woman. Looking at me from my bedside were my two little boys. They had been taken the night before across the snow-laden fields to my brother's house, but had risen at daybreak and had "come home to take care" of me!

My little maid Julia left me Christmas morning. She said it was too lonesome, and her "mistis" always let her choose her own places. I engaged "Anarchy" at twenty-five dollars a week for all her nights. But her hands, knotted by work in the fields, were too rough to touch my babe. I was propped upon pillows and dressed her myself, sometimes fainting when the exertion was over.

I was still in my bed three weeks afterwards, when one of my boys ran in, exclaiming in a frightened voice, "Oh, mamma, an old gray soldier is coming in!"

He stood—this old gray soldier—and looked at me, leaning on his sabre.

"Is this the reward my country gives me?" he said; and not until he spoke did I recognize my husband. Turning on his heel, he went out, and I heard him call:—

"John! John! Take those horses into town and sell them! Do not return until you do so—sell them for anything! Get a cart and bring butter, eggs, and everything you can find for Mrs. Pryor's comfort."

He had been with Fitz Lee on that dreadful tramp through the snow after Averill.[1] He had suffered cold and hunger, had slept on the ground without shelter, sharing his blanket with John. He had used his own horses, and now if the government needed him the government might mount him. He had no furlough, and soon reported for duty; but not before he had moved us, early in January, into town—one of my brother-in-law's houses having been vacated at the beginning of the year. John knew his master too well to construe him literally, and had reserved the fine gray, Jubal Early, for his use. That I might not again fall into the sad plight in which he had found me, he purchased three hundred dollars in gold, and instructed me to prepare a girdle to be worn all the time around my waist, concealed by my gown. The coins were quilted in; each had a separate

---

[1] General W. W. Averell on December 8, 1863, started a long raid through the Allegheny Mountains and, striking the supply line of the Virginia & Tennessee Railroad at Salem, Virginia, on the sixteenth, destroyed a store of cereals and wrecked bridges and track. General Robert E. Lee was so disturbed that he gave up the idea of spending Christmas with his family. General Jubal Early sent General Fitzhugh Lee in pursuit of Averell, but bad weather prevented his scotching the foe. See D. S. Freeman, *R. E. Lee*, III, 215; *Lee's Lieutenants*, III, 325.

section to itself, so that with scissors I might extract one at a time without disturbing the rest. . . .

11. BELLE EDMONDSON—SMUGGLING FROM MEMPHIS

At eighteen Belle Edmondson was living with her family at their plantation house near Nonconnah in Shelby County, Tennessee, where her father had large holdings of land and slaves. A war romance ended sadly when her Confederate soldier boy was transferred to Mobile and transferred his affections. Perhaps because of this unhappy love affair, Belle, according to family tradition, volunteered as a secret agent for the Confederacy. After near-by Memphis was occupied by Federal troops in June 1862, she engaged in the dangerous business of smuggling contraband between the lines. Her father served as a volunteer scout and her two brothers were with General Forrest.

During the war years Belle kept a diary which is a lively account of life on the plantation and her activities in occupied Memphis, the center of drug and cotton smuggling.

near Nonconnah

March   Sunday 13   1864

Today is the first anniversary of the happiest day in my life—just one short year ago, twas then on Friday morning, he came for me to walk on the hill to listen to the echoes of our triumph at Fort Pemberton (Greenwood)[1]—I rushed on to meet my fate, oh! God that it had never overtaken me—yet tis the brightest spot in my sad life—his love. . . . Oh! who in the course of his life has not felt some joy without a security, and without the certainty of a morrow! Time hath power over hours, none over the soul. Time had power over his heart, yet none over my true and holy love. Today he woos the daughter of a more sunny clime—Miss Sallie Anderson of Mobile, may she never know the pangs of a deceived heart. . . .

March   Monday 14   1864

. . . We have been delighted by the visit of a Rebel Major, Maj. Allen, who spent the day with us. . . . Maj. A. went down to Col.

---

[1] On March 11, 1863, this small work at the head of the Yazoo River beat off a Federal attack.

Perkins to stay until Thursday, when I will have returned from Memphis—having attended to his wants. . . . we had a pleasant evening—music, conversation, &c. Anna Nelson and I have made our arrangements to go into Memphis tomorrow and not return till next day. Oh! Lord, deliver me from getting in any trouble with the Yanks, this will be a hard trip, I have a great risk to run. . . .

March   Tuesday 15   1864

Anna Nelson and I started to Memphis about 9 o'clock, suffered very much with the cold, stopped at Mr. Roberts to warm—from there we passed through the Pickets to the Pigeon Roost Road—found Mr. Harbut's after much searching—did not reach Memphis until 10 o'clock, left our horse & buggy at Mr. Barbier's, went up town— and not one thing would the Merchants sell us, because we did not live in their lines. I consoled myself with a wheel that could not turn —could not spin—went to see my friend Mrs. Facklen, she went up town and bought the things for me—poor deluded fools, I would like to see them thwart a Southerner in such an undertaking as I had. Spent a very pleasant evening with Mrs. Facklen's family—all Rebels, and we talked just as we please!

Mrs. F. and I did not go to sleep until 2 o'c, this being the first time I had seen her since she returned from Dixie. I have finished all my provisions, and will have nothing to do tomorrow except fixing my things for smuggling.

March   Wednesday 16   1864

Went up Street directly after Breakfast to finish a little job I forgot on yesterday. At one o'clock Mrs. Facklen, Mrs. Kirk and I began to fix my articles for smuggling, we made a balmoral of the Grey cloth for uniform, pin'd the Hats to the inside of my hoops— tied the boots with a strong list, letting them fall directly in front, the cloth having monopolized the back & the Hats the side—All my letters, brass buttons, money, &c in my bosom—left at 2 o'clock to meet Anna at Mr. Barbier's—started to walk, impossible that— hailed a hack—rather suspicious of it, afraid of small-pox, weight of contrabands ruled—jumped in, with orders for a hurried drive to Cor Main & Vance—arrived, found Anna not ready, had to wait for her until 5 o'clock, very impatient—started at last—arrived at Pickets, no trouble at all, although I suffered horribly in anticipation of trouble. Arrived at home at dusk, found Mr. Wilson & Harbut, gave them late papers and all news. Mrs. Harbut here to meet her Bro. Bro't Mr. Wilson a letter from Home in Ky. Worn out. 8 yds. Long cloth, 2 Hats, 1 pr Boots, 1 doz. Buttons, letters, &c. 2 Cords, 8 tassels. . . .

March   Wednesday 23   1864

Tate & I went to Memphis this morning bright and early. Stopped at Mrs. Apperson's first—from there to Cousin Frazer. Tate met me at Mrs. Worsham's room. We then went up street, walked until three o'clock, attended to all affairs entrusted to our care, ready to leave at half past three. All of the Yankee Cavalry moving, destination not known—could hear no particulars. Think they are going after Forrest, who we think is on his way to Kentucky.[1] . . . We came through white Picketts. I think we will not try them again—the Negroes are ten times more lenient. We came by Wash Taylor's, got two hats for soldiers—came through Yankee Camp. If the Lord forgives me I will never do it again. Yankee soldier drove our horse in Nonconnah for us—seemed to be a gentleman, for which we were very grateful. Found Mr. Harbut awaiting our report. Mr. John & Henry Nelson & Mr. Harbut took Tea with us. Jim & Mr. Pugh completed the list for a nice Rebel meeting. Brought a great deal through lines this eve—Yankee pickets took our papers.

March   Wednesday 30   1864

It seems I can never go to Memphis without some disagreeable arrangements and sayings. I was greatly disappointed in my trip. Tate and I went together. I stopped at Mrs. Facklen's on Union St. She went on up to Cousin Frazer's in the buggy. Mrs. Facklen and Mrs. Kirk in great distress, old Hurlbut[2] gave her ten days to abandon her house. She took an old Yankee Officer, his Wife & two children to board with her, hoping he would recall the heartless order to make her and her little children homeless. I did not smuggle a thing through the lines except some letters. Mr. Tommery gave me a permit to bring 2 Gals Whiskey and 5 bbs Tobacco—which I got home safely.

March   Thursday 31   1864

Jim & Mr. Pugh are trying to find a way to join Forrest. They

---

[1] Forrest was indeed making for Paducah, Kentucky.
[2] The Union general Stephen A. Hurlbut, in command at Memphis.

had not been gone more than five minutes when four Yankees, belonging to 6th. Ill. Cavalry came riding in, asked if we had seen any Confederates. Of course we said no. I think they came to steal, but we were polite to them, and they left—only wanted some milk, which they got. Tate & Nannie went to town today. Mr. Perryman got them a pass—they got home safe, but saw Anna Nelson and Sallie Hildebrand arrested and carried back with a Negro guard, for smuggling a pair of boots.

April   Tuesday 5   1864

I was awakened at daylight by a servant with a note from Miss Hudson who has succeeded in getting all she wants out of Memphis, and promised to take the things I had for Mrs. Hudson to her. I regreted not having all the things through the lines, but sent what I had.

April   Thursday 7   1864

Tate and Nannie went to the Picketts this morning, were turned back, the lines closed. Capt. Barber & Mr. Kirk cannot get their things. I had not the heart to see them disappointed, so rob'd old Mr. McMahon of 2d. Mo. Mr. Kirk took his Boots, Capt. Barber his uniform. I will get him more through the lines before he comes for them. Nannie &c very busy sewing all day. Nannie & I made two shirts for a Kentucky'n who is so far from home, and no one to take an interest in his need. I sent him a pair of Pants too.

April   Monday 11   1864

Helen, Father, the children and myself spent the day alone, the rest all in Memphis. Joanna came home, succeeded in getting Father's permit for supplies, brought no news. Miss Perdue & Noble banished, leave tomorrow. I expect I will be next. I was so happy to hear Miss Em is expected today, my future plans depend upon her advice. Mr. McMahon, 2d. Mo. Cavalry came this eve. I was so disappointed about letting his things go—though he seemed perfectly satisfied, as he had replenished his wardrobe from Yankee Prison in Grierson's raid.[1] He has been quite sick, is now on his way to Camp at Jackson, Tennessee. He has his fine horse again. God grant him a safe journey, for he is a splendid Soldier.

---

[1] At the beginning of the Vicksburg campaign a raid by Grierson's Federal cavalry played havoc with railroads and supply depots in Mississippi.

April   Wednesday 13   1864

This has indeed been an exciting day, heavy firing all last night
& this morning. Forrest has captured Fort Pillow.[1] The firing we
heard was between the Fort and Gun Boats. The Yanks in Memphis
are frightened to death.

April   Thursday 14   1864

Father heard a rumor[2] this evening that our Virginia General
(Robert Lee) had ruined the left wing of Grant's Army. God grant
it may be so. Grant is a fool to think he can whip Gen. Lee. Gen.
Forrest still at Fort Pillow last account we had.

April   Saturday 16   1864

Another day of excitement—about 30 Yanks passed early this
morning, only six came in for their breakfast. They did not feed
their horses—they behaved very well, and seemed to be gentlemen,
in fact we so seldom see gentlemen among the Yankees that we can
appreciate them when they are met with.

April   Tuesday 19   1864

No Yanks today. No news from Forrest. We have not seen any
one today, or heard a word of news. Joanna and Bettie went to
Memphis today. Sallie went with them—got a Permit. I am going
to try my luck in the city tomorrow. Father is not willing I
should go.

April   Wednesday 20   1864

Tate and I arrived in Memphis quite early, put the horse up, then
walked up street together. Met Nannie and Anna Perkins. Nannie
gave me two letters, one from St. Lewis to Mr. Welch, an exile in
La Grange, Georgia, one from New York from a stranger, asking
assistance through me to communicate with Mrs. Van Hook at
Selma, Alabama. I received a letter from Maj. Price at Selma, by
Mrs. Flaherty. I dined with Mrs. Jones, and Mrs. Kirk—went round
for Hat after dinner, she went with me to see Capt. Woodward, to

---

[1] On April 12, 1864, General N. B. Forrest and his swift-moving troops stormed and
captured Fort Pillow, on the river forty miles north of Memphis. It was a bloody
affair, and Forrest was accused of having committed an atrocity, but no clear case
was ever made against him and the "massacre" seems rather to have been due to an
overstubborn defense, unskillfully conducted.
[2] A false report.

know what I must do in regard to an order which I heard was issued for my arrest. He advised me to keep very quiet until he could see the Provost Marshall and learn something in regard to it.

April   Thursday 21   1864

I went round according to appointment, met Capt. Woodward at 11 o'clock. Col. Patterson went with me. Capt. W. had not seen the Provost Marshall. He went as soon as I left, came round to Mrs. Facklen's after dinner, and brought bad news—though having approached Capt. Williams as aid for a heroine of Jericho, he could not treat me as the order read—it was issued from old Hurlbut. I was to be arrested and carried to Alton on first Boat that passed—for carrying letters through the lines, and smuggling, and aiding the Rebellion in every way in my power—he sent me word I must not think of attending Jennie Eave's wedding, or go out of doors at all, he would be compelled to arrest me if it came to him Officially, but as my Father was a Royal Arch Mason, and I a Mason, he would take no steps, if I would be quiet. . . .

12. MARY BYSON—"SISTER SUSAN HAS LOST THREE SONS"

Mary Byson of Red River, Texas, and her family, though far from the scene of battles, have not been spared their tragic consequences. Her correspondence with her friend Margaret Butler of Louisiana continued through the war years.

Red River Texas March 21/64

My dear Margaret

The Federals have not come to this part of the country though we have been expecting them all last fall. Our army may be able to keep them out this spring, at least I hope so. Horse-stealing and murder are going on in this part of the country—supposed to be done by some Missouri Bushwhackers who came here last fall but it is thought some of the people in the country are concerned in it.

Times are hard but I do not think we ought to complain. We have plenty of meat and bread and flour and sugar for the next year. I have been wearing homespun dresses this winter to save my calico and knit my stockings keeping my bought ones for summer. I am in hopes the war will end this year. Sister Susan has lost three sons since the war commenced. . . .

We hear of news but do not know when to believe any as so much is only rumor. . . .

Ever yours affectionately
M. Byson

13. SUSAN BRADFORD—"TODAY I HAVE NO SHOES"

To find a substitute for shoe leather taxed the ingenuity of many a Southern woman. Some made shoes from old felt hats; some knit them. Sometimes ladies appeared with their feet wrapped in lint. Mrs. Pryor, in Petersburg, made shoes from an old carpet, and Judith McGuire, in Richmond, made them from parts of a canvas sail rescued from a vessel wrecked on the James River. Parthenia Hague has told what she did. Her cousin Rob had tanned some squirrel skins for Susan Bradford. Now Susan has another bright idea.

After the war she married Nicholas Ware Eppes, a young Confederate soldier. They lived in Tallahassee and enjoyed a long, happy life together. In her late years she produced two books, The Negro of the Old South *and* Verses from Florida. *In 1926 her war diary,* Through Some Eventful Years, *was published. She died·on July 2, 1942, in her ninety-sixth year, survived by three daughters, Susan, Alice and Martha.*

Pine Hill Plantation
Leon County, Florida

April 7th, 1864.—Today I have no shoes to put on. All my life I have never wanted to go bare-footed, as most Southern children do. The very touch of my naked foot to the bare ground made me shiver. Lula my Mammy scolds me about this—even yet she claims the privilege of taking me to task when she thinks I need it.

"Look here, chile," she says, "don't you know you is made outen the dus' er de earth? Don't you onderstand dat when you is dead you is gwine back ter dat dus'?"

"Yes, Lula," I answer meekly.

"Well, den, what is you so foolish fur? Better folks dan you is gone bare-footed."

I listen to all she has to say but a thought has come to me and I have no time to argue the point. Until the shoes for the army are finished, Mr. McDearnmid will not have time to make any shoes for any one else, this is right, for our dear soldiers must come first in everything, but I will stop writing now and get to work.

April 9th, 1864.—Today I have on railroad stockings and slippers. Guess what these slippers are made of? Whenever I go to uncle Richard's I see an old black uncle, hard at work plaiting shucks and weaving the plaits together into door mats. It seemed to me a lighter braid might be sewed into something resembling shoes, so I picked out the softest shucks and soon had enough to make one slipper. So pleased was I that I soon had a pair of shoes ready to wear. They are a little rough so I have pasted inside a lining of velvet. Everybody laughed, but I feel quite proud.

14. VIRGINIA McCOLLUM STINSON—

YANKEES IN CAMDEN, ARKANSAS

Virginia was the wife of George H. Stinson, who had lost an eye at Shiloh and come home to Camden to work in the quartermaster department. She had three small children, the youngest a baby. Her brother-in-law John M. Daly had been killed at the Battle of Corinth. After the war Mrs. Stinson wrote her recollections of the occupation of Camden by enemy troops under General Frederick Steele. She seems to have accepted the responsibility for her household—the children, Aunt Sallie a trusted old cook, and three other servants. The younger sister Kate, that "saucy little rebel," apparently divided her time between Mrs. Stinson's and Mrs. Daly's.

On the morning of April 15th, 1864 all the women on West Washington Street and other streets in Camden who could were busy cooking rations for our dear men in grey. Everybody was excited for the news all day long was "the Yankees are nearing town." Women were flying about in the town to pay their last calls. They were not dressed in silk or fine hats or bonnets. There had been no "Spring Opening" for three years. They wore sunbonnets or maybe nothing at all on their heads. I could not go out visiting on account of my feeble health, so my good neighbors came to see me.

When the cry came "the Yankees are in sight," all the visitors rushed home and said good-bye. We did not know when we would meet again, for we women had resolved we would stay in our homes and save our household goods and stores.

Kate, my young lady sister, ran in the house and said, "Sis the Yankees are almost here." Such a noise they did make, shooting guns and pistols, and the tramp of feet and yelling of voices—it was distressing indeed. I gathered my household together and closed my doors and blinds. No glad welcome was extended them, our hearts were lifted to God in prayer for protection. We peeped through the blinds and saw them rush in our vacant lot, then in a short time our grounds were covered with the blue coats. They were as thick as blackbirds in springtime and chattering in louder voices. They began to take a look at our house, then came to the back door. Aunt Sallie went to the door to see what was wanted. I had given her all the keys to the smoke house and store room and told her to claim everything on the place. The Yankees demanded the keys from her. She said: "You can't have them." They replied, "We must have them because we need meat, flour and meal." Sister Kate went out to help Aunt Sallie. She would not let the doors be broken open, but unlocked them and let them take whatever they wished, but when they were taking nearly all of the meat from the smoke house, Kate said, "You surely don't mean to rob my sister of all the meat she has?" They then decided to leave some. They only left two of the smallest hams in the lot, but we had some stored away that they could not find.

Their robbery was begun about 6 P.M. and lasted until midnight. What a night of terror it was. Next morning they began to rob us again; this time I went to the store-room door myself. As Aunt Sallie opened it fifteen Yankees were there to grab whatever they could lay their hands on. I spoke to them in this pathetic manner: "Haven't you men mothers, wives or sister in your northern homes? If so, how would you like for our Southern soldiers to rob them as you are robbing me?" One or two looked ashamed, while the others were defiant and kept taking. Sister Kate had gone for a guard over at Gen. Steele's headquarters, which was at my neighbors, Mrs. Maj. Graham's home. While the Yankees were still taking rice and flour their commanding officers rode right up to my back door with a guard and robbing ceased. Kate told what a time she had to get a guard.

Before the Yankees occupied Camden a Confederate officer's wife, a Mrs. Maj. Sneed, who boarded with our sister Mrs. Daly, told us in case the Yankees came that she was well acquainted with Col. Mantor, one of Gen. Steele's staff officers, and if we needed help to go to him for he was a gentleman. So Kate applied to him for a guard for her sisters, but Col. Mantor did not treat her as a perfect gentleman should a lady. At last Kate told him, "I would not have asked you at all, but a lady of your acquaintance, Mrs. Maj. Sneed, told me that you were a gentleman and would aid helpless women and children." He then flew around and said: "Why didn't you tell me that at first?" "I did not think it necessary for I thought you were a perfect gentleman." He ordered guards to be sent in haste. The same day the guard came, Mrs. Graham advised me to take a Federal officer to board. A very nice one applied for board that day. This officer's regiment camped on a vacant lot east of my home. After the guard came and the Federal officer, I had no more serious trouble. The Federal officer also took interest in saving things for me. My husband had given me a bale of cotton that he took for debt, so the Federal officer had his men roll it in the barn for safe keeping.

Next morning after the Yankees came, Mr. Dan Fellows and Mr. Skelton came to see if I needed anything. Each one of these men had a water bucket with meal and salt, they feared the Yankees had left me little to eat. Mr. Skelton, who was always full of fun, said to me "Why Mrs. Stinson, you were strongly reinforced last night." At the same time pointing to the thousand Yankees on my left I replied, "that is true, but I prefer men in grey instead of blue." Things began to be a little easier for us. The Federal officer was a perfect gentleman and so thoughtful of our comfort, but the guard was just the opposite, not at all refined and would eavesdrop every time any of my friends called to see me. I never thought of his doing such a mean thing as that until Aunt Sallie caught him one day with his ear at the key hole of my room and she warned us to be careful what we had to say. After that all of our conversation was in a whisper.

Aunt Sallie and I felt that we had our hands full, a boarder and that guard to lodge and feed and seven of our own household to care for and our larder quite low. We did the best we could for them, gave them rye-coffee, bread, rice, and meat. Sister Kate dined with us several times, but she and the guard were not on good terms. The Federal officer seemed to enjoy the hot discussions Kate and the guard had. They soon found her to be a saucy little rebel, she cared not what she said, I constantly reminded her that silence was golden, for I feared the guard would capture her on account of her freedom of speech.

The Yankees took possession of all the cows, sheep and hogs they could drive into the vacant lots to slaughter them. One afternoon Kate saw them driving a lot of cows in my pasture, she spied one of my cows in the drove—she rushed out with a big stick and told the men not to drive her sister's cow to slaughter. The cow was trying to get to my barn-yard, so it was easy for Kate to drive her in. I did not know she was going to do it until I saw her running after the cow. I trembled for her safety among all those rough men, but she saved the cow. . . . After the battle of Poison Springs,[1] only thirteen miles from Camden, one of her friends, a young Confederate officer who was taken prisoner and brought to Camden, asked to visit Kate and he was allowed to do so under guard. At first he went to see our sister, Mrs. Daly, but as he did not find Kate there, he came to my house. I did not see him at all, but he made Kate quite a long visit. Yet he was between two fires, for my mean guard stood at the parlor door and the guard that came with him near by. So the soldier and Kate were watched real closely, that he did not know how to convey a letter to Kate that he had written some time before he came. This letter told of the whereabouts of our men and also of our brother Hugh, who was a warm friend of the officer. At last he picked up a book off the table, turned the leaves and tried to attract Kate's attention and watched the guards, when a good chance came he slipped the letter in the book, still kept it in his hands, finally Kate understood what the book contained. As soon as he took his leave she watched our guard and took the book and concealed the letter— never told me anything about it, but slipped off to our sisters and had a chance to read it without our guard watching her.

These were trying times to us, we were almost like prisoners in our own homes, but our faith in God was strong. Only one thing stirred my Southern blood to heat, was when a negro regiment passed my home going to fight our own dear men at Poison Springs. How fierce they did look, it was then that I gave vent to my feelings, but I must say our good old family servants were loyal to us. . . .

As the days moved slowly on we got through some how, each day we prayed that the Yankees would leave, but we saw no signs. Not a word could we hear from our dear men and not a word could they hear from us. After the Yankees had been here a week, rumors came

[1] April 18, 1864.

that a battle was to be fought right here in town. In fact they made preparations for it. Placed cannon at Ft. Southerland and made ready at Ft. Simmons, even fired off guns, so that our windows rattled and the earth trembled beneath our feet, props fell from transoms on our floors. The women and children were ordered to leave town. What a strain on our nerves. To run to the river bottom and leave our homes to the mercy of the Yankees and then what! Oh! where could we go? Not a horse nor a mule in town belonging to us. My sister Mrs. Daly was one of the impulsive ones, so she decided to pack up all her silver and valuables and a few clothes for herself and little son Richard and go down to the Dan Fellows home and get in his cellar until after the battle. She had only gone as far as Mr. Ben Johnson's house, when she met her neighbor Mr. John Silliman.

"Why Mollie where are you going?" Then she explained to him. "But give me the basket you are carrying, your fingers are bleeding, it is too heavy for your delicate hands. Don't be alarmed, I do not think we will have a battle today."

Her mind was soon quieted, and he saw that she got safely home. After she had been there a while a gentleman called, whom she had met at Clarksville, Tenn., an acquaintance of the Daly's—a Southern man, he told her he had been captured by the Yankees and was with them. She was glad to see him and asked his advice about the battle that was sure to come off early next morning. He told her he would help her to get out of town, that he had a mule that could be driven before our large buggy. How surprised I was that night when he and she came over to make arrangements for me, Aunt Sallie and the three children to pack up and go to the river bottom that night. I just told them I could not do it. Just think of me driving a strange mule and a buggy full of children and one a wee baby. She, Kate, the friend and the servants were to walk. Aunt Sallie said "Miss Mary Ann, Miss Virginia is not able to go." I then said I am going to stay at home and we can all die together.

While we were discussing that mule ride, some one knocked at the front door. My sister flew to the door and in a short time returned and said there was a Federal officer and two ladies who wanted to stay all night. She invited them in the parlor, but said to them, my sister has no more room vacant, then they asked to just let them stay in the parlor and with a fire and a quilt or two they could rest on the sofas and rocking chairs. They informed Kate there would be no battle the next morning, so our minds were at ease. I felt so distracted that I did not see the people. I consented for them to stay without seeing them, for my children needed my attention.

My sister went on home with her Tennessee friend, who afterwards proved to be a spy against his Southland. Then Aunt Sallie went in to see what manner of women we were giving lodging to that night. She came and whispered to me after she had returned from the room, that she didn't like their looks, they wasn't my style of ladies. And said, all your silk dresses and best clothes are in the parlor closet and the door is not locked, "I am going to lock it for no telling what kind of people they are."

I told her to go get something out of the closet and then lock the door, it would look bad to just go in and lock the door. Then she filled the key hole with paper, so not a sound could be heard from either room. The next morning the two women said they would like to have breakfast, and so we gave them a good one. After it was over they came to my room and offered me for lodging and breakfast a few pins, just a few rolls of pins, not even a paper. It made me angry because they said "they thought pins might be scarce down South," I thanked them and told them I had several papers of pins and had never been without. The officer that came with them the night before came for them and then I learned that he was Col. of the negro regiment that I saw pass my house a few days before. Then I had no use for him. He came in my room and spoke about what a cross baby I had, I told him she had colic and children suffering with such could not keep from crying. Indeed I was glad when he and his women left for I did not feel honored to have such people in my home.

My boarder, Capt. Rohadaback, the Federal officer, said he was glad I had gotten rid of those women for he had known them to go to peoples houses and almost take possession of the house, that I was fortunate to get them out of my house. It then flashed across my mind what kind of women they were. Oh, how thankful I was they had gone. We were kept in such a strain of excitement that we didn't know what would be next. If we could only hear from our dear ones in the army, to know that all were alive. And our father and mother who were seven miles from Camden on their plantation with fifty or sixty of their negroes, we feared to hear from them. After the Yankees had been here ten days, the morning of the last day, Capt. Rohadaback came hurriedly in and said, "Mrs. Stinson, I have orders to go away and may not return, I want to pay my board bill for the time I have been with you." So he paid me six dollars ($6.00) in green back, the first I had ever seen, but I was so distressed when he bid me good-by, for I felt I would be at the mercy of his regiment. Woman like I burst into tears and said "Oh! Capt. Rohadaback what will become of me and my little children, when you are gone." He tried to comfort me and said "I don't think my men will molest you at all."

I was not wise enough to know that Gen. Steele's whole army was going that very night, our guard went away too, at least I did not see him after Capt. Rohadaback left. The Yankee soldiers kept Aunt Sallie busy cooking rations for them all day. We could see from their movements they were up to something. At last they said they had orders to leave, but where they were going nobody knew. They threatened to burn the town before they left. How terrified we help-less women and children and faithful servants were. When night came on our nerves were completely unstrung. Just about dark the Yankees began shooting my chickens and they kept it up until they had killed every chicken except an old setting hen they did not find. What a night of terror it was. Aunt Sallie and I gathered our house-hold together save the sixteen year old negro boy who was persuaded by the Yankees to go with them, lots of silly negroes followed the Yankees off. The regiment east of me did not get off until morning. Aunt Sallie tried to get a guard but could not. My good friend, Mrs. Richmond, who was with Mrs. Graham, sent her only son Nat, who was only fourteen years old to stay with me. He was a brave boy and laughed at Aunt Sallie's terrors. But that night was a hard one for us for we sat up nearly all night.

What alarmed us most was the different squads of men around my house talking in low tones and once in a while a pistol shot off quite near my house. Then we feared they would fire our house, as one or two houses had been set on fire the first of the night.

No one but the children could sleep that night, our hearts were lifted to God in prayer for protection. Mother Elliott told me of her terror that night. She said her friend, Mrs. Norton, was with her, but she could not sleep and about midnight the mocking birds in the trees around her home began to sing so sweetly, both of them thought it was a good omen for they had not heard the birds sing so since the Yankees came and sure enough when morning came, not a blue coat was in our town. They silently folded their tents, wrapped the wheels of their wagons with cotton and left town without noise, and it was daylight when the last wagon left.

Camden looked like a deserted town, no noise or Yankees in town, Oh! what a relief it was to be free of them. We did not know what joy was in store for us that day—didn't know that our boys in grey were so near us, Oh! what joy when our dear men came marching in town—what waving of hands and handkerchiefs, women and children greeting their loved ones. My husband came that night, my brother Hugh McCollum and Col. Grinstead came with their regiment at noon and so many of my dear soldier friends in grey came. All that day and night and the next day too they were coming. We did not have much to give them to eat, for the Yankees had almost robbed us of all we had of some things, but for all that we divided cheerfully with them, but they were hurrying on in pursuit of the Yankees, so their stay with us was brief.

The Choctaw and Cherokee Indians who were Confederate soldiers came the second day. We gave them something to eat, they only asked for bread and sat on the ground to eat it. They were riding their Indian ponies and had their hats ornamented with gray peafowl's feathers, but they were very quiet, yet, the negroes were afraid of them.

Gen. Kirby Smith and staff officers came after the Yankees left, and asked permission to camp in our front yard. My husband and I were delighted to have them for our lawn is so large and is covered with giant oaks. The general and all his staff were perfect gentlemen and treated us so nicely. They would even ask permission to get water from our well and also for the use of the cooking stove to bake bread etc. They had a splendid cook, one that the General brought from his old home. Every morning a nice breakfast of hot rolls, beefsteak and genuine coffee was sent me with the compliments of Gen. Smith and staff. How neighborly they were. I tried to do all I could for them while they were here. When we got news that my brother Hugh was wounded at the battle of Jenkins ferry,[1] my husband started with my father and sister Kate to the battle field, but they met a courier the first night and he said that "Hugh had passed over the river" and his body would be sent home next day. Maj. Gen. Boggs one of Gen. Smith's staff came right away to see me and offer

[1] April 30, 1864.

aid and Major Feris another of the staff officers was so kind to me in my sorrow. They offered me conveyances or horses.

Maj. Feris was such a lover of home and his sweet wife and little girl, who he said he had not seen for a long time. He asked, as a favor from me, that I would let my little Lizzie, who was just the age of his little daughter come and sit on his knees so when I put on her fresh dress in the morning the nurse would take her to his tent which was in sight of my room door. He said seeing her reminded him of home, of his child that he had not seen in so long, and might never see again.

Gen. Kirby Smith and staff remained but a short time with us. They moved on to other fields of duty. I shall never forget him and his staff officers for their kindness to me and mine. . . .

15. VARINA HOWELL DAVIS—"THEY LEFT US ALONE WITH OUR DEAD"

Mrs. Davis had long since sold her horses and the fine carriage in which she and the children had ridden about the streets of Richmond. The grounds of the White House were neglected and inside the house spies were believed to have entered at will. It was from the high north piazza that the little son Joseph Emory Davis fell. Mrs. Chesnut, waiting in the drawing room after the accident, said she could hear through the livelong night the tramp of Jefferson Davis' feet above, as he paced up and down in grief.

In remembrance of her own grief, Mrs. Davis, in an article she wrote for the Montgomery Advertiser *in 1893, quoted with sympathy this letter from an unnamed Confederate woman to her husband:*

"Twenty grains of quinine would have saved our two children; they were too nauseated to drink the bitter willow tea and they are now at rest, and I have no one to work for but you. I am well and strong and am not dismayed. I think day and night of your sorrow. I have their little graves near me."

On April 30th, 1864, when we were threatened on every side, and encompassed so perfectly that we could only hope by a miracle to overcome our foes, Mr. Davis's health declined from loss of sleep so that he forgot to eat, and I resumed the practice of carrying him something at one o'clock. I left my children quite well, playing in my room, and had just uncovered my basket in his office, when a servant came for me. The most beautiful and brightest of my children, Joseph Emory, had, in play, climbed over the connecting angle of a bannister and fallen to the brick pavement below. He died a few minutes after we reached his side. This child was Mr. Davis's hope, and greatest joy in life. At intervals, he ejaculated, "Not mine, oh, Lord, but thine."

A courier came with a despatch. He took it, held it open for some moments, and looked at me fixedly, saying, "Did you tell me what was in it?" I saw his mind was momentarily paralyzed by the blow, but at last he tried to write an answer, and then called out, in a heart-broken tone, "I must have this day with my little child." Somebody took the despatch to General Cooper and left us alone with our dead. . . .

VII

BLOWS OF THE HAMMER

May-October 1864

On March 9, 1864, President Lincoln appointed Ulysses S. Grant lieutenant-general in supreme command of all the Union armies. According to Grant's plans of general strategy:

The Army of the Potomac, under General Meade but with Grant's personal direction, would attack General Lee's Army of Northern Virginia;

Ben Butler was to advance on Richmond up the south bank of the James River from Fortress Monroe;

Sigel would sweep through the Shenandoah Valley;

Sherman would move from Chattanooga for Atlanta against Joe Johnston's army;

Banks would go against Mobile.

As things developed the brilliant Beauregard promptly disposed of the egregious Butler on May 16 and bottled him up in the neck of land between the James and Appomattox rivers. Breckinridge and Imboden, with boys from the V.M.I., sent Sigel flying down the Valley after the Battle of New Market on May 15. When old David Hunter replaced Sigel he tried a little of the fire-and-destruction campaign that the Germans called "thoroughness" in World War I. He had some initial success, but General Jubal A. Early took good care of him. By June 22 "Old Jube" was well north in the Valley. In July he rode on, defeating Lew Wallace's little force at the Monocacy River on the ninth, getting within the suburbs of Washington, scaring the Federal government into conniptions and diverting a whole army corps from Grant. Then he drew back into the Shenandoah, where Sheridan succeeded Hunter.

In September Sheridan, now in general command of the Union cavalry, with fifty thousand men defeated Early's twenty thousand at Fisher's Hill near the north end of Massanutten Mountain and drove them back to New Market. Then all the way from Staunton to Winchester Sheridan put the fair Valley into utter desolation, with the real "thoroughness" at which Hunter was a novice. It was said *if a crow tried to fly across, it would have to carry its own rations. Early followed behind and while Sheridan was in Washington for a conference hit the Union army at Cedar Creek on October 19— hit it hard on front, flank and rear, and might have won a decisive victory, but Sheridan, riding "from Winchester twenty miles away," rallied his troops and put the Confederates to flight. Henceforth the Valley could not be used to subsist the army or to threaten Washington.*

These were diversions. The great hammer blows, the main attacks of Grant and Sherman, were different matters.

Grant, with 118,000 in the four corps of Hancock, Warren, Sedgwick and Burnside, crossed the Rapidan, and was promptly engaged by Lee in the desperate struggles of the Wilderness. It was a case of Grant's bludgeon against Lee's rapier, of Grant's determined resolution against Lee's mobility and skill. In the same jungle of ravines, copses and undergrowth close to suffocation where Hooker had been trapped and entangled the year before, Grant tried to slug it out, ever attempting movements by the left flank around Lee's right. There were the Battle of the Wilderness (May 5-7), of Spottsylvania Court House (May 8-18), of the North Anna and Totopotomoy Creek (May 23-28) and Cold Harbor (June 1-3). Cold Harbor was Grant's worst battle: he lost 5,000 men in the ten minutes of direct assault. By then, since the campaign had started, his casualties amounted to 55,000. That was too much for the North even with its vast resources. A storm of protest arose behind him.

Grant had been aiming straight for Richmond. He could not make it. Lee was ever in the way. Grant thought then he might shift around suddenly to the south and take Petersburg, the nexus of the roads to the Confederate capital. He nearly did it. But the advance was sluggish. Beauregard with a mere handful held it off till Lee in utmost urgency could bring in reinforcements on June 18.

Then began the siege of Petersburg, which was to last till the first of April, 1865. Grant had not destroyed Lee's army, but he had pinned it down. As part of the siege operations the Federals by tunneling placed a mine under a salient in the Confederate defense line. It was exploded on July thirtieth and a fierce combat resulted—all to Confederate advantage. Four Union divisions were trapped in the Crater—hoist with their own petard—and 4,000 Federals were lost there. Lee made the Petersburg lines as solid as human skill and ingenuity could make them.

*Starting his campaign on the same day as Grant, Sherman, with
100,000 men in three armies under Thomas, McPherson and Schofield, advanced directly south on Atlanta, important communications
center, focal point of the railroads between Richmond and the Deep
South. Opposed to him was Joe Johnston, the South's redoubtable
Fabian general, master of the strategic retreat. Never feeling himself
able to commit his force to an all-out engagement against superior
numbers, Johnston could attempt a blow only when things looked
peculiarly propitious. He sparred like a practiced boxer. He would
take a position behind breastworks, resist, and when Sherman,
marching first by the right and then by the left, would endanger
Johnston's flank, General Joe would slip out to a new stand farther
south. There were incessant cavalry clashes. There were notable
battles at Dalton, Resaca, Allatoona and New Hope Church in May,
at and all about Kennesaw Mountain in June, and at Smyrna Station
and the crossing of the Chattahoochee early in July.*

*Bragg came down to look things over for President Davis and
reported that the morale of the soldiers required a new commander
who would go on the offensive. Governor Brown of Georgia supported Bragg; the military were interfering with commercial traffic.
On July 17 Johnston was relieved and the command of the Army of
Tennessee given to lionhearted John B. Hood. Nothing was more
congenial to Hood than a stand-up fight. But at Peach Tree Creek on
July 20, the Battle of Atlanta on the twenty-second and Ezra Church
on the twenty-eighth he was unsuccessful and his losses were great.
The siege of the city began. On August 31 the last open railroad connection—the one to Macon—was broken in a fight at Jonesboro. On
September 1 Atlanta was evacuated by Hood and the next day
occupied by Sherman.*

*On August 23 the last but one of the open ports was closed to
blockade-runners when Admiral Farragut captured Mobile. The
Confederate women have told with what ingenuity they countered
the blockade, but such resourcefulness could not hold out forever.*

*On June 10 the Confederate Congress had authorized the use of
boys of seventeen and eighteen, of men between forty-five and fifty,
for military service.*

*How the Southern women felt as these great blows of the Northern
hammer rang in their ears is eloquently voiced by Louly Wigfall, the
daughter of Louis T. Wigfall, in the poem that is printed on the last
page of this collection.*

1. LORETA JANETA VELAZQUEZ—SPECIAL AGENT

Loreta was born in the West Indies in 1838, married a New Orleans planter named Roach and was living in St. James Parish, Louisiana, in 1861. After her husband's enlistment and early death in the Confederate cause, she raised a company of cavalry in Arkansas and equipped it at her own expense. Disguised as a man, she proceeded to Virginia where she took part in First Manassas and served for many months under Colonel Dreaux before her sex was discovered. She was ordered home, but instead, resuming her disguise, went to Columbus, Kentucky, and fought under General Polk in Kentucky and in Tennessee, where she was twice wounded. She was in New Orleans when Federals occupied the city in the spring of 1862. She married a Captain De Caulp who was soon killed in action.

Loreta was now engaged by the Confederate government as a spy and special agent. She passed freely between the lines. As a counter spy in Washington she managed without suspicion to become a member of the operating staff of Colonel Lafayette C. Baker, chief of the U.S. secret service. Her contemporaries described her as "the beautiful Confederate spy whose black eyes bewitched passes from Union generals."

Madame Velasquez was ordered to Canada in the spring of 1864, where Confederate commissioners were planning the "Northwest Conspiracy." This involved freeing the Confederate officers imprisoned on Johnson's Island in Sandusky Bay—10,000 were there at one time or another, though 3,000 filled capacity at any one time—at Camp Douglas, Chicago; Camp Morton, Indianapolis; and Camp Chase, Columbus; a total of about 26,000 men. The attempt on Johnson's Island was made unsuccessfully in September 1864.

On my arrival in Richmond, I immediately communicated with the authorities, delivered the messages and despatches submitted to me, sent letters to merchants in Wilmington and Savannah, as I had been directed to do, and gave all the information I could about the condition of things at the North, the proposed raid, and other matters.

Within a few days I heard, by special messenger, from the parties in Wilmington and Savannah. This man delivered to me a package which was to be taken through to Canada, and also orders and sailing directions for certain blockade-runners, and drafts which were to be cashed, and the money disposed of in certain ways for the benefit of the Confederate cause. I also received directions from parties in Richmond to confer with the Confederate agents, and if agreeable on all sides, to visit the prisons; it being thought that, as a woman, I would be able to obtain admission, and to be permitted to speak to the prisoners, where a man would be denied.

Then, freighted with my small, but precious package, several important despatches and other papers, and a number of letters for Confederates in Canada, I started to return. I would have been a rich prize for the Federals, if they should capture me; and, while on my way back, I wondered what Colonel Baker would think and say, in case some of his emissaries should chance to lay hands upon me, and conduct me into his presence, laden with all this contraband of war.

In consideration of the value of the baggage I was carrying, it was thought to be too great a risk for me to attempt to reach the North by any of the more direct routes, and I was consequently compelled to make a long detour by way of Parkersburg, in West Virginia. This involved a long and very tiresome journey, but it was undoubtedly the best course for me to pursue.

The wisdom in choosing this route was demonstrated by the result, and I succeeded in reaching Parkersburg without being suspected in the least by any one. At that place I found General Kelley[1] in command, and from him procured transportation to Baltimore, on the strength of my being an attaché of Colonel Baker's corps, which was a very satisfactory stroke of business for me, as it saved both trouble and expense.

The instructions under which I was moving required me to go to Baltimore, and from there inform the different parties interested of my arrival, and wait to hear from them as to whether they were ready to meet me at the appointed places, before proceeding farther. I was also to wait there for some drafts for large sums, which were to be cashed in New York, and the money taken to Canada. This involved considerable delay, which was particularly unpleasant just then, as I was getting very short of funds, and was, moreover, quite sick, the excitement I had gone through with— for this was a more

[1] General Benjamin F. Kelley, U. S. A.

exciting life even than soldiering—and the fatigue of a very long and tedious journey having quite used me up.

On arriving in Baltimore, fearing that I would not have enough money to see me through until I could obtain a remittance, I went to a store kept by a lady to whom I was told to appeal in event of being detained on account of lack of funds, and explaining who I was, and the business I was on, asked her if she would not assist me. She looked very hard at me, asked me a great many questions, and requested me to show her my papers. I said that this was impossible, as not only my honor and life were at stake, but that interests of great moment were involved in the preservation of the secrets I had in possession.

This, I thought, ought to have satisfied her; but it apparently did not, for she evidently regarded me with extreme suspicion. Her indisposition to trust me might have been caused by my rather dilapidated appearance, although my soiled travelling dress ought to have been proof of the fact that I had just been making a long, and very rough journey. Finally, another lady coming in, she walked back in the store with her, and I, supposing that she did not intend to take any more notice of me, arose to go out. She, however, seeing this movement, called for me to wait a moment. Shortly after she returned, and, handing me a sum of money, said, "I am a Union woman; but as you seem to be in distress, I will have to aid you. This is as much as I can afford to give."

I, of course, understood that this speech was intended for any other ears than mine that might be listening, and, merely giving her a meaning glance, walked out of the store, without saying anything further.

Having obtained this money, I went back to Barnum's Hotel, where I was stopping, feeling considerably relieved, so far as the exigencies of the moment were concerned, but not knowing to what poverty I might yet be reduced before I received my expected remittances. At first I was very much vexed at the behavior of the lady in the store, as I thought that the statement I made her, and the names of persons I mentioned as having referred me to her ought to have gained me her confidence at once. On reflection, however, I came to the conclusion that she might not be so much to blame after all, as she was obliged to be careful, on the one hand, not to be imposed upon, and, on the other not to be caught having secret dealings with the Confederates.

That night I was so sick that I had to send for a doctor. I offered him my watch for his services, stating that I was out of funds, and was detained in Baltimore through the non-arrival of money which I was expecting. He, however, refused to take it, and said that I might pay him if I ever was able, but that it would not matter a great deal one way or the other. The next day I was considerably better, and was able to go about a little, and I continued to improve with rest and quiet.

While stopping at Barnum's Hotel, I became acquainted with a young captain in the Federal army, and, as I made a practice of doing with all Federal officers—I did not know when they might be useful to me—I courted his friendship, and told him a story about myself similar to that I had told on several other occasions—that I had lost everything through the rebellion—that my husband was a U.S. army officer and had died about the outbreak of the war—had been so badly treated by rebels had been forced to come North. . . . I was especially bitter in my denunciations of the rebels. The captain was so affected by my pitiful narrative, that he introduced me to General E. B. Tyler, who was very affable and courteous, and who, learning that I was anxious to travel northward, and was short of money, kindly procured for me a pass to New York.

Finally, I received notice that one of the blockade-runners, with whom I was to communicate, was at Lewes, Delaware, and, on proceeding to that place, found an English brig, the Captain of which was anxiously waiting to receive instructions as to what port he was to sail for. The cargo was principally powder, clothing, and drugs, and the Captain was exceedingly glad to see me, as he wanted to get away as fast as he could, there being a liability that the Federal authorities might pounce upon him at any moment. I accordingly gave him his sailing papers, which contained directions for him to proceed to Wadling's Island, on the North of Cuba, where he was to transfer his cargo to another vessel, which was to run for any port it could make in the Confederacy. The Captain handed me the cards of several houses in Liverpool and Havre, which were extensively engaged in blockade-running, and I bade him adieu, wishing him a safe and pleasant trip.

This errand having been satisfactorily despatched. I went to Philadelphia, where I took a room at the Continental Hotel, and telegraphed for my papers, money package, etc., to be forwarded to me from New York by express. The next morning I received, in reply to this, my expected drafts, and also the following characteristic letter:

"Quebec, Canada.

"Mrs. Sue Battle: You will find enclosed a card of your government agent here, B——. Any orders you have for your government, if forwarded, we will execute and despatch quickly, according to your instructions. Messrs. B. & T. have several clippers, which they will put in the trade, if desired. I will drink your ladyship's good health in a bottle of good old Scotch ale. Let us hear from you at your earliest convenience. I will await your answer to return to Europe.

"With great respect, and hopes of success,

"I am, Madam, yours truly,

"R. W. L."

I now proceeded, without further delay, to New York, where I was met, at the Desbrosses Street ferry, by my associate in that city, who conducted me to Taylor's Hotel, where he had engaged a room for me. He said that he had been getting somewhat anxious for my safety, the more especially as he was informed that the detectives had received some information of my doings, and were on the watch for me. This made me a trifle uneasy, as I did not know but my friend, Colonel Baker, had discovered some facts about me which had served to convince him that I was not likely to be as valuable a member of his corps as he had supposed I would when he started me on my Richmond trip. Since my return to the North I had been endeavoring to keep myself concealed from Baker and all his people, as I did not wish to renew my acquaintance with the Colonel until I had visited Canada. That accomplished, I proposed to see him again, and to make use of his good offices for the purpose of putting into execution a still more daring scheme.

My New York accomplice said that he did not think I was in any immediate danger, although I would have to take care of myself. He himself had seen one of the detectives who were on my track, and, while I was evidently the person he was after, the description he had of me was a very imperfect one; so that, by the exercise of a little skill, I ought to be able to evade him. To put him on the wrong track, my accomplice had told this detective that he thought he knew the person he was searching for, and had procured a photograph of a very different looking woman, and given it to him.

Having cashed my drafts, and gotten everything ready, I started for Canada, carrying, in addition to valuable letters, orders, and packages, the large sum of eighty-two thousand dollars in my satchel. Mr. L., the correspondent whose letter has been quoted, was requested, by a telegraphic despatch, to meet me on my arrival in Canada.

Under ordinary circumstances, the great value of the baggage I was carrying would not have disturbed my peace of mind; but I knew that, in addition to the money I had with me, my capture would involve the officers of the Federal government obtaining possession of papers of the utmost importance, from which they would scarcely fail to gain quite sufficient information concerning the proposed raid to put them on their guard, and enable them to adopt measures for preventing the execution of the great scheme. It was not comfortable, therefore, for me to feel that the detectives were after me, and to be under the apprehension that one of them might tap me on the shoulder at any moment, and say, in that bland tone detectives use on such occasions, "Come, my good woman, you are wanted."

I was absolutely startled when, on approaching the depot, my companion, pointing to a man in the crowd, said, "There, that is the fellow to whom I gave the photograph. He is looking for you; so beware of him." Then, thinking it best that we should not be seen together by Mr. Detective, he wished me good luck, and said good-bye, leaving me to procure my ticket, and to carry my heavy satchel to the cars myself.

I watched the detective as well as I could without looking at him so hard as to attract his attention, and saw that he was rather anxiously surveying the people as they passed into the depot. . . .

After getting into the cars I lost sight of the detective until the arrival of the train in Rochester, and was congratulating myself that, not seeing the original of the photograph, he had remained in New York. At Rochester, however, to my infinite horror, he entered the car where I was, and took a seat near me.

When the conductor came through, after the train had started, the detective said something to him in a low tone, and showed him a photograph. The conductor shook his head on looking at it, and made a remark that I could not hear. I did, however, hear the detective say, "I'll catch her yet."

This whispered conference reassured me a little, as it showed that the officer was keeping his eye open for the original of the photograph which he had in his pocket. I concluded that I would try and strike up an acquaintance with this gentleman, in order to find out what he had to say for himself. . . .

I picked up my shawl and satchel and removed to the seat immediately back of him. The window was up, and I made a pretence of not being able to put it down, so that after a bit the detective's attention was attracted, and he very gallantly came to my assistance. When he had closed the window, I thanked him, with a rather effusive politeness, and he, probably feeling a trifle lonesome, seated himself beside me, and opened a conversation.

After passing the compliments of the day we launched into a general conversation, I attempting to speak with a touch of the Irish brogue, thinking that it would induce him to believe me to be a foreigner.

"You are going to Canada, are you not?" inquired my new-made friend.

"Yes, sir."

"Do you live there?"

"O, no, sir, I live in England. I am only going to Canada to visit some friends."

"Have you been in America long?"

"Only about eight months."

"How do you like this country?"

"O, I like living in England much better than I do here, and expect to go back as soon as I get through with my Canada visit. There is too much fighting going on here to suit me."

"O, you need not mind that; besides, the war will soon be over now."

"Do you think so? I will be glad when the fighting is over. It is terrible to hear every day of so many men being killed."

"O, that is nothing; we get used to it."

The detective now took out of his pocket the photograph which my associate in New York had given him, and which I was anxious to see, and handing it to me, said, "Did you ever see anybody resembling this? I am after the lady, and would like very much to find her."

"She is very handsome," I replied. "Is she your wife?"

"Wife! no," said he, apparently disgusted at the suggestion that he was in pursuit of a faithless spouse. "She is a rebel spy, and I am trying to catch her."

"Why, what has she been doing?"

"Well, she has been doing a good deal that our government would like to pay her off for. She is one of the smartest of the whole gang." This I thought was rather complimentary than otherwise. "I am on her track now, however, sure."

"But perhaps this lady is not a spy, after all. She looks too pretty and nice for anything of that kind. How do you know about her?"

"O, some of our force have been on the track of her for a long time. She has been working for these Copperheads and rebel agents here at the North, and has been running through the lines with despatches and goods. She came through from Richmond only a short time ago, and she is now on her way to Canada, with a lot of despatches and a big sum of money, which I would like to capture."

"I wonder how you can find out so much, when there must be a great many people coming and going all the time. Supposing that this lady is a spy, as you say, how do you know that she has not already reached Canada?"

"Maybe she has," he replied, "but I don't think so. I have got her down pretty fine, and feel tolerably certain of taking her before she gets over the line."

As he seemed inclined to change the subject, I was afraid to seem too inquisitive, and we dropped into a general conversation.

The detective seemed determined to be as polite to me as he could; and on leaving the cars he carried my satchel, containing eighty-two thousand dollars belonging to the Confederate government, and a variety of other matters which he would have taken possession of with the utmost pleasure, could he have known what they were. When we passed on board the boat I took the satchel from him, and thanking him for his attention proceeded to get out of his sight as expeditiously as I could.

When the custom-house officer examined my luggage, I gave him a wink, and whispered the pass-word I had been instructed to use, and he merely turned up the shawl which was on my arm, and went through the form of looking into my satchel.

On reaching the Canada shore I was met by Mr. L., who gave me a very hearty greeting; but I cautioned him to say as little as possible just then, as we might be watched. Glancing back, I saw my friend the detective, anxiously surveying the passing crowd. . . .

On my arrival in Canada I was welcomed with great cordiality by the Confederates there, who were eager to know all about my trip, how things were looking at Richmond, whether I had letters for so and so, and anything else that I was able to tell them. I distributed my letters and despatches according to instructions; mailed packages for the commanders of the cruisers Shenandoah and Florida, which I had received with especial injunctions to be particularly careful of, as they were very important; and then proceeded to the transaction of such other business, commercial as well as political, as I had on hand.

There were a good many matters of more importance than trade and finance, however, which demanded my immediate consideration, and many and long were the conferences held with regard to the proposed grand movement on the enemy's rear. There were a number of points about this grand scheme that I would have liked to have been informed of; but those who were making the arrangements for the raid were so fearful of their plans in some way getting to the ears of the Federal authorities, that they were unwilling to tell me, and other special agents, more than was absolutely necessary for the fulfillment of the duties intrusted to us. . . .

I was merely furnished with a general idea of the contemplated attack, and was assigned to special duties in connection with it. These duties were to visit Johnson's Island, in Lake Erie, and, if possible, other military prisons, for the purpose of informing the Confederates confined in them of what was being done towards effecting their release, and what was expected of them when they were released. I was then to telegraph to certain agents that the prisoners were warned, and such other information as I might deem it important for them to be possessed of, in accordance with an arranged system of signals. This being done, I was to proceed to the execution of other tasks, the exact details of which, however, were made dependent upon circumstances, and upon directions I might receive from the agents in the States, under whose orders I was to act.

This plan for a grand raid by way of the lakes excited my enthusiasm greatly, and I had very strong hopes of its success. . . .

2. SARAH ALEXANDER LAWTON—"HOW ALONE GENERAL LEE SEEMS!"

The daughter of A. L. Alexander of Washington, Georgia, Sarah Gilbert Alexander married Alexander Robert Lawton, member of the Savannah bar. He became a brigadier-general at the outbreak of hostilities, was in the Seven Days' battles, Second Manassas and An-

tietam—"Lawton's Georgians" were famous fighters—was wounded
at Sharpsburg in September 1862, and on August 7, 1863, appointed
quartermaster-general. Mrs. Lawton and the four children came from
Georgia to be with him in Richmond.

*In lieu of letters Mrs. Lawton sent extracts from her diary to
members of her family back home. This report of dark days went to
her sister, Mrs. George Gilmer Hull.*

Richmond—May 9 [1864] Monday. Mr. Lawton came upstairs
after dinner and said to me "I have made arrangements for all of
you to leave, day-after-tomorrow." It came like a thunder-clap upon
me. Our arms had seemed so successful that we were beginning to
breathe freely and to think the enemy were foiled. At least *I* cannot
go away.

May 10. Tired and sick tonight—after a sad and busy day—
preparing the children to go—they are all ready now. Corinne was
bitterly opposed to going—but her father talked to her a long time
and she now seems cheerful and reconciled.

May 11. They are gone. I feel sad and desolate enough—but
have not time to indulge it. I must pack my trunks, so as to be ready
for anything. . . .

Thursday—12th. Rain—but I went visiting. I had been at home
for several days and knew little of the state of feeling in town. We
heard last night that the children had safely reached the end of their
railroad journey, so I felt relieved about them. Mr. Lawton was kept
up late last night and waked up early this morning by business connected with getting a train of corn thro' to Gen. Lee's Army. Well,
I went visiting. I went first to Mrs. S's— found her tete a tete with
Mr. T.— made the acquaintance of that silver tongued Frenchman
and learned from his magnetic eyes the secret of his power over the
bewitching and bewitched lady.

I learned that on Tuesday there was great alarm in the city. Many
ladies sat up all night, dressed in all their best clothes with their
jewelry on. Congressmen besieged the war department all night—so
that Gen. Bragg[1] was called out of bed to go down to them after

[1] After General Bragg's unsuccessful Chattanooga campaign, General Joseph E.
Johnston had been put in command of the Army of Tennessee and Bragg called to
Richmond to be President Davis' chief-of-staff.

midnight. We knew nothing of all the excitement—absorbed in the grief of our expected family parting. We slept as we best could each in our quiet chamber. . . .

Friday—13th. Early this morning we were waked by the tidings that the Danville road was cut. We next learned that Gen. Stuart was dead—sad news. After breakfast I had a trunk or two to pack—while thus engaged, Mrs. Stanard sent for me to sit the morning with her. . . .

I had a very pleasant morning with Mrs. Stanard and returned home just before Mr. Lawton and the Doctor came to dinner. Mr. L. hurried off soon to be pall-bearer at Gen. Stuart's funeral. Not long after, the Doctor returned to his office—rain set in—I had a dreary afternoon—we are all alone this evening—a rare occurrence. The gentlemen are talking about how terrified the Congressmen are—how anxious to get horses. We are now hemmed in on all sides.

Sunday 15th. . . . The excitements yesterday were the cannon-nading at Drury's Bluff[1]—and the impressment of negroes to work on the fortifications. Jake was caught. Paul and Lysander took flight and hid—and all day Paul did not dare go out.

There is much feeling against Gen. Bragg and about Pemberton's being put in command of the artillery around the city. Members of Congress are much excited and there is indignation against the President on his account.

Today we had some cannonading at Drury's again—Beauregard is preparing to give the enemy battle. We expect a heavy fight in a day or two. A train went off on the Central Road today. Several families left on it, en route for the South.

Wednesday 25. For a week we have been more quiet. Business begins to receive attention. Letters are once more delivered. We are expecting, however, daily to hear of a terrible battle between Lee and Grant. We have all been much excited by the tidings that Gen. Johnston has retreated below Marietta and abandoned upper Georgia.

---

[1] About May 11 General Ben Butler advanced slowly until he reached Drewry's Bluff, halfway between Bermuda Hundred and Richmond. Beauregard had been gathering reinforcements. On the sixteenth he attacked Butler with vigor and with such success as to limit materially the usefulness of the Army of the James as a factor in the campaign.

May 30—Sunday. 9½ P.M. Gen. Lawton has just returned from a long ride. He has been out to Gen. Lee's headquarters at Atlee Station, 10 miles from town. He reports the Gen. very unwell and looking worn down. No wonder—the wonder is that he has kept up so long, with so intense a strain upon his mental powers. Gen. Lee seems to expect that the enemy will attack him tomorrow. He telegraphed for Beauregard who went up to him this afternoon. Butler is said to have been heavily reinforced—and I suppose Beauregard will not venture to stay long away from his command. We are all discussing the probability that Grant will not attack, but will cross the Chickahominy, thus forcing Gen. Lee to the city. A siege is far more to be dreaded by us than a battle.

Mr. Lawton was saying how alone Gen. Lee seems to be in his responsibilities. Ewell is out of the field—broken down,[1] Jackson gone, Longstreet wounded[2]—So few on whom he can rely for counsel.

June 19. Sunday. The enemy have been beleaguring Petersburg and shelling it. Refugees from there have been coming here and there are uncertain tidings of great battles—but nothing authentic is known. We here feel still very calm and cheerful and never think on the ifs of Grant's success. Household matters still fill up my daily life, as in peace times, and the struggle to live comfortably requires considerable effort and forethought. We continue to have all our wants supplied. I send to market every morning and get fresh vegetables. We have fresh meat in small quantities, some two or three times a week—the rest of the time, ham. I will append my market bills for a week.

Wednesday, 5½ lbs. of veal, $33.00. 1 peck green peas $12.

Thursday. Lettuce $1.50. Cherries, 2 qts for $3.00.

Friday, Squash. 1 doz. for $6. Asparagus, $3.00.

Saturday, Snap beans, $4. gooseberries $2.00. Butter, 4 lbs. for $48.00.

Sunday and Monday—nothing.

Tuesday, Lettuce $1.50. Beans, $4, Raspberries $20.

---

[1] Ewell, who had been in the thick of the fighting since the Wilderness campaign began, was "in danger of collapse under his burdens."—D. S. Freeman, *Lee's Lieutenants,* III, 433.

[2] Near the Plank Road in the Wilderness fighting on May 6 Longstreet had been seriously wounded by a ball mistakenly fired by one of his own men. It passed through his throat into his shoulder.

We have been to church this morning and tonight. I think all
the sermons we hear now show want of thought. Our ministers have
no time for study—they are so engaged with visits to the afflicted,
to hospitals, to the wounded and with funerals.

Tuesday 21. The air is full of sorrowful tales. Last week we
walked to the Armory to see Mrs. Gorgas.[1] She has just heard that
her brother-in-law was severely wounded. . . .

Friday—June 24. All our railroads cut[2]—Enemy fortifying on
the Weldon road. The Gen'l. getting very anxious about the supplies
of corn for the Army. The Doctor working hard with the sick and
wounded at Jackson Hospital. 2300 patients there—thermometer at
92— Daily prayer meetings. . .

3. JUDITH BROCKENBROUGH McGUIRE—
"GENERAL STUART DIED LAST NIGHT"

*After Chantilly in the spring of 1861 the McGuires found refuge
in Danville, Lynchburg, Charlottesville and other Virginia cities
and towns. In November 1863 they went to Richmond, where Mrs.
McGuire got a position in the Commissary Department and, as
always, helped in the hospitals.*

*General Stuart, the Bayard of the Confederacy, was only thirty-
one when he was mortally wounded by a pistol shot in a skirmish
with Sheridan at Yellow Tavern, six miles from Richmond, on May
11. When he was a young lieutenant at Fort Leavenworth, Kansas,
and she a girl in her teens, he had fallen in love with Flora, daughter
of Colonel Philip St. George Cooke, the most capable cavalry officer
in the United States Army. They were married in 1855. During
the crucial days of battle they had been able to snatch only fleeting
moments of happiness together. Mrs. Stuart was at Colonel Edmund
Fontaine's plantation at Beaver Dam when she heard the general
was wounded. She started at once for his bedside but Union raiders
had cut the communications and she did not reach Richmond till
four hours after he had died. The hymn for which he asked was
"Rock of Ages."*

[1] Brigadier-General Josiah Gorgas was chief of the Ordnance Department.
[2] This was only a rumor. Trains continued to roll into Richmond.

Richmond, Virginia
May 13, 1864

General Stuart died of his wounds last night, twenty-four hours after he was shot. He was a member of the Episcopal Church, and expressed to the Rev. Dr. Peterkin his resignation to the will of God. After much coversation with his friends and Dr. P., and joining them in a hymn which he requested should be sung, he calmly resigned his redeemed spirit to the God who gave it. Thus passed away our great cavalry general, just one year after the Immortal Jackson. This seems darkly mysterious to us, but God's will be done. The funeral took place this evening, from St. James's Church. My duty to the living prevented my attending it, for which I am very sorry; but I was in the hospital from three o'clock until eight, soothing the sufferers in the only way I could by fanning them, bathing their wounds, and giving them a word of comfort.

May 23.—Our young relative, Lieutenant G., a member of General Stuart's staff, has just been giving us a most gratifying account of General Stuart's habits. He says, that although he considered him one of the most sprightly men he has ever seen, devoted to society, particularly to that of the ladies, always social and cheerful, yet he has never seen him do any thing, even under the strongest excitement, unbecoming his Christian profession or his high position as a soldier; he never saw him drink, or heard an oath escape his lips; his sentiments were always high-minded, pure, and honorable, and his actions entirely coincided with them. In short, he considered him, whether on the field or in the private circle, the model of a Christian gentleman and soldier.

When speaking of his gallantry as an officer, Lieutenant G.'s admiration knows no bounds. He speaks of the devotion of the soldiers to him as enthusiastic in the extreme. The evening before his fatal wound, he sent his troops on in pursuit of Sheridan, under the command of General Fitz Lee,[1] as he was unavoidably detained for some three or four hours. General Lee overtook the enemy, and a sharp skirmish ensued, in which Sheridan's rear suffered very much. In the meantime, General Stuart determined to overtake General Lee, and, with his staff, rode very rapidly sixteen miles, and reached him about nightfall. They were halting for a few moments, as General Stuart rode up quietly, no one suspecting he was there,

[1] Major-General Fitzhugh Lee, eldest son of Sydney Smith Lee, who was an elder brother of Robert E. Lee.

until a plain-looking soldier crossed the road, stopped, peered through the darkness into his face, and shouted out, "Old Jeb has come!" In a instant the air was rent with huzzas. General Stuart waved his cap in recognition; but called out in rather a sad voice, "My friends, we won't halloo until we get out of the woods!" intimating that there was serious work before them. . . .

4. CORNELIA PEAKE McDONALD—HUNTER BURNS THE V.M.I.

Mrs. McDonald stayed in Winchester till the summer of 1863. Then she and the children became refugees in various parts of Virginia. The winter found them in Lexington, where, some months later, they were joined by Colonel McDonald, who had been seriously ill in Richmond.

In early June 1864 news came that General David Hunter was advancing toward Lexington with little Confederate opposition. He had defeated a small force of the Valley reserves, men and boys under General William E. Jones, at the Battle of Piedmont on the fourth. At Staunton he was reinforced by General George Crook and General W. W. Averell with cavalry from the Kanawha Valley. Hunter decided to move up the Shenandoah Valley to Lexington. Mrs. McDonald tells what happened. When Jubal Early came into the Shenandoah on June 18, things took a different turn.

Colonel McDonald died in December 1864. After Appomattox Mrs. McDonald went to Louisville, where three of her sons lived. She died there on March 11, 1909, but her body was taken to Richmond to lie beside her husband's in Hollywood Cemetery.

Meanwhile in 1875 she had filled out her wartime diary with a narrative. Then in 1934 Hunter McDonald, the "very cute" boy of the '60s, annotated and supplemented them. Dr. D. S. Freeman calls A Diary with Reminiscences of the War and Refugee Life in the Shenandoah Valley, 1860-1865, *"one of the most thrilling of the war books."*

June 11th [1864] the approach of the enemy was announced. Everybody connected with the army prepared to fly. Gen. Smith[1] departed with the corps of cadets, and Gen. McCausland,[2] after

---

[1] General Francis H. Smith, commandant of the Virginia Military Institute, who brought about 300 cadets into the concentration against Hunter.

[2] Brigadier-General John McCausland.

burning the bridge that led to the town, made good his retreat, leaving the terror-stricken people to their fears, and to the tender mercies of the enemy. My husband determined to go a few miles into the country, and remain till they had passed on their way. So he prepared to leave with Harry in an ambulance.

As he stood on the porch giving orders for his journey, he looked so little able to undertake even a short journey, that it filled me with misgivings. He spoke cheerfully of coming back, but in the morning he had told me that if he never saw me again, I must bring up the children as he would like to have them brought up, his boys to be true and brave, and his little girl modest and gentle. He also said that if his property should be confiscated, as he was sure it would be, I had a right to one-third which could not be taken from me; that if I could struggle on till the close of the war, I would have abundance. I scarcely heard what he said, for I felt that the future was nothing if only the terrible present was not here, portentous and dreadful, and I thought only of his going, and that he might not ever come back.

Will had gone off in another direction, on horseback, and when the ambulance had driven off with my husband and Harry we all felt lonely enough, and filled with apprehension.

Early the next morning the enemy began the bombardment of the town, imagining McCausland still there. Some shells went through the houses, frightening the inhabitants terribly. They were posted on the opposite bank of the river, and bombarded quite vigorously. Our house was struck in several places but no harm done. Indeed I was past being frightened by shot and shell. Nevertheless, I, the children and Flora retreated to the basement and waited there till the storm should be over. After a while there was a lull, and Flora, wishing to see what was going on, raised the window and put her head out.

Just as she did so, a piece of shell struck the window sill, knocking off a large piece.

No one looked out any more. At high noon the bombardment ceased, and soon through the deserted streets of the little town poured the enemy, coming in at every point. A troop rode by our house, Averill's cavalry. Two negro women rode at the head of the column by the side of the officers. We had shut all the doors and pulled down every blind, but peeped, to see without being seen. Looking down, Flora espied Hunter sitting on the front steps earnestly gazing at the passing soldiers. She immediately raised the window and called to him, "Hunter, are you not ashamed to be looking at those Yankees? Go under that porch, and dont you look at them again." Poor little fellow, perhaps he thought they were old friends. He retired under the porch, and did not emerge till they were all gone by.

We had been engaged all the morning in hiding the things we thought might be taken from us, among the rest a few hens and chickens that I had been trying to raise. The children quickly caught and transported them to a garret where we also put a few other things that might tempt them, the silver, etc. I was passing by the stairs and saw Hunter sitting on the lowest step crying bitterly. I stopped to kiss and comfort my poor little three year old baby and asked him what the matter was, when amid his sobs, he said "The Yankees are coming to our house and they will take all our breakfast, and will capture me and Fanny." Fanny was Nelly's doll which was nearly as large as he was, and who he had been taught by her to consider quite as important a member of the household. We remained as quiet as possible all the afternoon while the town was alive with soldiers plundering and robbing the inhabitants. Some came into our yard, robbed the milk house of its contents and passed on their way, picking up everything they could use or destroy. About four o'clock I heard a knock at the front door, and cautiously looking out before opening it I saw Maj. Quinn.[1] He came in, and I must plead guilty to having been glad to see at least one Yankee. He offered to remain at the house to prevent any annoyance to us or injury to property, and seated himself in the porch. Of course no marauding parties came near while he was there. I declined his offer to stay during the night, as I thought the sight they had had of him in the porch would serve to warn them off. The next morning a squad of men with an officer came to search for provisions and arms. They laughed when on examining the pantry they found only a half barrel of flour and a little tea, all the supplies we had; but their laughter was immense when on ascending to the garret they saw the hens and chickens running over the floor.

The next day, Sunday, we were constantly hearing of outrages inflicted on the towns people; breaking into houses and robbing them. I was too well used to those little affairs to think them very severe, but was intensely amused when I heard of their entry into

[1] A kind officer who had spent some time in Winchester during its early occupation.

Dr. Madison's neatly kept and well furnished house, carrying off molasses and preserves in pieces of old China, and wrapping up flour in Mrs. Madison's purple velvet cloak.

At sunset we saw a man led by with a file of soldiers. The children came in and told me that it was Capt. Matt White, that they were taking him out to shoot him. I thought they knew nothing about it and gave the matter no attention.

Sunday began a fearful work. The Virginia Military Institute with all the professors' houses was set on fire,[1] and the distracted families amid the flames were rushing about trying to save some of their things, when they were forced to leave them, officers standing by for the purpose. Not even their books and papers could they save, and scarcely any clothes. Col. Williamson was the only officer of the Institute who remained in the village, and he had to keep quiet and say nothing when his daughters were driven from their house and all its contents burned, even the old black mahogany desk where hidden away was a yellow lock of his wife's hair, and her letters tied up with a blue ribbon.

This one of his daughters told me, as if it was the greatest loss of all. One officer, Captain Prendergast,[2] knew Mrs. Gilham's brother, Col. Haydon, of the U.S. Army, and for his sake granted her the particular favor of removing some of her household goods, which after she had succeeded in removing, she was compelled to stay by with her little boys to guard. There she sat through the afternoon by her household goods, to keep them from being stolen by negroes and soldiers, and through the long night she remained at her post, and not a man dared to help her or offered to take her place. All the warehouses at the river, all the mills and buildings near were burned, all in flames at the same hour, and it really seemed as if the Evil One was let loose to work his will that day. The town people were so frightened that few dared to show themselves on the streets and Yankees and exultant negroes had their full satisfaction. Negroes were seen scudding away in all directions bearing away the spoils of the burning barracks—books, furniture, trunks full of the clothes of the absent cadets were among the spoils. . . .

[1] General John D. Imboden says that Hunter ordered the torch to be applied also to Old Washington College, but his officers protested. It became Washington and Lee University, when General R. E. Lee ended his years as its president. (*Battles and Leaders*, IV, 486.)

[2] General Franz Sigel refers to "Captain R. G. Prendergast, commander of my escort." (*Battles and Leaders*, IV, 489.)

They all held high carnival. Gen. Crook had his headquarters on a hill near me, in a large handsome house belonging to Mr. Fuller and as it was brilliantly lighted at night and the band playing it was quite a place of resort for the coloured population. . . .

We were told that they would leave on Tuesday; and when the time arrived the signal was given to depart. Some had already gone, when on looking down the street in the direction of Gov. Letcher's[1] house I saw it on fire. I instantly put on my bonnet and ran down there to help Mrs. Letcher as I was able, for though many persons were in town who knew her better than I did, none dared to leave their houses. I was too used to their ways to be afraid of them, and so in breathless haste got there in time to see the house enveloped in flames. Mrs. Letcher had consented to entertain two officers at her house, that she had been civilly asked to do. They had spent the night, and eaten breakfast with the family, sociably chatting all the while.

When they rose from breakfast, one of them, Capt. Berry, informed Mrs. Letcher that he should immediately set fire to her home. He took a bottle of benzine, or some inflammable fluid, and pouring it on the sofas and curtains in the lower rooms, applied a match, and then proceeded up stairs. Mrs. Letcher ran up stairs and snatching her sleeping baby from the cradle, rushed from the house with it, leaving everything she had to the flames. Lizzy ran up stairs and went into her father's room to secure some of his clothes, and had hung over her arm some of his linen, when Capt. Berry came near her with a lighted match, and set fire to the clothes as they hung on her arm. He then gathered all the family clothing and bedding into a pile in the middle of the room and set fire to them.

When I reached the scene, Mrs. Letcher was sitting on a stone in the street with her baby on her lap sleeping and her other little children gathered around. She sat tearless and calm, but it was a pitiable group, sitting there with their burning house for a background to the picture.

Some officers who had stayed all night at Mr. Matthew White's, and breakfasted there, had in reply to the anxious inquiries of the poor old Mother about her son who had been arrested some days before, assured her that he was in the jail just opposite her house; that he was temporarily detained, but would be immediately released. That afternoon as I sat by the window I saw a wagon pass on its

---

[1] John Letcher, Governor of Virginia, 1860-1864.

way up the street, and in it a stiff, straight form covered with a sheet. It was poor Matt White on his way to his Mother. He had been taken out to the woods and shot as the children had said, and had been left where he fell. Mrs. Cameron's daughters hearing the firing, went down to the place when the party had left, and finding the poor body, stayed there by it all night to keep it from being mangled by animals. No men were near to do it, and they kept up their watch till word could be sent to his parents where to find him; and that was not done till Tuesday evening, for no one could pass to the town till the troops had left.

The next day, Wednesday, was his funeral. Everybody who knew the family was there, I among the rest. We went to the cemetery and saw the poor fellow buried, and I turned and walked sadly away. . . . Soon I met Mrs. Powell, my dearest and most intimate friend. She looked very pale, and turned to me as if she would speak, but passed on. I thought it strange that she should pass me in that way but went on home. . . . I sat on the porch in the twilight, and one of the neighbors' little boys came and climbed up on the porch till he reached my ear. Holding to the balustrade he leaned over and whispered, "Did you know that Col. McDonald and Harry were killed and were lying in the woods fifteen miles from here?" I got up and called Allan and sent him up town to ascertain if there was any truth in what the child had said.

While Allan was gone the father of the child came and told me that it was true that they had been attacked, but that there was no certainty that they had been killed; that it was thought they were prisoners. . . .[1]

5. HENRIETTA BEDINGER LEE—"YOU BURNED MY HOME"

Colonel Edmund Lee and his wife lived at "Bedford" south of Shepherdstown far down in the Shenandoah Valley. On July 19, 1864, Mrs. Lee was alone with her young son Harry, a little daughter and the servants, when her home was burned by order of the invading General David Hunter. The next day, a refugee in Shepherds-

---

[1] Colonel McDonald and Harry were captured. Harry escaped, but the colonel was imprisoned in Cumberland, Maryland.

town, Mrs. Lee, gentle, dignified lady that she was, wrote this bitter denunciation to General Hunter.

Late in July when General Jubal Early heard of the burning of the homes of Mrs. Lee, Colonel Boteler and Alexander Hunter, a state senator, he sent General John McCausland on a raid to Chambersburg, Pennsylvania, to demand an indemnity of $100,000 in gold. The money not being forthcoming, the town was fired.

Mrs. Lee lived to a ripe old age, blessed with children and grandchildren. Harry, the little boy who saw Bedford in flames, became a much-loved clergyman in the Episcopal church.

Jefferson County, Virginia
July 20, 1864

General Hunter:

Yesterday your underling, Captain Martindale, of the First New York Cavalry, executed your infamous order and burned my house. You have had the satisfaction ere this of receiving from him the information that your orders were fulfilled to the letter; the dwelling and every out-building, seven in number, with their contents, being burned. I, therefore, a helpless woman whom you have cruelly wronged, address you, a Major-General of the United States army, and demand why this was done? What was my offence? My husband was absent, an exile. He had never been a politician or in any way engaged in the struggle now going on, his age preventing. This fact your chief of staff, David Strother, could have told you. The house was built by my father,[1] a Revolutionary soldier, who served the whole seven years for your independence. There was I born; there the sacred dead repose. It was my house and my home, and there has your niece (Miss Griffith), who has tarried among us all this horrid war up to the present time, met with all kindness and hospitality at my hands. Was it for this that you turned me, my young daughter, and little son out upon the world without a shelter? Or was it because my husband is the grandson of the Revolutionary patriot and "rebel," Richard Henry Lee, and the near kinsman of the noblest of Christian warriors, the greatest of generals, Robert E. Lee? Heaven's blessing be upon his head forever. You and your Government have failed to conquer, subdue, or match him; and disappointment, rage, and malice find vent on the helpless and inoffensive.

Hyena-like, you have torn my heart to pieces! for all hallowed

[1] Daniel Bedinger.

memories clustered around that homestead, and demon-like, you have done it without even the pretext of revenge, for I never saw or harmed you. Your office is not to lead, like a brave man and soldier, your men to fight in the ranks of war, but your work has been to separate yourself from all danger, and with your incendiary band steal unaware upon helpless women and children, to insult and destroy. Two fair homes did you yesterday ruthlessly lay in ashes, giving not a moment's warning to the startled inmates of your wicked purpose; turning mothers and children out of doors, you are execrated by your own men for the cruel work you give them to do.

In the case of Colonel A. R. Boteler, both father and mother were far away. Any heart but that of Captain Martindale (and yours) would have been touched by that little circle, comprising a widowed daughter just risen from her bed of illness, her three fatherless babies —the oldest not five years old—and her heroic sister. I repeat, any man would have been touched at that sight but Captain Martindale. One might as well hope to find mercy and feeling in the heart of a wolf bent on his prey of young lambs, as to search for such qualities in his bosom. You have chosen well your agent for such deeds, and doubtless will promote him.

A colonel of the Federal army has stated that you deprived forty of your officers of their commands because they refused to carry on your malignant mischief. All honor to their names for this, at least! They are men; they have human hearts and blush for such a commander!

I ask who that does not wish infamy and disgrace attached to him forever would serve under you? Your name will stand on history's page as the Hunter of weak women, and innocent children, the Hunter to destroy defenceless villages and refined and beautiful homes—to torture afresh the agonized hearts of widows; the Hunter of Africa's poor sons and daughters, to lure them on to ruin and death of soul and body; the Hunter with the relentless heart of a wild beast, the face of a fiend and the form of a man. Oh, Earth, behold the monster! Can I say, "God forgive you?" No prayer can be offered for you. Were it possible for human lips to raise your name heavenward, angels would thrust the foul thing back again, and demons claim their own. The curses of thousands, the scorns of manly and upright, and the hatred of the true and honorable, will follow you and yours through all time, and brand your name infamy! infamy!

Again, I demand why you have burned my home? Answer as you must answer before the Searcher of all hearts, why have you added this cruel, wicked deed to your many crimes?

6. ISSA DESHA BRECKINRIDGE—"I AM AN EXILE"

Issa, daughter of Dr. John R. Desha and granddaughter of Governor Joseph Desha of Kentucky, married Colonel William Campbell Preston Breckinridge of Lexington. Few families were so divided in allegiance. Within a year of the wedding the colonel was riding with John Hunt Morgan's cavalry, his father the Reverend Robert J. Breckinridge had become a prominent Unionist, his brother Joseph had enlisted in the Union Army and his brother Robert in the Confederate.

In the spring of 1864 Mrs. Breckinridge tried to get a pass into the Confederacy, but General W. T. Sherman wrote on April 24: "No person can now pass beyond our lines, save by making the circuit by some foreign country." In a few months she went to Canada; from there, in November, accompanied by her father, she journeyed to Washington. At last she got her pass—from President Lincoln— but by then all truce boats down the James River had ceased running. Back to Toronto she traveled, to stay till peace came.

When they were reunited in Lexington, Colonel Breckinridge resumed his law practice and edited the Observer. *His election to Congress took them to Washington, where Issa died in 1892, survived by three children.*

Queen's Hotel, Toronto, Canada
July 30, 1864

My own precious, loved and loving husband:

I hardly know where to begin. I am here an exile. On the night of the eighth Papa learned that the wives of all Rebel officers in Kentucky were to be sent South in the most disagreeable way and to land God knows where. He begged me to start the next day for Canada knowing that to go South at this season would be certain death to me and trembling at the thought at my being in the hands of our fiendish foes.

The night Papa heard of this, he saw General Stephen Burbridge[1] now Lord and Master of our poor suffering state. Burbridge told him the order was to be issued and to be indiscriminate and that it had come from Stanton. This was Sunday Morning. Monday noon I left home. Going forth a stranger in a strange land—all this was bitter but when I had to kiss our precious child [2] my last, long kiss, I felt that God had sent upon me more than I could bear—with every sorrow comes the thought I still have Willie and his love is everything to me.

I now count the days between this time and that in which I hope to go to you. Till then goodbye.

Your loving, trusting wife,

I. D. BRECKINRIDGE

7. SARA RICE PRYOR—IN BESIEGED PETERSBURG

During the siege, which began in the middle of June, the Pryor children had grown so accustomed to the differing boom of guns and varying screech of shells they amused themselves by naming them.

Roger Pryor was captured on November 27, 1864, and imprisoned in Fort Lafayette until a short time before the surrender at Appomattox.

After the Confederacy collapsed the Pryors went up to New York City on money raised by pawning Sara's jewelry. Roger embarked on a new career as a journalist and a distinguished career as a jurist, becoming a justice of the Supreme Court of the state. Sara won recognition for her stories and essays in national magazines and for her memoirs, published in 1904. She died in 1912, Roger in 1919. They had seven children.

Petersburg, Virginia, 1864

The month of August in the besieged city passed like a dream of terror. The weather was intensely hot and dry, varied by storms of thunder and lightning—when the very heavens seemed in league with the thunderbolts of the enemy. Our region was not shelled continu-

---

[1] General Stephen Gano Burbridge, U.S.A., had been assigned on February 15, 1864, to the command of the District of Kentucky, with broad civil as well as military powers.

[2] Ella, her two-year-old daughter.

ously. One shot from "our own gun," as we learned to call it, would be fired as if to let us know our places; this challenge would be answered from one of our batteries, and the two would thunder away for five or six hours. We always sought shelter in Mr. Campbell's bomb-proof cellar at such times, and the negroes would run to their own "bum-proofs," as they termed the cells hollowed under the hill.

My husband sent me a note by his courier, one hot August day, to tell me that his old aide, Captain Whitner, having been wounded, was now discharged from the hospital, but was much too weak for service in the trenches, so he had obtained for the captain leave of absence for two weeks, and had sent him to me to be built up. On the moment the sick man appeared in an ambulance. I was glad to see him, but a gaunt spectre arose before my imagination and sternly suggested: "Built up, forsooth! And pray, what are you to build him up with? You can no more make a man without food than the Israelites could make bricks without straw."

However, the captain had brought a ration of bacon and meal, with promise of more to come. I bethought me of the flourishing garden of my neighbor, whose onions and beets were daily gathered for her own family. I wrote a very pathetic appeal for my wounded Confederate soldier, now threatened with scurvy for want of fresh food, and I fully expected she would be moved by my eloquence and her own patriotism to grant me a daily portion from her garden. She answered that she would agree to send me a dish of vegetables fourteen days for fourteen dollars. Gold was then selling at the rate of twenty-five dollars in our paper currency for one dollar in gold, so the dish was not a very costly one. But when it appeared it was a very small dish indeed,—two beets or four onions. Homoeopathic as were the remedial agents, they helped to cure the captain.

One morning, late in August, Eliza came early to my bedside. I started up in alarm.

"Shelling again?" I asked her.

"Worse," said Eliza.

"Tell me, tell me quick—is the General——"

"No, no, honey," said my kind nurse, laying a detaining hand upon me, "You cert'nly sleep sound! Didn't you hear a stir downstairs in the night? Well, about midnight somebody hallooed to the kitchen, and John ran out. There stood a man on horseback and a dead soldier lying before him on the saddle. He said to John, 'Boy, I know General Pryor would not refuse to take in my dead brother.'

"John ran up to my room and asked me what he must do. 'Take him in,' I told him. 'Marse Roger will never forgive you if you turn him away.'"

"You were perfectly right," I said, beginning to dress myself. "Where is he?"

"In the parlor," said Eliza. "He had a man-servant with him. John brought in his own cot, and he is lying on it. His brother is in there, and his man, both of them."

The children were hushed by their nurse's story, and gathered under the shade in the yard. When breakfast was served, I sent John to invite my guest in. He returned with answer that "the captain don' feel like eatin' nothin'."

"Captain?" I asked.

"No'm, he ain't a captain, but his dead brother was. He was Captain Spann of South Carolina or Georgia, I forget which. His man came into the kitchen for hot water to shave his dead master, but I didn't ask many questions 'cause I saw he was troubled."

I went out to my ever blooming rose and found it full of cool, dewy blossoms. I cut an armful, and knocked at the parlour door myself. It was opened by a haggard, weary-looking soldier, who burst into tears at seeing me. I took his hand and essayed to lead him forth, but he brokenly begged I would place the roses upon his brother's breast. "Will you, for the sake of his poor wife and mother?"

Very calm was the face of the dead officer. His servant and his brother had shaven and cared for him. His dark hair was brushed from a noble brow, and I could see that his features were regular and refined. . . .

I persuaded the lonely watcher to go with John to an upper room, to bathe and rest a few minutes; but he soon descended and joined us at our frugal breakfast, and then Mr. Gibson, my good rector, came in to help and advise, and in the evening my husband returned, much gratified that we had received and comforted the poor fellow.

As August drew to a close, I began to perceive that I could no longer endure the recurrence of such scenes; and I learned with great relief that my brother-in-law had moved his family to North Carolina and had placed Cottage Farm, three miles distant from the besieged city, at my disposal. Accordingly, I wrote to General Bushrod Johnson,[1] requesting an army wagon to be sent me early the next

---

[1] Major-General Bushrod R. Johnson had helped Beauregard baffle Butler, and was constantly engaged in the defense of Petersburg.

morning, and all night was spent in packing and preparing to leave.

The wagon did not come at the specified hour. All day we waited, all the next night (without our beds), and the next day. As I looked out of the window in the twilight, hoping and watching, the cannonading commenced with vigor, and a line of shells rose in the air, describing luminous curves and breaking into showers of fragments. Our gun will be next, I thought, and for the first time my strength forsook me, and I wept over the hopeless doom which seemed to await us. Just then I heard the wheels below my window, and there was my wagon with four horses. . . .

8. AGNES—"I AM FOR A TIDAL WAVE OF PEACE"

Since we heard from our anonymous friend Agnes in January 1863 she has witnessed a bread riot of hungry women and children in Richmond; learned to make ink from the crimson sap of gall-oak nuts; plaited straw for a new hat; mended her china with white lead; attended Mrs. Davis' receptions and Tuesday "at-homes," and continued to keep Mrs. Pryor informed of life in the Confederate capital.

Richmond, August 26, 1864

You dear, obstinate little woman! What did I tell you? I implored you to get away while you could, and now you are waiting placidly for General Grant to blow you up. That awful crater! Do the officers around you consider it honorable warfare to dig and mine under a man and blow him up while he is asleep—before he has time to get his musket? I always thought an open field and a fair fight, with the enemy in front at equal chances, was the American idea of honest, manly warfare. To my mind this is the most awful thing that could be imagined. There is a strong feeling among the people I meet that the hour has come when we should consider the lives of the men left to us. Why let the enemy wipe us off the face of the earth? Should this feeling grow, nothing but a great victory can stop it. Don't you remember what Mr. Hunter[1] said to us in Washington? "You may sooner check with your bare hand the torrent of Niagara than stop this tidal wave of secession." I am for a tidal wave of peace—and I am not alone. Meantime we are slowly starving to death. Here, in

---

[1] R. M. T. Hunter of Virginia, who had been U. S. Senator with Jefferson Davis and was president *pro tem* of the Confederate Senate when President Davis was inaugurated in Richmond.

Richmond, if we can afford to give $11 for a pound of bacon, $10 for a small dish of green corn, and $10 for a watermelon, we can have a dinner of three courses for four persons. Hampton's cavalry[1] passed through town last week, amid great excitement. Every man as he trotted by was cutting and eating a watermelon, and throwing the rinds on the heads of the little negro boys who followed in crowds, on either side of the street. You wouldn't have dreamed of war—such shouting and laughing from everybody. The contrasts we constantly see look like insanity in our people. The President likes to call attention to the fact that we have no beggars on our streets, as evidence that things are not yet desperate with us. He forgets our bread riot which occurred such a little while ago. That pale, thin woman with the wan smile haunts me. Ah! these are the people who suffer the consequence of all that talk about slavery in the territories you and I used to hear in the House and Senate Chamber. Somebody, somewhere, is mightily to blame for all this business, but it isn't you nor I, nor yet the women who did not really deserve to have Governor Letcher send the mayor to read the Riot Act to them. They were only hungry, and so a thousand of them loaded some carts with bread for their children. You are not to suppose I am heartless because I run on in this irrelevant fashion. The truth is, I am so shocked and disturbed I am hysterical. It is all so awful.

Your scared-to-death

AGNES.

9. PHOEBE YATES PEMBER—
OUR EXCHANGE PRISONERS

Phoebe Yates, a native of South Carolina, married Thomas Pember of Boston, and was early left a widow. Possessed of executive ability and a tender heart, she made the journey to Richmond in the hope of helping the war wounded. She became superintendent of one of the wings of the immense Chimborazo Hospital. Dr. Freeman quotes T. C. de Leon, the Confederate commentator, who described her as "brisk and brilliant . . . with a will of steel, under a suave refinement, and [a] pretty, almost Creole accent [which] covered the power to ring in defi *on occasion." Dr. Freeman adds:*

---

[1] After General Stuart's death Major-General Wade Hampton of South Carolina had been promoted to command the cavalry.

"The story of Mrs. Pember's war on waste and thievery, of her struggle with indifference, and of her battle to save the lives of individual soldiers would be heartbreaking were it not told with an odd humor." [1] This distinctive humor flashes even in the autumn of 1864, amid the encircling gloom.

Early in September our hearts were gladdened by the tidings that the exchange of prisoners was to be renewed. The sick and wounded of our hospital (but few in numbers just then), were transferred to other quarters, and the wards put in order to receive our men from Northern prisons.

Can any pen or pencil do justice to those squalid pictures of famine and desolation! Those gaunt, lank skeletons with the dried yellow flesh clinging to bones enlarged by dampness and exposure! Those pale, bluish lips and feverish eyes, glittering and weird when contrasted with the famine-stricken faces,—that flitting, piteous, scared smile which greeted their fellow creatures, all will live forever before the mental vision that then witnessed it.

Living and dead were taken from the flag-of-truce boat, not distinguishable save from the difference of care exercised in moving them. The Federal prisoners we had released were in many instances in a like state, but our ports had been blockaded, our harvests burned, our cattle stolen, our country wasted. Even had we felt the desire to succor, where could the wherewithal have been found? But the foe,—the ports of the world were open to him. He could have fed his prisoners upon milk and honey, and not have missed either. When we review the past, it would seem that Christianity was but a name —that the Atonement had failed, and Christ had lived and died in vain.

But it was no time then for vague reflections. With beating heart, throbbing head and icy hands I went among this army of martyrs and spectres whom it was almost impossible to recognize as human beings; powerless to speak to them, choking with unavailing pity, but still striving to aid and comfort. There was but little variety of appearance. From bed to bed the same picture met the eye. Hardly a vestige of human appearance left.

The passion of sympathy could only impede my efforts if yielded to, for my hand shook too tremulously even to allow me to put the small morsels of bread soaked in wine into their mouths. It was all

[1] *The South to Posterity*, p. 115.

we dared to give at first. Some laid as if dead with limbs extended, but the greater part had drawn up their knees to an acute angle, a position they never changed until they died. Their more fortunate comrades said that the attitude was generally assumed, as it reduced the pangs of hunger and relieved the craving that gnawed them by day and by night. The Federal prisoners may have been starved at the South, we cannot deny the truth of the charge, in many instances; but we starved with them; we had only a little to share with any— but the subject had better be left to die in silence.

One among them lingered in patience the usual three days that appeared to be their allotted space of life on their return. He was a Marylander, heir to a name renowned in the history of his country, Richard Hammond Key, grandson of Francis Scott Key, author of "Star Spangled Banner," the last of seven sons reared in affluence, but presenting the same bluish, bloodless appearance common to them all. Hoping that there would be some chance of his rallying, I gave him judicious nursing and good brandy. Every precaution was taken, but the third day fever supervened and the little life left waned rapidly. He gave me the trinkets cut from gutta percha buttons that he had beguiled his captivity in making at Point Lookout,[1] to send to his family, handing me one of them for a souvenir; begged that he might be buried apart from the crowd in some spot where those who knew and cared for him might find him some day, and quietly slept himself to death that night. The next morning was the memorable 29th September, 1864, when the enemy made a desperate and successful attack, taking Fort Harrison,[2] holding it and placing Richmond in jeopardy for four hours. The alarm bells summoned the citizens together, and the shops being closed to allow those who kept them to join the city guards, there were no means of buying a coffin, or getting a hearse. It was against the rules to keep a body beyond a certain time on the hospital grounds, so little time was to be lost if I intended keeping my promise to the dead. I summoned a convalescent carpenter from one of the wards, made him knock

[1] U. S. prison in Maryland.

[2] An important point in the outer defense line southeast of Richmond, near the fortifications of Chapin's Bluff. On September 29, 1864, Federal troops captured it in a surprise move. Fearing that its loss might expose the capital, General Lee hastily gathered detachments for a counterattack and took the field in person. Three times the attack was delivered on the thirtieth, but to no avail. Lee had to extend his lines, which, with his depleted forces, was dangerous. During the fighting at Fort Harrison, Wade Hampton was stopping an advance of Federals that might have brought them to the Southside Railroad. See D. S. Freeman, *R. E. Lee,* III, 500-505.

together a rough coffin from some loose boards, and taking the seats out of my ambulance had it, with the body enclosed, put in. My driver was at his post with the guards, so taking the reins and kneeling in the little space at the side of the coffin I started for Hollywood cemetery, a distance of five miles.

The enemy were then in sight, and from every elevated point the masses of manoeuvering soldiers and flash of the enemy's cannon could be distinguished. Only stopping as I passed through the city to buy a piece of ground from the old cemetery agent, I reached Hollywood by twelve o'clock. Near the burying-ground I met the Rev. Mr. McCabe, requested his presence and assistance, and we stood side by side while the sexton dug the grave. The rain was pouring in torrents, while the clergyman repeated the Episcopal burial service from memory. Besides ourselves there were but two poor women, of the humblest class of life—Catholics, who passing casually, dropped upon their knees, undeterred by the rain, and paid their humble tribute of respect to the dead. He had all the honors of a soldier's burial paid to him unconsciously, for the cannon roared and the musketry rattled, mingling with the thunder and lighting of Heaven's artillery. The sexton held his hat over the small piece of paper on which I inscribed his name and birthplace (to be put on his headboard) to protect it from the rain, and with a saddened heart for the solitary grave we left behind I drove back to the city. The reverend gentleman was left at his home, and, perhaps, to this day does not know who his companion was during that strange hour.

I found the city in the same state of excitement, for no authentic news was to be heard, or received, except perhaps at official quarters; and it was well known that we had no troops nearer than Petersburg, save the citizens who had enrolled themselves for defense; therefore too anxious to return directly to the hospital, I drove to the residence of one of the cabinet ministers, where I was engaged to attend a dinner, and found the mistress of the establishment, surrounded by her servants and trunks preparing for a hasty retreat when necessary. Some persuasion induced her to desist, and the situation of the house commanding an extensive view of the surrounding country, we watched the advance of the enemy from the extreme northeast, for with the aid of opera-glasses we could even distinguish the colors of their uniforms. Slowly onward moved the bodies of dark blue, emerging from and disappearing into the woods, seeming to be skirting around them, but not to be diminishing the distance between, although each moment becoming more distinct, which proved their advance, while not one single Confederate jacket could be observed over the whole sweep of ground.

Half an anxious hour passed, and then, far away against the distant horizon, one single mounted horseman emerged from a thick wood, looked cautiously around, passed across the road and disappeared. He was in gray, and followed by another and another, winding around and cutting off the foe. Then a startling peal at the bell, and a courier brought the news that Wade Hampton and his cavalry were close upon the rear of the enemy. There was no occasion for fear after this, for General Hampton was the Montrose of the Southern army, he who could make any cause famous with his pen and glorious with his sword. The dinner continued in course of preparation, and was seasoned, when served, by spirits brightened by the strong reaction.

The horrors that attended, in past times, the bombardment of a city, were experienced in a great degree in Richmond during the fighting around us. The close proximity to the scenes of strife, the din of battle, the bursting of shells, the fresh wounds of the men hourly brought in were daily occurrences. Walking through the streets during this time, after the duties of the hospital were over, when night had well advanced, the pavement around the railroad depot would be crowded with wounded men just brought in, and laid there waiting for conveyance to the receiving hospitals. Some on stretchers, others on the bare bricks, or laid on a thin blanket, suffering from wounds hastily wrapped around with strips of coarse, unbleached, galling bandages of homespun cotton, on which the blood had congealed and stiffened until every crease cut like a knife. Women passing accidentally, like myself, would put down their basket or bundle, and ringing at the bell of neighboring houses, ask for basin and soap, warm water, and a few soft rags, and going from sufferer to sufferer, try to alleviate with what skill they possessed, the pain of fresh wounds, change the uneasy posture, and allay the thirst. Others would pause and look on, till the labor appearing to require no particular talent, they too would follow the example set them, and occasionally asking a word of advice, do their duty carefully and willingly. Idle boys would get a pine knot or tallow-dip, and stand quietly and curiously as torchbearers, till the scene, with its gathering accessories, formed a strange picture, not easily forgotten. Persons driving in different vehicles would alight sometimes in evening dress, and choosing the wounded most in need of surgical aid, put them in their places, and send them to their destination, continuing their way on foot. There was little conversation carried on, no necessity for introductions, and no names ever asked or given. This indifference to personality was a peculiarity strongly exhibited in hospitals, for after nursing a sick or wounded patient for months, he has often left without any curiosity exhibited as regarded my name, my whereabouts, or indeed any thing connected with me. A case in point was related by a friend. When the daughter of our general had devoted much time and care to a sick man in one of the hospitals, he seemed to feel so little gratitude for the attention paid, that her companion to rouse him told him that Miss Lee was his nurse. "Lee, Lee?" he said. "There are some Lees down in Mississippi who keep a tavern there. Is she one of them Lees?"

Almost of the same style, although a little worse was the remark of one of my sick, a poor fellow who had been wounded in the head and who, though sensible enough ordinarily, would feel the effect of the sun on his brain when exposed to its influence. After advising him to wear a wet paper doubled into the crown of his hat more from a desire to show some interest in him than from any belief in its efficacy, I paused at the door long enough to hear him ask the ward-master "who that was?" "Why, that is the matron of the hospital; she gives you all the food you eat, and attends to things." "Well!" said he, "I always did think this government was a confounded sell, and now I am sure of it, when they put such a little fool to manage such a big hospital as this."

The ingenuity of the men was wonderful in making toys and trifles, and a great deal of mechanical talent was developed by the enforced inaction of hospital life. Every ward had its draught-board and draughtsmen cut out of hard wood and stained with vegetable dyes, and sometimes chessmen would be cut out with a common knife, in such ornamentation that they would not have disgraced a drawing-room. One man carved pipes from ivy root, with exquisitely-cut shields on the bowls bearing the arms of the different States and their mottoes. He would charge and easily get a hundred and fifty dollars for a pipe (Confederate paper was then sixty cents for the dollar), and he only used his well-worn pocket-knife. Playing cards —the greatest comfort to alleviate the tedium of their sick life— were difficult to get a substitute for, so that the original packs had a hard time. They became, as may be supposed from the hands which used them, very dirty in a short time, and the corners in a particularly disreputable condition, but after the diffusion of the Oxford editions of the different books of the Bible sent from England as a donation, the soldiers took a lesson, and rounded the corners in imitation. A pack of cards after four years' use in a Southern hospital was beyond criticism.

The men had their fashions too, sometimes insisting upon having light blue pants drawn for them, and at other seasons preferring gray; but while the mania for either color raged, they would be dissatisfied with the other. When the quartermaster-general issued canvas shoes there was a loud dissatisfaction expressed in constant grumbling, till some original genius dyed the whitish tops by the liberal application of poke-berries. He was the Brummel of the day, and for many months crimson shoes were the rage, and long rows of unshod men would sit under the eaves of the wards, all diligently employed in the same labor and up to their elbows in red juice.

This fashion died out, and gave place to a button mania. Men who had never had a dream or a hope beyond a horn convenience to keep their clothing together, saved up their scanty means to replace them with gilt, and made neat little wooden shelves with a slit through the middle into which the buttons slid, so that they could be cleaned and brightened without taking them off, or soiling the jacket. With the glitter of buttons came the corresponding taste for gilt bands and tinsel around the battered hat, so that while our future was lowering darker and darker, our soldiers were amusing themselves like children who had no interest in the coming results.

The duty which of all others pressed most heavily upon me and which I never did perform voluntarily was that of telling a man he could not live, when he was perhaps unconscious that there was any danger apprehended from his wound. The idea of death so seldom occurs when disease and suffering have not wasted the frame and destroyed the vital energies, that there is but little opening or encouragement to commence such a subject unless the patient suspects the result ever so slightly. In many cases too, the yearning for life was so strong that to destroy the hope was beyond human power. Life was for him a furlough, family and friends once more around him; a future was all he wanted, and he considered it cheaply purchased if only for a month by the endurance of any wound, however painful or wearisome.

There were long discussions among those responsible during the

war, as to the advisability of the frequent amputations on the field,
and often when a hearty, fine-looking man in the prime of life would
be brought in minus an arm or leg, I would feel as if it might have
been saved, but experience taught me the wisdom of prompt measures. Poor food and great exposure had thinned the blood and broken
down the system so entirely that secondary amputations performed
in the hospital almost invariably resulted in death, after the second
year of the war. The blood lost on the battlefield when the wound was
first received would enfeeble the already impaired system and render
it incapable of further endurance.

Once we received a strong, stalwart soldier from Alabama, and
after five days' nursing, finding the inflammation from the wound in
his arm too great to save the limb, the attending surgeon requested
me to feed him on the best I could command; by that means to try
and give him strength to undergo amputation. Irritability of stomach
as well as indifference to food always accompanying gun-shot
wounds, it was necessary, while the fever continued, to give him as
much nourishment in as small a compass as possible, as well as easily
digestible food, that would assimilate with his enfeebled condition.
Beef tea he (in common with all soldiers and I believe men) would
not, or could not take, or anything I suggested as an equivalent, so
getting his consent to drink some "chemical mixture," I prepared
the infusion. Chipping up a pound of beef and pouring upon it a half
pint of water, the mixture was stirred until all the blood was extracted, and only a tea-spoonful of white fibre remained; a little salt
was added, and favored by the darkness of the corner of the ward in
which he lay, I induced him to swallow it. He drank without suspicion, and fortunately liked it, only complaining of its being too
sweet; and by the end of ten days his pulse was fairly good, and
there had been no accession of fever. Every precaution was taken,
both for his sake and the benefit of the experiment, and the arm
taken off by the most skillful surgeon we had. After the amputation,
which he bore bravely, he looked as bright and well as before, and
so on for five days—then the usual results followed. The system
proved not strong enough to throw out the "pus" or inflammation;
and this, mingling with the blood, produced that most fatal of all
diseases, pyaemia, from which no one ever recovers.

He was only one of numerous cases, so that my heart beat twice
as rapidly as ordinarily whenever there were any arrangements progressing for amputation, after any length of time had elapsed since

the wound, or any effort made to save the limb. The only cases under my observation that survived were two Irishmen, and it was really so difficult to kill an Irishman that there was little cause for boasting on the part of the officiating surgeons. One of them had his leg cut off in pieces, amputation having been performed three times, and the last heard from him was that he had married a young wife and settled on a profitable farm she owned in Macon, Georgia. He had touched the boundary lines of the "unknown land," had been given up by the surgeons, who left me with orders to stimulate him if possible. The priest (for he was a Catholic) was naturally averse to my disturbing what he considered the last moments of a dying man who had made his confession and taken his farewell of this world, and which ought to have been devoted to less worldly temptations than mint juleps; and a rather brisk encounter was the result of a difference of opinion on the subject; for if he was responsible for the soul, so was I for the body, and I held my ground firmly.

It was hard for an Irishman and a good Catholic to have to choose at this supreme moment between religion and whiskey; but though his head was turned respectfully towards good Father T—— his eyes rested too lovingly on the goblet offered to his lips to allow me to make any mistake as to the results of his ultimate intentions. The interpretation put by me on that look was that Callahan thought that as long as first proof brandy and mint lasted in the Confederacy this world was good enough for him, and the result proved that I was not mistaken. He always gave me the credit I have awarded to the juleps, and until the evacuation of Richmond kept me informed of his domestic happiness. . . .

10. KATE CUMMING—CHASING MY HOSPITAL

Stouthearted Kate has moved on with the Army of Tennessee into Georgia but her hospital has moved ahead of her and she is trying desperately to catch up with it.

General W. T. Sherman's plans of capturing Atlanta depended on the destruction of the railroads that centered there: the Georgia, running east to Augusta; the West Point, southwest to Montgomery; and the Central, south and southeast to Macon and Savannah. Late in July he marched down the Chattahoochee Valley to hit the West Point road. General Hood, fighting him at Ezra Church on the

*twenty-eighth, was repulsed and the line broken. At the same time
expeditions by Federal cavalry under George Stoneman and Edward
M. McCook against the railroads to Macon and Augusta did them
a lot of damage, though the forces were dispersed and the leaders
captured. No wonder Kate had railroad trouble.*

She stuck to her job till the war was over.

[Americus, Georgia]

August 19, 1864

We started from Newnan on the 15th instant, and very much
to our regret, as we had to leave so many of our old patients
behind. . . .

Mr. Williams of the Ninth Kentucky, one of our old patients, tried
to procure a permit to come with us, but he did not succeed. We were
very sorry, as he was anxious to get away from Newnan for fear of
being captured. He had been in the country at the time the hospital
was moved. . . .

We arrived at West Point about sundown the same day. Dr. W.
had put us under the care of the conductor, and he took us to a small
hotel—the Exchange. The landlord was moving, but informed us we
might lodge there for the night, as we had provisions with us; that
was all for which we cared. He gave us a room without even a wash-
bowl or pitcher in it; for the privilege of remaining in this delightful
room we paid the moderate sum of ten dollars.

We walked around the place; it is like many other of our small
towns—in a forlorn condition. . . .

There is quite a formidable fort built on a high hill, and from it
we had a very fine view of the surrounding country. The fort is
garrisoned by Massingale's battery. . . .

We had a pleasant walk on the bridge which the enemy were so
desirous of destroying. I believe the guard on it were Governor
Brown's[1] men. In the late raid through this portion of the country,
the enemy's object was the destruction of this bridge, as it is a very
important one to us. By its destruction we would lose one of the communications with the Gulf States, and at present they are the granary
of the Tennessee army; and, besides that, all communications between these states and both armies would be hindered, at least for
awhile. The river at this point is very wide.

---

[1] Joseph E. Brown, Governor of Georgia, 1857-1865, was an almost fanatical
defender of States' rights.

The late raiders did not come any further than Opelika, which is not many miles distance. There they destroyed a large portion of the railroad and government property. . . .

We were informed that morning that the Federals had cut the road between that point and Atlanta, and as the train did not come in at its usual time, we were confident the report was true, but the arrival of the train proved it false. We left about 4 P.M. on the 16th.

When a few miles beyond Opelika the locomotive ran off the track, and we came near having a very serious accident. I was reading, and knew nothing of it until I heard some ladies scream. I then felt a motion as if the train was about to upset. I saw several of the cars ahead of us plunge off the road, and men jumping from them; many took to the woods, as they were fearful of an explosion.

We remained on the car all night. Next morning men who had come from Opelika were at work trying to clear the track, but the job looked like an endless one. Every car excepting the one we were on (it being the last) was off the track.

One of our old patients made us some coffee, and we, like all the rest, ate our breakfast on the roadside. We were in the woods, and no sign of a habitation near. As there was little or no hope of our leaving there for some time, a gentleman who had found an empty house a little ways back came and took his party, Mrs. W., and myself to it. We found it quite a nice retreat. It had been a school-house, and the benches and desks were left standing. We had books, and altogether had quite a pleasant day. Our gentleman friend was Senator Hill,[1] of Legrange, Georgia. . . . Mr. Hill gave us some nice biscuit and ham, his servant made our coffee for dinner; and altogether we had a most delightful repast.

Miss Augusta Evans,[2] the authoress, was on the train, going to Columbus, where she has a badly wounded brother. From her I learned that all was quiet in Mobile, although we have had a naval battle, and Forts Morgan, Powell, and Gaines were taken. The battle was a desperate one, and we have lost our splendid ram, the Tennessee. Admiral Buchanan was severely wounded; himself and whole crew are prisoners. . . .

About 3 P.M., a wood-car came from Columbus, on which we all got. We cut branches of trees and held them over us for protection

---

[1] Senator Ben Hill was a much more liberal supporter of the Confederacy than Governor Brown.
[2] See page 211 *supra*.

from the sun. We reached Columbus without further accident in time to catch the Macon train. We arrived at the latter place about 4 A.M., the 17th. Went to a hotel and paid ten dollars for a bed, and as much more for breakfast. We called on Drs. Bemiss and Stout, and learned from them that our hospital had gone to Americus, Georgia. These two gentlemen were low spirited; they do not like the idea of coming so far South at this season, and think it will be deleterious to the wounded. . . .

The train to Americus had already gone and Mrs. W., being fearful that if we remained in the hotel another day our exchequer would be empty, we called on our old friend, Dr. Cannon, who has charge of the Wayside Home. I knew he could tell us where we could procure a boarding house more suited to our means. His two daughters were with him, and were keeping house in two rooms, refugee style; one of the rooms was parlor, bed-room, and dining-room, the other a kind of dressing-room. It astonishes me to see how well every body manages now-a-days; they put up with inconveniences as if they had been used to them all their lives. The war seems to have raised the minds of many above common every-day annoyances. Dr. C. insisted on us remaining with his family, and as Mrs. W. was half sick, and we were both worn out, we were only too thankful to accept the kind invitation. The family seem to be perfectly happy, as much so, I expect, as they ever were in their home in Tennessee.

Dr. Nagle and an officer who is stationed at Andersonville, where the prisoners are kept, spent the evening with us. The prisoners and their behavior was the principal topic of conversation, and from all we could learn we did not like the prospect of being so near them (Americus is ten miles below Andersonville). This officer informed us that no less than a hundred died daily. He said they were the most desperate set of men that he had ever seen. There were two parties among them, the black republicans and the copperheads, and they often have desperate fights, and kill each other. This officer said it was revolting to be near such men, and did not like his position.

Dr. C. sent us to the depot on the 19th in an ambulance. The train stopped a little while at Fort Valley, where the Buckner and Gamble Hospitals, of our post, have remained. There we saw a few familiar faces. The train remained about a half an hour at Andersonville, so we had time for a good view of the prisoners' quarters. I must say that my antipathy for prison-life was any thing but removed by the sight. My heart sank within me at seeing so many human beings crowded so closely together. I asked a gentleman near why we had so many in one place. He answered that we would not have men enough to guard them were they scattered. O, how I thought of him who is the cause of all this woe on his fellow-countrymen—Abraham Lincoln. What kind of a heart can he have, to leave these poor wretches here? To think how often we have begged for exchange; but this unfeeling man knows what a terrible punishment it is for our men to be in Northern prisons, and how valuable every one of them is to us. For this reason he sacrifices thousands of his own. May Heaven help us all! But war is terrible.

Arrived at Americus to-day, the 19th. . . .

11. MARY ANN HARRIS GAY—THE BATTLE FOR ATLANTA

Miss Gay was born in Jones County, Georgia, March 19, 1829. She and her mother were living in Decatur when war broke out. Her half sister Missouri Stokes taught school in the neighborhood, and her half brother Thomas J. Stokes was with the 10th Texas Infantry. Now in July 1864 the residence was being used as headquarters for Sherman's advance army.

Miss Gay wrote her book Life in Dixie during the War *especially for her only nephew, Thomie Stokes of Atlanta, but he died before it was published. Joel Chandler Harris supplied the introduction. "It is a gentle, a faithful and a tender hand that guides the pen," he says; "a soul nerved to sacrifice that tells the tale."*

Decatur, Georgia

No news from "the front;" no tidings from the loved ones in gray; no friendly spirit whispering words of cheer or consolation. Shut up within a narrow space, and guarded by Federal bayonets! not a ray of friendly light illuminated my environment.

The constant roaring of cannon and rattling of musketry; the thousand, yea, tens of thousands of shots blending into one grand continuous whole, and reverberating in avalanchan volume over the hills of Fulton, and the mountain heights of old DeKalb—told in thunder tones of the fierce contest between Federal and Confederate forces being waged without intermission for the possession of Atlanta.

The haughty, insolent boast of the enemy, now that Joe Johnston was removed from the command of the Army of the Tennessee, that they would make quick work of the rebellion, and of the complete subjugation of the South, had in no way a tendency to mitigate anxiety or to encourage hope. Thus surrounded, I sought and obtained permission to read Federal newspapers. The United States mail brought daily papers to the officers in command of the troops quartered in our yard; and through this medium I kept posted, from a Northern standpoint, concerning the situation of both armies. While there was little in these dispatches gratifying to me, there was much that I thought would be valuable to my people if I could only convey it to them; and I racked my brain day and night, devising ways and means by which to accomplish this feat. But the ways and means decided upon were, upon reflection, invariably abandoned as being impracticable.

In this dilemma, a most opportune circumstance offered an immediate solution of the difficult problem. In the midst of a deep study of the relative positions of the two armies, and of the hopes and fears animating both, a tall, lank, honest-faced Yankee came to the door of the portico and asked "if Miss Gay was in."

I responded that I was she, and he handed me a letter addressed to myself. I hastily tore it open and read the contents. It was written by a reverend gentleman whose wife was a distant relative of my mother, and told that she was very ill. "Indeed," wrote he, "I have but little hope of ever seeing her any better, and I beg you to come to see her, and spend several days."

I showed the letter to my mother, who was sitting near by, and, like myself, engaged in studying the situation. She strenuously objected to my going, and advanced many good reasons for my not doing so; but my reasons for going counteracted them all in my estimation, and I determined to go.

Taking Telitha with me, I carried the letter to the Provost Marshal, and asked him to read it and grant me the privilege of going. After reading the letter, he asked me how I obtained it, and received my statement. He then asked me if I could refer him to the party who brought it to me. Leaving the letter with him, I ran home and soon returned with the desired individual who had fortunately lingered in the yard in anticipation of usefulness. Convinced that the invitation was genuine, and for a humane purpose, this usually morose marshal granted me "a permit" to visit those poor old sick people, for the husband was almost as feeble as his wife. I told the obliging marshal that there was another favor I should like to ask of him, if he would not think me too presumptuous. "Name it," he said.

I replied: "Will you detail one or more of the soldiers to act as an escort for me? I am afraid to go with only this girl."

To this he also assented, and said it was a wise precaution. He asked when I wished to come home.

"Day after to-morrow afternoon," I told him, and received assurance that an escort would be in waiting for me at that time.

It now became necessary to make some important preparations for the trip. A great deal was involved, and if my plans were successful, important events might accrue. A nice white petticoat was called into requisition, and, when I got done with it, it was literally lined with Northern newspapers. "The Cincinnati Enquirer," and "The New York Daily Times;" "The Cincinnati Commercial Gazette," and "The Philadelphia Evening Ledger," under the manipulation of my fingers, took their places on the inner sides and rear of the skirt, and served as a very stylish "bustle," an article much in vogue in those days. This preparatory work having been accomplished, it required but a few moments to complete my toilet, and, under the auspices of a clear conscience and a mother's blessing, doubtless, I started on a perilous trip. The ever-faithful Telitha was by my side, and the military escort a few feet in advance.

After a walk of a mile and a half, I reached my destination for that day. I found the old lady in question much better than I had expected. Nervous and sick himself, her husband had greatly exaggerated her afflictions. By degree, and under protest, I communicated to these aged people my intention of carrying information to Hood's headquarters, that might be of use to our army. Both were troubled about the possible result if I should be detected; but my plans were laid, and nothing could deter me from pursuing them.

The rising sun of another day saw Telitha and me starting on our way to run the gauntlet, so to speak, of Federal bayonets. These good old people had given me much valuable information regarding the way to Atlanta—information which enabled me to get there without conflict with either Confederate or Federal pickets. Knowing the topography of the country, I took a circuitous route to an old mill, Cobb's I believe, and from there I sought the McDonough road. I didn't venture to keep that highway to the city, but I kept within sight of it, and under cover of breast-works and other obstructions, managed to evade videttes and pickets of both armies. After walking fourteen or fifteen miles, I entered Atlanta at the beautiful home of Mrs. L. P. Grant, at the southern boundary of the city. That estimable lady never lost an opportunity of doing good. On this occasion, as upon every other offering an opportunity, she remembered to do good. She ordered an appetizing lunch, including a cup of sure-enough coffee, which refreshed and strengthened me after my long walk. Her butler having become a familiar personage on the streets of Atlanta, she sent him as a guide to important places. We entered the city unchallenged, and moved about at will. The force of habit, probably, led me to Mrs. McArthur's and to Mrs. Craig's on Pryor Street. The head of neither of these families was willing to accompany me to Confederate headquarters, and without a guide I started to hunt them for myself. What had seemed an easy task now seemed insurmountable. I knew not in what direction to go, and the few whom I asked seemed as ignorant as myself. Starting from Mrs. Craig's, I went towards the depot. I had not proceeded very far before I met Major John Y. Rankin. I could scarcely restrain tears of joy. He was a member of the very same command to which my brother belonged. From Major Rankin I learned that my brother, utterly prostrated, had been sent to a hospital, either in Augusta or Madison.

Preferring not to stand upon the street, I asked Major Rankin to return with me to Mrs. Craig's, which he did, and spent an hour in pleasant conversation. Mrs. Craig was a delightful conversationalist, and while she was entertaining the major with that fine art, I retired to a private apartment, and with the aid of a pair of scissors ripped off the papers from my underskirt and smoothed and folded them nicely, and after re-arranging my toilet, took them into the parlor as a trophy of skill in outwitting the Yankee. Telitha, too, had a trophy to which she had clung ever since we left home with the tenacity of an eel, and which doubtless she supposed to be an offering to "Marse Tom," and was evidently anxious that he should receive it. Having dismissed Mrs. Grant's butler as no longer necessary to my convenience, Major Rankin, myself and Telitha went direct to the headquarters of his command. The papers seemed to be most acceptable, but I noticed that the gleanings from conversation seemed far more so. The hopefulness and enthusiasm of our soldiers were inspiring. But alas! how little they knew of the situation, and how determined not to be enlightened. Even then they believed that they would hold Atlanta against Herculean odds, and scorned the idea of surrender. At length the opening of Telitha's package devolved on me. Shirts, socks and soap, towels, gloves, etc., formed a compact bundle that my mother had sent to our soldiers.

I now turned my thoughts to our negroes, who were hired in different parts of the city. Rachel, the mother of King, hired herself and rented a room from Mr. John Silvey. In order that I might have an interview with Rachel without disturbing Mr. Silvey's family, I went to the side gate and called her. She answered and came immediately. I asked her if she realized the great danger to which she was continually exposed. Even then "shot and shell" were falling in every direction, and the roaring of cannon was an unceasing sound. She replied that she knew the danger, and thought I was doing wrong to be in Atlanta when I had a home to be at. I insisted that she had the same home, and a good vacant house was ready to receive her. But she was impervious to every argument, and preferred to await the coming of Sherman in her present quarters. Seeing that I had no influence over her, I bade her good-bye and left.

Telitha and I had not gone farther than the First Presbyterian Church, not a square away from the gate upon which I had leaned during this interview with Rachel, before a boomshell fell by that gate and burst into a thousand fragments, literally tearing the gate into pieces. After this fearfully impressive adventure, unfortified by any "permit" I struck a bee line to Mrs. Grant's. An old negro man belonging to Mrs. Williams, who had "come out" on a previous occasion, was there, and wanted to return under my protection to his home within the enemy's lines. Very earnest assurances from Mrs. Grant to that effect convinced me that I had nothing to fear from betrayal by him, and I consented that he should be a member of my company homeward bound. Two large packages were ready for the old man to take charge of, about which Mrs. Grant gave him directions, *sotto voce*. Putting one of them on the end of a walking cane he threw it over his right shoulder, and with his left hand picked up the other bundle. Telitha and I were unencumbered. We had not proceeded very far before we encountered our pickets. No argument was weighty enough to secure for me the privilege of passing the lines without an official permit. Baffled in this effort, I approved the action of the pickets, and we turned and retraced our steps in the direction of Atlanta, until entirely out of sight of them, and then we turned southward and then eastward, verging a little northward. Constant vigilance enabled me to evade the Yankee pickets, and constant walking brought me safely to the home of my aged and afflicted friends, from which I had started early in the morning of that day. These friends were conservative in every act and word, and, it may be, leaned a little out of the perpendicular towards that "flaunting lie," the United States flag; therefore they were favorites among the so-called defenders of the Union, and were kept supplied with many palatable articles of food that were entirely out of the reach of rebels who were avowed and "dyed in the wool."

A few minutes sufficed to furnish us with a fine pot of soup (and good bread was not lacking), of which we ate heartily. The old negro man was too anxious to get home to be willing to spend the night so near, just for the privilege of walking into Decatur under Yankee escort, and said he was "going home," and left me.

The next day my escort was promptly on hand, and in due time I was in Decatur. . . .

Not many mornings subsequent to the adventure just related, I discovered upon opening the door that the Yankee tents seemed to be vacant. Not a blue-coat was to be seen. What could it mean? Had they given up the contest and ignominiously fled? As if confirmatory of the gratifying suggestion, the booming of cannon in the direction of Atlanta was evidently decreasing. Then again I thought perhaps the wagon train had been sent out to forage upon the country, and as it would now have to go forty-five and fifty miles to get anything, it required an immense military escort to protect it from the dashing, sanguinary attacks of the "rebels."

Before the sun had attained its meridian height, a number of our scouts appeared on the abandoned grounds; and what joy their presence gave us! But they left us as suddenly as they came, and on reflection we could not think of a single encouraging word uttered by them during their stay. Suspense became intolerable. With occasional lulls, the roaring of cannon was a continuous blending of ominous sound.

In the midst of this awful suspense, an apparition, glorious and bright, appeared in our presence. It was my brother. He had left Madison a few days before, where he had been allowed to spend a part of his furlough, instead of remaining at the Augusta hospital. His mother's joy at meeting her beloved son, and under such circumstances, was pathetic indeed, and I shall never forget the effort she made to repress the tears and steady the voice as she sought to nerve him for the arduous and perilous duties before him. . . .

The shades of night came on, and darker grew until complete

blackness enveloped the face of the earth, and still the low subdued tones of conversation between mother, son and daughter, mingled with unabated interest. Hark! Hark! An explosion! An earthquake? The angry bellowing sound rises in deafening grandeur, and reverberates along the far-off valley and distant hill-tops. What is it—this mighty thunder that never ceases? The earth is ablaze—what can it be? This illumination that reveals minutest objects? With blanched face and tearful eye, the soldier said:

"Atlanta has surrendered to the enemy. The mighty reports are occasioned by the blowing up of the magazines and arsenals."

Dumbfounded we stood, trying to realize the crushing fact. Woman's heart could bear no more in silence, and a wail over departed hopes mingled with the angry sounds without. . . .

12. MARY RAWSON—"THEY TOOK POSSESSION OF ATLANTA QUIETLY"

The young daughter of E. E. Rawson of Atlanta kept a war diary which ended with the occupation by Sherman at the beginning of September 1864. Her father was a member of the City Council. When Sherman sought to justify his order of evacuation he addressed himself to James M. Calhoun, Mayor, E. E. Rawson, and S. C. Wells. Mary married Captain John D. Ray of the 1st Georgia Volunteers.

Atlanta, Georgia August 31, 1864

This day witnessed the downfall of the hopes of the citizens of Atlanta. Today Gen. Hood commenced his evacuation of our city. The gentlemen who did not wish to fall into the hands of the federals might have been seen in the afternoon of this day in company of the last of the soldiers, wending their way slowly out of the now desolate Atlanta; as night threw around our home its sable shadows, silence reigned broken only by pleasant converse with our now absent friends. How different from the few last nights preceeding; the pleasure and repose of these evenings was disturbed by the noise of exploding shells and the sharp crack of the death-dealing musketry. Oh! how much more pleasure there would have been had it not been for the expectation of the scene of the coming morrow. Nine oclock comes and we retire for the night, but sleep and dreams were soon interrupted by rapid and loud explosions. On arising a most beautiful spectacle greeted our sight. The Heavens were in a perfect glow while the atmosphere seemed full of flaming rockets, crash follows crash and the swift moving locomotives were rent in pieces and the never tiring metalic horse lay powerless while the sparks filled the air with innumerable spangles. This great exhibition was occasioned by the burning of the military stores which could not be removed with the soldiers. This crashing had scarcely ceased when our attention was called in another direction by a bright light which proved to be the burning of some more Government provisions.

After a time, it seemed to us an unending time, the morning dawned and the bright sun arose which ushered in another eventful month, September 1864. Although the commencement of this day was outwardly so pleasant, language falls short in expressing the suspense and anxiety experienced by everyone. Time after time had we been told of the severity of Gen. Sherman until we came to dread his approach as we would that of a mighty hurricane which sweeps all before it caring naught for justice or humanity.

The forenoon passed slowly with nothing of importance transpiring except a visit from Mr. Tenny, informing us that a few cavalry had been left to dispute every inch of ground through the city, as he said. With dinner time came Father, who said that the Federals had taken possession of the city. Oh! What a relief to me, I had expected them to enter in disorder exulting loudly in the success of their enterprise. Atlanta was taken possession of quietly. About ten oclock in the morning the mayor, two councilmen with the principle citizens went out to invite them in. After some hesitation they marched in under the command of Gen. Slocume.[1] Gen. Sherman was at this time preparing to encounter Gen. Hood near Jonesboro.[2] Immediately upon entering the town the stars and stripes were seen floating from the flag pole on the Franklin building. Father's store was used as a signal station; the signals were given with a blue flag having a large white star in the center and in the evening they used beautiful lanterns which were moved in different directions. . . .

Friday 2d. passed without particular event occurring. Saturday, this morning the sun and the bright azure are shut out by lowering clouds from which the rain pours in torrents. At ten this morning

[1] Major-General Henry W. Slocum, corps commander.
[2] Sherman had moved twenty-two miles southwest of Atlanta to strike the Central Railroad near Jonesboro. On August 31, General William J. Hardee, facing west from Jonesboro, attempted, without success, to drive the Federals into Flint River, but the next day drove Sherman back from Jonesboro.

Father had a visit from the provost marshal and several other officers, who wished us to give up our beautiful home for headquarters
for the general. This request Father told him it was impossible to
comply with for where could we find another home of any kind?
They finally gave up the idea of taking it from us and seemed much
pleased with our old school house instead. Oh how I felt to see the
beloved old playground in front of the school covered with tents and
the beautiful little shade trees cut down. Besides how could I see
Miss Maria's and Miss Anne's cherished pet flowers trampled down
by those who could not appreciate their beauty and fragrance. Oh it
was too much and Mattie and I shed tears to think of the desolation.
We were the only ones left of the pleasant class of seven who used
to assemble daily at the Pine Hill seminary. How many friends were
scattered in the great stampeed previous to the desertion of Atlanta.
Many of the girls had gone further South with their parents and one
dear class mate left us for another and I hope better world, during
the enclosure of our city by both Armies. But I forget myself. I was
speaking of the visit of the officers. When they prepared to leave I
was amused as well as astonished to see the behavior of the grooms.
One of them happening to be in our bomb-proof, his master called
"Jack come out of that proof and get my horse" and how he did fly
to obey his orders, brought his horse and equiped him for his rainy
journey by buttoning on his oilcloth coat and after much elaborate
brushing he gently placed him on his saddle and they went away. All
this I witnessed from the dining room window. . . .

The darkness now set in and I had a fine view of Gen. Gearys[1]
headquarters with the tents surrounding it—my window presenting
a good prospect of the city. The house was illuminated from the basement to the attic and the camp fires spread all over the hills filling
the atmosphere with a light smoke with the piramid of light issueing
from the windows of the generals home. . . . It grows late and I
must retire to bed not having a very flattering anticipation of the
coming Sabbath and carried to dreamland by the music of the bugle.

Sunday. At ten today our hearts were made sad by hearing the
familiar chimes of the church bells. How often has this been the
signal to us for leaving our homes to hear the word of God ex-

---

[1] General John W. Geary, U. S. A. He had been first postmaster, first alcalde, first
mayor of San Francisco, and governor of Kansas. Sherman was accustomed to entrust
civil affairs to him.

pounded. Today these peals serve only to send innumerable squads of soldiers to our own loved churches. The hills as well as the once crowded thorough-fare of Atlanta are covered with blue-coats wending their way to the different places of worship. Noon and dinner time come and afterwards Capt. Seymore called. Pa told him of the frequent depredations committed on our potato patch and he immediately sent us a guard. This afternoon as we stood in the upper front veranda, we noticed a great dust and what appeared to be a vast number of soldiers marching; besides, for the first time since the city was taken we heard the air of Yankee-doodle. After watching the soldiers some time one of the guards came around the terrace and saluted his fellow with the interrogation did you see the Johnnies? They were bringing in some captured Confederates and by close observation we could distinguish the two bodies of infantry, prisoners and the victors. These men were taken to one of the freight depots where a great many of the ladies visited them carrying delicacies.

Monday has been a quiet day for us. This evening George Zimmerman came over to request that Father would call the next morning to see his mother, and Gen. Sherman had ordered all ladies whose husbands were in "Rebel service," as he said, to leave the city in five days and Mr. Zimmerman being absent he had no one to advise with.

Tuesday. While we were at breakfast this morning Grand-father came and told us that Aunty had been ordered to leave her beautiful home to give place to a *Yankee colonel* who had given her only half a day to move all her property. O cruel soldier. I concluded I would go with Father and see Miss Delia and as Grand-pa urged me I would go to Grand-Mas on my return. I found Miss Delia indignant at the thought of being driven from home. O, she said, I would not live among them and if I had had any idea of them coming I would have gone ere this. But not withstanding her anger I had a very pleasant visit. I went according to promise to see Grand-Ma. The house was all in confusion, occasioned by the bringing in of Aunty's furniture. Then I went to Aunty's to see if I could not render some assistance and by constant running to and fro we succeeded in getting most of her valuables removed. But all this time the officers were there dictating as to what should be carried away and what should remain and continually repeating the injunction of haste, haste, forgetting that haste makes waste. Tongue cannot express her trouble in leaving, she has no home to go to elsewhere.

On returning to my home I found Mother in great anxiety, caused by the information derived from the guard first and confirmed by Mr. Tenny and Mr. Andrews that all citizens should be compelled to vacate the city, though they still had choice of which home they would prefer. We could be sent farther down in Dixie or we could attempt the ice and snow of the Northern winter. Father did not think the report at all reliable, but went to the provost marshal to inquire, but on reaching the office the door was closed; and a notice tacked on the door, saying that no one would be admitted until the next day, he then called on Gen. Geary and asked him concerning the order but he had heard nothing of it. So wearied out by walking and anxiety he returned home without any cheering news.

Wednesday. 7th. Today the first report on leaving the breakfast room was a confirmation of the one received yesterday. Father immediately set out for the headquarters of Gen. Slocume and afterwards to the provost and afterwards home again. At noon we gathered around Father to hear Gen. Shermans order read. During the forenoon he had seen Gen. Geary, Col. Beckworth, Capt. Forbes and Capt. Seymore. These had all expressed it as their opinion that the command referred to these men who in some way had been in the Confederate service and that all others could remain quietly in their home. The question now was. What explanation to give the order. There was also another law written forbidding any person to sell cotton or tobacco, as such comodities would be impressed for the government use. Pa was kept constantly moving to and fro trying to get authority to dispose of his tobacco for some mere pittance though this was finally proved to be impracticable, unless a special permit could be obtained from Sherman.

Thursday. 8th. The order compelling all persons to evacuate the city was today plainly written out. All those whose husbands were in the service were to leave on Monday, while the remainder were given fifteen days to pack and leave.

Fathers property mostly consisted in land and Confederate money so we had not means enough to venture North, unless Pa could get something for his tobacco.

Friday. 9th. Father made a visit to Col. Beckworth and Col. Eason to find if no disposition could be made of the tobacco, but ill fated weed though much loved and longed for by Yankee soldiery, you seem as ever to be only a source of trouble to those who possess and use you. No success was experienced and evening found us as undecided as in the morning.

Saturday dawns and another day of continued exertion and restless anxiety slowly passes. All of this time we had been wasting our precious fifteen days. Another appeal was made today to Col. Beckworth and he promised to see Gen. Sherman and obtain a written paper allowing us to dispose of our provisions and tobacco if he could. With this assurance we prepared to spend the approaching Sabbath.

Sunday. This morning Mother concluded that although we had not the slightest idea of our future home, we had better commence the task of packing. Scarcely was the work begun when we heard that all those who went South would have their trunks searched and all goods not ready made be removed. Now came the question as to how we could secrete them and so take them with us. We finally prepared two trunks to go either way by folding pieces of goods between ready made clothes and by tearing the cloth into pieces of sufficient length to make dress skirts and a great many other ways we found of hiding our goods. While we were in the midst of our work Aunt Charlotte came over from Grandmas and told us they had already opened Auntys trunks twice and came to preform the same detestable office again, when Aunty refused decidedly to open her baggage any more and Col. Beckworth coming in at that moment gave him a sound cudgening. Aunt Charlotte expressed her determination to follow her master and mistress wherever they go. Dear old Granny may you be well protected and carefully nursed during your old age and when life is over be laid gently to rest by those who can and do appreciate you.

This afternoon on hearing martial music, we looked up from the front porch where we were sitting to see the street filled with cavalry and infantry pack mules and army wagons and cattle crowded promiscously together, the cavalry and infantry ensigns floating in unison together. The musicians all riding on white horses. After making the signal for the march to commence they rode silently along until they passed in front of Gen. Gearys headquarters when simultaneously they broke into the old soul stirring "Hail Columbia"; the suddenness of the music startled me. They then, (after finishing the piece) slowly and silently marched through the city. A few minutes after this Mother went over to see my Grandparents and Aunty; and I went to have a little talk with Mattie; her father had determined to go to the North and so it seemed probable that the friends of seven years would be separated. We finally parted, I with a beautiful sprig of honeysuckle in my hair, placed there by Mr. Andrews who remarked that this would be the last time he would deck my hair for me.

Monday. 12th. This morning on leaving the breakfast table I hastily tied on my hat and veil previous to going to bid my dear kindred goodbye, for this was the day appointed for them to go. Arriving at the house I found two huge Army wagons and two ambulances at the gate and men hurrying to and fro with trunks and other baggage. At last they all came out and took their places in the ambulance and after a sad adieu they slowly departed. Then I returned home and all along the street in front of Mrs. Zimmermans I noticed many vehicles for taking them away and even more sadly than at first if possible I continued my walk.

Tuesday. 13th. This morning Father concluded to go himself to see Gen. Sherman and ask if he could get a written order permitting him to sell his provisions. About ten oclock he came back bringing the papers signed by the General, then came a long conversation with Mother which terminated in the resolve to brave the severities of the cold North West. We immediately prepared to emigrate to the prairies of Iowa. . . .

13. HENRIETTA HUNT MORGAN—"A BETTER SON
     NEVER LIVED"

On September 4, 1864, four days after John Hunt Morgan left Mattie in Abington, Virginia, for his last raid, he was shot by a Union soldier in Greeneville, Tennessee. Now it is his mother's turn to speak—to speak to the bereft wife whom she had never seen. She writes from Hopemont, her home in Lexington, Kentucky.

The daughter of John Wesley Hunt and widow of Calvin Morgan of Lexington, Henrietta was the mother of eight children. Her name-sake daughter was the wife of General Basil Duke, John Hunt Morgan's right hand and chronicler; her daughter Kitty, the wife of the great General Ambrose P. Hill. Besides John Hunt, Henrietta gave four sons to the Confederacy: Richard, Charlton, Calvin and Thomas. Thomas had been killed only three months ago—and now there is this culminating grief! Key, her youngest son, named for kinsman Francis Scott Key, was a boy of fifteen.

A daughter was born to Mattie Ready Morgan after John Hunt's death. Some years later Mattie married James Williamson, a Confederate veteran who became a circuit judge at Lebanon, Tennessee.

October 1st 1864

My Dear Dear Mattie, What words of comfort can I offer, my precious one, when my own heart is lashed and torn bleeding with this last terrible wound? Weak and worn and not at all healed from the great sorrow that has weighed me down the past eighteen months, my heart is faint, my nerves shattered, I lie awake night after night, count each strike of the clock, dread both night and day, tremble to open a letter. How gladly would I gather you and all together and fly to some far-off land, where there would be no sound of strife, but Oh! the dear ones can never be restored. How hard it is to resign my children. God gave them to me, to lose. It cannot be wicked that I feel the struggle so great to resign them. God forgive me if it is! I love you, dear Mattie, as having been a part of my boy. I hope the time may someday come when I can evince to you my full appreciation of the love you bore my noble son. A better son and brother never lived, so gentle, watchful to guard me from the disagreeables of life. From his youth to the last time I saw him he considered his mother!

Poor dear Charlton truly says he has lost a father, brother and friend. Trust in my love, dear child. I shall cherish it, for his sake and your own. My children are my all—are you not one? Although the circle is getting smaller and smaller, we must be a united family. Consider me as your own mother. Command my services in any way, at any time. You have my heart.

For two weeks, although confined to my room and on the bed, I could not help hoping there was some mistake. If a servant would step in and remark, "Miss Henrietta, many persons think it is not so," I felt like falling on my knees to embrace them with a feeling of gratitude for those little words of comfort. I wanted every hour to pour out my heart to God, and plead for his life to be spared a few years longer. After my prayers for a little while I would be comforted, but when the terrible letters came from dear Dick and Basil, it was all over, my hope was all all gone. I had to bow my head to the rod. It is selfish in me so to indulge and not try to comfort you. Forgive it, for it is my nature. After a while my letters shall be more tranquil, I will try not to indulge in such lamentations! My children are sincerely attached to you; command them at all times as brothers and sisters. I had a letter from dear Dollie of the 18th, the first for a long time; I was happy to know she and the children were well and comfortable. How anxious she must be all the time about her husband. I hear Henrietta has left Abingdon. Her whereabouts I do not know, poor dear child. I hoped Basil and Dick would have recruited a little before going into active service. Frank, my baby—do use your sisterly influence to keep him from the front. I heard you were going to Augusta; I was very glad you would be with your relations. I have a dear kind brother who will do all in his power to comfort you. I trust, my dear, there may still be a *blessing* in store for you and all. The last letter from you was the 1st of September. Your dear husband had left the day before soon to be back. How well it is the veil cannot be lifted from the future. God bless you and shield you from all future sorrow is the unceasing prayer of your unknown, tho devoted Mother

HENRIETTA MORGAN

VIII

WINTER OF DESPERATION

November 1864-March 1865

The recent antagonists, Hood and Sherman, now marched away from each other. Hood was going northwest to destroy Sherman's lines of communication, to recapture Nashville and perhaps keep on to the Ohio River.

Sherman dispatched first Thomas and then Schofield to hold Nashville. Schofield might have been destroyed at Spring Hill, Tennessee, on November 29, but somehow his army was allowed to slip by. When Hood attacked him the next day at Franklin, in a charge that for desperate valor rivaled Pickett's at Gettysburg, 4,500 Confederate were killed or wounded in an hour. Schofield proceeded to Nashville. There George H. Thomas waited patiently till he had assembled a massive force, twice as strong as Hood's. Then at the Battle of Nashville, December 15 and 16, he overwhelmed Hood and put his army to rout all the way back to the Tennessee River, the only complete rout suffered by any major Confederate force.

Meanwhile Atlanta was put to the torch on November 15. Sherman took up his march to Savannah and the sea; four infantry corps, one cavalry, 68,000 men, spread wide on four great roads. He had no reason to worry about supply lines. He had accumulated vast stores and had a rich and fertile country to live on. The orders for foraging were liberal, and at that were abused. The general effect of pillage and demolition was like that created by Sheridan in the Shenandoah. Through that broad swath was a scene of desolation "where stood chimneys only, amid ruins. The very birds of the air and the beasts of the field had fled."

General Hardee was in charge of the defense of Savannah, but with so small a force that he could not make it effective. On December 20 he took his men across the river into South Carolina, and the next day Sherman was in the city. He wired Lincoln, "I beg to present you, as a Christmas gift, the city of Savannah."

After recuperating for a month, Sherman turned north. His army found a gruesome satisfaction in punishing South Carolina for the

344

part she had played in starting the war, and the destruction wreaked
was worse than in Georgia. On February 17 Charleston was evacu-
ated and Columbia went up in flames. Wilmington, North Carolina,
last port of the Confederacy, was surrendered on the twenty-second.

Meanwhile, in Virginia the armies of Grant and Lee stayed locked
in the siege of Petersburg. Sheridan's cavalry ranged far and wide.

On February 3, 1865, Alexander Stephens, Robert M. T. Hunter
and John A. Campbell met President Lincoln and Secretary of State
Seward on a steamer at Hampton Roads for an informal peace talk.
It came to nothing.

And on February 6 Robert E. Lee was appointed general-in-chief
of all Confederate armies.

1. MARY ANN HARRIS GAY—"LEAD, BLOOD AND TEARS"

"All who cannot support themselves without applying to the
United States Commissary for assistance," Sherman had ordered,
"must go outside our lines, either north or south. . . ." But Mary
Ann Gay and her mother did not leave their home in Decatur. She
writes now of the situation in late November after Sherman's de-
parture from the burned city and countryside of Atlanta for the
March to the Sea.

Could Winston Churchill have read Miss Gay's book before he
warned the British people to expect "blood, sweat and tears"?

After mingling renewed vows of allegiance to our cause, and ex-
pressions of a willing submission to the consequences of defeat—
privations and evil dire, if need be—with my morning orison; yet
I could not be oblivious to the fact that I was hungry, very hungry.
And there was another, whose footsteps were becoming more and
more feeble day by day, and whose voice, when heard at all, was full
of the pathos of despair, who needed nourishment that could not be
obtained, and consolation, which it seemed a mockery to offer.

In vain did I look round for relief. There was nothing left in the
country to eat. Yea, a crow flying over it would have failed to discover a morsel with which to appease its hunger; for a Sheridan[1] by
another name had been there with his minions of destruction, and
had ruthlessly destroyed every vestige of food and every means of

---

[1] In the Shenandoah, Sheridan had "burned, blasted, slaughtered, destroyed."

support. Every larder was empty, and those with thousands and tens of thousands of dollars were as poor as the poorest, and as hungry too. Packing trunks, in every house to which refugees had returned, contained large amounts of Confederate money. We had invested all we possessed except our home, and land and negroes, in Confederate bonds, and these were now inefficient for purchasing purposes. Gold and silver had we none. A more favored few had a little of those desirable mediums of purchase, and sent a great distance for supplies; but they offered no relief to those who had stayed at home and borne the brunt of battle, and saved their property from the destroyers' torch.

What was I to do? Sit down and wait for the inevitable starvation? No; I was not made of such stuff. I had heard that there had been a provision store opened in Atlanta for the purpose of bartering provisions for munitions of war—anything that could be utilized in warfare. Minie balls were particularly desirable. I therefore took Telitha by the apron and had a little talk with her, and when I was through she understood that something was up that would bring relief to certain organs that had become quite troublesome in their demands, and she was anxious to take part in the performance, whatever that might be. I went also to my mother, and imparted to her my plans of operation, and she took that pathetic little backward step peculiar to herself on occasions which tried her soul, and with quivering lip she assented in approving, though almost inaudible words.

With a basket in either hand, and accompanied by Telitha, who carried one that would hold about a peck, and two dull case-knives, I started to the battle-fields around Atlanta to pick up the former missiles of death to exchange for food to keep us from starving.

It was a cold day. The wind was very sharp, and over the ground, denuded of forest trees and undergrowth, the wind was blowing a miniature gale. Our wraps were inadequate, and how chilled we became in that rude November blast! But the colder we were, the faster we walked, and in an incredibly short time we were upon the battle-field searching for lead.

I made it a point to keep very near the road in the direction of Atlanta, and soon found myself on the very spot where the Confederate magazine stood, the blowing up of which, by Confederate orders, shook the very earth, and was distinctly heard thirty-five or forty miles distant. An exclamation of glad surprise from Telitha carried me to her. She had found a bonanza, and was rapidly filling her basket with that which was more valuable to us than gold. In a marshy place, encrusted with ice, innumerable bullets, minie balls, and pieces of lead seemed to have been left by the irony of fate to supply sustenance to hungry ones, and employment to the poor, as all the winter those without money to send to more favored and distant points found sure returns from this lead mine. It was so cold! our feet were almost frozen, and our hands had commenced to bleed, and handling cold, rough lead cramped them so badly that I feared we would have to desist from our work before filling the baskets.

Lead! Blood! Tears! O how suggestive! Lead, blood and tears, mingled and commingled. In vain did I try to dash the tears away. They would assert themselves and fall upon lead stained with blood. "God of mercy, if this be Thy holy will, give me fortitude to bear it uncomplainingly," was the heart-felt invocation that went up to the throne of grace from over lead, blood and tears, that fearful day. For relief, tears did not suffice. I wanted to cry aloud; nature would not be satisfied with less, and I cried like a baby, long and loud. Telitha caught the spirit of grief, and cried too. This ebullition of feelings on her part brought me to a realization of my duty to her, as well as to my poor patient mother to whom the day must seem very long, and I tried to stifle my sobs and lamentations.

At length our baskets were filled, and we took up our line of march to the desolated city. There were no labyrinths to tread, no streets to follow, and an occasional question secured information that enabled us to find the "commissary" without delay. Telitha was very ambitious that I should appear a lady, and wanted me to deposit my load of lead behind some place of concealment, while we went on to deliver hers, and then let her go back for mine. But I was too much a Confederate soldier for that, and walked bravely in with my heavy, precious load.

A courteous gentleman in a faded grey uniform, evidently discharged because of wounds received in battle, approached and asked what he could do for me. "I have heard that you give provisions for lead," I replied, "and I have brought some to exchange." What seemed an interminable silence ensued.

"What would you like in exchange?" he asked.

"If you have sugar, and coffee, and meal, a little of each if you please," I timidly said. "I left nothing to eat at home." The baskets of lead were removed to the rear and weighed, and in due time returned to me filled to the brim with sugar, flour, coffee, meal, lard, and the nicest meat I had seen in a long time.

"O, sir," I said, "I did not expect so much."

Joy had gone out of my life, and I felt no thrill of that kind; but I can never describe the satisfaction I experienced as I lifted two of those baskets, and saw Telitha grasp the other one, and turned my face homeward. . . .

2. A SOLDIER'S WIFE—"THINGS IS WORSE AND WORSE"

This poor woman lived in Nansemond County, Virginia, near the girlhood home of LaSalle Corbell. She was the mother of four small children. Her husband was on duty with General Pickett.

B —— N ——, Dec. 17, 1864

My Dear B ——: Christmus is most hear again, and things is worse and worse. I have got my last kalica frock on, and that's patched. Everything me and children's got is patched. Both of them is in bed now covered up with comforters and old pieces of karpet to keep them warm, while I went 'long out to try and get some wood, for their feet's on the ground and they have got no clothes, neither: and I am not able to cut the wood, and me and the children have broke up all the rails 'roun' the yard and picked up all the chips there is. We haven't got nothing in the house to eat but a little bit o' meal. The last pound of meet you got from Mr. G——is all eat up, and so is the chickens we raised. I don't want you to stop fighten them yankees till you kill the last one of them, but try and get off and come home and fix us all up some and then you can go back and fight them a heep harder than you ever fought them before. We can't none of us hold out much longer down here. One of General Mahone's[1] skouts promise me on his word to carry this letter through the lines to you, but, my dear, if you put off a-comin' 'twon't be no use to come, for we'll all hands of us be out there in the garden in the old graveyard with your ma and mine.[2]

---

[1] The fiery Major-General William Mahone.
[2] After he got her letter the husband of a "Soldier's Wife" went home without a furlough, and on his return to camp was arrested as a deserter and found guilty. He appealed to Mrs. Pickett, who in turn appealed to her husband. The execution was postponed and three days later an order came from Richmond, reprieving all deserters.

3. REBECCAH C. RIDLEY—HOOD IS DEFEATED
AT NASHVILLE

Chancellor Bromfield Lewis Ridley of Fair Mont plantation near Murfreesboro, Tennessee, and his wife Rebeccah had a daughter Bettie who kept a war journal. When Bettie died from "congestion of the lungs" in November 1864, Mrs. Ridley carried it on. She names in this entry the five sons whom she gave to the Confederate cause. Bromfield, the youngest, was a lieutenant on the staff of General A. P. Stewart at the age of nineteen and after the war wrote Battles and Sketches of the Army of Tennessee. *Mrs. Ridley had witnessed the Battle of Stone's River at New Year's 1863. Her husband had to leave home, taking the young daughter Sallie with him. Fair Mont was burned in February and Mrs. Ridley moved into the only building spared, the old kitchen.*

Jefferson, Tennessee
December, 18, 1864

After my Dear Bettie's death Lavinia C. came over to stay with me. O how lonely and desolate I felt, husband far away in North Carolina, Sallie in Georgia, my 5 sons all in the Army, exposed to mortal peril, by bullit, and I desolate, my houses burned, and nearly all my household treasures in ashes—my negroes refractory and insolent and not supporting themselves—what little they make I have to divide with them, and the Yankees get the balance. The negroes are so utterly worthless they will not put up fences and burn the rails to keep from cutting wood. I employed Mr. Brown to live with me another year.

Lavinia and I have employed our time in sewing, knitting and reading until December 1, when the booming of cannon toward Columbia told us hostilities had commenced and Hood's Army was advancing on Nashville. A series of battles took place all along—on Friday a terrible battle was fought at Franklin. Hood took the place but lost 13 Generals 6 killed 7 wounded. The Southerners pressed the Yankees back to Nashville and Murfreesboro. I heard Brom was on the way and went to meet him and how rejoiced I was to see him after 2 years absence—grown to be a large fine looking man. He came home with me, but was running about so I saw but little. We went up to the hill—Brom with us—in a short time a company of

Yanks who had escaped from the stockade passed by retreating rapidly to Murfreesboro. We had a big scare fearing they would come by and catch Brom, but they were running for life. He rode after them with 3 others—took a shot at them. He stayed until 8th when he returned to his command. We have had a severe sleet for 3 days. The ground has been covered with snow and ice—freezing our poor unprotected soldiers—some of them I understand are barefooted, none have tents— or a sufficiency of blankets and all have to depend on the country for subsistance—poor fellows, how my heart bleeds for them. They come in at the houses to warm, and get something to eat, and some of our citizens who pretend to be very Southern grudge them the food they eat—say they will be eat out. In these terrible conditions Hood attacked Nashville on Wednesday 14th.[1] The noise of cannon was terrific all day—we all felt as if our fate was at stake. . . . At night all was still, about 1 o'clock someone woke me, it was Brom! My Heart died within me. I asked hastily what is the matter? He said "I came for my clothes and servant. The waggons are ordered to Franklin. I rode all night and went into Battle, it raged all day, we were driven back, lost 20 pieces of cannon. I have eat nothing."

I got him something to eat, he looked so sad, had traversed the road between our house and camp 60 miles in all, and galloped all day in the Battle Field carrying dispatches, got off his horse to deliver a message to Gen. Seares,[2] when a cannon ball passed between them, taking a pice out of Gen. S. leg, and the concussion knocked Brom down, without injury, tho thank God. He got leave to ride home that night—30 miles for his clothes and servant—threw himself on the bed—took 2 hours sleep, the first he had in 36—rode 4 miles in the morning, bought a horse and returned by 9 o'clock, and went off with his servant behind him. He looked so sad at parting—said "farewell, Mama, I hope I will see you again." I was satisfied Hood was defeated—but they fought all day Thursday—the soldiers and waggons passed rapidly by—such gloom and sorrow in every heart. Nature seems to mourn with us—it has been dark, and lowering and drizzling for 2 days—not a ray of sunshine, and but little hope in our hearts. The Yankees we hear are visiting their wrath on the defenseless citizens, taking off their food, bed clothes,

[1] The battle began at six in the morning of the fifteenth, the Federals attacking, and lasted through the sixteenth.
[2] Brigadier-General C. W. Sears.

breaking their table ware. We have looked for them all day, but suppose they are all after Hood's Army, and I fear awfully they will overtake and destroy a good many at the river before they cross. Only one of my sons poor Brom is with Hood's Army. George, I hear is sick at Withville [Wytheville], Va. Luke in Macon, Ga. Jerome in Newnan, Ga. Charlie in N.C. with his papa. Farewell to my hope of seeing husband and daughter. . . .

4. MARY ELLEN ARNOLD—RUNNING THE BLOCKADE

Mary Ellen Lyman of Massachusetts married Amory Appleton of the same state. They had one son, George Lyman Appleton—the George of her diary. After Amory Appleton's death in the early 1850s she married Charles S. Arnold of Savannah. He died in 1856.

George while serving in the Confederate Army was taken seriously ill with measles and incapacitated for further duty. When Sherman laid siege to Savannah early in December 1864 Mrs. Appleton and George escaped to Wilmington, North Carolina. They got passage on the blockade-running steamer Hansa *bound for the Bahamas. From Nassau they went on to St. Thomas in the Virgin Islands and from there got a ship to Europe, where they remained till November 1869.*

Mrs. Appleton's journal is barely legible. It is written in short, clipped notations, evidencing the excitement she was under. A sense of danger emerges dramatically from the pages of the dilapidated little book.

St. Thomas—West Indies
Feb. 16th 1865

Left Wilmington, N. Carolina, Thursday, Dec. 31—at noon— pouring rain—on the Hansa—blockade running steamer anchored at mouth of Cape Fear River, until Sunday evening Jan. 3, 1865. Everything being ready lights put out etc. start at midnight, papers, money & valuables in small packages, ready to be saved or destroyed should the blockading vessels overtake us or drive us ashore—pass safely through however, the small steamer heavily laden with cotton in the hands of a daring crew—resolved to lose all rather than be caught—goes on safely till Wednesday morning at daylight when a sail is discovered. A Yankee cruiser the Vanderbilt sees us, & starts in pursuit. All steam is crowded on, over the safety valve, a heavy weight placed, and on we rushed. Shot after shot is fired at us but we keep our distance—the coral reefs appear in sight under the green water. Our Bahama pilot sits like a statue on the wheel house—first raising one hand, then the other to guide the helmsman at the wheel. Bale after bale of cotton, worth nearly its weight in gold is thrown into the sea to lighten us, accompanied by the sighs of the men at such a sacrifice—about 80 bales are over. The water becomes too shallow for our pursuers and we are safe. The 20th shot is fired and falls harmless behind us. The crew of the Hansa give cheer after cheer and dip their flag, Confederate, three times to the discomfited foe.

Our names had been written down before leaving the Cape Fear River, in the order in which we were to have taken to the boats in case of need. Mine was in the Starboard Life boat with George and 22 others, under the charge of Cannop—1st mate, a man calm resolved, kind and gentlemanly. Captain Atkinson, English; first mate Cannop, English; 2nd mate McLeod, Scotch. Crew and passengers in all nearly one hundred souls and I the only woman on board. 3 mate Dickson—Doveton, Chief Engineer, and Wells, Bahama pilot. At 11 o'clock A.M. on Wed. Jan. 6th 1865, reach Nassau, New Providence.

5. MRS. WILLIAM LAMB—FORT FISHER
IS BOMBARDED

Wilmington, North Carolina, was the last open port of the Confederacy. On a sandy peninsula guarding the Cape Fear River, entrance to the port, was Fort Fisher. On December 20, 1864, appeared Admiral David Porter's fleet and land forces led by Ben Butler and Godfrey Weitzel. At midnight on the twenty-third an old gunboat stocked with powder was exploded near the fort. General Butler pinned great faith to this contraption but it was a complete fizzle. Christmas morning, while sixty Union vessels threw their shells, troops were landed for attack. But the Federals heard that Confederate reinforcements were expected from Wilmington. Butler got scared and withdrew that afternoon. He was relieved, as big a fiasco as his "powder ship," and bustled off to Massachusetts.

Commandant of the fort was handsome, gallant, thirty-year-old

Colonel William Lamb. A Norfolk boy, he had married a Providence, Rhode Island, girl. He enlisted as a captain in a Virginia regiment and rose to the rank of colonel. Mrs. Lamb was living in Norfolk with her father-in-law, the mayor of the city, when it was occupied by the Federals in May 1862. About the same time her third child was born and soon after they joined the colonel at Fort Fisher. The little boy Willie was sent to Providence to be with the grandparents. For a while Mrs. Lamb lived in the upper room of a pilot's house near the fort and then in a cottage built by garrison soldiers. It was to this cottage that the body of Rose Greenhow was brought when it was washed ashore, and it was Mrs. Lamb who dried Rose's clothes before a pine-knot fire.

Confederate Point, North Carolina
"The Cottage," January 9th, 1865

My Own Dear Parents:

I know you have been anxious enough about us all, knowing what a terrible bombardment we have had, but I am glad that I can relieve your mind on our behalf and tell you we are all safe and well, through a most merciful and kind providence. God was with us from the first, and our trust was so firm in him that I can truly say that both Will and I "feared no evil."

I stayed in my comfortable little home until the fleet appeared, when I packed up and went across the river to a large but empty house, of which I took possession; a terrible gale came on which delayed the attack for several days, but Saturday it came at last in all its fury; I could see it plainly from where I was, I had very powerful glasses, and sat on a stile out doors all day watching it— an awful but magnificent sight. . . .

The shelling was even more terriffic on Sunday, and I, not knowing how long it might continue concluded to go to Fayetteville, and started Sunday noon in a small steamer, with the sick and wounded, to Wilmington, where I was obliged to stay for several days in great suspense, not able to get away and not able to hear directly from Will, as the enemy had cut the wires—and then a martyr to all kinds of rumors—one day heard that Will had lost a leg, &c., &c., but I steadfastly made up my mind to give no credit to anything bad. At last, I heard again, that we had driven our persecutors off, and I returned again to the place I went first, and the next day Will came over for me and took me to the fort, which I rode all over on horseback, but we did not move over for nearly a week. The fort was strewn with missiles of all kinds, it seemed a perfect miracle how any escaped, the immense works were literally skinned of their turf, but not injured in the slightest; not a bomb-proof or a magazine—*and there are more then one*—touched; the magazine the enemy thought they had destroyed was only a caisson; the men had very comfortable quarters in the fort—pretty little whitewashed houses—but the shells soon set fire to them, making a large fire and dense smoke, but the works are good for dozens of sieges—plenty of everything; particularly plenty of the greatest essential—*brave hearts*. Our beloved General Whiting was present, but gave up the whole command to Will, to whom he now gives, as is due, the whole credit of building and defending his post, and has urged his promotion to brigadier-general, which will doubtless be received soon, though neither of us really care for it.

We expect the Armada again, and will give him a *warmer* reception next time. The fort, expecting a longer time of it, was reserving their heaviest fire for nearer quarters. Butler's "gallant troops" came right under one side of the fort, but our grape and canister soon drove them off, and *not* Porter's shell, which did not happen to be falling that time; they left their traces sufficiently next morning.

The "gallant fellow" who stole the horse from inside the fort, was doubtless so scared he didn't know much *where* he was. The *true* statement of the thing is, that an officer, unauthorized by Will or the general, sent a courier outside the fort with a message to some troops outside, and soon after he left the fort, was attacked and killed by a Yankee sharpshooter hidden under a bridge. The poor body fell and the *horse* was taken, and the flag spoken of, in the same way, was shot from the parapet and blew outside, when it was taken. When any of them see the *inside* of the fort they'll never live to tell the tale.

Ah, mother! you all, at home peacefully, do not know the misery of being driven from home by a miserable, cruel enemy! 'Tis a sad sight to see the sick and aged turned out in the cold to seek a shelter. I cannot speak feelingly because of any experience myself, as God is so good to us, and has so favored us with life, health and means, and my dear, good husband has provided me a comfortable home in the interior, where I can be safe.

Will has worried so much about you, dear mother, thinking you would be so anxious about us. He often exclaims, when reading some of the lying accounts: "How that will worry Ma!"

How is my darling Willie? We do so want to see our boy. I think Will will have to send for him in the spring. Kiss the dear one dozen of times for his father and mother.

Though it was a very unpleasant Christmas to me, still the little ones enjoyed theirs. Will had imported a crowd of toys for them and they are as happy as possible with them.

I have not heard from my dear home since last August, and you can imagine how very anxious I am to hear, particularly of dear sister Ria. Is she with George? Do write me of all the dear ones I love so much. How I would love to see you all, so much, and home!

I forgot to tell you of the casualties in the fight. Ours were only three killed; about sixty wounded; they were all.[1]

6. JUDITH BROCKENBROUGH McGUIRE—
"I THOUGHT OF THE GAYETY OF PARIS"

Mrs. McGuire had hoped to make Christmas cheerful for her small family in Richmond. She had even aspired to a turkey, but turkeys were priced from $50 to $100 and so were out of the question. Her son John was in a Northern prison, and her daughters were refugees some distance from Richmond. For many months her diary had been written on brown wrapping paper; now even scraps of that were hard to find.

Richmond, Virginia

January 8th, 1865.—Some persons in this beleaguered city seem crazed on the subject of gayety. In the midst of the wounded and dying, the low state of the commissariat, the anxiety of the whole country, the troubles of every kind by which we are surrounded, I am mortified to say that there are gay parties given in the city. There are those denominated "starvation parties," where young persons meet for innocent enjoyment, and retire at a reasonable hour;

[1] The Federals renewed the attack on Fort Fisher on January 15, 1865, and this time meant business. After contesting every redoubt, the noble little band of defenders fell before the heavy bombardment of a great fleet and the assault of a large land force. Colonel Lamb, wounded in the left hip, was captured. Through the efforts of General Bragg, Mrs. Lamb was able to follow him to his Northern prison.

but there are others where the most elegant suppers are served—cakes, jellies, ices in profusion, and meats of the finest kinds in abundance, such as might furnish a meal for a regiment of General Lee's army. I wish these things were not so, and that every extra pound of meat could be sent to the army. When returning from the hospital, after witnessing the dying scene of a brother, whose young sister hung over him in agony, with my heart full of the sorrows of hospital-life, I passed a house where there were music and dancing. The revulsion of feeling was sickening. I thought of the gayety of Paris during the French Revolution, of the "cholera ball" in Paris, the ball at Brussels the night before the battle of Waterloo, and felt shocked that our own Virginians, at such a time, should remind me of scenes which we were wont to think only belonged to the lightness of foreign society. The weddings, of which there are many, seem to be conducted with great quietness. There seems to be a perfect mania on the subject of matrimony. Some of the churches may be seen open and lighted almost every night for bridals, and wherever I turn I hear of marriages in prospect.

January 16th.—Fort Fisher has fallen; Wilmington will of course follow.[1] This was our last port into which blockade-runners were successful in entering, and which furnished us with immense amount of stores. What will be the effect of this disaster we know not; we can only hope and pray.

January 21st.—We hear nothing cheering except in the proceedings of Congress and the Virginia Legislature, particularly the latter. Both bodies look to stern resistance to Federal authority. The city and country are full of rumours and evil surmising; and while we do not believe one word of the croaking, it makes us feel restless and unhappy.

7. MALVINA BLACK GIST—THE TREASURY NOTE DEPARTMENT LEAVES COLUMBIA

John Black of Newberry, South Carolina, had a daughter Malvina, born on November 12, 1842, and brought her as a child to live in Columbia. When she grew up she married the son of Governor William H. Gist, Major William Moreno Gist, who within a few

---

[1] Wilmington fell on the twenty-second.

*months was killed in a skirmish the day before the Battle of Chicka-
mauga and buried in an unknown grave. Then the sprightly, intelligent Malvina took a job in the Treasury Note Department. Bills
bearing the signature "M. Gist" are still extant. Her brother, a scout,
was a prisoner in the North.*

*She began a diary five days after Sherman left Savannah on his
march through South Carolina and continued it through May 5, 1865.*

Columbia, S.C., February 6, 1865.—This wild talk about the
Federal Army and what it's going to do is all nonsense. Coming here!
Sherman! Why not say he's going to Paramaribo? One is about as
likely as the other, notwithstanding that papa shakes his head so
solemnly over it, and mamma looks so grave. He is always shaking
his head over something, it seems to me, and she forever looking
grave. I do hope I shall be able to get around being old, somehow.
Old people's weather is all bad weather; their horoscope all background; their expectation all disappointment; their probabilities all
failures. No doubt I am foolish—mamma says I am—but there's
a certain satisfaction in being young and foolish rather than old and
wise.

February 7.—While I cannot sign the bills as rapidly as Nannie
Giles can, today I finished up four packages of the denomination of
fifty dollars. Mr. Tellifiere says I am a treasury girl worth having,
and that I did a big day's work, and a good day's work. Took my
vocal lesson and paid Signor Torriani for my last quarter. He is
gloriously handsome in the Italian way, which is a very striking way.
I also sent check to the milliner for the $200 due on my new bonnet,
and paid $80 for the old lilac barege bought from Mary L——. Miss
P—— does not yet agree to let me have the congress gaiters for $75,
and unless she does she may keep them herself, to the end of time!
'Tis a pretty come to pass when $75 of Confederate currency is not
the equivalent of an ordinary pair of Massachusetts made shoes!
J. C. called this evening. He is pleasant, but stops right there, and
that isn't the place to stop. A man must know how to be disagreeable
to be dangerously attractive, I think.

February 8.—Saw that young Englishman again today. He isn't
half the idle dreamer he pretends to be. In truth (but let me whisper
it softly), *I believe he's a spy!* I can't see, otherwise, why he is so

tremendously and eagerly interested in matters Confederate. Nor is he smart enough to make me believe it's *me!* . . .

February 10.—This being German day, I went as usual for my lesson. If I must say it, old Frau's dressing is all top-dressing, and her conversation never more than a mild diversion. Its absorbing theme today was the same as with every one else—Sherman's movements; is he coming here? And what will he do when he does? These are the questions which embody the vague forebodings, the monstrous prophecies that fill the air. I marvel at the ease with which some people lose their heads. You would think Sherman was a three-tailed bashaw, to hear some of them talk.

February 11.—The dawning of a doubt is a troublesome thing, for if a doubt does not out and out destroy faith, it assuredly chastens it to an uncomfortable degree. Is he coming, that terrible Sherman, with all his legions? Well, and if he does, Beauregard is coming too, and Hampton[1] and Butler[2] are already here, so where's the sense of getting worried? I shall continue to possess my soul in peace.

February 12.—The situation becomes more alarming—that much I am fain to confess. My father's head is not the only one shaking now; they are all shaking—all the men's heads in town. No one can tell what a day will bring forth. Steady, now, nerves! Courage now, heart! My grandsires fought for liberty in the war of the Revolution; my great-grandmother faced the British, nor quailed so much as an eyelash before them! Is it for me to be afraid? I am not afraid.

February 13.—We were greatly startled yesterday by the firing of cannon in the upper part of the city. It proved to be a call for Colonel Thomas' Regiment of Reserves. I am sorry the weather is so cold. Our ill-clothed, ill-fed troops must suffer acutely in such bitter weather. Today I accompanied my mother to the Wayside Hospital, carrying some jelly and wafers for the sick. One of the inmates, a convalescent soldier, played with much taste and skill on the banjo. Came home to find my father much excited about me, having heard Mayor Goodwyn[3] say that he has no hope at all of holding the city.

[1] On January 6, 1865, while on leave of absence, General Hampton, commander of the Cavalry Corps, Army of Northern Virginia, was assigned to the command of all the cavalry in the operations against Sherman.

[2] Major-General M. Calbraith Butler, C. S. A.

[3] Colonel F. J. Goodwyn.

And my father does not consider the track of a great army the safest place for young women; hence he wants me to leave; go; get out of the way! But where? Where shall I fly from Sherman's army?

Tuesday, February 14.—Such a day! It was like "a winnowing of chaos." Very little work was done at the Treasury Department in the midst of such excitement and confusion. We are to remove at once to Richmond, and I am told Colonel Joseph Daniel Pope, Mr. Jamison, and many of the employees of the printing establishment, have already departed. I do not know if this be true; I hear too many contradictory reports for all of them to be true. One thing, however, appears to be quite true—*Sherman is coming!* And I never believed it before. This afternoon, we could distinctly hear firing in the distance, and at this writing (8:30 P.M.) we can see the sky arched with fire in the direction of the Saluda factory. Must I go with the department to Richmond? In such case, my parents will be entirely alone, Johnny having gone, also, to the front. Does this not clearly show the dire extremity to which we are reduced, when boys of sixteen shoulder the musket? There are other reasons why I should like to remain here to receive Sherman: it is high time I was having some experiences out of the ordinary, and if anything remarkable is going to happen, I want to know something about it; it might be worth relating to my grandchildren! Anyhow, it is frightfully monotonous, just because you are a woman, to be always tucked away in the safe places. I want to stay. I want to have a taste of danger. *Midnight.*—But I am overruled; I must go. My father says so; my mother says so. Everything is in readiness—my trunks packed, my traveling clothes laid out upon the chair, and now I must try to catch a little sleep. And then on the morrow—what? What will be the next stroke upon the *Labensuhr?* God only knows.

February 15.—(Waiting at the depot). Going as usual to the department this morning, I found orders had been issued for our immediate removal to Richmond. Barely had I time to run home, dash a few articles into my trunk, say good-bye, and join the others here. We girls are all together—Elise, Ernestine, Sadie, Bet, and myself. We have been seated in the train for hours and hours. Oh! this long waiting; it is weary work! A reign of terror prevails in the city, and the scene about me will ever live in memory. Government employees are hastening to and fro, military stores are being packed, troops in

motion, aids-de-camp flying hither and thither, and anxious fugitives
crowding about the train, begging for transportation. All kinds of
rumors are afloat, every newcomer bringing a new version. The latest
is that Hardee[1] has refused to evacuate Charleston, and will not
combine forces with Hampton in order to save the capital. I am
strangely laden; I feel weighted down. Six gold watches are secreted
about my person, and more miscellaneous articles of jewelry than
would fill a small jewelry shop—pins, rings, bracelets, etc. One of
my trunks is packed with valuables and another with provisions.
Shelling has begun from the Lexington heights, and under such conditions this waiting at the depot has a degree of nervousness mixed
with impatience. We catch, now and again, peculiar whizzing sounds
—shells, they say. Sherman has come; he is knocking at the gate.
Oh, God! turn him back! Fight on our side, and turn Sherman back!

8. EMMA FLORENCE LeCONTE—"POOR OLD COLUMBIA!"

*Young Emma LeConte was the daughter of the distinguished
scientist Joseph LeConte, friend and pupil of Agassiz of Harvard.
He lived at Midway, Georgia, and then at Athens, where he was
professor of geology and natural history in the state university. In
1856 he was called to the faculty of the South Carolina state university at Columbia. When the university was turned into a hospital
in June 1862 Emma remained on the campus with her mother and
sister Sallie, while her father carried out one of the notable powder-
making enterprises attempted by the Confederacy. She was sixteen
when Sherman came. Her journal runs from December 1864 to
August 1865.*

Columbia, South Carolina
February 14, 1865. What a panic the whole town is in! I have not
been out of the house myself, but Father says the intensest excitement prevails on the street. The Yankees are reported a few miles

[1] General Hardee, in command of the department of South Carolina, Florida and
Georgia, had escaped from Sherman at Savannah and moved north. Beauregard
arriving to take charge, Wade Hampton urged on him the importance of evacuating
Charleston and transferring the garrison of 16,000 men to a stand before Columbia.
Instead, when the city was abandoned on the seventeenth the garrison was sent on
a long march to North Carolina. The last troops to leave were those from Fort
Sumter.

off on the other side of the river. How strong no one seems to know. It is decided if this be true that we will remain quietly here, father alone leaving. It is thought Columbia can hardly be taken by raid as we have the whole of Butler's cavalry here—and if they do we have to take the consequences. It is true some think Sherman will burn the town, but we can hardly believe that. Besides these buildings, though they are State property, yet the fact that they are used as a hospital will, it is thought, protect them. I have been busily making large pockets to wear under my hoopskirt—they will hardly search our persons. Still everything of any value is to be packed up to go with father. I do not feel half so frightened as I thought I would. Perhaps because I cannot realize they are coming. I hope still this is a false report. Maggie Adams and her husband have promised to stay here during father's absence. She is a Yankee and may be some protection and help. . . . I look forward with terror, and yet with a kind of callousness to their approach. . . .

February 15. Oh, how is it possible to write amid this excitement and confusion! We are too far off to hear and see much down here in the Campus, but they tell me the streets in town are lined with panic-stricken crowds, trying to escape. All is confusion and turmoil. The Government is rapidly moving off stores—all day the trains have been running, whistles blowing and wagons rattling through the streets. All day we have been listening to the booming of cannon— receiving conflicting reports of the fighting. All day wagons and ambulances have been bringing in the wounded over the muddy streets and through the drizzling rain, with the dark clouds overhead. All day in our own household has confusion reigned too. The back parlor strewed with clothing etc., open trunks standing about, while a general feeling of misery and tension pervaded the atmosphere. Everything is to go that can be sent—house linen, blankets, clothing, silver, jewelry—even the wine—everything movable of any value. Hospital flags have been erected at the different gates of the Campus —we hope the fact of our living within the walls may be of some protection to us, but I fear not. I feel sure these buildings will be destroyed. I wish mother could have sent more furniture to different friends in town, but it is too late now. . . . I have destroyed most of my papers, but have a lot of letters still that I do not wish to burn, and yet I do not care to have them share the fate of Aunt Jane's and Cousin Ada's in Liberty Co., which were read and scattered along the roads. I will try to hide them. One of my bags is filled. The other I will pack tonight. Henry will stay with us, and vows he will stand by us through thick and thin—I believe he means it, but do not know how he will hold on. It is so cold and we have no wood. The country people will not venture in town lest their horses should be impressed. So we sit shivering and trying to coax a handful of wet pine to burn. Yonder come more wounded—poor fellows—indeed I can write no more.

Night. Nearer and nearer, clearer and more distinctly sound the cannon—Oh, it is heart-sickening to listen to it! . . . Just now as I stood on the piazza listening, the reports sounded so frightfully loud and near that I could not help shuddering at each one. And yet there is something exciting—sublime—in a cannonade. But the horrible uncertainty of what is before us! My great fear now is for father—Oh, if he were only gone—were only safe!

The alarm bell is ringing. Just now when I first heard it clang out my heart gave a leap, and I thought at once, "It's the Yankees!" So nervous have I grown that the slightest unusual sound startles me. Of course I knew it was a fire, yet it was with a beating heart I threw open the window to see the western horizon lit up with the glow of flames. Although we are composed, our souls are sick with anxiety. . . .

Later—They have passed our first line of breastworks. No firing tonight. Father and Uncle John leave tonight or tomorrow morning.

February 16. How can the terror and excitement of today be described! I feel a little quieter now and seize the opportunity to write a few lines. Last night, or rather early this morning, father left. After the last lines in my entry last evening, I went downstairs and found in the back parlor with father a man calling himself Davis. I had heard father speak of him before. He met him in Georgia while making his way back home with Sallie, and he was kind to them during that difficult journey. He calls himself a Confederate spy or scout and is an oddity. I only half trust him—he evidently is not what he pretends to be. He says he is a Kentuckian and is both coarse and uneducated, but wonderfully keen and penetrating. . . . He has taken an unaccountable fancy to father—as shown by his hunting him up—and he assures him again and again that he will have us protected during the presence of the Yankees here. He claims great influence with the Yankee officers and entire knowledge of the enemy's movements. All the evening he seemed exceedingly uneasy that Father should so long have deferred his departure and very impatient to get him off. He offered to lend him a horse if that would facilitate his leaving. Father is not uneasy, for our authorities assure him that all is right, but I do not like this man's evident anxiety. Can he know more than the Generals? About half-past twelve father took leave of us. Thus to part! Father starting on an uncertain journey—not knowing whether he may not be captured in his flight, and leaving us to the mercy of the inhuman beastly Yankees—I think it was the saddest moment of my life. Of course father feels very anxious about us, and the last words the man Davis said to him were to assure him that he might feel easy about us. I wonder if there is any confidence to be put in what he says! Hardly, I suppose. We said goodbye with heavy hearts and with many presentiments of evil.

After father was gone I sat up still, talking with Davis. I could not sleep, and besides I wanted to hear that father was safely off. We asked our guest how he thought Columbia would be treated—he said he would not tell us—it would alarm us too much. Does he really know all he pretends, or is he only guessing? It was three o'clock before I lay down and fell into a disturbing doze which lasted until seven. Davis stayed and slept on the ground floor, but was gone before we awoke.

The breakfast hour passed in comparative calm. About nine o'clock we were sitting in the dining room, having just returned from the piazza where we had been watching a brigade of cavalry passing to the front. "Wouldn't it be dreadful if they should shell the city?" someone said. "They would not do that," replied mother, "for they have not demanded its surrender." Scarcely had the words passed her lips when Jane, the nurse, rushed in crying out that they were shelling. We ran to the front door just in time to hear a shell go whirring past. It fell and exploded not far off. This was so unexpected. I do not know why, but in all my list of anticipated horrors I somehow had not thought of a bombardment. I leaned against the door, fairly shivering, partly with cold, but chiefly from nervous excitement. After listening to them awhile this wore off and I became accustomed to the shells. They were shelling the town from the Lexington heights across the river, and from the campus their troops could be seen drawn up on the hill-tops. Up the street this morning the Government stores were thrown open to the people and there was a general scramble. Our negroes were up there until frightened home by the shells. The shelling was discontinued for an hour or two and then renewed with so much fury that we unanimously resolved to adjourn to the basement and abandon the upper rooms. Sallie and I went up to our rooms to bring down our things. I was standing at my bureau with my arms full when I heard a loud report. The shell whistled right over my head and exploded. I stood breathless, really expecting to see it fall in the room. When it had passed I went into the hall and met Sallie, coming from her room, pale and trembling. "Oh Emma" she said, "this is dreadful!"

We went downstairs—mother stood in the hall looking very much frightened. "Did you hear——" "Yes indeed"—and at that instant another whistled close overhead. This was rather unpleasant and we retreated to the basement without further delay, where we sat listening as they fell now nearer, and now farther off. Sallie suffered most —she would not be left alone, and would not allow me to go to the outer door to look about, but would call me back in terror. The firing ceased about dinner time. . . .

During the afternoon a rapid cannonade was kept up and I do not think the forces could have been more than half a mile from here. Dr. Thomson says they are only skirmishing. Davis says we have received re-inforcements, but he thinks we cannot hold the town as we have given up the strongest position. He was here this morning during the shelling and stood talking to me in the dining room for some time, giving me a picture of the confusion in town. Our soldiers had opened and plundered some of the stores. He brought me a present of a box of fancy feathers and one or two other little things he had picked up. He says the bridge will be burned and the town evacuated tonight.

10 o'clock P.M.—They are in bed sleeping, or trying to sleep. I don't think I shall attempt it. Davis was here just now to tell the news—it is kind of him to come so often to keep us posted. I went up to see him—made Henry light the gas and sat talking to him in the hall, while through the open door came the shouts of the soldiery drawn up along the streets ready to march out. Perhaps the Yankees may be in tonight—yet I do not feel as frightened as I thought I would. . . . We have moved into the back basement room. I opened the door which gives from our present sleeping room on the back yard just now, and the atmosphere was stifling with gun-powder smoke. Henry had to cut down a tree in the yard today for fuel. . . .

February 17. . . . At about 6 o'clock while it was still quite dark and all in the room were buried in profound slumber, we were suddenly awakened by a terrific explosion. The house shook—broken windowpanes clattered down, and we all sat up in bed, for a few seconds mute with terror. . . . We lit the candle, and mother sent Jane to inquire of Henry the cause. Of course he did not know. I went out of doors. The day was beginning to break murkily and the air was still heavy with smoke. All continuing quiet we concluded that the authorities had blown up some stores before evacuating. . . . After breakfast the cannon opened again and so near that every report shook the house. I think it must have been a cannonade to cover our retreat. It did not continue very long. The negroes all went uptown to see what they could get in the general pillage, for all the shops had been opened and provisions were scattered in all directions. Henry says that in some parts of Main Street corn and flour and sugar cover the ground. An hour or two ago they came running back declaring the Yankees were in town and that our troops were fighting them in the streets. This was not true, for at that time every soldier nearly had left town, but we did not know it then. . . . Mother is downright sick. She had been quite collected and calm until this news, but now she suddenly lost all self-control and exhibited the most lively terror—indeed I thought she would grow hysterical. . . . By-and-by the firing ceased and all was quiet again. It was denied that the Yankees had yet crossed the river or even completed their pontoon bridge, and most of the servants returned up town. They have brought back a considerable quantity of provisions—the negroes are very kind and faithful—they have supplied us with meat and Jane brought mother some rice and crushed sugar for Carrie, knowing that she had none. How times change! Those whom we have so long fed and cared for now help us. . . . A gentleman told us just now that the mayor had gone forward to surrender the town.

One o'clock P.M.—Well, they are here. I was sitting in the back parlor when I heard the shouting of the troops. I was at the front door in a moment. Jane came running and crying, "O Miss Emma, they've come at last!" She said they were marching down Main Street, before them flying a panic-stricken crowd of women and children who seemed crazy.

I ran upstairs to my bedroom windows just in time to see the U.S.

flag run up over the State House. O what a horrid sight! What a degradation! After four long bitter years of bloodshed and hatred, now to float there at last! That hateful symbol of despotism! I do not think I could possibly describe my feelings. I know I could not look at it. I left the window and went downstairs to mother. In a little while a guard arrived to protect the hospital. They have already fixed a shelter of boards against the wall near the gate—sentinels are stationed and they are cooking their dinner. The wind is very high today and blows their hats around. This is the first sight we have had of these fiends except as prisoners. The sight does not stir up very pleasant feelings in our hearts. We cannot look at them with anything but horror and hatred—loathing and disgust. The troops now in town is a brigade commanded by Col. Stone.[1] Everything is quiet and orderly. Guards have been placed to protect houses, and Sherman has promised not to disturb private property. . . .

Later—Gen. Sherman has *assured* the Mayor, "that he and all the citizens may sleep as securely and quietly tonight as if under Confederate rule. Private property shall be carefully respected. Some public buildings have to be destroyed, but he will wait until tomorrow when the wind shall have entirely subsided." . . .

February 18. What a night of horror, misery and agony! It even makes one sick to think of writing down such scenes. Until dinner-time we saw little of the Yankees, except the guard about the campus, and the officers and men galloping up and down the street. . . . We could hear their shouts as they surged down Main Street and through the State House, but were too far off to see much of the tumult. . . . I hear they found a picture of President Davis in the Capitol which was set up as a target and shot at amid the jeers of the soldiery. From three o'clock till seven their army was passing down the street by the Campus, to encamp back of us in the woods. Two Corps entered the town—Howard's and Logan's[2]—one, the diabolical 15th which Sherman has hitherto never permitted to enter a city on account of their vile and desperate character. Slocum's Corps remained over the river, and I suppose Davis' also. The devils as they marched past looked strong and well clad in dark, dirty-looking blue. The wagon trains were immense. Night drew on. Of course we did not expect to sleep, but we looked forward to a toler-

---

[1] Colonel George A. Stone, with men from Iowa.
[2] Major-General O. O. Howard and Major-General John A. Logan.

ably tranquil night. . . . At about seven o'clock I was standing on the back piazza in the third story. Before me the whole southern horizon was lit up by camp-fires which dotted the woods. On one side the sky was illuminated by the burning of Gen. Hampton's residence a few miles off in the country, on the other side by some blazing buildings near the river. Sumter Street was brightly lighted by a burning house so near our piazza that we could feel the heat. By the red glare we could watch the wretches walking—generally staggering —back and forth from the camp to the town—shouting—hurrahing —cursing South Carolina—swearing—blaspheming—singing ribald songs and using such obscene language that we were forced to go indoors. The fire on Main Street was now raging, and we anxiously watched its progress from the upper front windows. In a little while, however, the flames broke forth in every direction. . . . Guards were rarely of any assistance—most generally they assisted in the pillaging and the firing. The wretched people rushing from their burning homes were not allowed to keep even the few necessaries they gathered up in their flight—even blankets and food were taken ·from them and destroyed. The firemen attempted to use their engines, but the hose was cut to pieces and their lives threatened.

The wind blew a fearful gale, wafting the flames from house to house with frightful rapidity. By midnight the whole town (except the outskirts) was wrapped in one huge blaze. Still the flames had not approached sufficiently near us to threaten our immediate safety, and for some reason not a single Yankee soldier had entered our house. . . . Henry said the danger was over, sick of the dreadful scene, worn out with fatigue and excitement, we went downstairs to our room and tried to rest. I fell into a heavy kind of stupor from which I was presently roused by the bustle about me. Our neighbor Mrs. Caldwell and her two sisters stood before the fire wrapped in blankets and weeping. Their house was on fire, and the great sea of flame had again swept down our way to the very Campus walls. . . . Jane came in to say that Aunt Josie's house was in flames— then we all went to the front door—My God! what a scene! It was about four o'clock and the State House was one grand conflagration.

Imagine night turning into noonday, only with a blazing, scorching glare that was horrible—a copper colored sky across which swept columns of black rolling smoke glittering with sparks and flying embers, while all around us were falling thickly showers of burning flakes. Everywhere the palpitating blaze walling the streets with solid masses of flames as far as the eye could reach—filling the air with its terrible roar. On every side the crackling and devouring fire, while every instant came the crashing of timbers and the thunder of falling buildings. A quivering molten ocean seemed to fill the air and sky. The Library building opposite us seemed framed by the gushing flames and smoke, while through the windows gleamed the liquid fire.

The College buildings caught. . . . All the physicians and nurses were on the roof trying to save the buildings, and the poor wounded inmates left to themselves, such as could crawled out while those who could not move waited to be burned to death. The Common opposite the gate was crowded with homeless women and children, a few wrapped in blankets and many shivering in the night air. Such a scene as this with the drunken fiendish soldiery in their dark uniforms, infuriated, cursing, screaming, exulting in their work, came nearer the material ideal of hell than anything I ever expect to see again. . . .

The State House of course is burned, and they talk of blowing up the new uncompleted granite one. . . . We dread tonight. O, the sorrow and misery of this unhappy town! From what I can hear their chief aim, while taunting helpless women, has been to "Humble their pride—Southern pride." "Where now," they would say, "is all your pride—see what we have brought you to. This is what you get for setting yourselves up as better than other folks." . . .

Sunday, February 19. The day has passed quietly as regards the Yankees. . . . I rose, took off my clothes for the first time in three days, and after bathing and putting on clean clothes felt like another being. This morning fresh trouble awaited us. We thought the negroes were going to leave us. While we were on the back piazza Mary Ann came to us weeping and saying she feared the Yankees were going to force Henry to go off with them, and of course she would have to go with her husband. He did not want to go and would not unless forced. . . . The others, Maria and her children, want to go I think. They have been dressed in their Sundays best all day. . . .

February 20. . . . Shortly after breakfast—O joyful sight—the two corps encamped behind the Campus back of us marched by with all their immense wagon trains on their way from Columbia. They tell us all will be gone by tomorrow evening. . . .

Of course there was no Service in any of the churches yesterday
—no Church bells ringing—the Yankees riding up and down the
streets—the provost guard putting up their camp—there was nothing to suggest Sunday. . . .

February 21. A heavy curse has fallen on this town—from a beautiful city it is turned into a desert. How desolated and dreary we feel
—how completely cut off from the world. No longer the shrill whistle
of the engine—no daily mail—the morning brings no paper with
news from the outside—there are no lights—no going to and fro. It is
as if a city in the midst of business and activity were suddenly smit-
ten with some appalling curse. One feels awed if by chance the
dreary stillness is broken by a laugh or too loud a voice. . . .

February 22. I have seen it all—I have seen the "Abomination of
Desolation." It is even worse than I thought. The place is literally
in ruins. The entire heart of the city is in ashes—only the outer
edges remain. On the whole length of Sumter Street not one house
beyond the first block after the Campus is standing, except the brick
house of Mr. Mordecai. Standing in the centre of town, as far as the
eye can reach nothing is to be seen but heaps of rubbish, tall dreary
chimneys and shattered brick walls, while "In the hollow windows,
dreary horror's sitting." Poor old Columbia—where is all her beauty
—so admired by strangers, so loved by her children! . . .

Everything has vanished as if by enchantment—stores, merchants,
customers—all the eager faces gone—only three or four dismal looking people to be seen picking their way over heaps of rubbish, brick
and timbers. The wind moans among the bleak chimneys and whistles through the gaping windows of some hotel or warehouse. The
market a ruined shell supported by crumbling arches—its spire
fallen in and with it the old town clock whose familiar stroke we miss
so much. After trying to distinguish localities and hunting for familiar buildings we turned to Arsenal Hill. Here things looked more
natural. The Arsenal was destroyed but comparatively few dwellings.
Also the Park and its surroundings looked familiar. As we passed
the old State House going back I paused to gaze on the ruins—only
the foundations and chimneys—and to recall the brilliant scene en-
acted there one short month ago. And I compared that scene with its
beauty, gayety and festivity, the halls so elaborately decorated, the

surging throng, to this. I reached home sad at heart and full of all I had seen. . . .

February 23. . . . Somehow I feel we cannot be conquered. We have lost everything, but if all this—negroes—property—all could be given back a hundredfold I would not be willing to go back to them. I would rather endure any poverty than live under Yankee rule. . . . I would rather far have France or any other country for a mistress—anything but live as one nation with the *Yankees*—that word in my mind is a synonym for all that is mean, despicable and abhorrent. . . .

9. CHARLOTTE ST. JULIEN RAVENEL—
"THE ENEMY COMES TO OUR PLANTATION"

The young daughter of Henry William Ravenel, well-known botanist, lived at Pooshee plantation in Berkeley County, South Carolina. The plantation and the surrounding countryside were protected only by a few old men and young boys. After the Federal occupation of Charleston and the burning of Columbia in the middle of February 1865 roving bands of Union soldiers, white and black, burned and pillaged the neighborhood, as Charlotte tells in her journal.

Mrs. Chesnut says: "Potter's raid . . . ruined us. It burned our mills and gins, and a hundred bales of cotton. Indeed, nothing is left now but the bare land, and debts incurred for the support of these hundreds of Negroes during the war." This was Brigadier-General Edward E. Potter who commanded the Beaufort District in South Carolina after January 1865.

Pooshee

The 1st of March is a day which we will never forget; everything went on as usual until nine o'clock at night when we heard several pistol shots in the negro yard. I ran up stairs to tell Pennie who had gone to bed and by the time I got back we heard a noise at the back door; our hearts sank when we heard them talking, for they were negroes without an officer, what we had always dreaded. They asked for the master of the house, and when Grand Pa went out, they asked in the most insolent manner for his horses, wagons, meat and poultry. They then asked if there were any fire arms in the house, and told there was none but a plantation gun. They said they would not believe that such a house could be without a gun and that they would have it or shed blood. They then went off into the yard to get the things. They emptied the smoke-house; took what poultry they wanted, and then went to the store room under the house, took a few things from there and told the negroes to go in and take the rest;—which they did, cleaning out the store room and meat room. There were a great many things there for Aunt Bet had moved over her provisions. The plantation negroes took about twenty bushels of salt; twenty of rice; fifteen of grist, besides several jars of lard, molasses; all of Hennie's soap, a box of Pineland crockery and a good many other things. They left us with one quart of salt in the house and would not bring any of it back, until Pa stated the case to a *white* Yankee the next day and he went around and made them bring some of it back.

When the negro soldiers first went to the store room they sent for Grand Pa. It made our blood curdle to hear our aged relative spoken to in the manner they did. We were all in the hall and could hear everything that went on below. After some very impudent language we heard a gun click. I will never forget that moment as long as I live. The wretch had his gun pointed at Grand Pa, and though we found out afterwards that they did not dare to take life, we did not know it at the time.

After this they called up the negroes and told them they were free, and if they worked for Grand Pa again they would shoot them. They then went off with three horses, a wagon and a buggy. They told the negroes that the army would be through the next day to take our clothes and other things. Three of us sat up in the hall for the rest of the night, and though the others retired to their rooms there was rest for no one. It must have been too mortifying to poor Grand Pa for his negroes to behave as they did, taking the bread out of our mouths. I thought better of them than that. I have attempted to describe that dreadful night, but nothing can come up to the reality.

The next morning everything looked so desolate that it made us feel sad, most of the house servants came in crying, and said they were willing to do for us, but were afraid. Of course we would not put them in any danger, so sent them all off. We sat down to breakfast to a plate of hominy and cold corn bread that had been cooked the day before for one of our soldiers. The very night before we had

sat down to an elaborate supper;—such are the fortunes of war! We
cleaned up the house and cooked dinner, looking all the time for our
friends for such we considered the officers. Just as our dinner was
put on the table a party rode up; we were so glad to see them that
we all went in the piazza. The officer came forward and bowed very
politely. Pa then told him how we had been treated the night before
and asked what guarantee we would have against such treatment in
the future.

Capt. Hurlbut who was in command of the party said that the
black soldiers had no authority to come without an officer and if
found, they would be punished. He said that Gen'l. Potter would be
along soon and we might get a protection from him, but afterwards
he said that he would write a paper which might do us good, and
certainly would do no harm. I do not remember the words; but the
sense of it was, that we had very wisely remained at home, while
many had flocked to other parts of the Confederacy. He said that
everything had already been taken from us, and he would advise
that we would not be further molested. He then spoke to the negroes,
told them they were free and could either go away or stay at home,
but if they remained on the place, they must work, for no one could
live without working. He told them they would be better off if they
stayed at home.

Soon after Col. Hartwell and staff arrived. They all agreed in saying that the marauders would be punished and the Colonel signed the
paper. One of his staff got quite familiar; played with Aunt Ria's
baby, little Maria, and ended by kissing her. We laugh and tell the
baby she has caught a Yankee beau, and she always laughs and
seems to enjoy the joke. In a very short time Gen'l Potter and his
staff came up in the piazza. Then the army commenced passing
through the yard, about three regiments of infantry, one white and
two colored passed through, besides artillery and cavalry. Each one
stopped and the men ran in every direction after poultry. They
marched the colored regiments right by the piazza; I suppose as an
insult to us. The negroes were collected in the yard and cheered them
on. Hennie and Sister asked the General if he could not leave us a
guard that night, but he said there was no use; his army did not
straggle, and that he could not leave a guard at every place he
passed. The General did not make a favorable impression on us; he
was very short in his manner, but his staff were very polite. One of
them told us to try the General again.

You must not be too surprised at our staying out in the piazza with so many men, for there were a great many of us to keep company, and then we had never seen such a sight in our lives before. The last of the army had not left the yard before we saw the General returning; he said he had determined to take up his headquarters here that night. We were all, of course, delighted for we could not have been better guarded. They had the parlor for their sitting room, and one chamber for the General. The wagon train camped just in front of the house, and two regiments in the field in front. There was a sentinel at the front and one at the back door all night. The camp fires looked very pretty at night. Did we ever imagine that Pooshee would be headquarters for a Yankee army? About two hundred head of poultry and a great many sheep were killed; the negroes' own did not escape! We recognized one of the prisoners (that our scouts had here the first of the week) driving a cart, and Lieut. Bright and his men were prisoners that night in the wash room, one of them asked to be allowed to speak to some of the girls who were at the back door; he seemed to be a gentleman.

During the course of the next day soldiers were continually passing through. Our protection paper was of great use, for we were not molested again and from that day to this 9th of March we have been in comparative quiet.

Wantoot house has been burned, also seven unoccupied houses in Pineville. Some of the residents there were shamefully treated, even their clothes taken from them. Uncle Rene was among the fortunate ones; he only had a ham stolen from his house but all of his poultry. They went into the house at Woodboo, though a Mrs. Williams was living there to protect it, opened every drawer and box in the house; dressed themselves in Uncle Thomas's and the boys' new clothes, leaving their old ones behind.

At Northampton they were told by the negroes that a good many things were hid in the house, so made a thorough search. They actually threatened to hang Mr. Jervey, and had the rope brought. For some time they had been told that treasure had been buried. The people about here would not have suffered near as much if it had not been for these negroes; in every case they have told where things have been hidden and they did most of the stealing. The negroes here have behaved worse than any I have heard of yet.

Daddy Sandy is as faithful as ever. He is sorry that the Yankees have been here. George still comes about the house, but does not do much. Daddy Billy, who we all thought so much of, has not come in since they were made free. He pretends to be hurt because Hennie told him he could go if he wanted to. Hennie's maid Annette has taken herself off. Kate comes in regularly to attend in the bed rooms night and morning.

We have to do our own cooking now, and you don't know how nicely we do it. We take it by turns to cook dinner in the panty, two going together every day. I have not touched my needle for a week; would you believe that? The field negroes are in a dreadful state; they will not work, but either roam the country, or sit in their houses. At first they all said they were going, but have changed their minds now. Pa has a plan to propose to them by which they are to pay Grand Pa so much for the hire of the land and houses; but they will not come up to hear it. I do not see how we are to live in this country without any rule or regulation. We are afraid now to walk outside of the gate.

IX

OUR CONFEDERACY IS GONE
WITH A CRASH

March-May 1865

In Richmond on March 18 the Confederate Congress adjourned. As Sherman marched north from ruined Columbia desperate efforts were made to concentrate against him. Hardee's men came from Savannah, Bragg's from Wilmington, the garrison from Charleston, and what was left of the noble Army of Tennessee all the way from Tupelo. But only 20,000 could be mustered. Under Joseph E. Johnston they fought Sherman's 80,000 in a three-day battle at Bentonville, North Carolina (March 19-21). Undefeated, they retired in good order and spirit toward the center of the state.

In the entrenchments at Petersburg Lee's army had spent an agonizingly cold and hungry winter. Supplies—what there were of them —came over the only line still open, the South Side Railroad. Young General John B. Gordon made a gallant attempt, on March 25, to break through at Fort Stedman and wreck Grant's own supply line. He nearly succeeded, but in confused fighting was driven back to the trenches. On March 31 Sheridan, with a great detachment of infantry and cavalry, went out four miles west of the entrenchments, encountered Pickett and Bushrod Johnson at Dinwiddie Court House, was repulsed; but the next day, coming on with his immoderately superior forces, won the Battle of Five Forks, the last important battle of the war.

Petersburg and Richmond were evacuated on April 2. The President and his government fled south with the treasury and the records. Lee moved his men westward seeking to reach the Richmond & Danville Railroad for the southwest. Thwarted, he turned toward Lynchburg, and the skeleton army marched and fought and struggled on, until the hopelessness of it all became ineluctable. Then Appomattox and the surrender on April 9.

In the last bivouac General Lee issued his Farewell Address to his soldiers:

"After four years of arduous service marked by unsurpassed courage and fortitude, the Army of Northern Virginia has been compelled to yield to overwhelming numbers and resources. . . . I
determined to avoid the useless sacrifice of those whose past services
have endeared them to their countrymen. . . . Officers and men can
return to their homes and remain until exchanged. . . . I bid you all
an affectionate farewell"

*Mobile fell on April 12. On the eighteenth General Johnston sur-
rendered to Sherman near Durham, North Carolina. On May 4
General Richard Taylor surrendered the troops in the Deep South,
and on the same day, meeting at Washington, Georgia, the Cabinet
decided it was useless to continue the struggle anywhere. On May 26
General Kirby Smith surrendered his Trans-Mississippi Department.
A total of 157,000 Confederate soldiers surrendered to a total of
797,800 Federals.*

*But 258,000 gray ghosts were marching from Fort Sumter to
Appomattox in the Army of Confederate Dead.*

*And the Southern women, who had danced with them and worked
and prayed for them, shed tears that were both sad and proud.*

1. MALVINA BLACK GIST—"WE MAY HAVE TO FLY FROM RICHMOND"

*Arriving at Richmond after their flight from the doomed city
of Columbia, Malvina and the other members of the Confederate
Note Department were established in the Ballard Hotel. They became protégées of George A. Trenholm of Charleston, who had
succeeded Christopher G. Memminger as Secretary of the Treasury
in June 1864.*

*In 1867 Malvina married Clark Waring and spent the rest of her
life in Columbia. She wrote three novels, a number of short stories
and several books of verse. She died in 1930 at the age of eighty-
eight, survived by three children.*

BALLARD HOUSE, RICHMOND, March 1, 1865—We have taken
Richmond, if the Yankees haven't! Yes, we are here; but had some
trouble to get settled. The fashionable mode of living is room-keep-
ing, and we are strictly in the fashion. And now how nicely comes in
that trunk of provisions my thoughtful papa made me bring, much

against my own wishes. On opening it, we found meal, hominy, flour, a side of bacon, some coffee, tea, and a quantity of potatoes. They will help us along wonderfully, as all food products bring a tremendous price in this beleaguered city. Ernestine went to market this morning and paid $10 for a steak for our breakfast. At that rate we can only afford to take a savory smell occasionally! Ernie is simply angelic in spirit—she never loses patience, never gets cross, never says anything she oughtn't to say, even against the Yankees! The city is crowded to suffocation, the streets thronged with soldiers in uniform, officers gaily caparisoned, and beautiful women, beautifully dressed, though not in the latest Parisian toilettes. I should say there is no more brilliant capital among all the nations. Are there great and somber tragedies going on around us? Is there a war? I thought so before I reached Richmond!

March 2.—Our department quarters here are not nearly so comfortable as those left behind in Columbia. They do well enough, however. I have not had a chance to mention that handsome officer we saw on the train after leaving Greensboro. He was of the blonde type, with tawny, flowing mustache, and hair bright as "streaks from Aurora's fingers." Tall and broad-shouldered, he was attired in a captain's uniform, and deeply absorbed in reading a book. What was the book? Lise and I were wild to find out. We did find out, and, I hope, without exciting the least suspicion on his part. The book was "Quits." Knowing the story so well, and his face being so expressive, we could almost guess the contents of the pages as he turned them over. But after awhile he did not appear so deeply interested in it, and when our train had to be exchanged for another he stepped forward, raised his hat, and asked to be allowed to remove our packages. He was very grave and dignified. Were we wrong in accepting the attention? Sadie says we must not accept the slightest attention from unknown men while thus traveling. We have been thrust forth from the same environment of our homes and cannot afford to take any risks. Sadie is as proper as a dowager duchess of eighty. But, ah! the strange exigencies of these times! What is to become of us? There is no longer the shadow of a doubt—our homes are in ashes.

March 3.—I find myself regarding Lise with increasing admiration and affection. She is surely the most graceful girl in existence, combining a lot of downright amiability with a vast amount of tact.

Also, she has a deal of fun and mischief. That blond stranger must have noticed all of this with his eyes, so darkly blue.

March 4.—A letter from home! It reached me by hand through the department—is most reassuring and at the same time most delightfully comprehensive. They are all safe—thank God, my dear ones. Johnny came through without a scratch, and so did my new Steinway. It was a night of untold horrors (the 17th), but in the general conflagration our house was saved. My father and mother made friends even among their enemies, and through their exertions and old Maum Nancy's the family were fed and protected during the whole time. A number of Federal officers were quartered with the family until the morning of the 20th. One of them, whom mamma describes as "a most attractive young lieutenant," examined my music, tried my piano, playing with no little skill, and then inquired, "Where is she; the young lady who plays?" And when my father answered, "Gone to Richmond," he laughingly rejoined, "Ran away from the Yankees! Now, where was the use of that? We are just as sure to catch her there as here." Are you, Mr. Lieutenant? I fancy not; Sherman's army can't expect to over-run the whole earth; we are safe enough in Richmond. And yet I regret again not being there. I might have conducted the argument on both sides, for a while, with that attractive young lieutenant, and who knows? perchance make one Yankee's heart ache a little. What fun! What an opportunity! What a chance to get even have I lost!

March 5.—Oh! the seduction, the novelty, the fascination of this life in Richmond! If patriotism is its master-chord, pleasure is no less its dominant note, and while it is as indescribable as the sparkle of champagne, it is no less intoxicating. Last night the parlor was full of visitors, and the same may be said of almost every night— officers, privates, congressmen, senators, old friends and new ones, from all parts of the country. They are finding out our whereabouts and paying their devoirs. And what do you think, my little book? The blonde captain was among them. Strange things are the most natural, I have begun to think, for our strange acquaintance has come about in the most natural way. Dr. S—— knows his relatives in Maryland, and we are acquainted with his relatives in Carolina, so not even Sadie could gainsay the fitness of the acquaintance—nor Ernestine, who is an anxious mother to the last one of us.

March 7.—He is just as charming a gentleman as I thought he would be—I refer to the captain, of course. Last night I saw him gazing at Bet's hair in the most admiring manner. It is magnificent. I should be awfully vain of it, were it mine—but she is not. Bet is as levelheaded as a girl can be, and as sweet and modest as a violet.

March 8.—Wish I had been taught to cook instead of how to play on the piano. A practical knowledge of the preparation of food products would stand me in better stead at this juncture than any amount of information regarding the scientific principles of music. I adore music, but I can't live without eating—and I'm hungry! I want some chicken salad, and some charlotte russe, and some oxpalate, and corn muffins! These are the things I want; but I'll eat anything I can get. Honestly, our cuisine has become a burning question. Dear, sweet Ernie bears the brunt, and has to, because the rest of us are simpletons! She'll be canonized some of these days, or deserves to be, if she isn't.

March 9.—Little book, give me your ear. Close! There! Promise me never to breathe it! Blank loves Blank! Yes, he does! And she doesn't care for him—not a pennyworth! It is a dreadful state of affairs, to be sure. Why must there be so much loving and making of love? How much nicer to just keep on being friends with everybody (except one) and nothing more. It is a shame that I have so little time to devote to my journal. We meet so many delightful people and so many famous people. The other day, attended a review of Gary's Brigade, by Generals Fitzhugh Lee and Longstreet, in an open field between the Nine Mile and Darby Town roads. We went in an army ambulance, attended by a number of our gentlemen friends. Fitz. Lee passed very near us. It was the sight of a lifetime; it thrilled and pulsated all through me. When the review was over, we were speedily surrounded by a throng of gallants, officers and privates—the noble privates, heroes, I love them! They bear the yoke and do the fighting, while some of the officers don't do anything but ornament the army. Mind, I don't say all—*some*. Do you think we women give no heed to these things? I know what kind of a heart a man carries under his brass buttons. We spoke to many of our own State troops, some of them gaunt and battle-scarred veterans, and some of them young in service but with the courage of veterans in them. Whether we get whipped in this fight or not, one thing will be forever indisputable—our soldiers are true soldiers and good fighters. Sometimes I fear that we are going to get the worst of it—but away with all fears!

To doubt the end were want of trust in God.

So says Henry Timrod, in his *Ethnogenesis,* and he is a poet, and the poet has a far-seeing eye. It opens beautifully—this poem, I mean—

    Hath not the morning dawned with added light?
      And shall not evening call another star
  Out of the infinite regions of the night
    To mark this day in Heaven?

I hear Timrod's health is poor. What a pity! I hope he will live to sing us many songs.[1] I must not forget to chronicle the fact that I saw my gallant cousin, Robert D——, out at the review. We greeted each other with unfeigned pleasure.

March 10.—The drawing room was again crowded last night, and we got up an important dance on the spur of the moment. General Kershaw,[2] General Gary,[3] and General Ruggles[4] were present; also our friends, the congressman, the captain, the major, and the M.P. Oh! yes. We know Mr. Connelly, an Irish M.P. and Southern sympathizer. He seems to have plenty of money, and lives here in great style for war times; owns a steam yacht, and we are to have an outing on it before long. There are so many interesting things I could and ought to write about, but I just can't, because I am so hungry! And having nothing to eat, I am going to bed to fill up on sleep.

March 11.—Thank goodness! I'm not hungry tonight, and for a very good reason; we dined with the Secretary of the Treasury and his family, the Trenholms. It was a symposium to us poor Treasury girls, attractive and impressive. We discussed the varied menu, elegantly prepared and daintily served, with a Confederate appetite, sharply whetted for long-denied delicacies. Mr. Morgan, the young

---

[1] He died in Columbia, South Carolina, October 6, 1867.
[2] Major-General Joseph B. Kershaw.
[3] Major-General M. W. Gary.
[4] Brigadier-General Daniel Ruggles.

midshipman, was there, quite *en famille.* I did not hear when the wedding is to be. I suppose after the war. Everything is going to take place after the war. As we arose from the table, President and Mrs. Davis were announced. This famous man *honoris causa,* I had already seen before in Columbia, but this was my first glimpse of his wife. She was graciousness itself. Some people whom I have heard talk, and who look upon Mr. Davis as a mere function of government, are disposed to regard him as a conspicuous failure, but, in the name of reason, how can one man please everybody? His role is certainly one of great difficulty. Socially, he may rub some persons the wrong way, but not so with us. He was pleasant, polished and entertaining. . . .

March 15.—The Trenholms are exceedingly kind to us. Whenever that majordomo of theirs makes his appearance with that big basket of his, plenty prevails in this section of the Ballard. Heaven bless them! To demolish the contents of that basket is like getting into a home kitchen. Will the time ever come when we can have real coffee to drink again? Our trunk of provisions is gone, and we often feel *gone* without them! Ernestine says Lise and I are completely spoiled for any other life than this surging, intoxicating stream of brass buttons, epaulettes, and sword-belted manhood. It may be so; I am afraid it is. There is an air of military inspiration around us; it pervades our being; we exist in a tremor of ecstasy, or else foreboding. Our Richmond life holds a little of everything, save *ennui*—not a grain of that in it.

March 16.—It is a hard thing to say, but I am going to say it. I don't admire all the men who wear the Confederate uniform! I would rather dig holes in the ground than talk to some of them!

March 17.—I could eat a tallow candle if I had a good one. But I have accepted an invitation to dine with the Trenholms—in my dreams! . . .

March 20.—A great joy has come to me this day, an unlooked-for, an inexpressible joy! A card was brought to me, and I took it with a sigh, because so many cards are brought in and we have so little time for rest. But the name upon that particular card made my heart thump and thump so fast I thought it would thump clean out of my body. It was my dear brother's name—the scout, who has been in prison two years, first at Camp Chase[1] and recently at Fort Delaware.[2] Without stopping as usual to give a last touch to my hair, I rushed into his presence and into his arms. He's the rowdiest, shabbiest, patchiest looking fellow you ever saw, but as handsome as ever, and the same old darling. We talked and talked; we crowded the talk of two long years of separation into two short hours of face to face. It is a thrilling romance, the way he escaped from prison. In a dead man's shoes it was! That man's name was Jesse Tredway, and he died in his bunk after his name had been entered on the list of exchange. My brother put his dead comrade in his own bunk and said nothing. He answered to his name in the roll call and quietly took his place in the ranks of the outgoing prisoners. The details of that journey homeward, the recital of his adventures and narrow escapes from detection all along the route, is something to be heard from his own lips in order to be appreciated. The recital made the blood tingle in my veins and then suddenly run cold; made my pulses throb and then suddenly cease almost to throb at all. Think of it! The recklessness of the deed, and his subsequent anxiety and fear of detection every moment. In the soft veil of the night, in the white light of the morning, under the noonday sun, under the midnight stars, even in the stillness of sleep, never to be rid of the fear of detection. His very life hung upon the issue, for he had made up his mind to shoot down the first man who remanded him back to prison. Thank God! he was never detected, never remanded back! He will now journey on without delay, on foot, for the most part. He has no money to pay his passage—but what of that? It is a pleasure to him to walk on God's fair earth again, no longer a shut-up animal in a cage; the earth is full of a new glory for him, the glory of sweet liberty. The exile has returned to his home.

March 23.—Congressman Farrow asked me today if I were feeling well. Come to think of it, I do not feel well. My nerve forces seem to be all out of tune, and my digestion is impaired—in fact, a general *malaise* appears to be the result of hardtack on my constitution.

March 25.—My head aches; I have no appetite (and nothing fit to eat, either); my senses are dull. Heaven grant I may not be ill in

[1] In Ohio.
[2] In Delaware.

Richmond! At this particular epoch, it is the place for everything else, but no place to be sick in.

March 29.—Mr. Duncan brings us the weightiest news. The Confederacy is going to the dogs—or, did he say the devil? That young lieutenant was right. We may have to fly from Richmond as we did from Columbia. It is a profound secret as yet; but he warns us to be ready to leave on quick notice. Are we to be driven to the wall? I can't believe it! But somehow—somehow—my heart is as barren of hope tonight as the great Sahara of water.

March 30.—Indeed, something very serious is astir in military circles. After arranging everything, the M.P. has had to give up the projected outing on the James? It is not safe—a fight is brewing. Doubtless I should worry more if I felt better; when the head is so confused with pain, and the nerves unstrung, all other matters are secondary.

March 31.—Feel better today. Mr. Connelly gave us a collation in the hotel in lieu of the abandoned picnic. Very swell, despite the blockade. Must have cost him a pretty sum. I told Mr. Duncan I would not leave Richmond, so full of a certain charm is the life here; but of course have had to give in, and now am ready for another flight as soon as he notifies us. . . .

2. JUDITH BROCKENBROUGH McGUIRE—
"THE SOUND OF CANNON IS EVER IN OUR EARS"

Mrs. McGuire has now been a refugee for four years and is fifty-two years old. She keeps up her vocation in the Commissary Department and her avocation in the hospitals.

March 10th, 1865. Still we go on as heretofore, hoping and praying that Richmond may be safe. I know that we ought to feel that whatever General Lee and the President deem right for the cause must be right, and that we should be satisfied that all will be well; but it would almost break my heart to see this dear old city, with its hallowed associations, given over to the Federals. Fearful orders have been given in the offices to keep the papers packed, except such as we are working on. The packed boxes remain in the front room, as if uncertainty still existed about moving them. As we walk in every morning, all eyes are turned to the boxes to see if any have been removed, and we breathe more freely when we find them still there.

To-day I have spent in the hospital.

March 11th. Sheridan's raid through the country is perfectly awful, and he has joined Grant, without being caught. Oh, how we listened to hear that he had been arrested in his direful career! It was, I suppose, the most cruel and desolating raid upon record— more lawless, if possible, than Hunter's. He had an overwhelming force, spreading ruin through the Upper Valley, the Piedmont country, the tide-water country, until he reached Grant.[1] His soldiers were allowed to commit any cruelty on non-combatants that suited their rapacious tempers—stealing every thing they could find; earrings, breastpins, and finger-rings were taken from the first ladies of the land; nothing escaped them which was worth carrying off from the already desolated country. And can we feel patient at the idea of such soldiers coming to Richmond, the target at which their whole nation, from their President to the meanest soldier upon their army-rolls, has been aiming for four years? Oh, I would that I could see Richmond burnt to the ground by its own people, with not one brick left upon another, before its defenceless inhabitants should be subjected to such degradation!

Fighting is still going on; so near the city, that the sound of cannon is ever in our ears. Farmers are sending in their produce which they cannot spare, but which they give with a spirit of self-denial rarely equalled. Ladies are offering their jewelry, their plate, any thing which can be converted into money, for the country. I have heard some of them declare, that, if necessary, they will cut off their long suits of hair, and send them to Paris to be sold for bread for the soldiers. . . . Some gentlemen are giving up their watches, when every thing else has been given. . . .

[1] "As the spring opened, Grant called to himself Sheridan's force, which had wintered in the Valley. Sheridan marched through that unhappy country; struck the remnants of Early's little army at Waynesboro, on March second; drove and scattered them, with large captures; crossed the Blue Ridge, destroyed miles of the Virginia Central Railroad and the James River canal, and, with little opposition, marched eastward through Virginia to the White House on the Pamunkey. From there, on March nineteenth, he reported his troops for duty with the armies immediately under Grant."—*The Story of the Confederacy,* by Robert S. Henry, pp. 453, 454.

March 12th.—A deep gloom has just been thrown over the city by the untimely death of one of its own heroic sons. General John Pegram fell while nobly leading his brigade against the enemy in the neighborhood of Petersburg. But two weeks before he had been married in St. Paul's Church. . . . All was bright and beautiful. Happiness beamed from every eye. Again has St. Paul's been opened to receive the soldier and his bride[1]—the one coffined for a hero's grave, the other, pale and trembling, though still by his side, in widow's garb. . . .

March 31st.—A long pause in my diary. Every thing seems so dark and uncertain that I have no heart for keeping records. The croakers croak about Richmond being evacuated, but I can't and won't believe it. . . .

There is hard fighting about Petersburg, and General A. P. Hill has been killed.[2] . . .

3. MARY D. WARING—"THEY MARCHED INTO MOBILE TO THE TUNE OF 'YANKEE DOODLE'"

After the Battle of Mobile Bay (August 5, 1864), in which Admiral Franklin Buchanan's great ram the Tennessee *had, practically alone, engaged Admiral Farragut's fleet, Union forces had taken the two great Confederate forts, Morgan and Gaines, guarding the bay. Piles driven into the Mobile River rendered the city itself safe for the time being. General Dabney H. Maury, Betty Maury's cousin, was in command at the barricade, which was protected by Spanish Fort. After the Battle of Nashville he was reinforced by four brigades, including General Randall L. Gibson's, from Hood's army. General Maury surrendered to the Union fleet and land forces under General Gordon Granger on April 12.*

Mary was the young daughter of Moses and Ellen Smoot Waring of Mobile. In her war diary she made note of personal affairs, events in the city, war news. Like Esther Alden and many another Southern

---

[1] She was the beautiful Hetty Cary, Constance's cousin, who came to Richmond from Baltimore early in war days and immediately became the toast of the town. General Chesnut said, "If there was no such word as 'fascinating,' you would have to invent it to describe Hetty Cary."

[2] On the last day of fighting in the trench lines at Petersburg.

girl, she could not bring herself to record the fall of the Confederacy. Her journal ended abruptly on April 16 in the middle of a sentence.

Betty married Lieutenant Thomas Locke Harrison, a graduate of the Naval Academy at Annapolis, who had served under Buchanan at Mobile Bay. They had two children. She and her husband are buried in Magnolia Cemetery at Mobile.

Mobile, Alabama

Mar. 27th, 1865. Today the enemy commenced operations by an attack on Spanish Fort, where some of our best troops under Gen. Gibson, were stationed. The firing was heavy and continuous, while the booming of heavy Artillery was heard distinctly on this side, rendering us very uneasy as to the fate of our brave and gallant boys stationed in and around the fort. Being unaccustomed to such heavy firing, we were, of course, much startled and excited until we gradually became used to the sound.

Tuesday March 28th. Heavy firing is still kept up at the Fort, from both sides. The wharves and all high places in the city, filled with persons, impelled, some by curiosity, but many more by anxiety, watching the firing. It has been impossible to do work of any description, or to compose the mind, for reading, writing, practicing or any thing else. I have been wandering around, like a restless spirit, trying to compose myself, but finding every effort to do so, impossible, finally give up the attempt, so great is my anxiety about Marion, and many of my friends stationed there.

Wednesday March 29th/65 Tidings from the Eastern Shore, relative to the proceedings of yesterday, are very encouraging, our boys still frustrating all efforts of the enemy to take the fort. Our casualties, considering the heavy cannonading, are slight, and our wounded receive the kindest care and attention at the Hospitals. This morning, as I started down town, I met Fanny, who being desirous of seeing the firing at Spanish fort, went with me round to Cousin Pidge's, where we had a very good view from the third story. We each stationed ourselves at the windows with an opera-glass apiece, and spent our whole morning in gazing at different objects on the bay. We could very readily discern the vessels of the enemy, also many of their transports coming in with fresh troops, and we imagined that we could see the "Nashville" [1] tho' I hardly imagine our sight was keen enough for that. After passing an hour or two, in this manner, we went down to Cousin P's room, where she had a nice lunch prepared for us, & which we did full credit. . . .

Thursday, March 30th, 1865. The cannonading last eve, was fierce and heavy in the extreme, the firing, as we learned this morning, being *chiefly our gunboats* shelling the woods. So rapid and so distinct was the booming of the "big guns" that our fears and anxiety were not a little excited, tho' very little damage was done. . . .

Monday, Apr. 3rd. Just one week today since the bombardment commenced, and our *dear,* gallant men fought hard and bravely. They certainly deserve our highest commendation and admiration, and all the encouragement we can heap upon them. Our thoughts are constantly for them and with them, and I trust that we may ever succeed in our noble cause.

Tuesday April 4th. The fighting all last night and today has been excessively heavy, and makes us feel much anxiety and fear for our brothers and friends. This evening the firing is terrific, not a moment elapsing between the booming of "heavy artillery." I trust our noble little fort will stand defiant to the assaults of the enemy.

Wednesday, April 5th. Our casualties of yesterday were very small, considering the tremendous bombardment of the whole day. All will end well, I trust, for us.

Thursday, April 6th. Today I have been exceedingly busy, making a tobacco-bag, for one of the soldiers to whom our Society are preparing to send a handsome present in the form of a box of provisions. It was filled with every thing which these war times was capable of sending. I also busied myself with making a large sponge cake for Cousin Tom.

Friday, April 7th. It has been comparatively quiet and uneventful today, only we are still kept excited and uneasy about the firing. Tonight we meet at Mrs. Muldons' and, I fear, will not be permitted long to meet and work for our dear Confederate soldiers, as things

[1] Confederate gunboat.

begin to look threatening. After picking considerable lint and rolling bandages, we dispersed hoping to have, at least, one more meeting in peace and in Confederate lines. . . .

Sunday April 9th. Bright and early this morning I was awakened with "Spanish Fort is evacuated" while I could hardly believe it. Still I had to believe the evidence of my own eyes, for our soldiers were passing by in squads, from an early hour, dirty, wet and completely worn out, having been compelled to march through a marsh for a distance of four miles, in order to make their escape. Poor fellows, how discouraging it must have been to abandon the fort after having so bravely defended it for two weeks. All day long they have been coming in. . . . Mrs. Hall came in with any quantity of bad news—viz:—that the enemy had charged the breast works, at Blakely, taking them & capturing the whole garrison, which was sad news, indeed, for us. Our course was now clear to us, and we felt distressed at the idea of the occupation of our dear little city, by our detested enemy. We sat up until late, brooding over our misfortune. . . .

Monday, Apr. 10th 1865. This morning, we were much startled by the ringing of the alarm bell: the object of which was to call troops together to prepare for evacuation. Never have I experienced such feelings as now take possession of me—perfectly miserable, as may be imagined. Everybody is excited and running around, gathering what information they can. . . . It is with a heavy heart that I bid my friends "good bye" not knowing whether I shall ever see them again or not. . . .

Tuesday, April 11th 1865. All excitement still this morning. We are all perfectly miserable at the idea of being separated, for an indefinite period of time, from our dear brothers and friends. . . . The day has passed away without my accomplishing a thing except watching our soldiers as they passed by, and now and then seeing a friend and saying *Adieu.* How sad the word. . . . This afternoon about dinner time, the 1st La. Regiment which has been stationed in Mobile for the past six or eight months, passed by on their way to the boat, seemingly in good spirits. . . .

Wednesday, April 12th. I awoke this morning with a most deserted and desolate feeling. All our troops got off some time during the night, and the city is entirely free of "gray coats" except some few Scouts who will decamp upon the entrance of the enemy.

Our feelings can be better imagined than described, as we were momentarily expecting the intelligence that the enemy were nearly to the city. Meanwhile, quite a commotion has sprung up, down the street, and the people threatened with a *mob*. A quantity of commissary stores having been left by our military authorities, and being turned over to the poor, each one of that class, helping himself freely, and endeavoring to carry off as much as possible—each one tries to be first, and consequently much scuffling and rioting ensues —which is soon quelled by the citizens, who appear with loaded guns & various weapons.

About 12 o'clock, the Mayor, accompanied by many gentlemen, went down the bay to surrender the city to Gen. Granger, and soon they were on their way to the city. The Yankee troops did not come in until about four o'clock in the afternoon, when they were marched in to the tune of "Yankee Doodle." When I heard *that,* and the cheering of the men, I began to realize what *had* and was taking place, as before *that,* I had been so much excited that I hardly had time for thought. . . . My feelings this afternoon and tonight, have been any thing but pleasant. I believe I was never so gloomy—but there will be a bright day for us yet.

Thursday, April 13th. The city is filled with the hated Yanks, who differ in the greatest degree from our poor dear soldiers. Really I feel quite strange in my own city, seeing so many new and strange countenances. To do them justice, however, I must admit, though reluctant to do so, that they are very quiet and orderly, and they entered the city with extra-ordinary order and quiet, so different from what we had anticipated, from the numerous accounts of their behavior in captured cities. We are thankful for it and hope such conduct will be preserved throughout their stay here.

4. VARINA HOWELL DAVIS—"WITH HEARTS BOWED DOWN BY DESPAIR WE LEFT RICHMOND"

Except for a brief while in the spring of 1862 when Richmond was first threatened, Mrs. Davis had been in the city. In the White

House she had borne two children. A little son, as we have seen, had been killed by falling from the north balcony.

The last photograph of the First Lady was taken in the winter of 1864. It shows her in a cheap muslin dress; her face is gaunt and lined but she bears herself proudly. She maintained her receptions down to the final weeks.

"Providence has seen fit," said Mrs. Chesnut, "that I should have known three great women, and Mrs. Jefferson Davis is one of them."

She was captured with her husband on May 10, 1865, at Irwinville, Georgia. She shared with him the last months of his two-year imprisonment in Fortress Monroe; she nursed him and cleaned his cell in the casemate dungeon. On his release she went with him to Canada and to England. They lived for several years in Memphis and finally retired to a new home, "Beauvoir," near Biloxi, Mississippi. After his death on December 6, 1889, she devoted herself to writing a tribute to him, Jefferson Davis: ex-president of the Confederate States of America.

She died in New York on October 16, 1906, and was buried beside her husband in Hollywood Cemetery, Richmond, where so many of the Confederate great rest in peace.

Darkness seemed now to close swiftly over the Confederacy, and about a week before the evacuation of Richmond,[1] Mr. Davis came to me and gently, but decidedly, announced the necessity for our departure. He said for the future his headquarters must be in the field, and that our presence would only embarrass and grieve, instead of comforting him. Very averse to flight, and unwilling at all times to leave him, I argued the question with him and pleaded to be permitted to remain, until he said: "I have confidence in your capacity to take care of our babies, and understand your desire to assist and comfort me, but you can do this in but one way, and that is by going yourself and taking our children to a place of safety." He was very much affected and said, "If I live you can come to me when the struggle is ended, but I do not expect to survive the destruction of constitutional liberty."

He had a little gold, and reserving a five-dollar piece for himself, he gave it all to me, as well as all the Confederate money due to him. He desired me not to request any of the citizens of Richmond to take

[1] Richmond was evacuated April 2.

care of my silver plate, of which we possessed a large quantity, for, said he, "They may be exposed to inconvenience or outrage by their effort to serve us."

All women like bric-a-brac, which sentimental people call their "household goods," but Mr. Davis called it "trumpery." I was not superior to the rest of my sex in this regard. However, everything which could not be readily transported was sent to a dealer for sale, and we received quite a large draft on a Richmond bank as the proceeds, but in the hurry of departure the check was not cashed.

Leaving the house as it was, and taking only our clothing, I made ready with my young sister and my four little children, the eldest only nine years old, to go forth into the unknown. Mr. Burton N. Harrison,[1] the President's private secretary, was to protect and see us safely settled in Charlotte, where we had hired a furnished house. Mr. George A. Trenholm's lovely daughters were also to accompany us to remain with friends there.

I had bought several barrels of flour, and intended to take them with me, but Mr. Davis said, "You cannot remove anything in the shape of food from here, the people want it, and you must leave it here."

The deepest depression had settled upon the whole city. . . .

The day before our departure Mr. Davis gave me a pistol and showed me how to load, aim, and fire it. He was very apprehensive of our falling into the hands of the disorganized bands of troops roving about the country, and said, "You can at least, if reduced to the last extremity, force your assailants to kill you, but I charge you solemnly to leave when you hear the enemy are approaching; and if you cannot remain undisturbed in our own country, make for the Florida coast and take a ship there for a foreign country."

With hearts bowed down by despair, we left Richmond. Mr. Davis almost gave way, when our little Jeff begged to remain with him,

[1] Burton Harrison was to be imprisoned with President Davis at Fortress Monroe. His fiancée, Constance Cary, who was staying with relatives in New Jersey, had no news of him for months. She went to Washington and worked to secure his release. At last she succeeded and he visited her and her mother there. Constance went to Europe late in 1866 and on her return she and Burton were married, November 26, 1867, in Saint Ann's Church at Morrisania, New York, where her aunt lived. Burton practiced law in New York City, and Constance became popular as a writer of vivacious short stories, novels, plays, essays. Her autobiography, *Recollections Grave and Gay,* appeared in 1911. She died in Washington November 21, 1920, survived by two sons.

and Maggie clung to him convulsively, for it was evident he thought he was looking his last upon us.

As we pulled out from the station and lost sight of Richmond, the wornout engine broke down, and there we sat all night. There were no arrangements possible for sleeping, and at last, after twelve hours' delay, we reached Danville. A hospitable and wealthy citizen of that place invited me to rest with his family, but we gratefully declined and proceeded to Charlotte.

The baggage cars were all needing repairs and leaked badly. Our bedding was wet through by the constant rains that poured down in the week of uninterrupted travel which was consumed in reaching our destination. Universal consternation prevailed throughout the country, and we avoided seeing people for fear of compromising them with the enemy, should they overrun North Carolina. We found everything packed up in the house we had rented, but the agent, Mr. A. Weill, an Israelite, came to meet us there, and gave us every assistance in his power; and when he found there were no conveniences for cooking, he sent out meals from his own house for several days, refusing, with many cordial words, any offer to reimburse him for the expense incurred, and he offered money or any other service he could render.

Mr. Harrison, after seeing us safely established in Charlotte, fearing he might be separated from Mr. Davis, and hoping to be of use, set out for Richmond to rejoin him. . . .

5. PHOEBE YATES PEMBER—"THE WOMEN OF THE SOUTH STILL FOUGHT THEIR BATTLE"

Her four years' labor as matron in Chimborazo Hospital ably concluded, Mrs. Pember set down her impressions of the occupation of Richmond. Then she went to live with relatives in Savannah, carrying with her all she possessed—a box of Confederate money and one silver ten-cent piece.

Her account of hospital experiences was published in 1879—A Southern Woman's Story. *It is introduced by this quotation:*

"Whatsoever is beginning that is done by human skill;
Every daring emanation of the mind's imperfect will;
Every first impulse of passion, gush of love or twinge of hate;
Every launch upon the waters, wide-horizoned by our fate;

> Every venture in the chances of life's sad, aye, desperate game;
> Whatsoever be our object, whatsoever be our aim—
>   'Tis well we cannot see
>   What the end will be."

Richmond, Virginia
April 2, 1865

No one slept during that night of horror, for added to the present scenes were the anticipations of what the morrow would bring forth. Daylight dawned upon a wreck of destruction and desolation. From the highest point of Church hill and Libby hill, the eye could range over the whole extent of city and country—the fire had not abated, and the burning bridges were adding their flame and smoke to the scene. A single faint explosion could be heard from the distance at long intervals, but the *Patrick Henry* was low to the water's edge and Drewry but a column of smoke. The whistle of the cars and the rushing of the laden trains still continued—they had never ceased—and the clouds hung low and draped the scene as morning advanced.

Before the sun had risen, two carriages rolled along Main street, and passed through Rocketts just under Chimborazo hospital, carrying the mayor and corporation towards the Federal lines, to deliver the keys of the city, and half an hour afterwards, over to the east, a single Federal blue-jacket rose above the hill, standing transfixed with astonishment at what he saw. Another and another sprang up as if out of the earth, but still all remained quiet. About seven o'clock, there fell upon the earth the steady clatter of horses' hoofs, and winding around Rocketts, close under Chimborazo hill, came a small and compact body of Federal cavalrymen, on horses in splendid condition, riding closely and steadily along. They were well mounted, well accoutered, well fed—a rare sight in Southern streets, —the advance of that vaunted army that for four years had so hopelessly knocked at the gates of the Southern Confederacy.

They were some distance in advance of the infantry who followed, quite as well appointed and accoutered as the cavalry. Company after company, regiment after regiment, battalion after battalion, and brigade after brigade, they poured into the doomed city—an endless stream. One detachment separated from the main body and marching to Battery No. 2, raised the United States flag, their band playing the Star Spangled Banner. There they stacked their arms. The rest marched along Main Street through fire and smoke, over burning fragments of buildings, emerging at times like a phantom army when the wind lifted the dark clouds; while the colored population shouted and cheered them on their way.

Before three hours had elapsed, the troops had been quartered and were inspecting the city. They swarmed in every highway and byway, rose out of gullies, appeared on the top of hills, emerged from narrow lanes, and skirted around low fences. There was hardly a spot in Richmond not occupied by a blue coat, but they were orderly, quiet and respectful. Thoroughly disciplined, warned not to give offense by look or act, they did not speak to any one unless first addressed; and though the women of the South contrasted with sickness of heart the difference this splendidly-equipped army, and the war-worn, wasted aspect of their own defenders, they were grateful for the consideration shown them; and if they remained in their sad homes, with closed doors and windows, or walked the streets with averted eyes and veiled faces, it was that they could not bear the presence of invaders, even under the most favorable circumstances.

Before the day was over, the public buildings were occupied by the enemy, and the minds of the citizens relieved from all fears of molestation. The hospitals were attended to, the ladies being still allowed to nurse and care for their own wounded; but rations could not be drawn yet, the obstructions in the James river preventing the transports from coming up to the city. In a few days they arrived, and food was issued to those in need. It had been a matter of pride among the Southerners to boast that they had never seen a greenback, so the entrance of the Federal army had thus found them entirely unprepared with gold and silver currency. People who had boxes of Confederate money and were wealthy the day previously, looked around in vain for wherewithal to buy a loaf of bread. Strange exchanges were made on the street of tea and coffee, flour and bacon. Those who were fortunate in having a stock of household necessaries were generous in the extreme to their less wealthy neighbors, but the destitution was terrible. The sanitary commission shops were opened, and commissioners appointed by the Federals to visit among the people and distribute orders to draw rations, but to effect this, after receiving tickets, required so many appeals to different officials, that decent people gave up the effort. Besides, the musty corn-meal and strong cod-fish were not appreciated by fastidious stomachs—few gently nurtured could relish such unfamiliar food.

But there was no assimilation between the invaders and invaded. In the daily newspaper a notice had appeared that the military bands would play in the beautiful capital grounds every afternoon, but when the appointed hour arrived, except the Federal officers, musicians and soldiers, not a white face was to be seen. The negroes crowded every bench and path. The next week another notice was issued that the colored population would not be admitted; and then the absence of everything and anything feminine was appalling. The entertainers went alone to their own entertainment. The third week still another notice appeared: "colored nurses were to be admitted with their white charges," and lo! each fortunate white baby received the cherished care of a dozen finely-dressed black ladies, the only drawback being that in two or three days the music ceased altogether, the entertainers feeling at last the ingratitude of the subjugated people.

Despite their courtesy of manner, for however despotic the acts, the Federal authorities maintained a respectful manner—the newcomers made no advance towards fraternity. They spoke openly and warmly of their sympathy with the sufferings of the South, but committed and advocated acts that the hearers could not recognize as "military necessities." Bravely-dressed Federal officers met their former old class-mates from colleges and military institutions and inquired after the relatives to whose houses they had ever been welcome in days of yore, expressing a desire to "call and see them," while the vacant chairs, rendered vacant by Federal bullets, stood by the hearth of the widow and bereaved mother. They could not be made to understand that their presence was painful. There were few men in the city at this time; but the women of the South still fought their battle for them; fought it resentfully, calmly, but silently! Clad in their mourning garments, overcome but hardly subdued, they sat within their desolate homes, or if compelled to leave that shelter went on their errands to church or hospital with veiled faces and swift steps. By no sign or act did the possessors of their fair city show that they were even conscious of their presence. If they looked in their faces they saw them not: they might have supposed themselves a phantom army. There was no stepping aside with affectation to avoid the contact of dress, no feigned humility in giving the inside of the walk: they simply totally ignored their presence.

Two particular characteristics followed the army in possession— the circus and booths for the temporary accommodation of itinerant venders. The small speculators must have supposed that there were no means of cooking left in the city, from the quantity of canned edibles they offered for sale. They inundated Richmond with pictorial canisters at exorbitant prices, which no one had money to buy. Whether the supply of greenbacks was scant, or the people were not disposed to trade with the new-comers, they had no customers.

In a few days steamboats had made their way to the wharves, though the obstructions still defied the ironclads, and crowds of curious strangers thronged the pavements, while squads of mounted male pleasure-seekers scoured the streets. Gayly-dressed women began to pour in also, with looped-up skirts, very large feet, and a great preponderance of spectacles. The Richmond women sitting by desolated firesides were astonished by the arrival of former friends, sometimes people moving in the best classes of society, who had the bad taste to make a pleasure trip to the mourning city, calling upon their heart-broken friends of happier days in all the finery of the newest New York fashions, and in some instances forgiving their entertainers the manifold sins of the last four years in formal and set terms.

From the hill on which my hospital was built, I had sat all the weary Sunday of the evacuation, watching the turmoil, and bidding friends adieu, for even till noon many had been unconscious of the events that were transpiring, and now when they had all departed, as night set in, I wrapped my blanket-shawl around me, and watched below me all that I have here narrated. Then I walked through my wards and found them comparatively empty. Every man who could crawl had tried to escape a Northern prison. Beds in which paralyzed, rheumatic, and helpless patients had lain for months were empty. The miracles of the New Testament had been re-enacted. The lame, the halt, and the blind had been cured. Those who were compelled to remain were almost wild at being left in what would be the enemy's lines the next day; for in many instances they had been exchanged prisoners only a short time before. I gave all the comfort I could, and with some difficulty their supper also, for my detailed nurses had gone with General Lee's army, and my black cooks had deserted me.

On Monday morning, the day after the evacuation, the first blue uniforms appeared at our quarters—three surgeons inspecting the hospital. As our surgeon was with them, there must have been an amicable understanding. One of our divisions was required for use by the new-comers, cleared out for them, and their patients laid by the side of our own sick so that we shared with them, as my own commissary stores were still well supplied. Three days afterwards an order came to transfer my old patients to Camp Jackson. I protested bitterly against this, as they were not in a fit state for removal, so they remained unmolested. To them I devoted my time, for our surgeons had either then left or received orders to discontinue their labors.

Towards evening the place was deserted. Miss G. had remained up to this time with me, but her mother requiring her presence in the city, she left at sunset, and after I had gone through all my wards, I returned to my dear little sitting-room, endeared by retrospection, and the consciousness that my labors were nearly over, but had been (as far as regarded results) in vain. . . .

6. JUDITH BROCKENBROUGH McGUIRE—
"LIKE A VIVID, HORRIBLE DREAM"

*"My heart would break if the Federals occupied Richmond,"
Mrs. McGuire had said. Now the Union flag waved from the roof
of the Capitol, and the invading General Godfrey Weitzel had moved
into the White House.*

Richmond, Virginia

April 3.—Agitated and nervous, I turn to my diary to-night as the means of soothing my feelings. We have passed through a fatal thirty-six hours. Yesterday morning we went, as usual, to St. James's Church, hoping for a day of peace and quietness, as well as of religious improvement and enjoyment. The sermon being over, as it was the first Sunday in the month, the sacrament of the Lord's Supper was administered. While the sacred elements were being administered, the sexton came in with a note to General Cooper, which was handed him as he walked from the chancel, and he immediately left the church. It made me anxious; but such things are not uncommon, and caused no excitement in the congregation. The services being over, we left the church, and our children joined us, on their way to the usual family gathering in our room on Sunday. . . .

John remarked to his father, that he had just returned from the War Department, and that there was sad news—General Lee's lines had been broken, and the city would probably be evacuated within twenty-four hours. . . .

In an hour J. received orders to accompany Captain Parker to the South with the Corps of Midshipmen. Then we began to understand that the Government was moving, and that the evacuation was indeed going on. The office-holders were now making arrangements to get off. Every car was ordered to be ready to take them south. Baggage-wagons, carts, drays, and ambulances were driving about the streets; every one going off that could go. The people were rushing up and down the streets, vehicles of all kinds were flying along, bearing goods of all sorts and people of all ages and classes who could go beyond the corporation lines. We tried to keep ourselves quiet. We could not go south, nor could we leave the city at all in this hurried way. . . .

Last night, when we went out to hire a servant to go to Camp Jackson for our sister, we for the first time realized that our money was worthless here, and that we are in fact penniless. About midnight she walked in, escorted by two of the convalescent soldiers. We collected in one room, and tried to comfort one another. . . .

Oh, who shall tell the horror of the past night! Union men began to show themselves; treason walked abroad. About two o'clock in the morning we were startled by a loud sound like thunder; the house shook and the windows rattled; it seemed like an earthquake in our midst. It was soon understood to be the blowing up of a magazine below the city. In a few hours another exploded on the outskirts of the city, much louder than the first, and shivering innumerable plate-glass windows all over Shockoe Hill. It was then daylight, and we were standing out upon the pavement. The lower part of the city was burning.

About seven o'clock I set off to go to the central depot to see if the cars would go out. As I went from Franklin to Broad Street, and on Broad, the pavements were covered with broken glass; women, both white and coloured, were walking in multitudes from the Commissary offices and burning stores with bags of flour, meal, coffee, sugar, rolls of cotton cloth, etc., coloured men were rolling wheelbarrows filled in the same way. I went on and on towards the depot, and as I proceeded shouts and screams became louder. The rabble rushed by me in one stream. "Who are those shouting? What is the matter?" I seemed to be answered by a hundred voices, "The Yankees have come." I turned to come home, but what was my horror, when I reached Ninth Street, to see a regiment of Yankee cavalry come dashing up, yelling, shouting, hallooing, screaming! All Bedlam let loose could not have vied with them in diabolical roarings. I stood riveted to the spot; I could not move nor speak. Then I saw the iron gate of our time-honoured and beautiful Capitol Square, on the walks and greensward of which no hoof had been allowed to tread, thrown open and the cavalry dash in. I could see no more. . . . I came home. . . .

The Federal soldiers were roaming about the streets; either whiskey or the excess of joy had given some of them the appearance of being beside themselves. We had hoped that very little whiskey would be found in the city, as, by the order of the Mayor, casks were emptied yesterday evening in the streets, and it flowed like water through the gutters; but the rabble had managed to find it secreted in the burning shops, and bore it away in pitchers and buckets. . . .

The fire was progressing rapidly, and the crashing sound of falling timbers was distinctly heard. Dr. Read's church was blazing. The War Department was falling in; burning papers were being wafted about the streets. The Commissary Department, with our desks and papers, was consumed already. Warwick & Barksdale's mill was sending its flames to the sky. Cary and Main Streets seemed doomed throughout; Bank Street was beginning to burn, and now it had reached Franklin. . . . Almost every house is guarded; and the streets are now (ten o'clock) perfectly quiet. The moon is shining brightly on our captivity. God guide and watch over us!

April 5.—I feel as if we were groping in the dark; no one knows what to do. The Yankees, so far, have behaved humanely. . . .

April 6th.—Mr. Lincoln has visited our devoted city to-day. His reception was any thing but complimentary. Our people were in nothing rude or disrespectful; they only kept themselves away from a scene so painful. There are very few Unionists of the least respectability here; these met them (he was attended by Stanton and others) with cringing loyalty, I hear, but the rest of the small collection were of the low, lower, lowest of creation. They drove through several streets, but the greeting was so feeble from the motley crew of vulgar men and women, that the Federal officers themselves, I suppose, were ashamed of it, for they very soon escaped from the disgraceful association. . . .

April 10th.—Another gloomy Sabbath-day and harrowing night. We went to St. Paul's in the morning, and heard a very fine sermon from Dr. Minnegerode—at least so said my companions. My attention wandered continually. I could not listen; I felt so strangely, as if in a vivid, horrible dream. Neither President was prayed for; in compliance with some arrangement with the Federal authorities, the prayer was used as for all in authority! How fervently did we all pray for our own President! Thank God, our silent prayers are free from Federal authority. . . .

Thursday Night.—Fearful rumours are reaching us from sources which it is hard to doubt, that it is all too true, and that General Lee surrendered on Sunday last, the 9th of April. . . . We do not yet give up all hope. General Johnston is in the field, but there are thousands of the enemy to his tens. The citizens are quiet. The calmness of despair is written on every countenance. . . .

Good-Friday.—As usual, I went to the hospital, and found Miss T. in much trouble. A peremptory order has been given by the Surgeon-General to remove *all* patients. . . . The ambulances were at the door. Miss T. and myself decided to go at once to the Medical Director and ask him to recall the order. We were conducted to his office, and, for the first time since the entrance of the Federal troops, were impolitely treated.

We had no service in our churches to-day. An order came out in this morning's papers that the prayers for the President of the United States must be used. How could we do it? . . .

Sunday Night.—Strange rumours are afloat to-night. It is said, and believed, that Lincoln is dead, and Seward much injured.[1] As I passed the house of a friend this evening, she raised the window and told me the report. Of course I treated it as a Sunday rumour; but the story is strengthened by the way which the Yankees treat it. I trust that, if true, it may not be by the hand of an assassin, though it

[1] Lincoln was shot in Ford's Theater the night of April 14 and died a little after seven o'clock Saturday morning the fifteenth. Secretary of State Seward was assaulted in his bedroom but was able to resume his duties in May.

would seem to fulfil the warnings of Scripture. His efforts to carry out his abolition theories have caused the shedding of oceans of Southern blood. . . . But what effect will it have on the South? We may have much to fear.

7. MRS. W. T. SUTHERLIN—PRESIDENT DAVIS IN DANVILLE

Major Sutherlin and his wife opened their home in Danville, Virginia, to President Davis in flight from Richmond on April 3, 1865. A Cabinet meeting was held there, Secretary of War John C. Breckinridge alone being absent, and there the President's last proclamation was written. A marker on the house claims it as the "last capitol of the Confederacy, April 3-10, 1865."

When President Davis had been at our house for three days he said that he could not impose on our hospitality longer, and made arrangements to establish his headquarters at the old Benedict house, on Wilson Street. I told him that he might take his cabinet to any place he pleased, but as for himself he must be our guest so long as he remained in the city, and he yielded to the request. He remained here five days after that time, and was, of course, in a most anxious frame of mind, but was always pleasant and agreeable. One morning he and Mr. Sutherlin went down town and soon returned in an excited manner, and I knew something had happened. I met them at the door and President Davis told me almost in a whisper that Lee had surrendered and that he must leave town as soon as possible.

Making a few hurried arrangements, he offered his hand to me to say good-by, and I asked him the question: "Mr. Davis, have you any funds other than Confederate money?" and he replied in the negative. "Then," said I, offering him a bag of gold containing a thousand dollars, "take this from me." I offered the money without having consulted Mr. Sutherlin, but knew it would be all right with him.

Mr. Davis took my hand and the tears streamed down his face. "No," said he, "I cannot take your money. You and your husband are young and will need your money, while I am an old man, and," adding after a pause, "I don't reckon I shall need anything very long."

He then put his hand in his pocket and took out a little gold pencil which he asked me to keep for his sake. . . .

8. JUDITH BROCKENBROUGH McGUIRE—
"GENERAL LEE HAS RETURNED"

With a breaking heart Mrs. McGuire closes the pages of her diary. It was published anonymously shortly after the war, as "By a Lady of Virginia."

Richmond, Virginia

April 16, 1865.—General Lee has returned. He came unattended, save by his staff—came without notice, and without parade; but he could not come unobserved; as soon as his approach was whispered, a crowd gathered in his path, not boisterously, but respectfully, and increasing rapidly as he advanced to his home on Franklin Street, between 8th and 9th, where, with a courtly bow to the multitude, he at once retired to the bosom of his beloved family.

When I called in to see his high-minded and patriotic wife, a day or two after the evacuation, she was busily engaged in her invalid's chair, and very cheerful and hopeful. "The end is not yet," she said, as if to cheer those around her; "Richmond is not the Confederacy." To this we all most willingly assented, and felt very much gratified and buoyed by her brightness. I have not the heart to visit her since the surrender, but hear that she still is sanguine, saying that, "General Lee is not the Confederacy," and that there is "life in the old land yet." He is not the Confederacy; but our hearts sink within us when we remember that he and his noble army are now idle, and that we can no longer look upon them as the bulwark of our land. He has returned from defeat and disaster with the universal and profound admiration of the world, having done all that skill and valour could accomplish.

The scenes at the surrender were noble and touching. General Grant's bearing was profoundly respectful; General Lee's as courtly and lofty as the purest chivalry could require. The terms, so honourable to all parties, being complied with to the letter, our arms were laid down with breaking hearts, and tears such as stoutest warriors may shed. "Woe worth the day!" . . .

[Final entry] May 4.—General Johnston surrendered on the 26th of April. "My native land, good-night!"

9. MARY CUSTIS LEE—"our poor unhappy country"

After she left beloved Arlington and near-by Ravensworth there had been months of weary wandering for Mrs. Lee. She had visited relatives or friends at Chantilly; in Loudoun, Fauquier, Clarke counties, at Kinloch, Annefield, Meida and Audley; at Hot Springs, Shirley and Marlbourne; at Hickory Hill in Hanover County and elsewhere. At times she had been within the Federal lines. In October 1863 she came to Richmond to live on Leigh Street. From January 1, 1864, to June 1865 the home of the Robert E. Lees was a larger house at 707 East Franklin Street, called "The Mess" because it had been occupied by some staff officers.

Always confident of Confederate success, she had watched her family serve and suffer in the war. Of her sons, Custis had been on President Davis' staff; had, as major-general, seen in the last days the field action for which he had longed, and been captured at Sayler's Creek. W. H. F. ("Rooney"), also a major-general, had been wounded at Brandy Station on the march to Gettysburg, taken prisoner and closely confined at Fortress Monroe until February 1864, when he was exchanged, and then been in the thick of things in the Wilderness and before Appomattox. Young Rob had left the University of Virginia to enlist as a private in the Rockbridge Artillery under Stonewall Jackson, and risen to the rank of captain.

Mrs. Lee had been with her daughter Annie when she died at Warren White Sulphur, North Carolina, October 20, 1862. She had been in Richmond near Charlotte, Rooney's high-born wife, when she died in December 1863 while he was a prisoner of war and soon after the death of their young son.

Long a severe sufferer from arthritis, Mrs. Lee was forced to use crutches and a rolling chair. The last days of the Confederacy were, of course, sad and shocking for her. They were the harder to bear because for a short time after the evacuation of Richmond she had to leave her home, which was threatened by fire. Back in the Franklin Street house she devoted her time to knitting and making bandages while she awaited her husband's return from Appomattox. Two weeks after the surrender she wrote this letter to her cousin Mary Meade. In R. E. Lee Dr. Freeman quotes from it to show how bravely she rallied from the crushing blow of final defeat.

Richmond, April 23, 1865

I have just heard, my dear cousin Mary, of an opportunity to Clarke County & write to tell you we are all well as usual, and thro' the mercy of God all spared thro' the terrible ordeal thro' which we have passed. I feel that I could have blessed God if those who were prepared had filled a soldier's grave. I bless Him that they are spared I trust for future usefulness to their poor unhappy country. My little Rob has not yet come in, but we have reason to think he is safe. Tho' it has not pleased Almighty God to crown our exertions with success in the way & manner we expected, yet we must still trust & pray not that *our will* but His may be done in Heaven & in earth. I could not begin to tell you of the startling events that have been crowded into the last few weeks. But I want you all to know that when Gen'l Lee surrendered, he had only 8 thousand 7 hundred muskets; that the enemy by their own account had nearly 80 thousand men well provisioned & equipped, while ours had been out 7 days with only 2 days rations; that they were fighting by day & marching all night without even time to parch their corn, their only food for several days; that even in this exhausted state they drove back hosts of the enemy, but could not follow up their advantage; that had Grant demanded *unconditional* surrender, they had determined to sell their lives as dearly as possible & cut their way thro' his encircling hosts; but the conditions he offered were so honourable, that Gen'l Lee decided it was wrong to sacrifice the lives of these brave men when no object would be gained by it. For my part it will always be a source of pride & consolation to me to know that all mine have perilled their lives, fortune & even fame in so holy a cause. We can hear nothing *certain* from the rest of the army or from our President. May God help and protect them. We can only pray for them. Our plans are all unsettled. Gen'l Lee is very busy settling up his army matters & then we shall *all* probably go to some of those empty places in the vicinity of the White House. Fitzhugh has gone on there to see what we can do; but this place is an utter scene of desolation. So is our whole country & the cruel policy of the enemy has accomplished its work too well. They have achieved by *starvation* what they never could win by their valor; nor have they taken a *single town* in the South, except Vicksburg, that we have not *evacuated*. . . .

Love to all friends. Ever & affectionately yrs,

M. C. LEE

10. ELIZA FRANCES ANDREWS—"AND THIS IS THE END OF THE CONFEDERACY"

Eliza was one of the seven children of Judge Garnett Andrews of Washington, Georgia. In her view the family was not rich, owning only some two hundred slaves. "Our chief extravagance," she says, "was the exercise of unlimited hospitality." Her father bitterly opposed secession, but her brother enlisted in the Confederate Army, and twenty-four-year-old Eliza gave her heart to the Cause.

Near "Haywood," the Andrews' house on the north side of the town square, was the old bank building where Jefferson Davis signed his last official paper as President of the Southern Confederacy on May 3. On the same spot today a room is designated: "The Last Cabinet Meeting Chapter of the United Daughters of the Confederacy."

Eliza became a schoolteacher after the war and wrote poems, short stories, three novels and two books on botany. In 1908 she edited and published her old war diary.

April 25, Tuesday. [Washington, Georgia.]—Little Washington is now, perhaps, the most important military post in our poor, doomed Confederacy. The naval and medical departments have been moved here—what there is left of them. Soon all this will give place to Yankee barracks, and our dear old Confederate gray will be seen no more. The men are all talking about going to Mexico and Brazil.

The Irvin Artillery[1] are coming in rapidly; I suppose they will all be here by the end of the week—or what is left of them—but their return is even sadder and amid bitterer tears than their departure, for now "we weep as they that have no hope." Everybody is cast down and humiliated, and we are all waiting in suspense to know what our cruel masters will do with us. . . . Till it comes, "Let us eat, drink and be merry, for tomorrow we die." Only, we have almost nothing to eat, and to drink, and still less to be merry about.

The whole world seems to be moving on Washington now. An average of 2,000 rations are issued daily, and over 15,000 men are said to have passed through already, since it became a military post, though the return of the paroled men has as yet hardly begun. . . .

---

[1] The first military company organized in Washington. Eliza Andrews said it "contained the flower of the youth of the village."

April 27, Thursday.—The navy department has been ordered away from here—and Washington would seem a very queer location for a navy that had any real existence. Capt. Parker[1] sent Lieut. Peck this morning with a letter to father and seven great boxes full of papers and instruments belonging to the department, which he requested father to take care of. Father had them stored in the cellar, the only place where he could find a vacant spot, and so now about all that is left of the Confederate Navy is here in our house, and we laugh and tell father, that he, the staunchest Union man in Georgia, is head of the Confederate Navy.

April 28, Friday.—I was busy all the morning helping to get ready for a supper that father gave to Gen. Elzey[2] and staff. . . . We had a delightful evening, in spite of the clouds gathering about us. . . . We had several sets of the Lancers and Prince Imperial, interspersed with waltzes and galops, and wound up with an old-fashioned Virginia reel, Gen. Elzey and I leading off.

April 29, Saturday.—Visitors all day, in shoals and swarms. Capt. Irwin brought Judge Crump[3] of Richmond to stay at our house. Capt. Irwin seems very fond of him, and says there is no man in Virginia more beloved and respected. He is Assistant Secretary of the Treasury or something of the sort, and is wandering about the country with his poor barren exchequer, trying to protect what is left of it, for the payment of Confederate soldiers. He has in charge, also, the assets of some Richmond banks, of which he is, or was, president, *dum Troja fuit*. He says that in Augusta he met twenty-five of his clerks with ninety-five barrels of papers not worth a pin all put together, which they had brought out of Richmond, while things of real value were left a prey to the enemy.

April 30, Sunday.—When I came in from church in the afternoon, I found Burton Harrison, Mr. Davis's private secretary, among our

[1] Captain William Parker had been head of the Naval Academy at Richmond. Before the city was taken over by the Federals he and sixty of the cadets had gone south guarding the government money. They escorted Mrs. Davis from Charlotte to Abbeville, South Carolina; proceeded to Washington, Georgia, and returned to Abbeville, where they stored the treasure in a warehouse before they were disbanded. The boys walked back to Richmond.

[2] Arnold Elzey, of Maryland, made a brigadier on the field of First Manassas, was seriously wounded in the Seven Days' fighting. When partly recovered, he was commissioned major-general and put in command of the Department of Richmond, where he organized the government clerks into a "Local Defense" brigade.

[3] William Wood Crump, a distinguished Virginia jurist.

guests. He came in with Mrs. Davis, who is being entertained at Dr. Ficklen's. Nobody knows where the President is, but I hope he is far west of this by now. . . . Mr. Harrison probably knows more about his whereabouts than anybody else, but of course we ask no questions. Mrs. Davis herself says that she has no idea where he is, which is the only wise thing for her to say. The poor woman is in a deplorable condition—no home, no money, and her husband a fugitive. She says she sold her plate in Richmond, and in the stampede from that place, the money, all but fifty dollars, was left behind. . . .

May 1, Monday.—Crowds of callers all day . . . Men were coming in all day, with busy faces, to see Mr. Harrison, and one of them brought news of Johnston's surrender, but Mr. Harrison didn't tell anybody about it except father. While we were at dinner, a brother of Mrs. Davis[1] came in and called for Mr. Harrison, and after a hurried interview with him, Mr. Harrison came back into the dining-room and said it had been decided that Mrs. Davis would leave town tomorrow. . . .

May 2, Tuesday.—Mr. Harrison left this morning, with a Godspeed from all the family and prayers for the safety of the honored fugitives committed to his charge. . . .

May 3, Wednesday.—About noon the town was thrown into the wildest excitement by the arrival of President Davis. He is traveling with a large escort of cavalry, a very imprudent thing for a man in his position to do, especially now that Johnston has surrendered, and the fact that they are all going in the same direction to their homes is the only thing that keeps them together. He rode into town ahead of his escort, and as he was passing by the bank, where the Elzeys board, the general and several other gentlemen were sitting on the front porch, and the instant they recognized him they took off their hats and received him with every mark of respect due the president of a brave people. When he reined in his horse, all the staff who were present advanced to hold the reins and assist him to dismount, while Dr. and Mrs. [M. E.] Robertson hastened to offer the hospitality of their home. About forty of his immediate personal friends and attendants were with him, and they were all half-starved, having tasted nothing for twenty-four hours. Capt. Irwin came running

[1] Jefferson Howell.

home in great haste to ask mother to send them something to eat, as it was reported the Yankees were approaching the town from two opposite directions closing in upon the President, and it was necessary to hurry him off at once. There was not so much as a crust of bread in our house, everything available having been given to soldiers. There was some bread in the kitchen that had just been baked for a party of soldiers, but they were willing to wait, and I begged some milk from Aunt Sallie, and by adding to these our own dinner as soon as Emily could finish cooking it, we contrived to get together a very respectable lunch. We had just sent it off when the president's escort came in, followed by couriers who brought the comforting assurance that it was a false alarm about the enemy being so near. By this time the president's arrival had become generally known, and people began flocking to see him; but he went to bed almost as soon as he got into the house, and Mrs. Elzey would not let him be waked. . . . The party are all worn out and half-dead for sleep. They traveled mostly at night, and have been in the saddle for three nights in succession. Mrs. Elzey says that Mr. Davis does not seem to have been aware of the real danger of his situation until he came to Washington, where some of his friends gave him a serious talk, and advised him to travel with more secrecy and dispatch than he has been using.

Mr. Reagan[1] and Mr. Mallory are also in town, and Gen. Toombs[2] has returned, having encountered danger ahead, I fear. Judge Crump is back too, with his Confederate treasury, containing, it is said, three hundred thousand dollars in specie. He is staying at our house, but the treasure is thought to be stored in the vault at the bank. . . .

May 4, Thursday.—I sat under the cedar trees by the street gate nearly all the morning, watching the stream of human life flow by, and keeping guard over the horses of some soldier friends that had left them grazing on the lawn. Father and Cora went to call on the President, and in spite of his prejudice against everybody and everything connected with secession, father says his manner was so calm and dignified that he could not help admiring the man. Crowds of people flocked to see him, and nearly all were melted in tears. Gen. Elzey pretended to have dust in his eyes and Mrs. Elzey blubbered

[1] John H. Reagan, of Texas, postmaster-general.
[2] Robert Toombs, whose home was in Washington, Georgia, after being Secretary of State in the Confederate Provisional Government became a brigadier-general and fought in the Seven Days, at Antietam and in the Atlanta campaign.

outright, exclaiming all the while, in her impulsive way: "Oh, I am such a fool to be crying, but I can't help it!" When she was telling me about it afterwards, she said she could not stay in the room with him yesterday evening, because she couldn't help crying, and she was ashamed for the people who called to see her looking so ugly, with her eyes and nose red. She says that at night, after the crowd left, there was a private meeting in his room, where Reagan and Mallory and other high officials were present, and again early in the morning there were other confabulations before they all scattered and went their ways—and this, I suppose, is the end of the Confederacy. . . .

The Confederate Flag
"Requiescat in Pace"

The hands of our women made it!
    'Twas baptized in our mother's tears!
And drenched with blood of our kindred,
    While with hope for those four long years,
Across vale and plain we watched it,
    Where the red tide of battle rolled
And with tear-dimmed eyes we followed
    The wave of each silken fold.

As high o'er our hosts it floated,
    Through the dust and din of the fight,
We caught the glint of the spear-head
    And the flash of its crimson light!
While the blood of the men who bore it
    Flowed fast on the reddened plain,
Till our cry went up in anguish
    To God, for our martyred slain!

And we wept, and watched, and waited
    By our lonely household fire,
For the mother gave her first born,
    And the daughter gave her sire!
And the wife sent forth her husband,
    And the maiden her lover sweet;
And our hearts kept time in the silence
    To the rhythmic tread of their feet. . . .

LOUISE WIGFALL WRIGHT

BIBLIOGRAPHY

and

INDEX

BIBLIOGRAPHY

Full bibliographical description and credit are supplied for first listings. Additional selections from the same sources are referred back to the first listing.

CHAPTER I. THE UNION IS DISSOLVED (December 1860-May 1861)

1. South Carolina Secedes from the Union
   Diary of Emma E. Holmes, 1861-1862. Manuscript Room, Duke University Library.
2. Florida Passes the Ordinance of Secession
   Susan Bradford Eppes, *Through Some Eventful Years*. Macon, Ga.: The J. W. Burke Company, 1926. (By permission of Susan W. Eppes and Alice B. Eppes.)
3. "We Are a Free and Independent People"
   Augusta J. Kollock to her brother, January 22, 1861. Susan M. Kollock, ed., "Letters of the Kollock and Allied Families," *The Georgia Historical Quarterly*, XXXIV, 3 (September 1950), 229-231. (By permission of The Georgia Historical Society.)
4. Montgomery Welcomes Jefferson Davis
   Eleanor Noyes Jackson to her sister, February 19, 1861. Jefferson Davis Scrapbook, Manuscript Room, Alabama State Department of Archives and History.
5. "I Could Not Command My Voice To Speak"
   Varina Howell Davis, *Jefferson Davis: A Memoir by His Wife*. New York: The Belford Company, 1890.
6. Charleston Prepares for War
   Caroline Howard Gilman to her children, March 12, 1861. "Letters of a Confederate Mother," *The Atlantic Monthly*, CXXXVII (April 1926), 505-506. (By permission of *The Atlantic Monthly*.)
7. Fort Sumter Surrenders
   Diary of Emma E. Holmes, 1861-1862. (*See* I, 1.)
8. "Our Home Grew Lonely"
   Mary Anna Jackson, *Memoirs of Stonewall Jackson, by His Widow*. . . . Louisville, Ky.: The Prentice Press, 1895.
9. "The Prospects before Us Are Sad"
   Mary Custis Lee to her daughter, April 20, 1861. Rose Mortimer Ellzey MacDonald, *Mrs. Robert E. Lee*. Boston: Ginn & Company, 1939. (By permission of J. Lewis Scoggs.)
10. "I Heard the Drums Beating in Washington"
    [Judith Brockenbrough McGuire], *Diary of a Southern Refugee during the War, by a Lady of Virginia*. New York: E. J. Hale & Son, 1867.
11. I Set My House in Order
    Mary Custis Lee to her husband, May 9, 1861. *Mrs. Robert E. Lee*. (*See* I, 9.)

413

12. "They Are the Finest Set of Men"
Varina Howell Davis to Clement Claiborne Clay, Jr., May 10, 1861. Clay
Papers, Manuscript Room, Duke University Library.

CHAPTER II. THE CONFEDERACY IS INVADED
(May 1861-February 1862)

1. Virginia Is Invaded
[Judith Brockenbrough McGuire], *Diary of a Southern Refugee.* (See
I, 10.)
2. "We Left Washington"
Diary of Betty Herndon Maury. Manuscript Division, Library of Congress.
3. "A Battle Has Been Fought at Manassas"
From: A DIARY FROM DIXIE by Mary Boykin Chesnut. Copyright,
1905, D. Appleton & Company. Reprinted by permission of the publishers
Appleton-Century-Crofts, Inc.
4. "My Home Was Converted into a Prison"
Rose O'Neal Greenhow, *My Imprisonment and the First Year of Abolition
Rule in Washington.* London: Richard Bentley, 1863.
5. Our New Home
Varina Howell Davis, *Jefferson Davis.* (See I, 5.)
6. "Our Cause We Know Is Just"
Leora Sims to Mary Elizabeth Bellamy, November 14, 1861. Copy of letter
in possession of Mrs. Mary Verner Schlaefer, Jr., Columbia, South Carolina.
(By permission of Mrs. Mary Verner Schlaefer, Jr.)
7. "I Hope This State of Affairs Will Not Last Long"
Mrs. Dorian Hall to her son, January 6 and 9, 1862. William Hall Collec-
tion, Military Records Division, Alabama State Department of Archives and
History.
8. Hard Times in Texas
Mary Byson to Margaret Butler, January 16, 1862. Butler Family Papers,
Department of Archives, Louisiana State University.
9. Old Capitol Prison
Rose O'Neal Greenhow, *My Imprisonment.* (See II, 4.)
10. Personal Observations at Some of the Camps and Hospitals
Mary H. Johnstone to Alexander H. Stephens, February 3, 1862. Alexander
H. Stephens Papers, Library of Congress.
11. "My Husband Was a Prisoner at Fort Henry"
Louisa Frederika Gilmer to her father, February 10, 1862. Gilmer Papers,
Southern Historical Collection, University of North Carolina.
12. The Union Flag Was Raised in Nashville
Miss A. M. B., "Foraging Around Nashville," *Our Women in the War; The
Lives They Lived; The Deaths They Died.* Charleston, S. C.: The News and
Courier Book Presses, 1885.
13. The Inauguration of Jefferson Davis as Permanent President
Constance Cary Harrison, "A Virginia Girl in the First Year of the War,"
The Century Illustrated Monthly Magazine, XXX (August 1885), 610.

CHAPTER III. A FRIGHTING SPRING (March-May 1862)

1. "The Daring, Reckless Captain Morgan Visits Murfreesboro"
Diary of Alice Ready. Southern Historical Collection, University of North
Carolina.

2. "Write Me What Your Horse Is Named"
   Loulie Gilmer to her father, March 16, 1862. Gilmer Papers, Southern Historical Collection, University of North Carolina.

3. Winchester Is Occupied by the Enemy
   Cornelia Peake McDonald, *A Diary with Reminiscences of the War and Refugee Life in the Shenandoah Valley, 1860-1865,* ed., Hunter McDonald. Nashville, Tenn.: Cullom & Ghertner, 1934. (By permission of Hunter McDonald.)

4. "My Boy Is Gone from Me"
   Margaret Lea Houston to her mother, March 17, 1862. Temple Houston Morrow Collection, University of Texas Library.

5. The Aftermath of Shiloh
   Kate Cumming, *A Journal of Hospital Life in the Confederate Army of Tennessee from the Battle of Shiloh to the End of the War.* . . . Louisville, Ky.: John P. Morton & Company, 1866.

6. Abraham Lincoln Was in Fredericksburg
   Diary of Betty Herndon Maury. (*See* II, 2.)

7. Enemy Ships Pass the Forts below New Orleans
   Sarah Morgan Dawson, *A Confederate Girl's Diary,* ed., Warrington Dawson. Boston: Houghton Mifflin Company, 1913. (By permission of Warrington Dawson.)

8. New Orleans Has Fallen
   Julia Ellen (LeGrand) Waitz, *The Journal of Julia LeGrand, New Orleans, 1862-1863,* ed., Kate Mason Rowland and Mrs. Morris L. Croxall. Richmond, Va.: Everett Waddey Company, 1911.

9. The Enemy Comes to Baton Rouge
   Sarah Morgan Dawson, *A Confederate Girl's Diary.* (*See* III, 7.)

CHAPTER IV. THEY CALLED THEM "GREAT DAYS"
(May-September 1862)

1. Stonewall Defeats Banks at Winchester
   Cornelia Peake McDonald, *A Diary with Reminiscences.* (*See* III, 3.)

2. In Richmond during and after Seven Pines
   Constance Cary Harrison, "A Virginia Girl." (*See* II, 13.)

3. "I Want To See You So Bad"
   Lucy Lowe to her husband, June 1, 1862. William Hall Collection, Military Records Division, Alabama State Department of Archives and History.

4. "Jackson Is Doing Great Things"
   Diary of Betty Herndon Maury. (*See* II, 2.)

5. "What Cannot Be Cured Must Be Endured"
   Amie Kelly to her husband, July 6, 1862. Letter in possession of Miss Maud McLure Kelly, Montgomery, Alabama. (By permission of Miss Maud McLure Kelly.)

6. "I Am Proud To Be Your Wife"
   Elizabeth McGavock Harding to her husband, July 17 and 27, August 5 and 29, 1862. Letters in possession of Mrs. Jesse E. Wills, Nashville, Tennessee. (By permission of Mrs. Jesse E. Wills.)

7. "We Appeal to You as Our Friend"
   Lucy Smith to Jefferson Davis and Alexander H. Stephens, August 20, 1862. Alexander H. Stephens Papers, Library of Congress.

8. "Gone Was My Small Paradise!"
   Sarah Morgan Dawson, *A Confederate Girl's Diary.* (*See* III, 7.)

9. "The Children All Want To See You"
Mary Frances Brooks to her husband, September 3, 1862. "Confederate Letters," Georgia State Archives.

10. "I Received My Commission"
Belle Boyd, *Belle Boyd: In Camp and Prison*. London: Saunders, Otley & Company, 1865

CHAPTER V. HIGH HOPES WANING (September 1862-May 1863)

1. "What Shall I Name the Baby?"
Cassie Selden Smith to her husband, October 10, 1862. Edmund Kirby Smith Papers, Southern Historical Collection, University of North Carolina.

2. "I Never Walk or Ride without My Pistol"
Cordelia Lewis Scales to Lou Irby, October 29, 1862. Percy L. Rainwater, ed., "The Civil War Letters of Cordelia Scales," *Journal of Mississippi History*, I (July 1939), 170-181. (By permission of Percy L. Rainwater and *Journal of Mississippi History*.)

3. We Hope To Reach Texas
Mary Williams Pugh to her husband, November 9 and 18, 1862. Richard L. Pugh Papers, Department of Archives, Louisiana State University.

4. "Accept My Best Wishes for Your Happiness"
Mary Cahal to Mrs. John Hunt Morgan, December 16, 1862. John Hunt Morgan Papers, Southern Historical Collection, University of North Carolina.

5. "New Orleans Is Full of Rumors"
Julia Ellen (LeGrand) Waitz, *The Journal of Julia LeGrand*. (*See* III, 8.)

6. "The Negroes Are Having a Merry Time"
Diary of Sarah L. Wadley, August 1859-April 1863. Southern Historical Collection, University of North Carolina.

7. "God Blessed Us with Victory at Fredericksburg"
Diary of Betty Herndon Maury. (*See* II, 2.)

8. "Come to Me, My Darling"
Martha Ready Morgan to her husband, January 6, 1863. John Hunt Morgan Papers, Southern Historical Collection, University of North Carolina.

9. "There Is Not a Bonnet for Sale in Richmond"
Agnes to Sara Rice Pryor, January 7, 1863. Mrs. Roger A. (Sara Rice) Pryor, *Reminiscences of Peace and War*. New York: The Macmillan Company, 1904. (By permission of The Macmillan Company.)

10. "I Wore My Pistol All the Time!"
Cordelia Lewis Scales to Lou Irby, January 27, 1863. "The Civil War Letters." (*See* V, 2.)

11. "We Are To Be Turned Out of Doors"
Diary of Betty Herndon Maury. (*See* II, 2.)

12. My Brother Is an Exchange Prisoner
Journal of Missouri Stokes. Mary Ann Harris Gay, *Life in Dixie during the War*. Atlanta, Ga.: Charles P. Byrd, 1897.

13. "My New Novel Is Dedicated to the Army of the Confederacy"
Augusta Jane Evans to General Pierre G. T. Beauregard, March 17, 1863. Beauregard Papers, Manuscript Room, Duke University Library.

14. "General Forrest Asked for a Lock of My Hair"
Emma Sansom. John Allan Wyeth, *Life of General Nathan Bedford Forrest*. New York: Harper & Brothers, 1899. (By permission of Harper & Brothers.)

15. "They Said My Husband Had Been Wounded"
    Mary Anna Jackson, Memoirs of Stonewall Jackson. (*See* I, 8.)

CHAPTER VI. HEARTBREAK (May 1863-April 1864)

1. In a Cave at Vicksburg
   Mary Ann Loughborough, *My Cave Life in Vicksburg, with letters of trial and travel.* New York: D. Appleton & Company, 1864.
2. "We Dance at Fort Sumter"
   Diary of Esther Alden. *Our Women in the War.* (*See* II, 12.)
3. Yankees Parade in Natchez
   Mrs. G. Griffin Wilcox, "War Times in Natchez," *Southern Historical Society Papers,* XXX (1902), 135-136.
4. "I Marry My General, the Hero of Gettysburg"
   LaSalle Corbell Pickett, *Pickett and His Men.* Atlanta, Ga.: The Foote & Davies Company, 1899.
5. "Somebody's Darling"
   Marie Ravenel de la Coste, "Somebody's Darling," *The Home Book of Verse,* ed., Burton Egbert Stevenson. New York: Henry Holt and Company, 1912.
6. "Charleston Is in Great Danger"
   Rose O'Neal Greenhow to Jefferson Davis, July 16, 1863; to Alexander Robinson Boteler, July 20, 1863. Jefferson Davis Papers, Manuscript Room, Duke University Library.
7. "An Arrow Struck the Wall Opposite My Window"
   Belle Boyd, *In Camp and Prison.* (*See* IV, 10.)
8. "Many Things Are Becoming Scarce"
   Susan Bradford Eppes, *Through Some Eventful Years.* (*See* I, 2.)
9. Dependent on Our Own Resources
   Parthenia Antoinette Hague, *A Blockaded Family: Life in Southern Alabama during the Civil War.* Boston: Houghton Mifflin Company, 1888.
10. Christmas in Petersburg
    Mrs. Roger A. (Sara Rice) Pryor, *Reminiscences.* (*See* V, 9.)
11. Smuggling from Memphis
    Diary of Belle Edmondson. Southern Historical Collection, University of North Carolina.
12. "Sister Susan Has Lost Three Sons"
    Mary Byson to Margaret Butler, March 21, 1864. (*See* II, 8.)
13. "Today I Have No Shoes"
    Susan Bradford Eppes, *Through Some Eventful Years.* (*See* I, 2.)
14. Yankees in Camden, Arkansas
    Virginia McCollum Stinson. Mrs. M. A. Elliott, ed., *The Garden of Memory: Stories of the Civil War.* Camden, Ark.: H. L. Grinstead Chapter, U. D. C., [n. d.].
15. "They Left Us Alone with Our Dead"
    Varina Howell Davis, *Jefferson Davis.* (*See* I, 5.)

CHAPTER VII. BLOWS OF THE HAMMER (May-October 1864)

1. Special Agent
   Loreta Janeta Velazquez, *The Woman in Battle: A Narrative of the Exploits, Adventures and Travels of Madame Loreta Janeta Velazquez, Other-*

wise Known as Lieutenant Harry T. Buford, Confederate States Army, ed., C. J. Worthington. Hartford, Conn.: T. Belknap, 1876.

2. "How Alone General Lee Seems!"
Sarah Alexander Lawton to her sister, May 9, 1864. Marion Alexander Boggs, ed., *The Alexander Letters, 1787-1900.* Savannah, Ga.: privately printed for G. F. Baldwin, 1910. (By permission of A. Leopold Alexander.)

3. "General Stuart Died Last Night"
[Judith Brockenbrough McGuire], *Diary of a Southern Refugee. (See* I, 10.)

4. Hunter Burns the V. M. I.
Cornelia Peake McDonald, *A Diary with Reminiscenses. (See* III, 3.)

5. "You Burned My Home"
Henrietta Bedinger Lee to General David Hunter, July 20, 1864. *Southern Historical Society Papers,* VIII (1880), 215-216.

6. "I Am an Exile"
Issa Desha Breckinridge to her husband, July 30, 1864. Breckinridge Papers, Manuscript Division, Library of Congress.

7. In Besieged Petersburg
Mrs. Roger A. (Sara Rice) Pryor, *Reminiscences. (See* V, 9.)

8. "I Am for a Tidal Wave of Peace"
Agnes to Sara Rice Pryor, August 26, 1864. *Reminiscences. (See* V, 9.)

9. Our Exchange Prisoners
Phoebe Yates Pember, *A Southern Woman's Story.* New York: G. W. Carleton & Company, 1879.

10. Chasing My Hospital
Kate Cumming, *A Journal of Hospital Life. (See* III, 5.)

11. The Battle for Atlanta
Mary Ann Harris Gay, *Life in Dixie. (See* V, 12.)

12. "They Took Possession of Atlanta Quietly"
Diary of Mary Rawson. "The Margaret Mitchell Memorial Library," Atlanta Historical Society, Atlanta, Ga.

13. "A Better Son Never Lived"
Mrs. Henrietta Morgan to her daughter-in-law, October 1, 1864. John Hunt Morgan Papers, Southern Historical Collection, University of North Carolina.

CHAPTER VIII. WINTER OF DESPERATION (November 1864-March 1865)

1. "Lead, Blood and Tears"
Mary Ann Harris Gay, *Life in Dixie. (See* V, 12.)

2. "Things Is Worse and Worse"
A soldier's wife to her husband, December 17, 1864. *Pickett and His Men. (See* VI, 4.)

3. Hood Is Defeated at Nashville
Rebeccah C. Ridley, "Behind the Lines in Middle Tennessee, 1863-1865: The Journal of Bettie Ridley Blackmore," ed., Sarah Ridley Trimble, *Tennessee Historical Quarterly,* XII (March 1953). (By permission of *Tennessee Historical Quarterly.*)

4. Running the Blockade
Journal of Mary Ellen Arnold. Arnold-Appleton Papers, Southern Historical Collection, University of North Carolina.

5. Fort Fisher Is Bombarded
Mrs. William Lamb, "The Heroine of Confederate Point: An Interesting

Contemporaneous Account of the Heroic Defense of Fort Fisher, December 24th and 25th, 1864, by the Wife of the Commandant, Colonel William Lamb," *Southern Historical Society Papers*, XX (1892), 301-306.

6. "I Thought of the Gayety of Paris"
[Judith Brockenbrough McGuire], *Diary of a Southern Refugee. (See* I, 10.)

7. The Treasury Note Department Leaves Columbia
Mrs. Malvina Gist Waring (Malvina Black Gist), "A Confederate Girl's Diary," *South Carolina Women in the Confederacy*, I, ed., Mrs. Thomas Taylor and others. Columbia, S. C.: The State Company, 1903.

8. "Poor Old Columbia!"
Journal of Emma Florence LeConte, December 31, 1864, to August 6, 1865. Southern Historical Collection, University of North Carolina.

9. "The Enemy Comes to Our Plantation"
Diary of Charlotte St. Julien Ravenel. Susan R. Jervey and Charlotte St. Julien Ravenel, *Two Diaries from Middle St. John's, Berkeley, South Carolina.* Charleston, S. C.: St. John's Hunting Club, 1921. (By permission St. John's Hunting Club.)

CHAPTER IX. OUR CONFEDERACY IS GONE WITH A CRASH
(March-May 1864)

1. "We May Have To Fly from Richmond"
Mrs. Malvina Gist Waring (Malvina Black Gist), "A Confederate Girl's Diary." (*See* VIII, 7.)

2. "The Sound of Cannon Is Ever in Our Ears"
[Judith Brockenbrough McGuire], *Diary of a Southern Refugee. (See* I, 10.)

3. "They Marched into Mobile to the Tune of 'Yankee Doodle'"
Journal of Mary D. Waring, July 26, 1863, to April 16, 1865. Manuscript Room, Alabama State Department of Archives and History.

4. "With Hearts Bowed Down by Despair We Left Richmond"
Varina Howell Davis, *Jefferson Davis. (See* I, 5.)

5. "The Women of the South Still Fought Their Battle"
Phoebe Yates Pember, *A Southern Woman's Story. (See* VII, 9.)

6. "Like a Vivid, Horrible Dream"
[Judith Brockenbrough McGuire], *Diary of a Southern Refugee. (See* I, 10.)

7. President Davis in Danville
Mrs. W. T. Sutherlin. J. William Jones, *The Davis Memorial Volume: Or Our Dead President, Jefferson Davis, and the World's Tribute to His Memory.* Richmond, Va.: B. F. Johnson & Company, 1889.

8. "General Lee Has Returned"
[Judith Brockenbrough McGuire], *Diary of a Southern Refugee. (See* I, 10.)

9. "Our Poor Unhappy Country"
Mary Custis Lee to Miss Mary Mead, April 23, 1865. *Mrs. Robert E. Lee.* (*See* I, 9.)

10. "And This Is the End of the Confederacy"
Eliza Frances Andrews, *The War-Time Journal of a Georgia Girl, 1864-1865.* New York: D. Appleton & Company, 1908.

11. "The Confederate Flag"
Mrs. D. Giraud (Louisa Wigfall) Wright, *A Southern Girl in '61: The Wartime Memories of a Confederate Senator's Daughter.* New York: Doubleday, Page & Company; Copyright 1905 by Doubleday & Company, Inc. (By permission of Doubleday & Company, Inc.)

INDEX

Maury, Nannie Belle, 42, 43, 44, 45, 51, 117, 121, 151, 208

Maury, Nanny, 46, 46n, 53, 118, 150, 207

Maury, Sally, 117, 207

Maury, Sue Crutchfield, 150, 152

Maury, Will A., 42, 43, 45, 117, 119, 150, 151, 152, 153

McCabe, Reverend, 320

McCausland, Brig.-Gen. John, 304, 304n, 305, 310

McClellan, Gen. George B., 83, 120, 120n, 139-140, 145, 166, 176

McClernand, Maj.-Gen. John A., 210n

McCollum, Hugh, 280, 284

McCollum, Kate, 277-282

McCook, Edward M., 326

McCulloch, William J., 188

McDearnmid, Mr., shoemaker, 259, 276

McDermid, see McDearnmid

McDonald, Allan, 94, 95, 100, 102, 144, 309

McDonald, Angus, 94, 140, 145, 304-309

McDonald, Cornelia Peake, 83, 94-106, 140-145, 304-309

McDonald, Donald, 94, 96

McDonald, Ellen, 94, 96

McDonald, Harry, 94, 95, 100, 144, 304, 309, 310

McDonald, Hunter, 94, 304, 305-306

McDonald, Kenneth, 94, 96, 101

McDonald, Roy, 94, 96

McDowell, Maj.-Gen. Irwin, 30, 60, 119, 213

McGavock, David Turner, 161, 163, 163n

McGavock, John, 157, 161, 161n, 162, 163

McGehee, ——, pres. of Florida Convention, 10

McGuire, John, 355, 397

McGuire, Rev. John P., 24, 34-42

McGuire, Judith Brockenbrough, 24-26, 30-42, 67, 276, 302-304, 355-356, 383-385, 397-400, 402

McLean, Mrs. Sumner, 60

McMahon, Mr., 273

McPherson, Gen. James B., 204, 204n, 289

McVay, Lieutenant, 254

Meade, Gen. George, 222, 287

Meade, Mary, 403

Memminger, Christopher G., 29n, 376

Mercer, ——, editor of Union, 162

Mercer, Ellen, 198

Miller, Mr., minister, 108, 110, 111

Miller, Mrs., 114

Miller, Mary Boykin, see Chesnut, Mary Boykin

Miller, Stephen Decatur, 55

Milroy, Maj.-Gen. R. H., 139

Milton, Gov. John, 8

Minis, ——, photographer, 218

Minnegerode, Doctor, 400

Minor, Frank, 47

Minor, John, 42, 43

Mitchel, Mrs., of Holly Springs, Miss., 205

Mitchel, Billie, 205

Mitchel, Gen. Ormsby M., 91, 91n

Monroe, John T., 128n

Montgomery, Col. L. M., 234, 234n

Moore, Andrew B., 29n

More, Hannah, 41

Morgan, Calvin, 342

Morgan, Charlton, 342

Morgan, Eliza, see La Noue, Eliza

Morgan, Frank, 343

Morgan, Henrietta Hunt, 341-343

Morgan, Henry, 121, 134

Morgan, James, 121, 122, 134

Morgan, Gen. John Hunt, 83, 85-93, 140, 156, 156n, 191-192, 198-200, 312, 341

Morgan, Key, 342

Morgan, Lydia Carter, 121, 168, 171

Morgan, Martha (Mattie) Ready, 83, 87, 90, 92, 191-192, 198-200, 341-343

Morgan, Miriam, 121, 122, 123, 129, 130, 134-138, 168, 170

Morgan, Judge Philip, 121, 168

Morgan, Richard, 342, 343

Morgan, Sarah, 121-123, 128-138, 140, 168-171

Morgan, Thomas, 342

Morgan, Judge Thomas Gibbes, 121

Morgan, Mrs. Thomas Gibbes, 122, 129, 134-138, 168, 169

Morgan, Thomas Gibbes, Jr., 121, 168

Morgan, Tom, 192

Morris, Anne, 153

Morrison, Doctor, 219

Morrison, Joseph, 219